Women and the White House

WOMEN
AND THE
WHITE HOUSE

Gender, Popular Culture, and Presidential Politics

Edited by

Justin S. Vaughn and Lilly J. Goren

To Ann —
Enjoy!
Cheers —
Lilly Goren

K UNIVERSITY PRESS OF KENTUCKY

Scholarly publisher for the Commonwealth,
serving Bellarmine University, Berea College, Centre College of Kentucky, Eastern
Kentucky University, The Filson Historical Society, Georgetown College, Kentucky
Historical Society, Kentucky State University, Morehead State University, Murray State
University, Northern Kentucky University, Transylvania University, University of Kentucky,
University of Louisville, and Western Kentucky University.
All rights reserved.

Editorial and Sales Offices: The University Press of Kentucky
663 South Limestone Street, Lexington, Kentucky 40508-4008
www.kentuckypress.com

17 16 15 14 13   5 4 3 2 1

Library of Congress Cataloging-in-Publication Data

Women and the White House : gender, popular culture, and presidential politics / edited
by Justin S. Vaughn and Lilly J. Goren.
     p. cm.
  Includes bibliographical references and index.
  ISBN 978-0-8131-4101-5 (hardcover : alk. paper) — ISBN 978-0-8131-4102-2 (epub)
  ISBN 978-0-8131-4103-9 (pdf)
  1. Women presidential candidates—United States. 2. Presidential candidates—United
States. 3. Women political candidates—United States. 4. Women—Political actvity—
United States. 5. Presidents—Family relationships—United States. I. Vaughn, Justin S.,
1978- II. Goren, Lilly J.
  HQ1391.U5W634 2013
  323.3'40973—dc23   2012030908

This book is printed on acid-free paper meeting the requirements of the American
National Standard for Permanence in Paper for Printed Library Materials.

Manufactured in the United States of America.

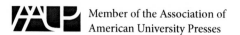 Member of the Association of
American University Presses

CONTENTS

1. The Mechanized Gaze: Gender, Popular Culture, and the Presidency   1
   Justin S. Vaughn and Lilly J. Goren

Part I: Framing Candidates, Understanding Voters

2. Puritan or Pit Bull: The Framing of Female Candidates at the National Level   25
   Linda Beail and Rhonda Kinney Longworth

3. Colbert Nation: Gender, Late-Night Television, and Candidate Humanization   49
   Mary McHugh

4. Soccer Moms, Hockey Moms, National Security Moms: Reality versus Fiction and the Female Voter   75
   Chapman Rackaway

Part II: Hollywood's Influence on Presidential Politics

5. Fact or Fiction: The Reality of Race and Gender in Reaching the White House   97
   Lilly J. Goren

6. Gendering the Presidency without Gender in the Presidency   121
   Joseph E. Uscinski

7. It's a Man's World: Masculinity in Pop Culture Portrayals of the President   135
   Justin S. Vaughn and Stacy Michaelson

Part III: "All the News That's Fit to Print"? Alternative Avenues for Political Information

8. Sitting with Oprah, Dancing with Ellen: Presidents, Daytime Television, and Soft News   163
   José D. Villalobos

9. The Checkout Line Perspective: Presidential Politics as Celebrity Popular Culture in *People* 181
   Elizabeth Fish Hatfield

10. Viral Videos: Reinforcing Stereotypes of Female Candidates for President 205
    Todd L. Belt

Part IV: Women in the White House: First Ladies, First Couples, First Families

11. High Culture, Popular Culture, and the Modern First Ladies 229
    MaryAnne Borrelli

12. The First Family: Transforming the American Ideal 249
    Melissa Buis Michaux

13. The Presidential Partnership: A Gender Seesaw 269
    Karen S. Hoffman

Acknowledgments 287
Selected Bibliography 291
Contributors 305
Index 311

1

THE MECHANIZED GAZE

Gender, Popular Culture, and the Presidency

Justin S. Vaughn and Lilly J. Goren

The 2008 election saw significant interaction between gender-driven popular culture and politics, from Hillary Clinton's shot-and-beer visits to working-class bars and Hillary nutcrackers in airport gift shops to Sarah Palin's self-identification as a "hockey mom" and T-shirts with pictures of pit bulls wearing lipstick. Add to that *Saturday Night Live* sketches (including those declaring "Bitch is the new black"), fashion breakthroughs, and the cementing of female-driven programming as an important political battleground, and the battle to become the forty-fourth president took on gender implications of significant proportions. Although popular culture has long influenced the dynamics of presidential elections, the 2008 election was unique in the overwhelming role that gender-driven popular culture and commodification played, providing a stunning reminder of how much gendered popular culture influences the ways American voters think about politics, especially presidential politics.

As scholars, we quickly realized the important lessons about gender and politics that popular culture was teaching us—and the rest of the citizens who were following the campaign's dynamics in real time. Indeed, by examining the intersecting relationships between popular culture, gender, and presidential politics, especially as perceived through the multiple lenses of the media, we can learn a great deal about the evolution of American attitudes toward the institution of the presidency, those who have occupied the office, and those who have attempted to occupy it. Perhaps more important, we can examine how these portrayals create a popular filter or prism through which the American electorate views and understands the leadership efforts of actual presidents in real time.

Although the notion that politics and popular culture have a mutually reinforcing relationship is not a new one, scholars are only beginning to understand the role gender plays in the dynamic intersections between the political and the cultural. The work that has been done (and that is referenced by the chapters throughout this volume) provides a foundation for the emergence of the remaining critical questions. Specifically, this volume is motivated by the need to untangle and investigate the way our contemporary political culture frames the role of gender in politics, particularly in how citizens are encouraged (if not instructed) to observe and engage with female political leaders; how concepts of presidential leadership and presidentiality are gendered in consistent and disparate ways across different forms of media; and how popular culture influences the way gender is performed by the women who make the White House their home.

To answer these central questions, we need research that is simultaneously engaged with contemporary political developments and in conversation with a broad range of existing scholarship so that we can continue to evolve and extend our theoretical understanding of the ways these powerful concepts and phenomena intersect while also rigorously observing the real-world implications of these intersections as they transpire. We have brought together the chapters in this volume in an attempt to do this, to examine the contemporary state of presidential politics, from the way we select our chief executives to the ways in which presidencies are performed, while consciously moving relevant academic debates concerning the central questions of this volume forward. In this sense, then, this volume is intended to serve a wide audience made up of scholars across several disciplines who are interested in these important intersections.

Studying Popular Culture

Academics from a range of disciplines have studied popular culture for a variety of reasons, not the least of which is that it is a realistic meeting place within any course or classroom—it is often the one place where faculty member and student can find an immediate source of commonality. But this relationship easily translates beyond any particular classroom to the broader space within our democracy where—because of the ease with which most Americans can access common cultural touchstones and phenomena—citizens of varied ages, partisan dispositions, class, gender, and religious beliefs can meet each other. As Joseph Foy explains, it is not just that Americans can meet each other through popular culture but that it is also the venue where Americans learn about the political system itself. According to Foy, "Many people first learn about important governmental offices, such as the presidency, Congress, the courts, and the public bureaucracy, and organizations such as interest groups and political parties not from a textbook or political science class, but from a TV show, a movie, or a song. Likewise, exposure to concepts such as civil rights and liberties, terrorism and torture, domestic and foreign policy, and even political philosophy and culture is often delivered through entertainment and that which is 'pop.'"[1] Foy's point is that not only is popular culture important to understand, but it fundamentally contributes to the knowledge that citizens have about the institutions of government, how they work, how one interacts with those institutions, and how elected representatives operate within political institutions. But these institutions and citizens are also interacting with the broader society, where "politics" is not an overt component but where an Aristotelian understanding of politics is distinctly at play—politics understood as the interactions of individuals within society in the myriad ways in which individuals interact, publicly and privately.[2] Political institutions and citizens do not operate in a discrete universe—they are embedded within a society where economics, religions, morals, opinions, and, most important, human interactions all regularly contribute to what we consider to be our culture. Exactly what that culture is is often contested, since it pulls in so many different threads and qualities that come together to form an often shifting or changing whole.

Cultural observers pay so much attention to popular culture because it is rich with information about the political disposition of a particular time or era and can often convey a variety of messages—sometimes competing messages— to cultural consumers. It is also important to consider popular culture's varied and numerous venues, from the most obvious (films, television, music, books) to the less often considered (magazines, newspapers, video games, fashion, all manner of interactive technological experience, even cultural occasions—such as royal weddings, sporting events, inaugurations, etc.), since all of these cultural artifacts contribute to the way that we, as citizens, think of ourselves, as members of particular communities, groups, parties, and nations. In this regard, although we often consider that there is a distinct separation between popular culture artifacts and ourselves, in reality we regularly interact with and shape popular culture, sometimes knowingly and sometimes unconsciously, while we are also influenced by popular culture. In this way our understanding of popular culture also contributes to our understanding of the working of democracy, be it a particular democracy (as in the United States) or democracy as a form of citizen rule. Democracy reflects the contributions of citizens to the shaping of norms and opinions not merely through overt political engagement (like voting) but also through cultural interaction (buying tickets to a movie on its opening night and contributing to its establishment as a blockbuster, adopting particular forms of fashion and contributing to a new trend as a result, etc.). These dimensions of democracy, though based in consumer culture and often considered more economic than political, contribute to the same fabric within society and contribute to the way in which citizens view themselves and their fellow citizens.[3]

CONCEPTUALIZING POPULAR CULTURE

The idea that popular culture simultaneously shapes and reflects American political reality, including the kinds of political leaders and politics that Americans accept and expect, is the theoretical foundation upon which this collection of essays is based. To better understand this foundation, however, we must first address the important question of what exactly we mean when we use the phrase "popular culture." Scholars of popular culture continue to have a now decades-long rich and ever-evolving debate about the precise definition of popular culture—an important intellectual task, to be sure.[4]

As Andi Zeisler has noted, defining popular culture is a task easier said than done.[5] To solve this problem, we follow in the footsteps of experts before us, deferring as did Lee Harrington and Denise Bielby to Chandra Mukerji and Michael Schudson's wise and inclusive attempt to reconcile terminological disputes, agreeing to their definition of popular culture as a concept that "refers to the beliefs and practices, and the objects through which they are organized, that are widely shared among a population."[6] Mary Stuckey and Greg Smith provide additional, intuitive discussion of popular culture, noting that it is "integrated into people's everyday lives," that it is "widely shared across a culture or subculture, but it is also intimately experienced in American living rooms and cars, in a darkened theater, at the beauty salon."[7]

We are particularly intrigued by the causal relationships between the popular culture individuals consume and the way those individuals relate to politics. Geoff Martin and Erin Steuter have written about mass production and passive consumption of popular culture, particularly as it relates to spreading norms of militarism in the age of the global war on terror, and have noted the ability of the public to appreciate popular culture "without the aid of special knowledge or experience."[8] Instead, the bulk of popular culture is consumed for the purposes of entertainment. Liesbet van Zoonen makes a persuasive argument that entertainment is an important, if not the main, ingredient of popular culture, building on John Street's observation that popular culture is a form of culture that is mass produced or made available to large numbers of people via media such as television.[9] This conception of popular culture can be reconciled with some of the most ambitious work being done on the relationship between presidents and popular culture. In particular, the ideas put forward in Jeff Smith's *The Presidents We Imagine* about the importance of storytelling and fictional portrayals of the presidency to the way the institution is understood and how it manifests in reality echo arguments similar to, if broader than, those of van Zoonen.[10] So too does Anne Norton's conceptualization of the president as an actor, in both the institutional and theatrical sense—as well as her reference to the candidate as a commodity, a subject we have also written about elsewhere—reinforce the entertainment-based notion of popular culture.[11]

THE FRAMEWORK FOR ANALYZING POPULAR CULTURE

Popular culture as a category for study and analysis evolved out of the economic changes that transpired with mechanization and the capacity to mass-produce items that are then consumed by the public at large. Although there were earlier forms of popular culture, the change introduced by industrialization provided a truly revolutionary method to disseminate ideas and artifacts in formats that were easily accessible and simple to distribute. The analytical framework for much of the modern intellectual interaction with popular culture came out of the Frankfurt School—which was influenced by interpretations of Karl Marx's understanding of the industrialization of society and the overarching role of economics in establishing the political and cultural dynamics of society. This particular point of confluence also harks back to some of the foundational ideas with regard to intersection of culture and politics or ideology, namely the possible concealment of the fact that those who do not hold power are ultimately subordinated to those who do and are thus deceived by the powerful and are unaware that they are being exploited and oppressed. The act of deception—which often employs culture to mask the reality of exploitation and oppression—is a hallmark of the economic condition within Marxian analyses of industrialized/industrializing societies. The Frankfurt School approach was the first to confront this new form of culture—a culture that is available to the population at large, not confined to particular classes or groups—and analyze what this shift was and what it might mean.

Whether one finds Marx's or the Frankfurt School's economic interpretation of society persuasive or not, mass access to cultural and political tropes has certainly become normalized over the past century and spans both developed and developing societies. What one sees and understands is contextualized by what is historically present: how one understands an experience is determined, in part, by the context in which that experience transpires. Walter Benjamin observed a change from sporadic or occasional interactions with particular aspects of culture to a broad-based consumption of culture that would inevitably contribute to an individual's understanding of his or her place within society.[12] In a more modern context, this can be seen in the way individuals experience their gender or race within society: not only is the individual born a particular sex or race, but our understandings of those experiences are framed by society. As George Lakoff explains, "Politics is about the narratives our culture and our circumstances make available to all of us to live."[13] The ways society frames those experiences become our cultural narratives, and those narratives also frame politics and our individual and group understandings of politics. Thus the historical context and the cultural frame contribute to our understanding of society as much as the political institutions that surround us.

This evolution of culture in the industrial age spurred members of the Frankfurt School and other cultural critics and intellectuals toward this area of analysis—examining how mechanization would transform and essentially make culture popular in ways that had not been possible before the industrial age. While there was some hope among many of these theorists that this had the potential to eliminate class from understandings of culture, many of their conclusions suggested that dominant and subordinate positions within society would remain unchanged. This also weaves into our understanding of politics in general—especially postindustrialization politics, when so much is available to all through a host of media. Popular culture is inevitably political because what informs it are not particularities but broad contours of power and control. More recent discussions of popular culture suggest that what we see in the various forms of culture that surround us indicates where power, especially political power, is lodged, and if that power shifts, it is often conveyed or the shift is demonstrated through cultural presentations. These more modern analyses see less autocratic control in the formulation of popular culture and a more permeable entity that shifts and moves, integrating influences from a host of sources.

The changing positions of power and the permeable nature of popular culture have been combined in contemporary debates. Judith Butler and Angela McRobbie both delineate the fluid nature of power within society and the way in which this comes through popular culture. Butler's proposition points to her conceptualization of the dynamic nature of power and popular perceptions:

> Distinct from a view that casts the operation of power in the political
> field exclusively in terms of discrete blocs which vie with one another

for control of policy questions, hegemony emphasizes the ways in which power operates to form our everyday understanding of social relations, and to orchestrate the ways in which we consent to (and reproduce) those tacit and covert relations of power. Power is not stable or static, but it is remade at various junctions within everyday life; it constitutes our tenuous sense of common sense, and is ensconced as the prevailing epistemes of a culture.[14]

McRobbie slightly reformulates Butler's premise, noting that "relations of power are indeed made and re-made within texts of enjoyment and rituals of relaxation and abandonment," highlighting the role that these texts and rituals (television shows, romantic comedies, popular literature) play in our digestion of the changing positions of dominance within society's framework.[15] Butler and McRobbie wrestle with where the locus of power is within society, particularly democratic society, and note that that locus changes and shifts, with those shifts often seen through the perceptions of culture. McRobbie's point is more precisely directed toward the issue of feminism and what is acknowledged and presented as the "standards" for women within Anglo-American society. Feminist scholars in particular have seen value in using popular culture as a text to explore the role and place of gender in society and the ways in which conceptions of gender change or remain static.[16]

This perspective, that popular culture has something to tell us about how gender is both marketed and consumed, as well as how our understandings of gender may change or shift, provides a foundation for much of the discussion that follows in the chapters within this book. And although dominant political and economic power may not have shifted to women, there has been quite a lot of movement since both first- and second-wave feminism, demonstrating that there is the possibility of movement both within political structures and within culture. This is what we find to be of particular interest and import to our democracy—that popular culture can be a foundational text or demarcation to measure cultural attitudes and to explore the place of gender within society.

EXECUTIVE POWER AND PRESIDENTIAL POLITICS

Within this framework we also need to contextualize executive power, as opposed to simple political power within dominant societal groups. Executive power is perceived and has been defined within Western political thought as stemming from the power of the father within the family and of the king over his subjects (both of these formulations extrapolate from the concept of divine dominion over humanity).[17] Thus it is generally singular, unilateral, male, and dominant. The American presidency, which crowns the executive branch and thus the institutions that exercise executive power, is defined by a kind of male power or quality. The last century has seen the rise of the executive branch within the American political system, the shift in institutional arrangements based on the expansion of the administrative capacities of the office and branch and the move to candidate-centered campaigns and elections.[18] This particular shift, especially with regard to candidate-centered campaigns and elections, has also contributed to the decline of the roles of the political parties within American politics.

The rise of candidate-centered campaigns, not only for the presidency, but across the spectrum of offices, has also contributed to the fusing of popular culture with American political culture—following along some of the paths outlined by the original popular culture theorists. This form of campaign inevitably turns the individual into a commodity and operates in the political marketplace just as a company's brand operates in the economic marketplace. This process has been aided by the rise of twenty-four-hour news and the telescoping of the time frame for information dissemination, as well as by the various new media outlets that provide constant news and analysis for citizen-consumers. There is certainly much more information available to the voters, but whether a citizen pursues deeper knowledge of candidates and policies or is in quest of more "horse-race" data is an ongoing research question within the fields of political science and communications studies.

In this respect, the candidate for president—especially—is sold across the country to a variety of consumers with differing tastes and influences, and thus campaigns and candidates have adapted to sell the individual and, to a lesser degree, the policies advocated by the candidate, in a manner that plays extensively on cultural demands and norms. Even the term *culture* has been integrated into our political vocabulary: "culture wars" are waged, "hipster culture" is seen in opposition to that of "cultural conservatives," and the list goes on.

Because of the shifted focus on the presidency and the executive branch through most of the twentieth century and into the twenty-first, the role of the president as the cultural leader of the country has also affected the way in which we conceive of the office itself. The policies are also commodified around the particular president: "Reaganomics" and "Obamacare" are two examples of this kind of branding—the former being a laudatory term, the latter currently a term used to criticize President Obama's health care reform policy. With the advent of the modern campaign, fused with the evolving media landscape, there is no escaping the mechanized manner in which a presidential campaign and ultimately the president in office is "sold" through a host of outlets and avenues.

The origins of the discussion of modern popular culture can be located in the changing economies within industrializing nations. The initial analysis was of how the new form of culture—mechanized and constructed in formats that themselves were mechanized—would shift the understanding of culture, from one that was clearly aesthetically based to one that would be much more political in nature. This analysis also emphasized the nonparticipatory nature of the new form of popular culture. It was seen as having been created or used by powerful economic and political organs within society, and it was used to control or anesthetize the populace into a kind of consumer conformity.

The more recent debates among cultural scholars across a range of academic disciplines is more focused on not only the value and substance of what makes up popular culture but what can be learned from popular culture about power and politics. Polls and voting may tell us a great deal about partisan political preferences, but popular culture presents sometimes conflicting, sometimes coordinated understandings of the roles that individuals and groups occupy within society. We have located this text within this contested research stream in an effort to tease out some of the cultural frameworks for understanding the role of gender within presidential politics. Gender is now inserted into this broader framework of popular culture and the modern presidential landscape. Just as gender is salable, running for office is a commitment to sell oneself, and into this framework we bring the historical commodification of women, who were—and in some places still are—generally considered property. American culture has grown out of these property transactions, and these experiences are part of our political, economic, and cultural history.

In the recent third-wave feminist era, the industrialized gaze is a defining characteristic of popular culture. Into this mix, we overlay the evolved position of candidate-centered politics and the defining characteristics of power as it is associated with the presidency and executive power. Any individual who runs for president will have to negotiate multiple perspectives and contexts, but women who run for the presidency have found themselves in particularly contested positions, and their partisan disposition (Democrat Hillary Clinton, Republican Sarah Palin, Republican Michele Bachmann) has contributed to some of the contested nature of how they are to be understood and perceived, both politically and, to an odd degree, symbolically.[19]

POPULAR CULTURE AND THE MASS MEDIA

A subject that is frequently raised in studies of popular culture is the mass media and whether it is a component of popular culture or something entirely distinct. Stuckey and Smith have noted the distinction between popular culture and mass media by effectively considering the former content that is disseminated by the latter. As they note, mass media are "defined by the channel that carries the content, not by content itself. Although people talk about 'television' or 'film' as if they were coherent entities, the medium itself is a delivery system that can relay vastly different forms of culture."[20] At the same time, we contend that there may be substantive differences in the kinds of culture being delivered across different types of media that make some medium-specific analyses of popular culture content valuable. This is particularly the case in the current media environment, where the commercial viability of media of all kinds has dramatically changed the dynamic in which the traditional understanding of media has been replaced by a less clearly delineated one that increasingly trades on celebrity, consumerism, and conveying information to citizens. Thus we have included several medium-specific chapters in this volume.

In the discussion of the media, there is also a need to explore the multidimensional nature of media coverage. Not all coverage is equal, and not all coverage of politicians, especially presidents or those seeking the presidency, is equal. The pace and constancy of the evolution of media in the United States also make it difficult to designate particular forms of media (print, television, radio, blogs, etc.) as the true arbiters of information. Because of the evolution not only of the media but also of the business structure that supports media, all of these components are currently in a fluid period. The media have become a much more regular component within popular culture, where the separation between news purveyors and newsmakers is often difficult to distinguish. This fusing of media and popular culture is also connected to the explosion of celebrity culture. Public figures have increasingly become celebrities—from politicians (this was a line of attack that the McCain campaign used against Obama in the summer of 2008) to news personalities, bloggers, and other journalists.

This fusion is even more pronounced within new media—which spend as much time focusing on popular culture as they do on information dissemination. And new media are explored, analyzed, and discussed (both academically and more broadly) as a subject of popular culture and our understanding of culture in general—as much as they function as a means of conveying information about culture. Thus new media are both a means of disseminating the cultural conversation and a subject of that conversation itself. They are also hybrid participants in the cultural conversation because of the ubiquity of the Internet—in this regard, new media have been altering the way in which candidates, campaigns, and public individuals must operate. As Nichola D. Gutgold notes in her book *Almost Madam President: Why Hillary Clinton "Won" in 2008*, "Today's media savvy candidate knows that the Internet is as viable a source for information as any and that the information on the Internet lives on in perpetuity. Campaigns must have the mechanism to respond quickly to Internet movements."[21] This has become almost a defining quality of recent campaigns—whether they are able to successfully interact with new media, respond to the constant demands of online culture, and make use of new media to aid and enhance their candidate's appeal.

Research has also indicated that demographic groups access media differently—older, more educated individuals tend to operate within a more traditional media platform, accessing information from print media and network news and, in some cases, from a few Internet sources. As the demographic groups change, the consumption of information changes; thus younger citizens move around among multiple Internet sources for information, not necessarily even accessing traditional media platforms for information.[22] In this fluid media environment, candidates, campaigns, and elected officials need to direct different messages to different demographic groups through different media outlets and resources. Christopher Cooper and Mandi Bates Bailey explain that "citizens who get their information from soft news media differ significantly from those who consume traditional hard news sources. Hard news consumers tend to be more educated, more interested in politics, older, and more likely to be males than soft news consumers."[23] In a sense, demographic and socioeconomic groups are now occupying the same space as gender groupings in accessing information.[24] But it is not only the difference among voters that is of interest; it is also important to explore the presentation and consumption of gender at the national level, as voters experience the growing presence of gender in the context of the institution of the U.S. presidency.

PRECEDENTS FOR EXPLORING GENDER, POPULAR CULTURE, AND THE PRESIDENCY

As a whole, this volume takes an interdisciplinary approach to the analytical examination of the increasingly important and multifaceted relationships between popular culture, gender, and presidential politics. In recent years, scholarly awareness of this important nexus has started to grow, and the rich body of literature concerning the relationship between popular culture and presidential politics (e.g., John Matviko's *The American President in Popular Culture*, Peter Rollins and John O'Connor's *Hollywood's White House*, and Jeff Smith's *The Presidents We Imagine*) has started to take notice of the driving force played by gender.[25] Michaele Ferguson and Lori Jo Marso have edited a volume, *W Stands for Women*, about the impact the George W. Bush administration had on shaping a new politics of gender, and Regina Lawrence and Melody Rose have authored a text on the gender and media politics of Hillary Clinton's run for the Democratic Party's presidential nomination.[26] A stand-alone text more directly related to the role of culture is Trevor and Shawn J. Parry-Giles's study of *The West Wing*, which looks at the seminal television program and how it promoted particular cultural messages about U.S. nationalism, especially with respect to gender and race.[27] Finally, Lori Cox Han and Caroline Heldman's *Rethinking Madam President* confronts, from multiple perspectives, the issues facing women as they pursue election to the presidency.[28] In that collection of essays, several scholars take up topics like media stereotypes, cultural barriers, and conceptions of masculinity in a comprehensive effort to answer a single central motivating question: Is the United States ready for a female president? Although our approach is different in that we are more explicitly interested in analyzing the role popular culture plays in shaping how Americans think about both gender and presidential politics and less interested in determining the extent to which the American electorate is amenable to female leadership, the intellectual efforts made in Han and Heldman's volume are significant, and the present volume owes it a great debt.

However, despite the excellence of the previous works noted above, a dramatic shortage of serious scholarly inquiries into the relationships between gender, popular culture, and presidential politics persists. It is into that void that this volume steps. We have assembled twelve contributions that cover several key cultural arenas while also making new theoretical contributions to the scholarly discourse of multiple academic disciplines. The chapters in this book about films, for example, do not just describe the relationship between popular culture and the institution of the American presidency but also offer unique scholarly arguments about that relationship, especially as seen through a gendered framework. This emphasis on the role of gender and how it frames and influences so much of our understanding of presidential electoral politics helped to guide our compilation of chapters for this volume. Many of the texts noted above do not include analyses of important and relevant subjects such as daytime soft news programs, print tabloids, or the first family. Our volume also reaches back into modern history—and, in some cases, further back to the inception of the American presidency—to provide comparative context for the discussions of popular culture. Although some of the chapters, by their very cultural area, concentrate most heavily on the most recent election, all chapters provide relevant historical context so that these discussions offer the reader not only an understanding of today's popular culture as it relates to our current president but also analyses of the evolution of popular culture as it intersects with the presidency and the individual president, especially as that intersection has varied over time.

As noted previously, the underlying concern of this volume is how popular culture simultaneously shapes and reflects American political reality, including the kinds of political leaders and politics that Americans accept and expect. By tightening our focus to the relationship between gender dynamics and this culture-politics linkage as it relates to the American presidency, we have been able to develop particularly strong insights not only about how gender-based factors drive the approach and methods through which women and men participate at the highest levels of American public life but also about how attitudes toward gender are reflected in the popular cultural artifacts that document broader cultural attitudes toward the most important symbolic representatives of American society.

PRESIDENCY AND PATRIARCHY: GENDERED INTERSECTIONS OF THE PRESIDENCY

The election of Barack Obama as the forty-fourth president was obviously a watershed event. At the same time, both before and since Obama's election, there have been women and minorities in growing numbers in positions of political power in the United States. Over the past half century, there have been a number of "firsts." President Ronald Reagan's appointment of Sandra Day O'Connor to the Supreme Court is a landmark example. Geraldine Ferraro's run as Walter Mondale's vice presidential candidate in 1984 was another important moment, and though it took place across the Atlantic Ocean, the long and notable tenure of British prime minister Margaret Thatcher was yet another watershed for the reality of women in political positions of power and significance. Further, the actual administrations in Washington, DC, have included greater gender diversity with each new administration.

It has really been only during the last twenty years or so, though, that women have been appointed to cabinet-level positions that are not "naturally" associated with their gender.[29] Although President Franklin Roosevelt appointed the first woman to a cabinet position (Frances Perkins as secretary of labor from 1933 to 1945), most of the cabinet positions that were held by women tended to be directly connected to what are generally perceived to be the natural/innate issue areas of their gender, such as the Department of Labor and the Department of Health and Human Services. The cabinet positions that are the oldest and thus among the most important in the functioning of the administration and advising the president have only recently started to open up to women. Janet Reno became the first (and, thus far, only) female attorney general. Furthermore, both a Latino (Alberto Gonzales) and an African American (Eric Holder) have held the post. Madeleine Albright became the first female secretary of state, followed by Colin Powell as the first African American secretary of state and Condoleezza Rice as the first female African American secretary of state, who, before that, served as the first female African American national security advisor. Hillary Clinton came to her position as secretary of state from her elected position in the U.S. Senate (and after her run for the Democratic presidential nomination in 2008). The presidential administrations of Bill Clinton, George W. Bush, and Barack Obama opened up significantly more positions of power to more women than any previous presidential administrations.

The president himself has always been a symbol of many things—including power, patriarchy, virtue, ability, and popularity. This office is defined by patriarchal characteristics and qualities—from the capacity of the president as commander in chief to the unbroken 225-year streak of only men filling this position (which distinguishes it from both monarchies, which are often led by women, and most other developed democracies, many of which have elected women to the highest executive office of prime minister, president, or chancellor). The president's particular role in foreign affairs (the appointment of ambassadors, the making of treaties, etc.) also reflects the acutely patriarchal qualities of the office; as Charlotte Hooper has noted in her *Manly States: Masculinities, International Relations, and Gender Politics*, "The focus on war, diplomacy, states, statesmen, and high-level economic negotiations has overwhelmingly represented the lives and identities of men. This is because of the institutionalization of gender differences in society at large and the consequent paucity of women in high office."[30] Although Hooper herself rejects the term "patriarchy," what she analyzes is the patriarchal nature of executive leadership. Linda Horwitz and Holly Swyers explain that "the notion of what a president should look like, or what is presidential, is fundamentally masculine. . . . Leadership is a masculine domain as established by God."[31]

Perceptions among the electorate that women and men handle different situations with different capacities contribute to Hooper's thesis and are discussed throughout the literature examining the different perceptions about male and female candidates. For example, Gina Serignese Woodall and Kim L. Fridkin explain that certain stereotypes voters hold will, at times, contribute to the embedded patriarchal dimensions of the White House, noting that "when the country is at war or when the US economy is in recession, economic issues, foreign policy, and defense issues will top the national agenda. These are precisely the issues that people believe men can handle better than women."[32] We have also noted that although women have been appointed as secretary of state and recently as national security advisor, there have been no female secretaries of the treasury or defense.[33] There are still clearly entrenched ideas about different capacities that men and women have, especially with regard to the conduct of war and defense policy. For example, Jennifer Lawless has found a distinct difference in perceptions of abilities based on gender, with a substantial majority thinking that men were much better equipped to handle military issues and defense policy decisions than were women. According to Lawless, "Citizens prefer men's leadership traits and characteristics, deem men more competent at legislating around issues of national security and military crises, and contend that men are superior to women at addressing the new obstacles generated by the events of September 11, 2011. As a result of this stereotyping, levels of willingness to support a qualified woman presidential candidate are lower than they have been for decades."[34] This is particularly important when considering the essential character of the American presidency, which, as Alexander Hamilton asserted, is to be characterized by unity, decision, secrecy, activity, and dispatch. The office requires many of the qualities, at least to a degree, of a traditional "executive"; in the minds of the Founders this meant an emphasis on issues of war, martial conduct, international relationships, and, particularly in Hamilton's opinion, the economic policy of the republic.[35] These are issues that are defined as masculine in quality and characteristic. Feminine issues tend to be those more closely associated with the home and family: education, health, human services, labor, and housing. Although research has indicated that male and female candidates are treated similarly in many respects, there remain fundamental conceptions of policy areas that are more specifically masculine and areas that are more specifically feminine. The particular emphasis of the presidency is on the issue areas that are generally defined as masculine.

The Path of the Volume

The chapters in this book are grouped into four thematically linked sections, each of which responds to the central questions identified earlier in this chapter that motivate the creation of this volume. Together, these sections examine the way culture shapes politics, how political reality shapes culture across a variety of cultural arenas, and how the two combine in the one dimension of the American presidency that has historically been dominated by women: the White House's domestic sphere, occupied by the first lady and the first family. Part I, "Framing Candidates, Understanding Voters," concerns the ways in which candidacies for the nation's highest office are often presented in gendered terms. The three chapters in this section use evidence from recent elections, especially the 2008 election cycle, to enter into broader discussions of the ways in which messages about candidates are conveyed, controlled, altered, and framed, particularly the different ways that male and female candidates are presented to the public and try to present themselves to the public.

Linda Beail and Rhonda Kinney Longworth start their investigation with Sarah Palin's run as John McCain's vice presidential candidate as the avenue into a discussion of the framing of female candidates for high national office. At the same time, they compare other female candidates to Governor Palin and the way she presented herself to the public and the way in which the public came to see her. They demonstrate that though the frames employed to present Palin to the electorate were not easily controlled, they were driven by the different kinds of relationships Palin had and developed with key voter blocs, including men as well as women. Mary McHugh explores the impact that late-night comedy has on this message framing, especially as these programs have become key venues for young adults (young men more than young women) to access political information. She shows that both gender and the extent to which a candidate is previously unknown shape the strength of what she calls the *Saturday Night Live* effect. In the final chapter in this section, Chapman Rackaway evaluates the actual voter, especially the female voter, who has become the center of media attention during presidential election cycles. Much has been made of soccer moms, security moms, and now hockey moms as distinct and important voting groups, but this chapter aims to determine whether these stereotypes are more media fabrication or reality, while also comparing the particular attention showered on female voters with attention paid to male voters. Rackaway finds that notions of empathy play a powerful role in explaining the difference between female and male voting patterns and, in doing so, identifies the philosophical and cultural underpinnings of gender differences that have previously been explained by motherhood. All three chapters present historical perspectives along with the most recent examples, and together amount to a well-rounded evaluation of the ways female candidates for the presidency and vice presidency frame themselves and are framed by media and political operations.

Part II, "Hollywood's Influence on Presidential Politics," takes up the relationship between popular culture and gendered considerations of presidential politics in a more traditional manner as the three chapters explore film and television productions that focus on the American presidency with an aim to discern what these productions teach us about how the presidency is integrated into the public consciousness in deeply gendered ways. Lilly Goren analyzes fictional presentations of both female presidents and minority male presidents to determine if there are patterns in what Hollywood thinks is appropriate and will sell tickets. Her chapter yields interesting insight into the way fictional presidents are elected or otherwise ascend to the presidency, especially in connection to their gender and race. Chapters 6 and 7 each explore how the gender bias associated with the presidency has been integrated into our fictional frameworks of film and television series. In chapter 6, Joseph Uscinski investigates the source of American ambivalence toward and discomfort with the idea of female presidential leadership. He argues that Hollywood has supplied messages that have reinforced this antipathy. In chapter 7, Justin Vaughn and Stacy Michaelson pay particular attention to the question of masculinity and the ways in which the fictional presidency has been conveyed in that context. They show that not only are successful presidents men who display masculine characteristics but women and unsuccessful male presidents are portrayed as antimasculinist and feminine.

Part III, "'All the News That's Fit to Print'?: Alternative Avenues for Political Information," continues the examination of gendered popular culture but moves the locus of attention away from Hollywood and toward a range of cultural artifacts that are often considered secondary in importance to more traditional cultural forms. However, we contend that it is essential to consider such a broad range of cultural artifacts because even though films, television shows, and music are generally considered the dominant modes of popular cultural expression in America, they are not the sole forms by which important information about society is communicated. Instead, numerous forms of cultural expression reach large audiences, even if not quite on the order of the dominant modes like film, television, and music. This section of the book takes up three of these areas, concentrating on what is now considered to be "soft news" venues: daytime talk shows, popular magazines and tabloids, and the Internet or blogosphere. First, José Villalobos explores the "Oprah Effect" in his chapter on how presidents and candidates reach millions of voters when they sit down to talk with hosts on gendered television programming. These engagements contribute to the way presidents and presidential aspirants are considered and consumed, especially by the important female voting demographic. Villalobos shows how this communication strategy is as controversial as it is effective and provides a comprehensive account of the strengths and weaknesses for candidates and citizens in this campaign strategy. In chapter 9, Elizabeth Hatfield considers the way in which the presidential image, especially the image of the president's family, is conveyed through popular entertainment print outlets and tabloids. Like that of daytime talk television, this market is predominantly female and has received considerably more attention in recent decades from presidential aspirants and scholars alike, as women have become more important factors in election strategy. Conducting an exhaustive analysis of *People*'s coverage of presidential families and, especially, the first ladies since the 1970s, she concludes that the personal dimension of this tabloid-style journalism influences elections by providing information to an audience of voters who may not be paying attention to other kinds of media outlets and, in doing so, helps these voters determine their vote choice based on how they feel about the candidates and their families as people. Finally, Todd Belt takes on the more informal effects of new media and the Internet as he focuses on the ways in which viral video candidate personas are increasingly determined by independent forces across the blogosphere in a way that is different and more difficult to anticipate for female candidates than for their male counterparts. His innovative empirical analysis of this new yet powerful phenomenon demonstrates that although frequently produced by amateurs, such videos mirror broader trends found in the more filtered mass media, particularly in the ways these videos gender the aspirants to high office and the office itself.

Part IV, "Women in the White House: First Ladies, First Couples, First Families," includes three chapters that each focus on gender in the White House. Although a man has formally occupied the presidency since the dawn of the Republic, gender has long exerted significant influence on the institution and the individuals who populate it. This section includes three chapters that deal directly with the human element of the institution, from the first lady to presidents and their relationships with their wives and families. These chapters are particularly noteworthy, as the only direct integration thus far of gender into the innermost circle of the presidency has been through the family that accompanies the elected president into the White House. The analyses of these influences give clear voice and understanding to the role that women have had—directly—in the institution of the presidency and our understanding of that office. Although the influence may be quite different than that of the president himself, any text that claims to take up the issue of gender and the presidency must also include a discussion of the role of the first lady, the first family, and the way the president and his wife operate both on the campaign trail and once they have entered the White House. In doing so, MaryAnne Borrelli examines the role first ladies have played in linking popular culture with domestic initiatives. Rooting the analysis in a broader historical discussion of how individual first ladies have attempted to make the institution their own, Borrelli focuses on three examples in the Obama administration of Michelle Obama continuing or renewing efforts by her predecessors in her own way. Melissa Buis Michaux and Karen Hoffman each examine the domestic life of presidents, as Michaux analyzes the ways portrayals of family within the White House have shaped and been shaped by trends in families throughout the nation, with a particular focus on what we can learn from the current occupants of the White House, while Hoffman focuses on the marriages of the presidents and first ladies and the balance between the public's expectations and the private realities of the relationship. Michaux demonstrates how Michelle Obama's embodiment of reconstructive feminism has challenged contemporary conceptions of not only the first lady but also the ideas we have about American ways of living, working, and belonging. Hoffman's examination of the first couple and how White House partnerships have been and continue to be constituted show that though the contributions of the first lady have changed over time, its gendered and gendering dimension persists.

Taken together, these chapters provide a multifaceted approach to the powerful and profound linkages between gender, popular culture, and the American presidency. The intersection between these subjects connects many avenues of research. By examining the ways candidates for the nation's highest office are gendered, the ways the institution itself is gendered by Hollywood and other important sources of cultural understanding and the ways that gender has exerted influence over the people within the actual White House we emerge better equipped not only to answer the common question of when the United States will elect its first female president but also more substantive questions such as what the public will expect from that trailblazing chief executive, how gender will affect the way she governs, and what tests and challenges she will face as both presidential aspirant and Oval Office occupant.

Notes

1. Joseph J. Foy, introduction to *Homer Simpson Goes to Washington: American Politics through Popular Culture*, ed. Joseph J. Foy (Lexington: University Press of Kentucky, 2008), 3.

2. See particularly book 1, chapter 2, of Aristotle's *Nicomachean Ethics,* trans. Robert C. Bartlett and Susan D. Collins (Chicago: University of Chicago Press, 2011).

3. Fashion has always considered itself political, and fashion designers and fashion magazine editors, while usually avoiding overt forms of partisan political commentary, are constantly making political commentary through their creations and the attempt to create the next global trend.

4. For an instructive introduction to academic discourse surrounding the definition of popular culture, see C. Lee Harrington and Denise D. Bielby, "Constructing the Popular: Cultural Production and Consumption," in *Popular Culture: Production and Consumption,* ed. C. Lee Harrington and Denise D. Bielby (Malden, MA: Blackwell, 2001), 1–15.

5. Andi Zeisler, *Feminism and Pop Culture* (Berkeley, CA: Seal Studies, 2008), 1.

6. Chandra Mukerji and Michael Schudson, "Introduction: Rethinking Popular Culture," in *Rethinking Popular Culture: Contemporary Perspectives in Cultural Studies,* ed. Chandra Mukerji and Michael Schudson (Berkeley: University of California Press, 1991), 3.

7. Mary Stuckey and Greg M. Smith, "The Presidency and Popular Culture," in *The Presidency, the Public, and the Parties,* 3rd ed. (Washington, DC: CQ Press, 2008), 212.

8. Geoff Martin and Erin Steuter, *Pop Culture Goes to War: Enlisting and Resisting Militarism in the War on Terror* (Lanham, MD: Rowman and Littlefield), 60.

9. Liesbet van Zoonen, *Entertaining the Citizen: When Politics and Popular Culture Converge* (Lanham, MD: Rowman and Littlefield, 2005), 10; John Street, *Politics and Popular Culture* (Cambridge: Polity, 1997), 7.

10. Jeff Smith, *The Presidents We Imagine: Two Centuries of White House Fictions on the Page, on the Stage, Onscreen, and Online* (Madison: University of Wisconsin Press, 2009).

11. Anne Norton, *Republic of Signs: Liberal Theory and American Popular Culture* (Chicago: University of Chicago Press, 1993), 87, 113; Lilly Goren and Justin Vaughn, "Profits and Protest: The Cultural Commodification of the Presidential Image," in *Politics and Popular Culture,* ed. Leah A. Murray (Newcastle upon Tyne: Cambridge Scholars Press), 85–99.

12. Walter Benjamin, "The Work of Art in the Age of Mechanical Reproduction," in *The Continental Aesthetics Reader,* ed. Clive Cazeaux (New York: Routledge, 1936), 325–26.

13. George Lakoff, *The Political Mind: Why You Can't Understand 21st-Century American Politics with an 18th-Century Brain* (New York: Viking, 2008), 35.

14. Judith Butler, Ernesto Laclau, and Slavoj Žižek, eds., *Contingency, Hegemony, Universality: Contemporary Dialogues on the Left.* (London: Verso, 2000), 13–14.

15. Angela McRobbie, "Post-Feminism and Popular Culture," *Feminist Media Studies* 4, no. 3 (2004): 262.

16. See Jennifer Baumgardner and Amy Richards, *Manifesta: Young Women, Feminism, and the Future.* (New York: Farrar, Straus and Giroux, 2000); Bonnie J. Dow, *Prime Time Feminism: Television, Media Culture, and the Women's Movement since 1970* (Philadelphia: University of Pennsylvania Press, 1996); Leslie Heywood and Jennifer Drake, eds., *Third Wave Agenda: Being Feminist, Doing Feminism* (Minneapolis: University of Minnesota Press, 1997); Joanne Hollows, *Feminism, Femininity, and Popular Culture* (Manchester: Manchester University Press, 2000); Amanda D. Lotz, *Redesigning Women: Television after the Network Era* (Urbana: University of Illinois Press, 2006); Suzanna Danuta Walters, *Material Girls: Making Sense of Feminist Cultural Theory* (Berkeley: University of California Press, 1995); Leslie Heywood and Jennifer Drake, eds., *Third Wave Agenda: Being Feminist, Doing Feminism, and the Future.* (New York: Farrar, Straus and Giroux, 1997); Charlotte Brunsdon, *The Feminist, the Housewife, and the Soap Opera* (New York: Oxford University Press, 2000); Suzanne Ferriss and Mallory Young, eds., *Chick Lit: The New Woman's Fiction* (New York: Routledge, 2006); Sherrie A. Inness, *Tough Girls: Women Warriors and Wonder Women in Popular Culture* (Philadelphia: University of Pennsylvania Press, 1999); Joanne Hollows and Rachel Moseley, *Feminism in Popular Culture* (New York: Berg, 2006).

17. For an extensive discussion of the dominant characteristics and qualities of executive power as have generally been integrated into the American system, see Niccolò Machiavelli, *The Prince,* trans. Harvey C. Mansfield (Chicago: University of Chicago Press, 1998); Thomas Hobbes, *The Leviathan,* 1651; John Locke, *Two Treatises of Government,* 1689; Harvey C. Mansfield, *Taming the Prince: The Ambivalence of Modern Executive Power* (New York: Free Press, 1989).

18. See Sidney M. Milkis, *The President and the Parties: The Transformation of the American Party System since the New Deal* (New York: Oxford University Press, 1993).

19. While much time was devoted to discussions of Hillary Clinton's cleavage on the campaign trail in 2008, less time was spent discussing her general wardrobe in comparison to the amount of coverage of Sarah Palin's fashion choices. Clinton's wardrobe fit into an expected rubric: conservative professional suits. She had added color to her wardrobe so that not all of her suits were black, but generally her wardrobe was not unlike most other elected officials—male or female. Palin, on the other hand, wore clothes that ran the gamut, from the outfit she wore while giving her extremely well-received speech at the Republican National Convention to flannel shirts and jeans and running clothes. There were endless discussions about Palin's shopping spree at Nordstrom during the Republican convention and the cost of her campaign wardrobe.

20. Stuckey and Smith, "Presidency and Popular Culture," 212.

21. Nichola D. Gutgold, *Almost Madam President: Why Hillary Clinton "Won" in 2008* (Lanham, MD: Lexington Books, 2009), 98.

22. For an insightful review of this literature as well as analysis that connects different media consumption patterns with political participation, see Ingrid Bachmann et al., "News Platform Preference: Advancing the Effects of Age and Media Consumption on Political Participation," *International Journal of Internet Science* 5, no. 1 (2010): 34–47.

23. Christopher A. Cooper and Mandi Bates Bailey, "Entertainment Media and Political Knowledge: Do People Get Any Truth out of Truthiness?," in Foy, *Homer Simpson,* 140.

24. See Chapman Rackaway's chapter in this volume on the differences between male and female voters for more information on the way different gender groups operate within the political environment.

25. John W. Matviko, ed., *The American President in Popular Culture* (Westport, CT: Greenwood, 2005); Peter C. Rollins and John E. O'Connor, eds., *Hollywood's White House: The American Presidency in Film and History* (Lexington: University Press of Kentucky, 2003); Smith, *Presidents We Imagine.*

26. Michaele L. Ferguson and Lori Jo Marso, eds., *W Stands for Women: How the George W. Bush Presidency Shaped a New Politics of Gender* (Durham, NC: Duke University Press, 2007); Regina G. Lawrence and Melody Rose, eds., *Hillary Clinton's Race for the White House: Gender Politics and the Media on the Campaign Trail* (Boulder, CO: Lynne Rienner, 2010).

27. Trevor Parry-Giles and Shawn Parry-Giles, *The Prime-Time Presidency: "The West Wing" and U.S. Nationalism* (Urbana: University of Illinois Press, 2006).

28. Lori Cox Han and Caroline Heldman, eds., *Rethinking Madam President: Are We Ready for a Woman in the White House?* (Boulder, CO: Lynne Rienner, 2007).

29. It should be noted that a parallel story can be told about the evolution of race in the presidency.

30. Charlotte Hooper, *Manly States: Masculinities, International Relations, and Gender Politics* (New York: Columbia University Press, 2001), 12.

31. Linda Horwitz and Holly Swyers, "Why Are All the Presidents Men? Televisual Presidents and Patriarchy," in *You've Come a Long Way, Baby: Women, Politics, and Popular Culture,* ed. Lilly J. Goren (Lexington: University Press of Kentucky 2009), 119.

32. Gina Serignese Woodall and Kim L. Fridkin, "Shaping Women's Chances: Stereotypes and the Media," in Han and Heldman, *Rethinking Madam President,* 81.

33. MaryAnne Borrelli has written at length about the complex, gender-driven patterns of presidential cabinet nominations. See MaryAnne Borrelli, *The President's Cabinet: Gender, Power, and Representation* (Boulder, CO: Lynne Rienner, 2002).

34. Jennifer L. Lawless, "Women, War, and Winning Elections: Gender Stereotyping in the Post–September 11th Era," *Political Research Quarterly* 57, no. 3 (2004): 480.

35. See *Federalist Papers* 69 through 77, particularly 69 and 70, http://Thomas.loc.gov/home/histdox/fedpapers.html.

Part I

FRAMING CANDIDATES, UNDERSTANDING VOTERS

2

PURITAN OR PIT BULL

The Framing of Female Candidates at the National Level

Linda Beail and Rhonda Kinney Longworth

Sarah Palin's vice presidential candidacy garnered tremendous levels of interest, polarizing the American public. From the day John McCain chose her as his running mate, much of what has been written about Palin has focused on discovering who she "really" is: establishing her credentials, exploring her issue positions, or predicting her political future. Is she smart enough to govern? Are her policy positions or familial situations hypocritical? Will she run for president?

But perhaps more interesting than defining who Sarah Palin is would be analyzing why she touches such a nerve with the American electorate. Why does she ignite such passionate loyalty—and such loathing? How did her candidacy mobilize new parts of the electorate? Using the notion of "framing" popularized by George Lakoff, we explain and analyze the narratives told by and about Sarah Palin in the 2008 election: she is simultaneously understood and debated as a frontier woman, hockey mom, ordinary citizen and political outsider, maverick reformer, beauty queen, and postfeminist role model.[1] We explore where those frames are rooted historically in popular and political culture, why they were selected, and how they resonated with the electorate. Finally, we discuss what the choices and perceptions of these frames tell us about American politics and the status of American women within that arena.

As Lakoff notes, "Frames are the cognitive structures we think with."[2] Simple narrative structures with archetypal characters and events help us categorize new information into familiar stories that make sense to us: for example, a "rescue" narrative involving a hero who triumphs over some evil misdeed of a villain to save an innocent victim.[3] Invoking these story frames is less a conscious, deliberate choice than the unconscious work of neural binding in our brains. And these schemas are not merely cognitive; they carry emotional content as well.[4] Thus frames powerfully structure the way we react to political events and why they matter to us. According to Lakoff, "Politics is very much about cultural narratives. For candidates it is about the stories they have lived and are living, the stories they tell about themselves, the stories the opposition tries to pin on them, and the stories the press tells about them. But in a deeper sense, politics is about the narratives our culture and our circumstances make available to all of us to live. . . . Cultural narratives define our possibilities, challenges and actual lives."[5] Research conducted over the last two decades demonstrates that while some frames succeed and others fail, in general "framing effects have the potential to fundamentally shape public opinion."[6] Psychologist Drew Westen concurs, stressing the importance of "networks of associations, bundles of thoughts, feelings, images and ideas that have become connected over time."[7] The metaphors and stories that are most influential appeal to our emotional and moral sensibilities. Westen's work urges Democrats, perhaps too focused on the rational merits of particular issue positions, to take note of the more savvy ways Republicans have couched their proposals in language and stories that connect with voters' hearts and values: "Political persuasion is about networks and narratives."[8] These narratives also create the criteria by which citizens judge which political information matters, because "frames influence not only what people think and feel about an issue but what they don't think about."[9] Thus the frames we employ help us to focus on some factors as extremely important while discarding other aspects as not relevant.

The Gendered Context of Elections

Female candidates have had to think carefully and strategically about how they frame themselves for the voting public. We know that the public perceives candidates differently according to their sex. Just as party labels serve as cues for voters to assume information about a candidate in the absence of full information, a candidate's gender is used to infer certain personality traits and leadership strengths.[10] Psychological studies show widespread agreement about the division of personality traits ascribed predominantly to men and those attributed to women. A typical woman is seen as warm, sensitive to others, compassionate, and kind, whereas a typical man is viewed as decisive, self-reliant, willing to take risks, and assertive.[11]

Men and women in the political sphere are not immune to such stereotypes. Both survey data and experimental studies of hypothetical candidates demonstrate that female politicians are thought of as more compassionate, caring, honest, empathetic, and accessible than their male counterparts.[12] However, experimental studies show that when asked to assess the qualities of a "good" politician, students ranked tough and aggressive traits as more important than warm and expressive traits.[13] Experimental research regarding women as presidential candidates in particular has found that voters prefer masculine leadership characteristics and rate male candidates as more "effective" than similarly qualified women at presidential duties.[14] Thus female candidates may be ultimately disadvantaged when it comes to gender stereotypes about candidate personality traits. In a historical study of presidential candidates, Erika Falk found that the emotions of women were covered by the media at a much higher rate than men in the same races. Certainly the most noted aspect of Patricia Schroeder's exploratory bid for the Democratic nomination in 1987 was her tears at the press conference announcing she would not run—reifying the stereotype that women are too emotional. In 1999, Elizabeth Dole was criticized for being too ladylike—full of "sugar" and "charm" but too polite, scripted, and like a Stepford wife.[15] Indeed, early attempts by women to run for the White House fit no workable narrative and were literally unthinkable. In a 1972 editorial entitled "Symbolic Candidacy," the *New York Times* opined, "The presidential candidacy of Representative Shirley Chisholm, the second-term Congresswoman from Brooklyn, is not a venture in practical politics. She candidly recognizes that she is not going to win."[16]

Based on these beliefs about gender-linked personality traits, female leaders have been given credit for handling certain political issues significantly better than men.[17] These include issues involving children and family, poverty, health, education, peace, the arts, consumers, and the environment. Of course, these beliefs about issue competence are not based solely and arbitrarily on gender-role stereotypes. Female officeholders often place a high priority on these issues themselves. The electorate certainly can and does pick up on such agenda priorities. Further, surveys have shown that male politicians benefit from perceptions that they are tougher, know the political system better, and can more ably handle a crisis. These views lead voters to prefer male leadership in dealing with issues of defense, the military, international diplomacy, foreign trade, big business, and crime.[18] Particularly after the September 11 terrorist attacks, surveys showed a rise in the salience of security issues, a strong preference for male leadership in military crisis, and a drop in willingness to consider a female presidential candidate.[19] Voters in focus groups interviewed by the Barbara Lee Family Foundation in 2002 were likely to trust male gubernatorial candidates more than females with economic issues and budgeting—foundational issues in presidential campaigns.[20] Finally, Kim Fridkin Kahn found that voters apply gendered stereotypes about issues and personality traits to female candidates for the U.S. Senate even more often than they do to male candidates, making these stereotypes especially important in races involving female candidates.[21]

Because voters often characterize leadership, competence, and power as "masculine," female candidates may meet with the most success when they stress those types of traits rather than "feminine" qualities of compassion and honesty more commonly attributed to them.[22] In other words, female candidates have to make strategic decisions in their campaigns: Do they play to their stereotypical strengths and build on that support, or do they play against type and emphasize traits and issues voters normally associate with both men and political officehold-ers? Recent advice to potential female candidates for executive office emphasizes striking just the right balance on that tightrope: successful women must be "effec-tive but appealing," "factual and tough" without being "personal and harsh."[23] In its guidebooks advising female candidates, the Barbara Lee Family Foundation bluntly tells them to avoid short hair or a "mannish" appearance. They also warn women about their tone of voice, citing focus group comments such as "She was a witch. That was so clear" and "I couldn't stand to listen to her voice. . . . I'd have to move if she were elected."[24] Female candidates are told they need to be strong and assertive but to avoid seeming aggressive and shrill.

Of course, female candidates are not completely in control of the messages and images of themselves that voters receive and react to. Frames presented by candidates are not merely accepted at face value. As Kim Fridkin Kahn found, even though female senatorial candidates emphasized "masculine" traits 91 percent of the time in their ads, news stories about those female candidates only mentioned such traits 41 percent of the time. The same media reports emphasized masculine traits for male candidates more than the candidates did themselves—reinforcing views perhaps already in voters' minds but not what candidates were trying to communicate.[25] Historically, female candidates for the White House have received less coverage than similarly qualified men. Men on average had twice the number of articles written about them, and those articles were 7 percent longer.[26] Men also get more "issue" coverage, while female can-didates are more often described in terms of their physical appearance. Numer-ous accounts of women's campaigns discuss the "lipstick watch," the attention paid to the candidate's clothing and hairstyles.[27] Media trainer Michael Sheehan sums up the obstacles in his title for a seminar for potential female officehold-ers: "Husbands, Hemlines, and Hairdos."[28]

In addition to having their appearance scrutinized, deflecting attention away from political issues and potentially trivializing or objectifying them as women, female candidates are also faced with questions about their personal lives. As Susan Carroll notes, "Voters are more likely to scrutinize a woman candidate's family situation. . . . When a man runs for office, his family is generally viewed as an important source of emotional and personal support. When a woman runs, her spouse and children are more often perceived as additional responsibilities that the candidate must shoulder."[29] Female candidates face a double bind with regard to marriage and family. Mary Sue Terry, a single woman running for governor in Virginia in 1993, was lesbian-baited and accused of not being able to understand the issues of ordinary Virginia families, while Jane Swift, former governor of Massachusetts, was criticized as too distracted from her job in the statehouse because she had an infant daughter and was pregnant with twins.[30] Media reporting on women running for the presidency found that this role continued to be highlighted, situating them with regard to their families much more often than male candidates.[31] In 1984, Geraldine Ferraro's historic nomination for vice president was eclipsed by unrelenting coverage and questions about her husband's finances and dogged by concerns about gender roles on the campaign trail. How would she and Walter Mondale interact onstage together—would they hug? What title would they give her husband? It is in this gendered context that contemporary women, including Sarah Palin in 2008, situate their candidacies for executive office.

FRONTIER WOMAN

One frame evoked by the Palin campaign was that of a ruggedly capable and independent frontier woman. In a profile introducing Sarah Palin as a rising star in the Republican Party, written more than a year before she was chosen as McCain's running mate, she was described in exactly that way: "She's as Alaskan as you can get. . . . She's a hockey mom, she lives on a lake, she ice fishes, she snowmobiles, she hunts, she's an NRA member, she has a float plane, and her husband works for BP on the North Slope. . . . She says her favorite meal is moose stew or mooseburgers."[32]

No delicate city girl, Palin happily takes on the challenges of the wilderness and seems resourceful enough to hunt or catch her own (favorite) food. As conservative commentator Kathleen Parker remarked in the *National Review*, "Palin's narrative is fun, inspiring and all-American in that frontier way we all seem to admire."[33] One of the *New York Times'* first pieces about her after her selection for the vice presidential slot featured a picture of the governor in her

Anchorage office, seated on a couch with a large bearskin draped over the back.[34] The bear's head is still attached to the pelt draped over the couch—mouth open, as if in midroar, with sharp teeth bared—appearing menacingly lifelike as Palin leans back against it. The juxtaposition of a petite, professionally dressed Palin against the enormous, fierce bear not only served to bring a touch of the state's unique, wild beauty into this well-governed space but also reinforced how at home Palin is on the Last Frontier, with a strength and spirit equal to that of this wild creature, and with grit and determination that belies her small stature.

Like "pretty prairie wives with rifles who could out-hunt their husbands and still get dinner on the table," Palin evokes the can-do spirit of American pioneer women over a century ago.[35] She holds down the fort at home with aplomb while her husband is absent for weeks on the northern oil fields and joins him in the physically demanding work of commercial fishing. Cindy McCain evoked this frame explicitly at campaign rallies, introducing Palin as "a true Western woman."[36] Palin even brought the self-reliance implied by the frontier image to her political agenda: "Alaska needs to be self-sufficient, she says, instead of relying heavily on 'federal dollars' as the state does today."[37] Like Annie Oakley, Palin—portrayed on the cover of *Newsweek* with a shotgun thrown jauntily over one shoulder—reminds us "anything you can do, I can do better." This is a familiar refrain for American female political candidates, who have often been asked to prove their competence and toughness in a traditionally masculine realm.

But it is not merely the proof of Palin's strength and self-sufficiency that is important about her image here. What is really key is the paradox of this wilderness tomboy with the feminine beauty, the sharpshooter in a pencil skirt and high heels. She remains charmingly feminine, even while retaining her outdoorsy assertiveness. After all, Annie Oakley may have been able to beat Wild Bill Cody in a shooting competition, but she still wanted him to fall in love with her. Palin is a "guy's girl," the sexually attractive woman who shares a man's interests and hobbies without requiring any concessions to feminine qualities, pursuits, or "weaknesses." This plucky western "gal" is "self-confident and in-charge, but not threatening. She likes to do the same things the boys like to do, to hunt, fish and play sports. . . . Palin represents the (symbolic) possibility of the perfect girlfriend or wife. 'She brings home the bacon, cooks it, and will wear the sexy apron while serving it to your friends, who all want to sleep with her.'"[38] These framing narratives are dynamic, not static; Palin or her partisans are not completely in control of how citizens respond to and redeploy this frame. For example, a much-googled photo of Palin depicted her clad only in a skimpy red, white, and blue bikini with a rifle draped seductively across her body. The photo is actually of another woman's body, with Palin's head photo-shopped onto it. But the popularity and supposed veracity of this pinup pose speak to how easily this frame asserting feminine empowerment can become sexually objectified in ways perhaps not originally intended.

This frontier woman frame has racial and class aspects to it as well. "Pioneer woman" conjures up an image that is typically white and rural—a demographic important as a voting base to the Republican Party, although one not necessarily energized by John McCain. At a campaign appearance, Sarah Palin met country music artist Gretchen Wilson, best known for her hit song "Redneck Woman." The song invites its audience to join in celebrating that label rather than accepting it as an insult from more elite types who look down on them. Palin told Wilson that she loved the song, saying, "Someone called me a 'Redneck Woman.' I told them, 'Thank you—that's a compliment.'" By contrast, in her speech accepting the vice presidential nomination, she famously mocked Obama's experience as a community organizer, a move that left some observers unsurprised, commenting, "No wonder, given that occupation's urban (read black, read poor, read black poor) connotations."[39] In emphasizing her rural, even "backwoods," affinities, Palin's frontier woman frame may have alienated some voters. More important, though, it attempted to evoke identification and approval from small-town white women (and men) who consider themselves down-to-earth, hardworking, patriotic folks not afraid to shoot a rifle, drink a beer, or get their hands dirty.

HOCKEY MOM

The McCain campaign, and Sarah Palin herself, made motherhood a central feature of her potential political appeal. When McCain announced that he had chosen her as his running mate, Palin introduced herself to the crowd (and the nation) as "just your average hockey mom from Alaska." Like many women in politics, she attributed the start of her political career not to deliberate ambition but to getting involved in the PTA at her children's school, which then led to other opportunities. As Republican consultant Leslie Sanchez opined, she presented herself as Everymom: "She takes the kids to practice . . . she knows what it is to meet a budget—not just for a state with $11 billion in income and expenditures or her state's seventh-biggest city, but for a family of seven. She knows what it's like to be a mother, and a wife, and to care for aging parents, and pay for the groceries, and the heat, and the mortgage, and to make the car payment. . . . Truth is, we all know a Sarah Palin."[40] Some voters responded positively to this framing of Palin's maternal qualities and experiences as particularly relevant: *Newsweek* quoted one as saying, "I'm voting for Sarah because she's a mom. She knows what it's like to be a mom."[41] Throughout the campaign, Palin was often pictured surrounded by her husband and five children; she was shown many times onstage after a speech or rally tenderly cradling her infant son, Trig. The ubiquity of these images may also reflect the novelty that a mother with so many small children at home, running for such high office, presented to the media. Pictures of Palin with her children appeared in all sorts of press coverage and media outlets, but this type of shot seemed particularly popular with more entertainment-oriented publications like *Us Weekly* and *People* magazine, which put pictures of Palin with her baby on the cover. Perhaps these images allowed her to be contained within the norms of traditional femininity, situated in a narrative of "celebrity mom," similar to music or movie stars with babies who fascinate the public.

Palin also embodies a specific, conservative, pro-life view that places a high value on motherhood. She states emphatically, "On April 20, 1989, *my life truly began. I became a mom*" (emphasis added).[42] By choosing not to terminate her pregnancy after discovering the fetus she was carrying had Down's syndrome and by featuring her five-month-old son prominently in speeches and photos, Palin became something of a heroine to antiabortion forces. Her staunch pro-life position, further emphasized in the views she expressed about her seventeen-year-old daughter's unwed pregnancy, seemed to underscore a commitment to mothering as one of women's primary roles or duties. She may have added an ambitious profession, but she has certainly not given up or limited her role as wife and mother in exchange for it.

In fact, one of Palin's initial charms was how effortlessly she seemed to embody not just Everymom, but Supermom. Female journalists described themselves as "intrigued" and "delighted" when McCain first picked Palin, seeing her as the personification of the successful working mother. Sarah Palin "seemed to have achieved what so many of us were struggling for: an enviable balance between career and family. . . . She was running a state and breast-feeding a newborn and yet, amazingly did not seem exhausted. There was something inspiring about seeing a woman so at ease with her choices."[43] Palin reinforced this image of being able to "do it all" with her (in)famous quote in a *People* magazine interview: "What I've had to do, though, is in the middle of the night, put down the BlackBerries and pick up the breast pump. Do a couple of things different and still get it all done."

Sarah Palin's life raised a lot of questions for women, leading commentators and bloggers to debate whether or not she is a "good mother." Can she do the "big job" and still take care of all those kids, especially with a special-needs baby? Is her daughter's unwed pregnancy proof that she was a neglectful or absent mother? Would a good mother subject her pregnant teen to the scrutiny of a presidential race? Is the fact that she went back to work three days after giving birth admirable or ludicrous and horrifying? If she can do it all, does that mean all the rest of us moms, stretched too thin and doing a double day, are supposed to somehow do it all, too—without "whining" for policies that support working families?[44] Can women do it all—and do they even want to?[45] As Michelle Cottle noted, pitching "Palin's Supermom-of-five status as one of her chief assets has opened yet another front in the endless and endlessly counterproductive Mommy Wars."[46]

Palin is, importantly, a "hockey mom"—not a soccer mom. Beginning with the 1996 presidential race, the "soccer mom" demographic has been identified as an important swing vote in American elections. Soccer moms, as defined by scholars of gender and politics, tend to be white, married, middle-class suburban women with school-age children.[47] In 2004, Republican strategists appealed to their fears about terrorism to turn "soccer moms" into "security moms." As Minnesota blogger Jay Weiner points out, the addition of "hockey moms" to the political lexicon in 2008 lends a slightly different connotation. Hockey moms describe themselves as more "tough," "competitive," "aggressive," than soccer moms, able to deal with the predawn practices, freezing rinks, and broken teeth that go along with the sport.[48] There is also a class component to the distinction. Although hockey is in reality a less affordable sport (it requires more expensive equipment and is played by those with a higher average household income than soccer), the image of hockey moms is more working class.[49] As Tina Kelley puts it, soccer moms are married to doctors or lawyers and drink wine; hockey moms' husbands are ironworkers or fishermen, and they drink beer.[50] As a self-proclaimed "hockey mom," Palin makes a geographically based, blue-collar appeal: here is a rural gal from Alaska or Minnesota, not an elitist Ivy League grad raising her kids in the suburbs of Westchester, Connecticut.

Palin reinforces her toughness and down-to-earth qualities in the most quoted line of her vice presidential nomination acceptance speech: "You know the difference between a hockey mom and a pit bull? Lipstick." No swooning Victorian lady here—this female politician will be as tenacious and direct as a pit bull. Note how she also reasserts her femininity. She may be tough, but she also cares about being pretty. She is still a woman, and she wears the lipstick to prove it. With this pithy one-liner, Palin uses her definition of motherhood to position herself again as that juxtaposition of both a tough candidate to be reckoned with and utterly feminine. It also offers a notable contrast to one of the other women prominent in the 2008 election season, Hillary Clinton. Where Clinton strove to be taken seriously as "one of the boys"—with her dark pantsuits and mastery of policy detail, resisting focus on her clothes, hair, or other "frivolous" distractions—Palin wryly, fearlessly references a girlish accoutrement like lipstick. She offers an alternative femininity to that of Clinton, who was caricatured as scary, too powerful, and emasculating in the national imagination for the past sixteen years. Although Clinton may have had a "likability problem," Palin was described with adjectives such as perky, feisty, winsome, and cute. The "hockey mom" frame offered voters a narrative in which they could relate to Sarah Palin as an everymom, admire her as a supermom, applaud her maternal values, or judge her parenting choices, even while reinforcing her strong conservative, white, working-class appeal.

THE OUTSIDER

The "outsider" image is a relatively common narrative frame employed by women (and men) running for political office. Given that the electorate, political power players, and various media will likely perceive women as outsiders regardless of how they present themselves, female candidates have frequently attempted to turn what might be seen as a disadvantage into a position of strength. The strategy presents itself easily given the nontraditional paths women often have followed into office, as well as the issues that drew them into politics initially. This was clearly the case with the Palin vice presidential candidacy.

Her selection as McCain's running mate was unabashedly focused on her status as an outsider. John McCain announced her as his running mate in part by saying, "She's not from these parts, and she's not from Washington." Both the language and visuals employed by the McCain/Palin campaign reinforced this status, as did the news and popular media coverage of her candidacy. The implication was that as an outsider, Palin would be a more legitimate representative of average people's interests than would insiders who are out of touch with ordinary Americans. As an outsider she is "just like us"—disconnected from and distrustful of those who hold political office. McCain described Palin as someone who "understands the problems, the hopes and the values of working people."[51]

Throughout the campaign, Palin talked at length of her small-town background and Main Street values. These are key words and concepts intended to convey that she understands and is in touch with ordinary citizens (unlike Washington insiders such as Joe Biden). Her speech delivery is casual and folksy—she drops her *g*'s ("our financial system needs some shakin' up and some fixin'");

"heck," "darn," "shoot," and "gee" are mixed in as well; she gestures enthusiastically and cutely, as if we are all in on the joke. She is the cool kid making subtle fun of the far less cool intellectual kids in this election contest—no overly cerebral phrasing or carefully detailed answers from her that might intimidate or alienate potential supporters. Sarah Palin aimed her remarks openly and directly to Joe Six Pack and Joe the Plumber—average, "real" men. This was even true in her family life—no formal "First Gentleman" title for her husband; instead, he was the "First Dude" of Alaska.

Sarah Palin is not the first to adopt this narrative frame. One need look no further than the man she ran for office with—John McCain—to see another. In fact, the outsider frame is far from uncommon in American politics. This often geographic, class-based frame has been around at least since Andrew Jackson ran for president on the platform of promoting the common man's involvement in America's political future. Since Jackson, politicians have periodically appealed to the notion that western and rural interests might view themselves as outsiders and therefore be open to supporting candidates in touch with "ordinary" lives and values. Ronald Reagan ran openly against Washington, pledging term limits for officeholders and objecting to "pointy-headed," entrenched bureaucrats. Democrat Bill Clinton may have been a Rhodes scholar, but he also put on his jogging shorts and stopped by McDonald's for Big Mac meals. Republicans nominated George W. Bush, who, despite his status as the son of a former president, had partied his way through early adulthood.

Republicans have employed the very effective targeted and oppositional strategy of appealing to what they refer to as "Main Street" values. This conception of Main Street references God, patriotism, hard work, and individualism in very particular ways that imply non-Republicans are less traditionally Christian, love their country less, and are lazy and whiny and expect other hardworking Americans to take care of them. In the end, Libby Copeland was left to ask, "Could central casting produce a more ideal messenger [than Sarah Palin] for the new Republican populism?"[52]

When Sarah Palin chose this frame and used these reference points, it was in no way accidental or without meaning. These are appeals to carefully constructed images and ideas. McCain and Palin likely aimed to connect with unhappy working-class white voters in the industrial Midwest and the South. These voters had been instrumental to winners in several recent presidential elections. Appeals focused on winning their support were not surprising. This frame characterizes one of the defining paradoxes of the presidential office itself—the tension between citizens' desires for a superhuman president who is smarter, more capable, and therefore more qualified to lead and their also very real desires for a president who is "just like us." Some candidates and presidents manage to balance these competing demands and expectations from the citizenry, but many are defeated by the double-edged sword of this paradox, either by failing to be "presidential" enough or by becoming "out of touch" with average Americans.

THE MAVERICK REFORMER

The McCain campaign viewed Sarah Palin as a kindred spirit to John McCain, particularly in her history of taking heat from fellow Republicans for bucking them on issues and spotlighting their ethical failings. Both candidates saw themselves as fiercely principled, honest, unafraid warriors. As *New York Times* columnist David Brooks argued, "The Palin pick allows McCain to run the way he wants to—not as the old goat running against the fresh upstart, but as the crusader for virtue against the forces of selfishness. It allows him to make cleaning out the Augean stables of Washington the major issue of his campaign."[53]

The McCain campaign hoped this antiestablishment story and imagery would appeal to voters in a decidedly anti-incumbent, "throw the rascals out" mood. Particularly prominent in the early stages of the campaign, this frame highlighted Palin's claims that she had told Congress "Thanks, but no thanks" to the Bridge to Nowhere. As a small-town mayor, state board member, and governor, she fought her own entrenched partisans, sold the state plane on eBay, fired the personal chef, and served as a whistle-blower when she observed ethically questionable behavior—she was a giant killer. She advocated transparency in one of the least transparent states in the country by forcing open bidding for oil contracts where there had been none in the past. She was often described as a breath of fresh air—a politician who "calls them as she sees them." It is not a tremendous surprise that she appealed to the man who ran the Straight Talk Express. Another central aspect to this frame is the willingness to fight the principled fight and "fight to win." Palin and McCain proudly embraced her image as an ultracompetitive sportswoman—"Sarah Barracuda" on the basketball court.

Of all the frames employed during the campaign, this is perhaps the one that lost the most focus and depth with observers; what it meant to be a maverick did not come through substantively. This was perhaps best illustrated in the widely viewed impersonations of Palin by Tina Fey on *Saturday Night Live (SNL)*. In one widely circulated clip of *SNL's* vice presidential debate skit, Fey's Governor Palin is asked how she and John McCain will solve the financial crisis:

Fey (as Sarah Palin): Ya know, John McCain and I, we're a couple of
mavericks. And gosh darnit, we're gonna take that maverick energy
right to Washington, and we're gonna use it to fix this financial crisis
and everything else that's plaguin' this great country of ours.
Queen Latifah (as Gwen Ifill, moderator): How will you solve the
financial crisis by being a maverick?
Fey (as Palin): You know, we're gonna take every aspect of the crisis
and look at it, and then we're going to ask ourselves, what would
a maverick do in this situation? And then, you know, we'll do
that.

The humor only works in this skit if voters understand and concur that the term
had become overused and was not clearly defined.

This frame became emblematic of a candidacy perceived to lack intellectual
seriousness or depth. By the end of the campaign, no one was quite sure what
being a maverick meant precisely, particularly in light of effective advertising
from the Obama campaign emphasizing the degree to which McCain's senate
voting record aligned with the preferences of incumbent president George W.
Bush. It was a concept without impact or solid cultural reference points.

THE SEXY PURITAN

From the beginning of her involvement on the national political stage, Sarah
Palin's looks and style have been central focal points in our collective experience
of her persona. In his July 2007 *Weekly Standard* article introducing Palin as
a rising Republican star, Fred Barnes mentioned her previous beauty pageant
involvement, noting that Palin won the Miss Wasilla beauty contest, was named
Miss Congeniality, and later competed in the Miss Alaska competition.[54] Pollster
Dave Dittman described Palin as "young and pretty," Rush Limbaugh referred
to her as a "babe," Tina Fey referenced the term "MILF," and countless others
commented on Palin's hair, eyeglasses, skirts, and shoes.

It was not just her attractive looks that were part of the image but her overall style and approach as well. Former Miss America Kate Shindle suggested,
"There's a touch of pageant world to Palin's voice, to her careful adherence to
sound bytes [sic], and that 'cheerful aggressiveness' [that is] part cheerleader,
part news anchor and part drill sergeant." The frame did not go unnoticed by
observers.[55] Columnist Maureen Dowd, for one, commented that "instead of
going home and watching 'Miss Congeniality' with Sandra Bullock, I get to stay
here and watch 'Miss Congeniality' with Sarah Palin. . . . She has a beehive and

sexy shoes, and the day she's named she goes shopping with McCain in Ohio for a cheerleader outfit for her daughter."[56]

In past election cycles, this open and direct talk of traditional femininity and attractiveness, sexiness, and wardrobe might have all been viewed as just the type of objectification that women and female candidates for office had experienced in the past. Feminist critics have commented on how these variables have been used to call into question the seriousness, readiness, or qualifications of female candidates and to disadvantage them with voters in some way. Most past female candidates for office in either party paid great attention to appearing strong, prepared, decisive, and like they belonged in the game.

Yet Palin seemed quite comfortable, almost amused, with this imagery and framing—even empowered by it. Copeland notes that this "traditional feminine warmth" is what set her in direct opposition to Hillary Clinton, who took the more common approach of projecting great strength and demonstrating experience.[57] Rather than responding by confronting and contradicting the stereotypical focus on her appearance, the McCain/Palin camp instead responded by trying to reframe the discussion altogether and turn the focus to their advantage. Palin embodied the argument that women could be strong without threatening traditional social values and practices, particularly men's traditional sense of masculinity. She could handle it all, happily, without whining about it along the way.

According to *Washington Post* staff writer Libby Copeland, "For many Palin supporters, her attractiveness does not weaken her appeal—rather, it balances those tales of valor on the tundra. Supporters have charged her critics with sexism but at the same time, at the GOP convention, delegates wore buttons that said 'Hottest VP from the Coolest State.'"[58] Through this frame Palin could be seen as less defensive, less shrill, and more authentic as a candidate. Republican speechwriter Landon Parvin suggested that "she's not a woman trying to deliver a speech like a man, and there is an integrity to that."[59] Or as one observer told a reporter, "She's a different kind of feminist . . . a strong woman who can wear a skirt and be proud of it."[60]

Tom Perrotta suggests that Sarah Palin embodies the most recent representation of a particular type of woman, the Sexy Puritan, which has become a familiar and potent figure in the ongoing culture wars between right and left in American politics. As his analysis suggests,

Sexy Puritans engage the culture wars on two levels—not simply by advocating conservative positions on hot-button social issues but by embodying non-threatening mainstream standards of female beauty and behavior at the same time. The net result is a paradox, a bit of cognitive dissonance very useful to the cultural right: You get a little thrill along with your traditional values, a wink along with the wagging finger. . . . The right has understood for a long time that harsh social messages seem a lot more palatable coming from an attractive young woman than a glowering old man.[61]

Palin as "Sexy Puritan" makes use of her sexuality as a powerful tool. Her flirtatious teasing of the electorate, in her stilettos and sexy librarian bun, modernizes and twists the socially conservative positions she espouses. Winking and playful, this type of "hot" conservative woman undermines the conventional wisdom that conservative views on abortion, abstinence, and homosexuality reflect repression, prudishness, or lack of libido. Having an attractive woman embrace the conservative message refutes charges that conservative issue positions merely oppress women and allow men to remain in control. Palin's sexiness is appealing and useful, even as she employs it to take moralistic positions.

However, much like the other frames, this one had potentially negative aspects that had to be confronted over the course of the fall campaign. Without the careful balancing of other narrative frames (e.g., frontier woman and maverick), the focus on traditional femininity and appearance had the potential to convey girlishness and a lack of seriousness and preparedness. Some would argue that over time the balance was lost and that this danger was realized both in the real political world and in satirical portrayals of Palin, particularly those on *SNL*. Near the end of the campaign, when it appeared clear that the McCain campaign was not going to prevail over Obama and Biden, the very McCain campaign operatives who embraced the positive aspects of Palin's traditional femininity were quick to leak "negative" stories about her shopping habits and diva-like qualities when the results turned against them in November. This seemed an easy criticism, more easily received and believed because of the earlier decision to present Palin through this frame.

A Contested Frame: Feminist Role Model or Victim of Sexism?

Sarah Palin did achieve a historic milestone in becoming the first Republican woman to gain the vice presidential nomination of her party. But whether this was a victory for gender equality remains a controversial question. Was Palin a feminist role model—younger, with a more expansive and less doctrinaire definition of empowerment—or an antifeminist throwback? Was she a victim of sexism during the campaign or a beneficiary of John McCain's chivalrous protection? Framing Palin in terms of feminism involved highly contested narratives throughout the election season.

From the moment she publicly accepted John McCain's invitation to be his running mate, Sarah Palin touted herself as an empowered role model for women. After noting Hillary Clinton's historic achievement in garnering 18 million votes in presidential primaries, Palin deftly cast herself as heir apparent to Clinton's mantle, asserting, "It turns out the women of America aren't finished yet, and we can shatter that glass ceiling once and for all." In her interview with Katie Couric, Palin described herself as a feminist. Independent Women's Forum president Michelle Bernard agrees with that label: to her, Palin "really represents what early generations of women fought for, which was the right to do whatever you want to do with your career. . . . Regardless of whether or not you agree with her political ideology, she really is a good representation of what the women's rights movement was about."[62]

Other women vehemently disagreed, seeing the Palin pick as "cynical tokenism" on the part of the McCain camp.[63] They rejected this narrative of a feminist role model: "To try to suggest Sarah Palin might garner the Hillary Clinton vote, that one woman is just the same as another, that biology trumps ideology, is the ultimate evidence of sexism."[64] Palin's supposed feminism was called into question by her absolutist antiabortion position; her support for abstinence-only sex education; her lack of advocacy for equal pay, flextime, health care reform, or child care policies; and her free-market, "no whining" approach to policies that might support women and children. Critics wondered if it was hypocritical of her to talk about her daughter's "choice" to have a baby when she would like to outlaw that choice or of "family values" Republicans to praise Bristol's decision not to have an abortion while conveniently ignoring the issue of teenage sex. Some cringed at Palin's willingness to use her looks or flirtatious charm as a political asset and were appalled by tabloid-style headlines shrieking "Babies, Lies & Scandal" and "Palin's Family Drama."[65] Outraged feminist Katha Pollitt summed up what she viewed as Palin's cooptation of feminist rhetoric:

> What can you say after you've said that her career shows that even right-wing fundamentalist women have taken in feminism's message of empowerment and that's good, but that Palin's example suggests women can do it all without support from society and that's bad? Count me as a feminist who never believed that being PTA president meant you

could be, well, President. The more time we spend on dippy rumina-
tions—how does she do it? Queen Bee on steroids or hockey mom
next door? How hot is Todd, anyway?—the less focus there will be on
the kind of queries that should come first with any vice presidential
candidate, and certainly would if Palin were a man.[66]

The debate about Sarah Palin as an example of women's progress quickly turned
to charges by the McCain campaign that she was a victim of sexist treatment
by the media.[67] Criticism that she was underqualified and ill-prepared to be a
heartbeat away from the presidency—which intensified after her disastrous
interviews with Charles Gibson and Katie Couric on national television—was
dismissed as condescending and antiwoman.

Thus the frame telling us how to read Sarah Palin—as feminist symbol or
as victim of sexism—became contested. Certainly there were moments during
the election season when her gender was exploited (whether to her advantage
or at her expense). One of the more striking examples, which provoked coverage of the resulting controversy at the *Washington Times* and Fox News sites,
is a picture taken by a wire service photographer at a campaign event in Pennsylvania. Taken from below and behind Palin as she stood onstage, it frames
the rapt face of a young male supporter directly between her legs. The young
man, mesmerized expression on his face, is positioned perfectly between the
V of her calves and high-heeled shoes, while the rest of Palin's body has been
completely cropped out of the frame. It is hard to imagine an image that is less
gender-neutral and more sexualized. Palin herself implied she was a victim of
"trashing" by feminists who should have shown her sisterly solidarity. At an
October 2008 rally in Carson, California, she informed the crowd of a quote
from Madeleine Albright found on her Starbucks cup: "There is a special place
in hell for women who don't support other women."[68] Palin implied that women
(perhaps especially former Hillary Clinton supporters?) who didn't support her
were actually the ones being sexist and antifeminist.

However, many observers rejected this narrative of sexist victimization.
Some, like CNN's Campbell Brown, threw the accusation of sexism back at
the McCain campaign, wondering if they were behaving in a sexist fashion by
shielding Palin from more tough media interviews and scrutiny—as if this delicate woman could not handle it and needed to be protected. Such "chivalrous"
protection confuses a sexist double standard (such as asking female politicians
how they can possibly be good mothers and hold public office but not asking
males about their parenting responsibilities and public life) with a legitimate

query about qualifications (e.g., a candidate's education and experience). "Conflating the two is not combating sexism, it is exercising chivalry, and chivalry is an insult to all smart, accomplished women everywhere."[69] In rejecting the stories of feminist triumph or sexist victimization, there is worry over the implications of Sarah Palin's performance for other women. "Should we feel sorry for Sarah Palin? No. But if she fails miserably, we might be excused for feeling a bit sorry for ourselves . . . [because] she's yanking us back to the old assumption that women can't hack it at these heights" of power.[70] Or as Amanda Fortini put it, "Palin reinforced some of the most damaging and sexist ideas of all: that women are undisciplined in their thinking; that we are distracted by domestic concerns or frivolous pursuits like shopping; that we are not smart enough, or not serious enough, for the important jobs."[71]

2008 and Beyond

Frames are relational and are not employed or understood in isolation from one another. In 2008, Sarah Palin's candidacy is best understood in reference not only to Hillary Clinton and John McCain but also in turns to Joe Biden, Barack Obama, and even Michelle Obama and Tina Fey. Race and class matter greatly here. The white, rural, working-class appeals of Palin made sense in light of her juxtaposition to Ivy League–educated women and an exoticized black candidate.

Relationship with the audience also matters in framing. A tremendous amount of airtime and ink in 2008 were devoted to the question of whether women would be confused or conflicted over the choice between "breaking the glass ceiling" by choosing to support a female (Palin) and voting for a ticket with policy positions that most closely resembled their preferred issue positions (Obama/Biden). The *New Republic* suggested that "by running as a spunky can-do Republican-style feminist mom who meets challenges head-on instead of whining about them, Palin may appeal to some working mothers, as the GOP intends. But it's more likely that a different demographic will find this winsome: anti-feminist men."[72] The most successful targets of this framing may not have been women alienated by the sexist treatment of Hillary Clinton and the elitism of Barack Obama but working-class men or traditional Republican voters, comforted by the traditional gender roles and partisan themes embodied by Sarah Palin. Indeed, Palin's 2008 experience certainly highlights the intersection of partisan themes with gendered experiences of female candidates. It matters whether the female candidates under analysis are Democrats or Republicans, as the audience they are relating to varies tremendously.

Further, frames are not static or easily controlled by their original authors. Consumers interpret, respond to, and reimagine them, sometimes in sympathy with the original author and sometimes not. In the 2008 contest, attempts to understand Sarah Palin's framing are virtually inseparable from Tina Fey's impersonation of her, with its resulting reinvention of these narratives. Fey's humorous mocking of Palin's grasp of foreign policy ("I can see Russia from my house") and beauty pageant activities (e.g., "fancy pageant walkin'" and talent portions of the competition) defined Palin as much as anything the McCain/Palin campaign did.

As framing scholars suggest, narrative frames are powerful because they reference enduring and well-known themes. So the narratives described here did not begin with Sarah Palin, and they will be reappropriated, reworked, and retold in the future. As we moved into the 2010 elections, Sarah Palin described herself with a new frame: a "Mama Grizzly," angry about trends in American politics and on the attack to protect her cubs and her values. The Mama Grizzly frame demonstrates continuity with many of the narratives and appeals used by Palin in 2008. It evokes the fierce spirit of the frontier woman (and the imminent dangers that must be fought in the wilderness). It takes the hockey mom one step further: from strong and aggressive to downright angry, provoked to fight back. The Mama Grizzly is on the attack, hostile to Washington insiders, Democratic incumbents, Republicans in name only, and the liberal "lamestream" media. She is the ultimate citizen outsider (from all the way out in the woods), hostile to all that is wrong with experts and entrenched political elites. And the Mama Grizzly is not alone. Both the media and Palin herself began to refer to a cadre of "commonsense conservative" women by the same label—Delaware senatorial candidate Christine O'Donnell, South Carolina gubernatorial candidate Nikki Haley, Nevada senatorial candidate Sharon Angle, and Minnesota congresswoman Michele Bachmann.

The narrative (and primary election successes) of Mama Grizzlies opens up space for a wider range of female candidates ideologically and extends beyond the usual advice to women on how to win office. Female office seekers have conventionally been told that remaining calmly and coolly competent is the path to success (defying those feminine stereotypes of emotion and weakness). But the Mama Grizzly frame makes space for women to express anger—albeit not the shrill hysteria (or the righteous indignation about sexism) voters might fear. The story of Mama Grizzlies is one of outraged populism in a feminine voice. They claim new political space for women's anger, aggression, and even violence—legitimized by protecting what they hold dearest. But they are not fighting to protect "cubs" traditionally by supporting child-centered public policies in areas like health care, education, day care, or social supports to prevent poverty. Instead, they are reclaiming issues traditionally thought of as "masculine"—reducing the size of government, the economy, free markets, lower taxes—as areas where women are needed to protect the futures of their children. They are roused as fierce Mama Grizzlies to protect American freedom and the future as only protective mothers can. Importantly, this recasting of issues and ideology is still couched in terms of motherhood and traditional femininity. These are not the caricatures of "angry feminists" rejecting men and family. Their attractive, stylish, feminine personas may be essential to their success in using harsh populist rhetoric and not in contradiction to it. The narratives surrounding Sarah Palin illustrate the ways in which the political arena continues to adapt to an ever-increasing diversity of female candidates and strategic approaches for women in politics. While women have still not escaped the expectations of traditional femininity, the meanings and bounds of that notion continue to be debated.

Notes

1. George Lakoff, *The Political Mind: Why You Can't Understand 21st-Century American Politics with an 18th-Century Brain* (New York: Viking, 2008).

2. Ibid., 22.

3. Ibid., 24.

4. Ibid., 27.

5. Ibid., 35.

6. James N. Druckman, "Competing Frames in a Political Campaign," in *Winning with Words: The Origins and Impact of Political Framing*, ed. Brian F. Schaffner and Patrick J. Sellers (New York: Routledge, 2010), 102.

7. Drew Westen, *The Political Brain: The Role of Emotion in Deciding the Fate of the Nation* (New York: Public Affairs, 2007), 3.

8. Ibid., 12.

9. Ibid., 264.

10. Virginia Sapiro, "If U.S. Senator Baker Were a Woman: An Experimental Study of Candidate Images," *Political Psychology* 2 (1982): 61–83; Monika McDermott, "Voting Cues in Low Information Elections: Candidate Gender as a Social Information Variable in Contemporary United States Elections," *American Journal of Political Science* 41, no. 1 (1997): 270–83; Kathleen Dolan, "The Impact of Candidate Sex on Evaluations of Candidates for the U.S. House of Representatives," *Social Science Quarterly* 85, no. 1 (2004): 206–17; Kira Sanbonmatsu and Kathleen Dolan, "Do Gender Stereotypes Transcend Party?" *Political Research Quarterly* 62, no. 3 (2009): 485–94.

11. Classic studies of gender trait stereotyping are Sandra Bem, "The Measurement of Psychological Androgyny," *Journal of Clinical and Consulting Psychology* 42 (1974): 155–62; Inge Broverman et al., "Sex-Role Stereotypes: A Current Appraisal," *Journal of Social Issues* 28 (1972): 59–78. These are replicated and reconfirmed in Deborah Prentice and Erica Carranza, "What Women and Men Should Be, Shouldn't Be, Are Allowed to Be, and Don't Have to Be: The Contents of Prescriptive Gender Stereotypes," *Psychology of Women Quarterly* 26, no. 4 (2002): 269–81; and Susan Rachael Seem and M. Diane Clark, "Healthy Women, Healthy Men, and Healthy Adults: An Evaluation of Gender Role Stereotypes in the Twenty-First Century," *Sex Roles* 55 (2006): 247–58.

12. Kim Fridkin and Patrick Kenney, "The Role of Gender Stereotypes in U.S. Senate Campaigns," *Politics & Gender* 5 (2009): 301–24; Barbara Burrell, *A Woman's Place Is in the House: Campaigning for Congress in the Feminist Era* (Ann Arbor: University of Michigan Press, 1994); Leonie Huddy and Nayda Terkildsen, "Gender Stereotypes and the Perception of Male and Female Candidates," *American Journal of Political Science* 37, no. 1 (1993): 99–147; Barbara Lee Family Foundation, *Positioning Women to Win* (Brookline, MA: Barbara Lee Family Foundation, 2007).

13. Shirley Rosenwasser and Norma Dean, "Gender Role and Political Office," *Psychology of Women Quarterly* 13, no. 1 (1989): 77–85; Jennifer Lawless, "Women, War, and Winning Elections: Gender Stereotyping in the Post–September 11 Era," *Political Research Quarterly* 57, no. 3 (2004): 479–90.

14. Lawless, "Women, War, and Winning"; Jessi L. Smith, David Paul, and Rachel Paul, "No Place for a Woman: Evidence for Gender Bias in Evaluations of Presidential Candidates," *Basic and Applied Social Psychology* 29 (2007): 225–33; Shirley M. Rosenwasser and Jana Seale, "Attitudes toward a Hypothetical Male or Female Presidential Candidate: A Research Note," *Political Psychology* 9 (1988): 591–98.

15. Erika Falk, *Women for President: Media Bias in Eight Campaigns* (Urbana: University of Illinois Press, 2008), 72; Eleanor Clift and Tom Brazaitis, *Madam President: Women Blazing the Leadership Trail* (New York: Routledge, 2003), 99–102.

16. Falk, *Women for President*, 125–26.

17. Huddy and Terkildsen, "Gender Stereotypes"; Paul S. Herrnson, Celeste Lay, and Atiya Stokes, "Women Running 'as Women': Candidate Gender, Campaign Issues, and Voter Targeting Strategies," *Journal of Politics* 65, no. 1 (2003): 244–55; Fridkin and Kenney, "Role of Gender."

18. Mark S. Leeper, "The Impact of Prejudice on Female Candidates: An Experimental Look at Voter Inference," *American Politics Quarterly* 19 (1991): 248–61; Carol M. Mueller, "Nurturance and Mastery: Competing Qualifications for Women's Access to High Public Office?," in *Women and Politics: Activism, Attitudes, and Office-Holding*, ed. Gwen Moore and Glenna D. Spitze (Greenwich, CT: JAI, 1986); Rosenwasser and Seale, "Attitudes"; Burrell, *Woman's Place*; McDermott, "Voting Choices."

19. Lawless, "Women, War, and Winning."

20. Barbara Lee Family Foundation, *Cracking the Code* (Brookline, MA: Barbara Lee Family Foundation, 2004).

21. Kim Fridkin Kahn, *The Political Consequences of Being a Woman: How Stereotypes Influence the Conduct and Consequences of Political Campaigns* (New York: Columbia University Press, 1996).

22. Lynda Lee Kaid et al., "Sex Role Perceptions and Televised Political Advertising: Comparing Male and Female Candidates," *Women & Politics* 4, no. 4 (1984): 41–53.

23. Clift and Brazaitis, *Madam President*; Barbara Lee Family Foundation, *Cracking the Code.*

24. Barbara Lee Family Foundation, *Cracking the Code.*

25. Kahn, *Political Consequences.*

26. Falk, *Women for President.*

27. Diane J. Heith, "The Lipstick Watch: Media Coverage, Gender, and Presidential Campaigns," in *Anticipating Madam President,* ed. Robert P. Watson and Ann Gordon (Boulder, CO: Lynne Rienner, 2003), 123–30; Falk, *Women for President*; Linda Witt, Karen M. Paget, and Glenna Matthews, *Running as a Woman: Gender and Power in American Politics* (New York: Free Press, 1994).

28. Clift and Brazaitis, *Madam President.*

29. Susan J. Carroll and Kelly Dittmar, "The 2008 Candidacies of Hillary Clinton and Sarah Palin: Cracking the 'Highest, Hardest Glass Ceiling,'" in *Gender and Elections: Shaping the Future of American Politics,* 2nd ed., ed. Susan J. Carroll and Richard L. Fox (Cambridge: Cambridge University Press, 2010), 46.

30. Clift and Brazaitis, *Madam President.*

31. Falk, *Women for President.*

32. Fred Barnes, "The Most Popular Governor: Alaska's Sarah Palin Is the GOP's Newest Star," *Weekly Standard,* July 16, 2007.

33. Kathleen Parker, "Palin Problem," *National Review,* September 26, 2008.

34. William Yardley, "Sarah Heath Palin, an Outsider with Charms," *New York Times,* August 29, 2008.

35. Libby Copeland, "Shooting from the Hip, with a Smile to Boot," *Washington Post,* October 1, 2008.

36. Ibid.

37. Barnes, "Most Popular Governor."

38. Bernadette Barker-Plummer, "Reading Sarah Palin," *Flow TV,* October 18, 2008, http://flowtv.org/2008/10/reading-sarah-palin-bernadette-barker-plummer-university-of-san-francisco/.

39. John Heileman, "The Sixty-Day War," *New York Magazine,* September 5, 2008.

40. Leslie Sanchez, "Palin Is a VP for the Rest of Us," CNN, September 4,

2008, http://articles.cnn.com/2008-09-04/politics/sanchez.palin_1_sarah-palin-life-choices-life-support?_s=PM:POLITICS.

41. Sam Harris, "When Atheists Attack," *Newsweek*, September 29, 2008, http://www.newsweek.com/id/160080.

42. Sarah Palin, *Going Rogue: An American Life* (New York: Harper, 2009), 51.

43. Amanda Fortini, "The 'Bitch' and the 'Ditz': How the Year of the Woman Reinforced the Two Most Pernicious Sexist Stereotypes and Actually Set Women Back," *New York Magazine*, November 16, 2008.

44. Katherine Marsh, "Whine Not: The Working Mothers' Case against Sarah Palin," *New Republic*, September 24, 2008, http://www.tnr.com/print/article/whine-not.

45. Ruth Marcus, "Palin Hits the Motherload," *Washington Post*, September 10, 2008.

46. Michelle Cottle, "Shattered," *New Republic*, September 24, 2008, http://www.tnr.com/article/shattered.

47. Susan J. Carroll and Richard L. Fox, eds., *Gender and Elections: Shaping the Future of American Politics* (New York: Cambridge University Press, 2006).

48. Jay Weiner, "She's Now a Household Phrase, but What Is a Hockey Mom?" MinnPost, September 5, 2008, http://www.minnpost.com/stories/2008/09/05/3407/shes_now_household_phrase_but_whats_a_hockey_mom.

49. Ibid.

50. Tina Kelley, "Soccer Moms Welcome Their Hockey-Loving Sisters to the Political Arena," *New York Times*, September 7, 2008.

51. John McCain, Running mate announcement speech, Dayton, OH, August 29, 2008.

52. Copeland, "Shooting from the Hip."

53. David Brooks, "What the Palin Pick Says," *New York Times*, September 2, 2008.

54. Barnes, "Most Popular Governor."

55. Copeland, "Shooting from the Hip."

56. Maureen Dowd, "Vice in Go-Go Boots?" *New York Times*, August 31, 2008.

57. Copeland, "Shooting from the Hip."

58. Ibid.

59. Ibid.

60. Kim Severson, "The Spotlight Arrives, to Some Unease, in a State That Savors Its Isolation," *New York Times*, August 31, 2008.

61. Tom Perrotta, "The Sexy Puritan," *Slate*, September 26, 2008, http://www.slate.com/id/2200814/.

62. Susanna Schrobsdorff, "Sister, Sister: What Some of America's Smartest, Most Successful Women Have to Say about Sarah Palin, Hillary Clinton, and the Meaning of the Word 'Feminist' in 2008," *Newsweek*, October 9, 2008, http://www.newsweek.com/id/163219.

63. Cottle, "Shattered."

64. Anna Quindlen, "Can You Say Sexist?" *Newsweek,* September 15, 2008, http://www.newsweek.com/id/157543.

65. On Palin's use of her looks and charm, see Fortini, "The 'Bitch' and the 'Ditz.'"

66. Katha Pollitt, "Lipstick on a Wing Nut," *Nation,* September 29, 2008.

67. Heileman, "Sixty-Day War."

68. Nico Pitney, "Palin Misquotes Albright: Place in Hell Reserved for Women Who Don't Support Other Women," *Huffington Post,* October 5, 2008, http://www .huffingtonpost.com/2008/10/05/palin-misquotes-albright_n_131967.html.

69. Barker-Plummer, "Reading Sarah Palin."

70. Emily Bazelon, "The Un-Hillary: Why Watching Sarah Palin Is Agony for Women," *Slate,* October 1, 2008, http://www.slate.com/id/2201330/.

71. Fortini, "The 'Bitch' and the 'Ditz.'"

72. Marsh, "Whine Not."

3

COLBERT NATION

Gender, Late-Night Television, and Candidate Humanization

Mary McHugh

"I can see Russia from my house." This line has become one of the most remembered lines from the 2008 presidential election campaign. It has been repeated often and now defines the public's perception of former Alaska governor Sarah Palin, John McCain's running mate on the failed Republican ticket. However, this line was spoken not by Governor Palin but by Tina Fey, playing Palin, during an opening sketch of NBC's *Saturday Night Live (SNL)* on September 13, 2008. Tina Fey's resemblance to and impersonation of Palin during the months prior to the November election brought *SNL* its highest ratings in many years. It also helped to reaffirm the importance of humor in presidential politics as it created a path for both the media and voters to understand and resolve the issue of gender and gender bias in the campaign. As we will see, long-term success for female candidates begins with, and depends on, candidate humanization that can occur through political satire in late-night comedy programs.

We know that the 2008 election was historic for many reasons. Many of the candidates seeking the presidency were not traditional ones. The winner of the Democratic Party nomination was going to be a first (either for race or gender) as a major-party nominee. Whoever won the general election was also going to be a first as president (race or age) or possibly as vice president (gender). Interest in and excitement about this campaign were higher than anyone could remember. During the campaign, the traditional news media struggled against relying on stereotypes (i.e., women were too weak to be president, Obama was an angry black man, McCain was old and senile) as they covered the race and needed to be careful not to insult or injure the various bases of support for these precedent-breaking candidates. The uniqueness of the candidates actually created an opportunity for late-night television, allowing programs to incorporate stereotypes into their humor, which often affected the campaign more directly than reporting by traditional media. Late-night talk shows such as *The Tonight Show* and *The Late Show* sprinkled their opening monologues with jokes and anecdotes about the race. Fake, or soft, news shows like *The Daily Show* and *The Colbert Report* were able to focus on the media's coverage of the election and the candidates, through humor, with an audience who interacted with the traditional news industry in a minimal way. The long-running program *SNL* led the way in parodying the candidates and the campaigns and provided a unique prism for the media and the voters. In 2000, David Letterman quipped, "The road to the White House runs through me."[1] In 2008, the road to the White House clearly did wind through many of the late-night comedy shows. This chapter shows not only how late-night comedy helped to humanize candidates but how these shows did more to help female candidates begin to crack the glass ceiling of presidential politics. Late-night comedy shows have set the stage for future, and possibly successful, attempts by female candidates by priming the public through humor for the legitimate consideration of a woman as both president and vice president.

A variety of research has been done in the fields of political science and communication studies on the impact of late-night television comedy shows on politics. As the number and success of these shows have grown, scholars continue to consider and debate their importance as sources of news and political information for different age groups, especially younger voters. Some authors have expressed concerns about the impact of these shows, which they believe are "debasing and trivializing political discourse."[2] Jody Baumgartner and Jonathan Morris discuss how jokes at the expense of political candidates led audience members of *The Daily Show* to rate those candidates more negatively.[3] Others have discussed the positive value of these types of shows. As Lauren Feldman and Dannagal Young write, "*The West Wing, NYPD Blue,* and *Oprah Winfrey* reveal that just as traditional news programs can persuade, teach, prime, frame and alter political efficacy and trust, so can entertainment programs."[4] Feldman and Young also believe that these programs can be a "gateway" to traditional news sources and that those who are watching such programs have a "desire to understand political humor" and "to be in on the joke."[5] Xiaoxia Cao agrees that "citizens can obtain political knowledge as a by-product of watching political comedy shows."[6] Dannagal Young and Russell Tisinger write, "Soft news may foster political attention among people who do not routinely tune into traditional news programs."[7] The Pew Research Center in 2007 released a study that indicated that within the younger age group one of six get their political information from late-night comedy shows and that this cohort relies on comedy shows more than newspapers, broadcast news, or cable news.[8] Clearly, these late-night comedy shows can be quite powerful among younger voters who don't necessarily watch the news. "For those who don't follow the media closely, satirical shows can hold even greater sway. If Stewart and Colbert and Maher are the ones installing the news in a viewer's mind—as part of their setup before instilling their humorous slant—then they're functioning as both messenger and comic massager; a one-stop plug-and-play for the iPod generation."[9]

As this brief overview of the existing research shows, there is much to explore in studying the impact of these programs. Much of this research has focused on the effect of satire on political engagement but not as much on its effect on our perceptions of gender and politics. The 2008 election is a good example of the effect of these shows on the recognition and discussion of the issue of gender in a presidential campaign. The late-night comedy shows confronted this issue directly through the use of subtle—and at times not so subtle—humor, impersonation, and sketch comedy. As Jeffrey P. Jones points out, "In popular culture, these interactions can be unscripted, more aggressive or crucial than journalism and often more far-reaching, moving from serious to humorous and back again in seconds. As such, popular culture forums offered fresh and alternative perspectives for which to assess candidates and their campaigns."[10]

It is helpful to categorize late-night comedy shows, as Cao does, into two different groups: late-night talk shows and political comedy shows.[11] NBC's *The Tonight Show with Jay Leno* and CBS's *The Late Show with David Letterman* are examples of traditional late-night talk shows. From Jack Paar to Johnny Carson to Jay Leno and David Letterman, the late-night talk show has been quite popular and successful. The mix of politics and entertainment allows viewers to tune in for a lighter alternative to the hard news of the day. Actors and entertainers actively seek appearances on these shows to promote themselves and their performances. Politicians find appearances on these shows to be equally advantageous. Every presidential and vice presidential candidate except Sarah Palin appeared on at least one of the major late-night talk shows during the 2008 campaign. Late-night talk show hosts are usually more polite and less confrontational with their guests than typical news show hosts. This softer approach is especially conducive for a politician who can use the appearance to talk to the public in his or her own words in a longer time format without major interruptions by the host or editing by a reporter. Politicians can show the viewers a more personal side, usually mixing in humorous stories and personal anecdotes while still covering their main talking points. This format has become a valid source of outreach for both candidates and officeholders. Interacting easily with the host, showing a sense of humor, and having the ability to laugh at oneself humanizes politicians and allows viewers to get a different perspective on them as "normal" people. Presidential candidates have grasped the importance of such appearances to their campaigns in this media-dominated era of presidential politics. This format was especially important in 2008, when nontraditional candidates needed to convince the public that their race or their gender should only be a description of who they were and not be considered a barrier to their ability to do the job. Appearances on these shows by Hillary Clinton gave viewers a firsthand chance to evaluate her personality and, of course, her gender as they considered her as a potential president. By not appearing on these shows, Sarah Palin most likely missed a crucial opportunity to showcase her personality and answer her critics in a nonthreatening environment.

The growing popularity of Comedy Central's mock news shows *The Daily Show* and *The Colbert Report* is also important to consider as we look at elections and presidential politics. *The Daily Show* continues to grow in both audience and influence. Paul Brewer and Emily Marquardt write: "*The Daily Show* has come to occupy a visible place in the media world and beyond."[12] Although both shows are viewed by fewer people than watch the major network shows, it is important to realize that they can still be relatively influential because of who is watching: "Among that young, educated, politically sophisticated minority are journalists, politicians, and other governing elites who render *The Daily Show* important because its potential impact on them and their likely status as opinion leaders in certain circles."[13] While both *The Daily Show* and *The Colbert Report* are similar to the network late-night shows with regard to the number of candidates that appear on them, they also provide a value in their format as fake news shows. These mock or fake news shows provide a humorous approach to the day's news and events. As *The Daily Show*'s website describes itself, "One anchor, six correspondents, zero credibility. If you're tired of the stodginess of the evening newscasts and you can't bear to sit through the spinmeisters and shills on the 24-hour cable news network, don't miss *The Daily Show with Jon Stewart,* the nightly half-hour series unburdened by objectivity, journalistic integrity or even accuracy."[14] This show, through its irreverent humor, intentionally criticizes the coverage of the news media themselves. The show provides "the satirical perspective of not only the stories dominating a news cycle but the tasks of information gathering and storytelling performed by journalists."[15]

Jon Stewart has been described as a "skeptical and bemused observer,"[16] with his facial expressions reinforcing the absurdity of a story or the way the news media covered it. Stephen Colbert has credited his program with helping to create a surge in popularity for any candidate who appears on the show (i.e., "The Colbert Bump"). The popularity of YouTube and the immediate posting of episodes on each show's website allow viewers to watch key interviews and sketches without having to stay up late to do so. Recognizing the impact and increasing importance of these shows, almost all of the presidential and vice presidential candidates appeared on *The Daily Show* and some on the *Colbert Report* during the 2008 election campaign, attracting large audiences and positive media coverage.

Besides the comedic careers that it has launched, *SNL* is probably best known for its ability to set the tone in popular and political culture. Some of the most memorable moments of its thirty-five seasons have come when it is spoofing a politician or a political event (a speech, a debate, etc.). Chevy Chase playing Gerald Ford, Dana Carvey playing George H. W. Bush, Darrell Hammond playing Bill Clinton, and Will Ferrell playing George W. Bush all captured the comedic foibles of those presidents' administrations. As the 2008 election had precedent-breaking candidates, *SNL* expanded its list to include these candidates, with Fred Armisen playing Barack Obama, Amy Poehler playing Hillary Clinton, and of course, Tina Fey playing Sarah Palin.[17] The common denominator of the long-lasting effect of *SNL*'s success is that characters have been memorable enough to shape the public's opinion of the actual politicians and their actions, even after their time in office has passed. Many students of politics believe that an *SNL* effect has played a role in several elections, including 2008. In 2000, an *SNL* parody of Vice President Al Gore's debate performance was used by Gore's campaign to show the candidate how bad the public's perception of him was in the hopes of correcting some of his flaws in time to rescue his campaign for the next debate. During the Clinton administration Darrell Hammond's spot-on impersonation of Bill Clinton reinforced the dual images of Clinton as a ladies' man and as a likable guy. Will Ferrell's portrayal of George W. Bush exaggerated Bush's cheerful personality and his perceived lack of qualifications for the job. During the 2008 campaign the show was so successful that it also produced three "bonus" Thursday night programs that focused solely on events surrounding the presidential election. When Lorne Michaels, the show's longtime executive producer, discussed the difference between *SNL*'s sketches and some of the other late-night programs, he said that "*Saturday Night Live* tends to be more affectionate and goofy than mean."[18] As

Ben Voth concludes, "Because the comedians are playing roles rather than making direct commentary—as in the case of Jon Stewart—*SNL* provides a means of comic correction wherein political players can accept their roles as comic clowns."[19] Being satirized by *SNL* gives a politician an instant sort of credibility and, often, media attention. As a recent article about *SNL* points out, "When it comes to stamping a politician in the public consciousness, '*Saturday Night Live*' has no equal. . . . *SNL* has become such a powerful cultural force that the show doesn't need merely to piggyback the political scene. It can lead, deciding what exactly becomes the characteristic trait worthy of lampooning."[20] Although most politicians do not appreciate being the center of jokes, showing that one has a sense of humor allows a candidate to connect with voters in a more humanizing way. As recent years have shown, the inclusion of female politicians brings gender into the discussion in both obvious and subtle ways. As Jones states, "There are moments when the show [*SNL*] produced stinging critiques that have affected public deliberation about the elections and/or candidates becoming water cooler moments as well as widely circulated video clips that are replayed across numerous media channels."[21] Comedic sketches and one-liners forced audiences to consider issues of bias and sexism more directly but less confrontationally than in almost any other forum. Both Hillary Clinton and Sarah Palin appeared on *SNL* in attempts to confront gender bias that developed during their respective campaigns.

These late-night comedy shows have become a prism through which their audiences view daily political events. The humanization of female candidates both as characters in sketches and during their appearances on these shows allowed gender bias to be recognized through humor and set the stage for the electorate to consider women as serious candidates.

The 2008 election gives us a unique (and understudied) opportunity to examine the role of late-night talk and comedy shows in three areas: in the way the candidates were presented or presented themselves, in the way media coverage of the campaign was critiqued, and in the way the campaigns readjusted strategies and schedules as a result of the appearances of or attention paid to the candidates on these shows. These areas are especially important in their effect on female candidates. This past presidential election campaign cycle found presidential candidates flocking to both the broadcast and cable television shows. During the 2008 campaign, the presidential candidates appeared over one hundred times, almost four times as often as in 2004.[22] Candidates even appeared on these shows to announce their candidacy (Fred Thompson on *The Tonight Show* and John McCain on *The Late Show*). Almost every candidate (and in some cases their spouses as well) found his or her way onto these shows (except Sarah Palin, who appeared only once on *SNL*). John McCain in fact created controversy for himself by canceling an appearance on the *Late Show* on September 24 in order to fly back to Washington to "take care of the economy." Host David Letterman skewered McCain for days afterward, which hurt the candidate's already sinking campaign and forced him to divert from his campaign schedule to go back to New York City to make an appearance and apologize.

Just as candidates benefit from the opportunity to speak to the public directly, the programs themselves also benefit. *The Tonight Show* garnered the most candidate appearances, as seen in the following list showing the number of candidate appearances on each show:

The Tonight Show (Jay Leno)	22
The Daily Show (Jon Stewart)	21
The Late Show (David Letterman)	19
The Colbert Report (Stephen Colbert)	15
Real Time (Bill Maher)	12
Saturday Night Live	8
Jimmy Kimmel Live!	5
Late Night (Conan O'Brien)	4
The Late Late Show (Craig Ferguson)	3[23]

John McCain's October 16 appearance on *The Late Show* gave the show its best ratings in three years. Michelle Obama's October 18 appearance on *The Daily Show* set a new record for ratings, only to be surpassed when her husband, Barack Obama, appeared on October 29.[24] The following list shows the number of appearances by each candidate:

John McCain	17
Mike Huckabee	16
Barack Obama	15
Hillary Clinton	7
Joe Biden	6
Jon Edwards	5
Dennis Kucinich	4
Fred Thompson	3
Chris Dodd	3[25]

Events and people surrounding both the primary and general election campaigns were a source of many of the shows' comedic themes and punch lines. In reviewing the shows and the content of the jokes, the *Media Monitor* found that during the general election (August 23–November 3) the McCain-Palin ticket was subject to four times as many jokes as Obama-Biden ticket. The content of the jokes regarding the McCain-Palin ticket centered on Palin's intelligence, physical appearance, and folksy ways and on McCain's age, personality, and intelligence. Jokes about Biden concerned his physical appearance, his lack of hair, and his personality quirks. Jokes about Obama were more cautious and were not usually direct attacks. Most of the jokes made fun of his rock star status and the silliness of his thirty-minute info-mercial that aired the week before the election. Interestingly, comics seemed to be careful with Obama, perhaps subconsciously not wanting to offend his supporters, and tended to tread cautiously on topics such as his race, his appearance, and his background.[26] Treatment of Palin (and of Hillary Clinton in the primary campaign) was not as cautious. The comics seemed to be less fearful of gender repercussions than racial ones, showing that gender bias was still less offensive to viewers. The Center for Media and Public Affairs tallied the number of jokes at each candidate's expense on late-night television as follows:

John McCain	1,359
George W. Bush	1,160
Barack Obama	769
Sarah Palin	712
Hillary Clinton	709
Mitt Romney	135
Joe Biden	107[27]

The following are some samples of the jokes.

McCain was asked how he's going to conserve energy. He said by taking three naps a day.—Jay Leno

Halloween, it's the dead walking among the living. That's what Halloween is. You know, they come back to life and they're dead but they're walking around. No, wait a minute, that's the McCain campaign. —David Letterman

I just got my 2009 Sarah Palin calendar. Pretty hot stuff. In one she is all sudsy with a sponge working on a moose. And in April it's Sarah Palin in a bikini firing a state trooper.—David Letterman

Tomorrow night, Sarah Palin will be on *Saturday Night Live*. When they told her, she said, "What night is that on?"—Jay Leno

The big story is Obama's world tour. Today he made history by being the first man to travel around the world in a plane propelled by the media's flash photography.—Stephen Colbert

The tour may strike some as presumptuous. In fact, I joked that Obama would be stopping in Bethlehem to visit the manger where he was born.—Jon Stewart[28]

In considering both the number of appearances made by candidates and the number of jokes made about them, Robert Lichter commented: "Talk shows have replaced editorial boards in vetting candidates for voters."[29] Another scholar suggested, "The satirical political messages offered via entertainment outlets like *The Tonight Show, The Simpsons, Saturday Night Live,* or *The Daily Show* are some of the more explicit examples of how audience members come into contact with entertainment-based political messages that are distinct from the storylines derived through traditional news conventions."[30] As the high ratings indicate, people were paying attention to these shows and forming opinions through them. Candidates paid attention to them as well by appearing on them and attempting to be part of the jokes. Joe Saltzman commented during the campaign, "The fact that the candidates go on *The Daily Show, Saturday Night Live,* and *The Tonight Show* means they believe the shows have impact on the voters."[31] Now we know that candidates avoid these shows at their own peril. They will miss connecting to an important part of the electorate if they do not appear. Female candidates especially need to make such appearances to dispel myths and stereotypes and confront issues of gender bias. As candidates become more reliant on getting their message out through these programs and voters get used to seeing candidates in this medium, it is not surprising to expect that presidents, once elected, will have to continue to appear on these programs to gain support for their administrations. Voters like to see their elected officials in this venue, and the humanization that began in the campaign will need to be continued while they are in office. As popular culture has become one of the more open and free-flowing arenas for communication about politics, these television shows take on added importance.[32] Thus the successful humanization of female candidates in late-night comedy might be the first step in the journey to electoral success.

The Writers' Strike

What made the impact of comedy shows on candidate humanization more noticeable and perhaps more important in 2008 than in other election cycles was the one-hundred-day writers' strike of 2007–2008. The Writers Guild of America, whose members include film and television writers, went on strike from November 5, 2007, to February 12, 2008, shutting down all of these programs. Some of the late-night talk shows were able to negotiate separate deals with the writers union and were able to go back on the air at the beginning of January. *SNL,* however, could not go live until the strike was settled. Thus from November until January, there were no new talk or comedy shows. By the time the shows came back on the air, primary and caucus voting had already begun, and political candidates had already begun to drop out. Without the strike, one wonders if there might have been a different electoral result.

Journalists were left to ponder the strike's potential effect on the campaign. As Paul Farhi playfully asked in the *Washington Post,* "Without late-night comedy, how will we really know what or whom to make fun of? With a few precious weeks before Iowa and New Hampshire will political journalists be forced to create their own caricature of the candidates without any help from *SNL,* Conan, or even that Scottish guy?"[33] Farhi's lament of a "parody void" was both humorous and somewhat serious. As much as the late-night talk shows were missed, most people decried the lack of new *SNL* episodes during an election year. Despite the down years that *SNL* had experienced, it seemed that each campaign year, it would regain its momentum and significance. In fact, the last *SNL* episode prior to the strike was the highest-rated show of the year (it included as host Brian Williams from NBC's *Nightly News* program and a surprise cameo appearance by Barack Obama). In coming back from the strike, the show announced plans to do four new episodes in four consecutive weeks beginning on February 23, 2008, and it seemed as if everyone was excited to see what the show would do with the campaign and a legitimate female candidate.

Saturday Night Live and the Clinton/Obama Primary Battle

SNL returned to the air on February 23 with an opening scene that parodied a debate between Barack Obama and Hillary Clinton that had taken place the week before. Fred Armisen played Barack Obama and Amy Poehler played Hillary Clinton. The main point of the sketch was to mock and exaggerate the media's fawning over Obama. Kristen Wiig, playing Campbell Brown from CNN, sums up the main point of the sketch (and thus the tone of the media coverage) in her opening lines:

> Like nearly everyone in the news media, the three of us are *totally* "in the tank" for Senator Obama. We *will* make every effort tonight to keep these biases hidden, but, should it become obvious, please remember we're only human. I, myself, have been clinically diagnosed as an Oba-maniac! While my associate, John King, just last week suffered his third Barack-Attack. [King nods] As for Jorge Ramos, he is clearly . . . just obsessed with Senator Obama, kind of . . . to an unhealthy degree, really . . . and, uh—well, I guess you could just call him a stalker! [Ramos nods][34]

The show also seemed to go out of its way to bring candidate Clinton back into the discussion. A "Weekend Update" sketch featured Tina Fey as a "women's correspondent" advocating for Clinton and her candidacy by directly confronting the issues of gender bias and equality. In this scene, the viewer gets a very good sense of some of the challenges that Clinton as a female candidate had to deal with during the primary campaign:

> Fey: And, finally, the most important women's news item there is: We
> have our first serious female presidential candidate in Hillary
> Clinton—[audience applauds]. And, yet, women have come so far
> as feminists that they don't feel obligated to vote for a candidate just
> because she's a woman. Women today feel perfectly free to make
> whatever choice Oprah tells them to. . . . I think what bothers me
> the most is when people say that Hillary is a bitch. And, let me say
> something about that: Yeah, she is! And so am I! And so is this one!
> [She points to Amy Poehler]
> Poehler: Yeah, deal with it!
> Fey: You know what? Bitches get stuff done. . . . So, I'm saying it's not too
> late, Texas and Ohio! Get on board! Bitch is the new black![35]

The use of the term "bitch" was clearly intentional in this sketch and was a term that most women could relate to. The repeated use of the term in the sketch in a celebratory manner can be seen as a direct satirical attack on the more common derogatory use of the term to demean women in leadership roles. Although the studio audience appreciated the comedy, the message of the sketch resonated beyond the set to the public and the media. The immediate reaction to the program was mixed, but during the following week these two scenes taken together created a major turning point in the campaign. The following week, during a debate between the real candidates Obama and Clinton, Clinton actually referenced the program's debate sketch, albeit in a very awkward way, and used it to bring further attention to the underlying charge being made by her and her followers about journalistic fairness in the coverage of the two candidates.

The next week on *SNL* the focus was on a debate in Ohio that aired on MSNBC. In this sketch, the actors playing moderators Brian Williams and Tim Russert seem to gang up on Clinton while fawning over Obama. The real Hillary Clinton, joined by Amy Poehler, her usual portrayer on *SNL*, makes an appearance to offer an "editorial response" in which they banter about Clinton's campaign, her clothes, and her personality, especially her laugh. This appearance showed a different side of Clinton's personality and her sense of humor. It also underscored and challenged the common stereotypes of most female candidates (criticisms of their clothes, looks, and personality). This episode quickly gained even more publicity than the prior week's, and media reaction to the two episodes was overwhelming. Some members of the media began to question and evaluate how fair they and their colleagues had been in their coverage of Clinton and Obama. We can see these themes emerging in some of the major newspapers and other media outlets at the time. For example, the *Boston Globe* put it this way:

> *Saturday Night Live,* the granddaddy of all political comedy shows, chose to build its Obama narrative around the idea that reporters were completely in his thrall. And its skits—on both Feb. 23 and March 1—presented Obama as an amiable guy inflated to hero status by a worshipful media. Clinton, by contrast, was presented as annoying but indefatigable—a scrappy underdog whose complaints of unfairness got laughed off by the media. As if to drive home the point, Tina Fey used the Feb. 23 "Weekend Update" segment to deliver a thinly veiled exhortation to young women to quit Obama and get with the Hillary bandwagon. In less than a minute, the *SNL* skit crystallized Hillary's

complaints [about unfair media treatment] and upgraded them from mere media inside baseball to the conventional wisdom.[36]

New York Times reporter Katharine Seelye commented that the change in the media's tone "stemmed at least in part by deeper scrutiny of Mr. Obama as the frontrunner and to rethinking by news organizations about whether they had been fair."[37] Howard Kurtz in the *Washington Post* echoed this theme by recounting an exchange between ABC reporter Jake Tapper and Obama in which the reporter asks the candidate some tough questions about his patriotism. Kurtz asks: "But did the exchange mark the end of a long period in which the media have gone easy on the man who could all but clinch the Democratic nomination in tomorrow's primaries? The Illinois Senator still hasn't faced the sort of negative onslaught that generally envelops presidential front-runners. But after a year of defying the laws of journalistic gravity, he is being brought back to earth."[38] Even candidate Obama admitted that the tone of the coverage had changed but blamed the Clinton campaign for whining about its treatment. Obama commented in an interview, "I am a little surprised that all the complaining about the refs has actually worked as well as it has for them."[39] The two episodes and Clinton's subsequent reaction to them definitely had an impact on coverage: "Some observers speculated that the comedic scrutiny actually altered press coverage; others countered that tougher Obama press was coming and that the late-night show simply showed great comic timing."[40] At that time it was still unclear how much impact it would have on the results of the primary campaign. As we know from centuries of political satire comedy can say things that candidates cannot. These *SNL* episodes showed the underlying problem of gender in the race and allowed Clinton, through her appearance and the other sketches, to become more humanized and actually more popular. It also forced the public and the media to take a closer look at their own biases and perceptions about the possibility of a woman being elected president.

    SNL in a third straight week looked at the primary race and showed more examples of sexism and stereotypes in the campaign. A sketch that mocked Clinton's infamous "3 A.M." ad also emphasized some of the problems facing a woman running for president. Can a woman be a strong leader? Can her experience be evaluated fairly by the media and by the voters? In this sketch the voice-overs are provided by Poehler as Clinton and Armisen as Obama. The pictures are mostly still photographs, but Clinton is dressed in curlers and pajamas with a beauty mask covering her face (all indicating an older matronly woman). The sketch raises the issues of leadership, experience, and gender and continues to mock the media's coverage of the election.

Poehler (as Hillary Clinton): Mr. President—

Armisen (as Barack Obama's Voice): Oh, my God! I am so [bleep]!! What do I do, Hillary? What do I *do?!*

Poehler (as Clinton): Mr. President, you can *start* by getting a *hold* of yourself.

Armisen (as Obama's Voice): [crying] I ca-an't!! Don't you see that I'm in a panic?! A blind, unreasoning, inexperienced PANIC!!

Poehler (as Clinton): For God's sake, Mr. President! Man up! Calm down and listen!

Armisen (as Obama's Voice): Okay . . .[41]

Although this sketch is critical of both Obama and Clinton, it does seem to have a message about gender. Clinton is shown to be tough and more masculine than Obama (she tells the president to "man up" and to "calm down") and seems to be a more qualified and experienced leader than Obama, who was actually elected. These different characterizations of gender seemed to be accepted by the audience (who laughed at the sketch) and later by the media that covered the program.

All the media attention paid to questions of fairness of media coverage seemed to energize Hillary Clinton and sparked her campaign to victories in Ohio and Texas, prolonging the nomination battle. Although much of the credit for the victories was due to the use of a new strategy (assuming the role of an underdog fighting from behind), some members of the media pointed out that *SNL* might have had a lot to do with her revival. As one reporter wrote, "In the weeks that followed, some commentators have cited the comedy bits as aids that helped revive Ms. Clinton's campaign with primary victories in Ohio and Texas. A study by Pew Research found that critical coverage of Obama increased after the sketches."[42] Even members of the news media have admitted that they asked themselves introspective questions about how fair they had been. CNN's Gloria Borger admitted, "I think the skit on *Saturday Night Live* made us look at ourselves. I would argue, however, that Barack Obama didn't get as soft coverage as everybody thought and that he did get some tough coverage. However, you took a look at the skit and you started asking some questions about being fair to both candidates."[43] Diane Sawyer also asked publicly, "Have all of us in the media used boxing gloves on Clinton and kid gloves on Obama? Have we been unfair?"[44]

Although the Clinton campaign enjoyed a new life after the wins in Texas and Ohio, it was too late for her to catch up. Would a full season of *SNL* have helped her? Would her campaign have figured out a more humanizing strategy earlier with the help of the late-night comedy mirror? Would a full season of *SNL* have drawn attention earlier to the media's affection for Obama or the sexism that was prevalent in the campaign? Amy Poehler was able to point out things as character Clinton that the real Clinton was unable to. The sketches on the program were able to poke fun at and draw attention to the images of women in the campaign. The publicity given to these sketches and the media discussion about and reaction to them brought issues of gender to the forefront. As entertainment correspondent Lola Ogunnaike from CNN's *American Morning* program pointed out, Clinton "could not articulate the feeling that Barack, in her mind, was getting, you know, softer questions from the anchors, from the pundits . . . from the other people. And so, Amy Poehler was able do that and as a result Hillary Clinton referenced it in a real-life debate."[45] Without the writers' strike we might have seen a different sort of campaign from both Hillary Clinton and Barack Obama. Although we will never know if the results would have been different without the writers' strike, the impact of *SNL* on the Clinton/Obama race and on the issue of gender bias after the strike can be clearly seen.

Saturday Night Live and Sarah Palin

Although the return of *SNL* for the end of the primary season was significant, the program's impact was never more evident than during the general election campaign. As the program dealt with issues of media bias and gender during the Obama/Clinton battle, the issue of gender bias again came forward when John McCain chose Sarah Palin to be his running mate. As a little-known Republican governor from Alaska, Palin needed to introduce herself to the American public. Her initial introduction was good: she was relatively young and fairly conservative and seemed initially to capture the interest of disaffected Clinton supporters. Her speech at the Republican convention was well received, and the McCain/Palin ticket received a bump from the convention, allowing it to close the gap on the Obama/Biden lead. From the time of McCain's announcement through the Republican convention and afterward, the media and the public were trying to learn as much as they could about this new face. In order to get her story and her qualifications out to the nation, the McCain campaign arranged for Palin to participate in one-on-one interviews with major news anchors. Her first major interview was with Charles Gibson from ABC's *World News Tonight* and did not go well. Palin sounded confused and unprepared. She was weak on foreign policy issues (she could not explain the Bush Doctrine) and seemed to be out of her league. Katie Couric from CBS's *Evening News* was also given an opportunity to interview Palin and to follow her campaign around for a few days. The interview was disastrous, with Palin looking even less qualified than she did with Gibson. Quickly, negative stories about Palin and doubts about her status on the ticket because of these interviews started to surface. *SNL*'s season premier was only a short time away, and the public and the media waited with anticipation. On September 13 the opening sketch of the season was a fictional joint appearance by Governor Sarah Palin, played by Tina Fey, and Senator Hillary Clinton, again being played by Amy Poehler. Here is part of the transcript from the show:

> Fey (as Sarah Palin): You know, Hillary and I don't agree on everythi—
> Poehler (as Hillary Clinton): [cutting in] ON ANYTHING!! I believe
>   that diplomacy should be the cornerstone of *any* foreign policy.
> Fey (as Palin): And I can see Russia from my house!
> Poehler (as Clinton): I believe that global warming is caused by man.
> Fey (as Palin): And I believe it's just God hugging us closer!
> Poehler (as Clinton): I *don't* agree with the Bush Doctrine.
> Fey (as Palin): [laughs] I don't know what that is![46]

The episode was the highest-rated edition of the show since 2002 according to Nielsen's preliminary ratings. The episode was also quickly available on the NBC website and YouTube, gaining countless millions of additional viewers.[47] Some of the dialogue between Fey and Poehler incorporated actual words and phrases used by Palin during her interviews, which, of course, reinforced the image that she, the campaign, and her party were trying to rehabilitate. The sketch also underscored the problems of gender bias facing Palin, which were unlike the issues that Clinton had faced. Clinton was seen as too smart and tough to be feminine; Palin was too feminine to be smart or to be a leader. Whereas Clinton had been seen as almost too masculine and aggressive, Palin's beauty and sexuality were prominent in many of the jokes about her, making it seem as if she was too feminine to be taken seriously on the national level. Where comedy had helped to humanize Clinton in the primaries, it seemed as if humor here was actually reinforcing gender stereotypes (that women in leadership positions cannot be both sexy and smart) against Palin. And, of course, Tina Fey's uncanny resemblance to Sarah Palin would make it difficult for the public to view Palin without thinking about the comedic Fey.

Two weeks later, on September 27, Fey's Palin character made another appearance on the program, joining again with Poehler, who this time plays Katie Couric in a sketch that spoofs the interview that the real Palin had with Couric on the *Evening News*. As we can see from the transcript, in this sketch, Palin's folksiness and shallowness seem to be the focus of the parody, with her answers befuddling the news anchor.

> Poehler (as Katie Couric): [shaking her head] What lessons have
> 　you learned from Iraq, and how, specifically, would you spread
> 　democracy abroad?
> Fey (as Sarah Palin): Specifically, we would make every effort possible to
> 　spread democracy abroad to those who want it!
> Poehler (as Couric): Yes, but, *specifically*, what would you do?
> Fey (as Palin): We're gonna promote freedom, usher in democratic values
> 　and ideals, and fight terror-loving terrorists.
> Poehler (as Couric): But, again—and, not to belabor the point—one
> 　specific thing?
> Fey (as Palin): [after an extended silence] Katie, I'd like to use one of my
> 　lifelines!
> Poehler (as Couric): I'm sorry?
> Fey (as Palin): I want to phone a friend!
> Poehler (as Couric): You don't have any lifelines.
> Fey (as Palin): Well, in that case, I'm just gonna have to get back to ya'![48]

Fey's performance received another good review, and the ratings for the episode were very high. *SNL* had again become "must-see TV," and we begin to see its influence on the campaign through the story lines that emerge from the traditional media and from the humor of the late-night talk shows. Taken in total, Palin's actual interviews and the humor that was culled from them on *SNL* turned her into more of a comedic (almost tragic) figure, damaging her image and the campaign itself. In coverage leading up the vice presidential debate, Palin was the topic of many jokes on the late-night talk shows. From August 29 through the vice presidential debate on October 2, Jay Leno and David Letterman combined to make her the butt of 180 jokes—more than the other three men involved in the race combined. For example, noting that Palin was getting ready for the debate, Jay Leno quipped, "I understand that she knows all three branches of government now." The same evening, David Letterman joked that being in Arizona "really helped her on foreign policy, because from Arizona she can see Mexico."[49] Both hosts seemed to pick up on the themes from *SNL* sketches that reinforced the gender stereotype that women in leadership positions cannot be both sexy and smart.

The vice presidential debate between Palin and Biden had the makings of a disaster for Sarah Palin. The expectations for her were very low, but by all accounts her performance was better than expected. After the debate was over, it seemed that everyone was waiting to see what *SNL* would do with the debate and Palin's performance. The public and the media were not disappointed. The first sketch on the episode following the debate depicted it with Queen Latifah playing the role of the moderator, Gwen Ifill. Cast member Jason Sudeikis played Senator Joe Biden, and Tina Fey again reprised her role as Governor Palin. The sketch mocked some of the answers given by both candidates during the debate. Biden's performance was also exaggerated, but Fey's Palin acted at times as if she were in a beauty pageant, at one point bringing out a flute for the talent portion of the show. Although all three of the impersonations received good reviews, Fey's portrayal of Palin again received the most attention. Ratings for the show were again very high (over 10 million watched it live, with countless others downloading it later), helping increase the season ratings by more than 50 percent over the season before.[50] The sketch again examined the stereotypes being used against Palin (as a beauty queen and nonintellectual) in the show's typical exaggerated manner.

After the two failed interviews and the many jokes at her expense, the Palin campaign was desperate. As pollster Dick Bennett from American Research Group explained, "Tina Fey has done more to hurt Sarah Palin and John McCain than anyone." Bennett went on to say that Republicans and independents who initially gave the McCain campaign a second look after the unexpected selection of the Alaska governor as McCain's running mate, helping to reinvigorate the McCain campaign, now pointed to Fey's parodying as a reason not to support the ticket. "Tina Fey made a joke of the criticisms about Palin and made them real to people."[51]

In an attempt to spark the campaign and help to reestablish her image, Sarah Palin agreed to appear on *SNL*, making it the only show that she would appear on during the campaign season. It was widely believed that Hillary Clinton's appearance on the program in February greatly humanized Clinton's image by allowing her to show a different side of her personality and that she could take a joke and laugh at herself. Palin needed to take advantage of the same opportunity to save her reputation and breathe life back into the McCain campaign. On October 18, Palin faced off with Tina Fey in an amusing skit where she also encounters actor Alec Baldwin, who talks to her as if she really were Tina Fey, and culminating in a scene in which Fey and Palin actually pass each other on camera. In this scene we see the discussion between Baldwin and Palin:

> Alec Baldwin: Hey, Lorne. Hey, Tina. Lorne, I need to talk to you. You can't let Tina go out there with that woman. She goes against everything we stand for. I mean, good Lord, Lorne, they call her . . . what's that name they call her? Cari . . . Cari . . . What do they call her again, Tina?
>
> Sarah Palin: Uh, that'd be Caribou Barbie.
>
> Baldwin: Caribou Barbie! Thank you, Tina. I mean, this is the most important election in our nation's history. And you want her—our Tina—to go out there and stand there with that horrible woman. What do you have to say for yourself?
>
> Lorne Michaels: Alec, this is Governor Palin.
>
> Palin: Hi there.
>
> Baldwin: I see. Uh—forgive me, but I feel I must say this—YOU . . . are way hotter in person.
>
> Palin: Why, thank you.
>
> Baldwin: I mean, seriously. I can't believe they let her play you.
>
> Sarah Palin: Thank you, and I must say that your brother Stephen is my favorite Baldwin brother.[52]

Palin also appeared during the "Weekend Update" section of the program as part of a rap number that again mocks her and her campaign. In her appearance, Palin showed herself to be a good sport with an engaging personality. More than 14 million people viewed the episode, the largest audience for an *SNL* episode since 1994. However, the reviews of Palin's performance varied, with most commentators concerned about the appropriateness of it. As one reporter wrote, "Governor Sarah Palin of Alaska made her point by going on *Saturday Night Live*. She proved she has a sense of humor at a time when the country is still debating whether to take her seriously as a potential commander in chief. It was definitely entertaining, but it was hard at times to tell whether it was a bold political tactic or a show-business audition."[53]

As we can see, Palin was still being defined by comedy and did not have the same success as Hillary Clinton did with her appearance. In fact some of the comedy actually reinforced the gender bias against her candidacy. Alec Baldwin refers to her at one point as "Caribou Barbie" and at another as "hot." The fact that she does not have any outward reaction to either term leaves it to the audience members to make their own judgments on the terms and their significance. Media analysis following the show did not react to these terms either, leaving the underlying questions about gender bias still unanswered. Although her appearance allowed voters to see her in a somewhat different light, she was unable to truly separate her identity from the comedic image that had developed.

After the 2008 election, members of the media examined the role that talk and comedy shows took during the campaign. The first thing noted was the huge ratings for all of the shows. "Politics has been very, very good to late-night television in 2008. During what turned out to be the most closely followed election since at least 1968, nothing was more appealing to late-night viewers than watching regular helpings of ridicule being dumped on the candidates—unless it was guest appearances by those same candidates."[54] When asked if "those comic takes have any impact on the election," Lorne Michaels responded, "I think we offer some perspective," adding, "But when people start getting into how we're changing things, I think we're not. I think we affect the media and maybe influence some people. I think we're a safety valve. Some pressure gets let off by what we do."[55] Jon Stewart weighed in on the issue but also downplayed the medium's importance: "It's always a feeling of high expectations. When the focus of the country turns to matters you've been dealing with, for a moment you could almost believe what you do matters. Then you go back and remember: Oh yeah, we don't."[56] Stewart also argues that it would be impossible for viewers to learn the news from his program because it "wouldn't make any sense."[57] Jay Leno agrees that the public is not necessarily swayed by the political humor, observing, "The audience has to know what you're talking about or else you'll be sunk."[58]

SNL and the rest of the late-night comedy shows all saw huge increases in their ratings during the months of the presidential race. Interest in the election was high, as the candidacy of Barack Obama drew new voters into the electorate and extremely large and energetic crowds at all his campaign events. As Seth Meyers noted, "This election was ideal for comedy because so many people are engaged with the story. It's the best for a writer when 70 million people see a debate because everyone knows the lines. We did 11.5 minutes on that debate sketch last week. We couldn't do that if everybody hadn't watched it."[59] And the ratings and news coverage suggest that people were watching and talking about it in record numbers.

Although it is difficult to determine exactly how much impact the political comedy shows had on the election, we do know that they had an effect. Poll results released after the election indicated that "non-traditional influencers also helped shape voter opinions. The '*Saturday Night Live*' effect absolutely impacted the election. We saw that 10 percent of voters said they were influenced by the skits. At the same time, the data shows that 59 percent of those who saw the skits voted for Obama and 39 percent voted for McCain."[60] McCain's choice of Palin as a running mate was a risky move that now seems to have backfired. In the course of the campaign, she was exposed to both hard news and soft news criticisms. She was unable to define herself before the media did. And, at least in part as a result of some of the gaffes she personally made during her early interviews with the media, she also became subject to ridicule that she was never able to overcome. As Dannagal Young explains, "When individuals are familiar with the biography and politics of a candidate, an impersonation highlights well-known flaws in an exaggerated way. But because Palin was widely unknown, Fey seemed to co-opt the governor's identity altogether, reconstructing her as a down-home, cute, but ignorant small town mayor, not quite ready for prime time."[61] This characterization has followed Palin since the election, ultimately having a great effect on how the news media have covered her.

The media priming found in late-night comedy has had an interesting effect on the gendering of the presidency as well. Researchers have shown that these shows have an effect on the way viewers, and thus voters, evaluate presidential candidates.[62] Appearances on these shows by Clinton and Palin clearly let the public know that they were legitimate presidential candidates, not just female candidates. They also showed that they were able to stand up to the contemporary versions of sexism. As Ellen Goodman wrote in 2007 about Clinton, "A woman moving into the power structure is expected to behave as if it's a fair and level playing field. Any woman who cries discrimination is likely to be decried as a whiner and women cannot whine their way to the top."[63] In their own ways, both Hillary Clinton and Sarah Palin needed to rely on humor in one way or another to confront gender bias in their campaign coverage. As one reporter commented, "Humor says you are not shrill, not bossy, not whiny, not a nag."[64] As female candidates, both needed to try to dispel the stereotypes about whether they were too strong to be feminine (Clinton) or too feminine to be a strong leader (Palin). By appearing with Letterman or Colbert or on *SNL*, these women were able to at least begin the conversation with viewers and voters about women reaching the historical achievement of becoming president. Both women were humanized by humor. They were both able to show their personalities in different lights. In fact, one wonders whether Palin would have been more successful in combating some of the stereotypes surrounding her if she had appeared on more comedy shows. Since 2008 she has begun to understand the importance of humanization. Her appearance on *The Tonight Show with Jay Leno* in March 2010 and her recurring role as a commentator on Fox News has helped to offset some of the more common criticisms of her and made her a frequently discussed potential candidate for the 2012 Republican nomination.

As the popularity of these late-night comedy shows continues to grow and spawn more shows, further attention needs to be paid to their influence on the political process. Since it is younger viewers (and voters) who are getting their news from these shows, it will be interesting to see how campaigns adapt to these programs and if there are any long-range implications for governing as a result of this sort of coverage. Since his election, President Obama has appeared on both *The Tonight Show* and *The Late Show.* He has also made a cameo appearance on the *Colbert Report* and has visited *The Daily Show.* Being able to talk directly to the public in a lighthearted atmosphere is as important to a president as it is to a candidate. Finding the proper balance between being "presidential" and being an average person is the obstacle facing a president when he appears on these shows. However, as the news media are as polarized as the political system, connecting with voters outside the traditional mainstream media is an enticing alternative for the president to communicate his message without the filter of an anchor or a reporter. During the 2008 elections, the late-night comedy shows were able to humanize candidates such as Barack Obama and gave the voters an opportunity to connect to these candidates in a very different way. As we look for more women to run for, and eventually achieve, the presidency, these shows will be even more important for female candidates. Candidate humanization is one way to help to solve the problems of gender bias in politics. As more and more women run for office, the equal opportunity of humor will help to normalize voters' perceptions of female candidates and neutralize some of the negative stereotypes that female candidates face. The "Colbert Bump" might eventually propel a woman to the White House or at least help to pave the way.

Notes

1. "The Comedy Campaign: The Role of Late-Night TV Shows in Campaign '08," *Media Monitor* 32 (2008): 1–8.

2. Xiaoxia Cao, "Political Comedy Shows and Knowledge about Primary Campaigns: The Moderating Effects of Age and Education," *Mass Communication and Society* 11 (2008): 44.

3. Jody Baumgartner and Jonathan S. Morris, "The *Daily Show* Effect: Can-

didate Evaluations, Efficacy, and American Youth," *American Politics Research* 34, no. 3 (2006): 341–67.

4. Lauren Feldman and Dannagal G. Young, "Late-Night Comedy as a Gateway to Traditional News," *Political Communication* 25, no. 4 (2008): 401.

5. Ibid., 403.

6. Cao, "Political Comedy," 46.

7. Dannagal G. Young and Russell M. Tisinger, "Dispelling Late-Night Myths: News Consumption among Late-Night Comedy Viewers and the Predictors of Exposure to Various Late-Night Shows," *Harvard International Journal of Press/Politics* 11, no. 3 (2006): 115.

8. Pew Research Center for the People and the Press, April 15, 2007.

9. Michael Cavna, "Comedians of Clout: In a Funny Way, Satirical Takes Can Color Perceptions of the Presidential Contenders," *Washington Post*, June 12, 2008.

10. Jeffrey J. Jones, *Entertaining Politics: Satiric Television and Political Engagement*, 2nd ed. (New York: Rowman and Littlefield, 2010) 5.

11. Cao, "Political Comedy," 44.

12. Paul R. Brewer and Emily Marquardt, "Mock News and Democracy: Analyzing *The Daily Show*," *Atlantic Journal of Communication* 14, no. 4 (2007): 250.

13. Dannagal G. Young, "*The Daily Show* as New Journalism," in *Laughing Matters: Humor and American Politics in the Media Age*, ed. Jody C. Baumgartner and Jonathan S. Morris (New York: Taylor and Francis, 2008), 256.

14. *The Daily Show* website, http://www.thedailyshow.com/about.jhtml.

15. R. Lance Holbert et al., "Primacy Effects of *The Daily Show* and National TV News Viewing: Younger Viewers, Political Gratification, and Internal Political Self-Efficacy," *Journal of Broadcasting & Electronic Media* 51, no. 1 (2007): 23.

16. Ibid.

17. Armisen gave rise to controversy by darkening his skin to play Obama, a move some likened to blackface. For an interesting media analysis of this controversy, see Joshua Alston, "The Dark Side of 'Corking Up,'" *Newsweek*, March 14, 2008, http://www.newsweek.com/2008/03/13/the-dark-side-of-corking-up.html.

18. Ben Voth, "*Saturday Night Live* and Presidential Elections," in *Laughing Matters: Humor and American Politics in the Media Age*, ed. Jody C. Baumgartner and Jonathan S. Morris (New York: Taylor and Francis, 2008), 232.

19. Ibid., 238.

20. Jason Zinoman, "Comedians in Chief Mustn't Be Prudent," *New York Times*, December 5, 2011.

21. Jones, *Entertaining Politics*, 10.

22. "The Comedy Campaign," 1.

23. Center for Media and Public Affairs, "Late-Nite Talk Shows Were Road to White House: Study Finds Candidates Appeared over 100 Times," December 29, 2008, http://www.cmpa.com/media_room_comedy_12_29_08.htm.

24. "The Comedy Campaign," 3.

25. Center for Media and Public Affairs, "Late-Nite Talk Shows."

26. "The Comedy Campaign," 4–6.

27. Center for Media and Public Affairs, "Late-Nite Talk Shows."

28. Quoted in "The Comedy Campaign," 7.

29. Quoted in Center for Media and Public Affairs, "Late-Nite Talk Shows Were Road to White House: Study Finds Candidates Appeared over 100 Times," December 29, 2008, http://www.cmpa.com/media_room_comedy_12_29_08.html.

30. Holbert et al., "Primacy Effects," 22.

31. Joe Saltzman, interview, "*Saturday Night Live* and the Election Cycle," Politics & Society, University of Southern California, May 9, 2008, http://politicsandsociety.usc.edu/2008/05/saturday-night-live-election-cycle.html.

32. Jones, *Entertaining Politics*, 5

33. Paul Farhi, "Pulling their Punch Lines: While Political Races Heat Up, Writers' Strike Leaves Late-Night Humorists Speechless," *Washington Post*, November 29, 2007.

34. *Saturday Night Live* transcripts, season 33, episode 5, "CNN Univision Debate," http://snltranscripts.jt.org/07/07edebate.phtml.

35. *Saturday Night Live* transcripts, season 33, episode 5, "Weekend Update with Amy Poehler & Seth Meyers," http://snltranscripts.jt.org/07/07eupdate.phtml.

36. Peter Canellos, "Swing in Momentum May Alter Media's Focus," *Boston Globe*, March 5, 2008.

37. Katharine Q. Seelye, "New Coverage Changes and So Does Tone of the Campaign," *New York Times*, March 5, 2008.

38. Howard Kurtz, "'Soft' Press Sharpens Its Focus on Obama," *Washington Post*, March 3, 2008.

39. Seelye, "New Coverage."

40. Cavna, "Comedians of Clout."

41. *Saturday Night Live* transcripts, season 33, episode 7, March 8, 2008, "Clinton Attack Ad," http://snltranscripts.jt.org/07/07gclinton.phtml.

42. Bill Carter, "Pro-Clinton? SNL Says You're Joking," *New York Times*, March 13, 2008.

43. Lisa de Moraes, "CNN, 'SNL' and TV Critics' Primary Concerns," *Washington Post*, July 12, 2008.

44. Quoted in "Press Takes a Harder Look at Obama—and Itself: PEJ Campaign Coverage, February 25–March 2, 2008," Journalism.org, Pew Research Center's Project for Excellence in Journalism, http://www.journalism.org/node/10004.

45. Quoted in "Presidential Candidates Using Pop Culture to Campaign; Lola Ogunnaike of CNN and Columnist Carl Hiassen Discuss Issue," *Today*, NBC News transcripts, May 6, 2008.

46. *Saturday Night Live* transcripts, season 34, episode 1, "A Non-Partisan Message from Sarah Palin & Hillary Clinton," http://snltranscripts.jt.org/08/08apalin.phtml.

47. Brian Stelter, "*SNL*'s Goals: Funny and Evenhanded," *New York Times,* September 17, 2008.

48. *Saturday Night Live* transcripts, season 34, episode 3, "CBS Evening News," http://snltranscripts.jt.org/08/08cpalin.phtml.

49. Quoted in Mark Leibovich, "Laugh or the World Laughs at You," *New York Times,* October 5, 2008.

50. Bill Carter, "An Election to Laugh About," *New York Times,* October 9, 2008.

51. Ira Teinowitz, "'*SNL*' Playing a Role: Insiders Differ on How Fey's Palin Act Might Affect Voting," *TV Week,* October 26, 2008, http://www.tvweek.com/news/2008/10/snl_playing_a_role.php.

52. *Saturday Night Live* transcripts, season 34, episode 5, "Palin Press Conference," http://snltranscripts.jt.org/08/08epalin.phtml.

53. Alessandra Stanley, "On '*SNL*' It's the Real Sarah Palin, Looking like a Real Entertainer," *New York Times,* October 20, 2008.

54. Bill Carter, "A Great Year to Be a Late-Night Satirist," *New York Times,* December 21, 2008.

55. Carter, "An Election to Laugh About."

56. Ibid.

57. Young and Tisinger, "Dispelling Late-Night Myths," 115.

58. Brewer and Marquardt, "Mock News," 251.

59. Carter, "An Election to Laugh About."

60. "Voters Sought Change in Leadership, but No Ideological Realignment Emerged, First View Election Night Survey Finds," Strat@comm, November 5, 2008, http://www.firstviewsurvey.com.

61. "Late Night Comedy's Effect on Voters," *Newswise,* University of Delaware, October 30, 2008, http://www.newswise.com/articles/view/545934/.

62. Patricia Moy, Michael A. Xenos, and Verena K. Hess, "Priming Effects of Late-Night Comedy," *International Journal of Public Opinion Research* 18, no. 2 (2008): 198–210.

63. Ellen Goodman, "The Gender Trap," *Truthdig,* November 8, 2007, http://www.truthdig.com/report/item/20071108_the_gender_trap/.

64. Emily Nussbaum, "Laugh Line: The Strange Gender-Humor Divide in Fake-Real News," *New York Magazine,* July 9, 2010, http://nymag.com/news/intelligencer/67152/.

4

SOCCER MOMS, HOCKEY MOMS, NATIONAL SECURITY MOMS

Reality versus Fiction and the Female Voter

Chapman Rackaway

A gap exists between men and women in political participation. This so-called gender gap, the difference in percentage of women and men who support a particular candidate or party, is largely a reflection of gender role differences. Men and women are different, and they vote accordingly. Women tend to favor the candidates of the Democratic Party and have for at least thirty years. Just as popular culture explores and magnifies gender differences, so does American politics. The gender gap has become a well-worn political cliché, moving beyond academic analysis and news assessments into popular culture.

Although a gender gap exists in the electorate, pop culture portrayals make the gap seem more persistent and larger than it actually is. The differences between men and women on display in popular culture are often exaggerated for comic or shock value, but nevertheless their focus on parenting roles and differences can inform our views of men and women as political actors. In presidential politics, the gender gap has as much to do with the conflicting portrayals of motherhood and fatherhood as it does with stereotypes or political preferences.

The Female Voter

In the century since female suffrage was guaranteed by the Nineteenth Amendment to the U.S. Constitution, female voting as a general trend has become an issue of great attention. Early voting studies did not pay attention to gender as a significant variable in the vote decision, focusing instead on sociopsychological factors or partisanship.[1] An assumption that women would vote as their husbands did led to this oversight, but in time that stereotype would be challenged.

Jeff Manza and Clem Brooks first noted the historical changes in voting trends and how female voting has evolved over time. While men began the era of female suffrage with much higher voting rates than women, by the 1980s the trend had reversed and women were more likely to cast a ballot than men were. Women also have significantly different value preferences than men do.[2] Pointing to changes in family roles, women's emergence in the workforce, and the rise of feminism, Manza and Brooks note that women do in fact vote differently from men, providing evidence for a gender-based gap in voting that emerges as a theme in other scholarship.

Michael Lewis-Beck and colleagues trace the gender gap as a preference for candidates back to the original National Elections Studies that prompted *The American Voter*. In the 1960s, there was little gender gap. Lewis-Beck et al. point to social mores of the time, when men were considered heads of households and would hold sway over their wives' political ideas. The male-female voting difference was minimal. In partisan terms, women were slightly more loyal to the Republican Party.[3]

Although Carol Mueller suggests that a gender gap has existed since the fight for women's suffrage began, most see a significant shift among female voters as a late-twentieth-century occurrence.[4] Valerie O'Regan, Stephen Stambough, and Gregory Thorson point to a shift occurring as women more fully began integration into the workforce in the 1960s.[5] Karen Kauffman and Jon Petrocik look to the 1980 election as the true beginning of the gender gap, however. The authors point to Republican nominee Ronald Reagan's stances on the Equal Rights Amendment and abortion rights, among others, as the pivotal elements that shifted the women's vote both to be distinct from the male vote and to align with Democratic candidates.[6]

Others see the gender gap not as a function of changes in the female voting population but in a growing unanimity of male voters. Alternatively, Margaret Trevor points to gender differences based on socialization factors. Trevor claims that conventional wisdom that pointed to the Democratic Party making women's issues a central component of their platforms in the 1970s is illusory because those women were socialized more toward Democratic issues in the first place.[7] Similar to Manza and Brooks, Kauffman and Petrocik show that men and women prefer different policies, place different priorities on issues, and feel differently about social welfare policies. As men coalesced more around conservative candidates, the gap between genders appeared. However, Kauff-man and Petrocik believe that female voting was more consistent over time but men changed their voting behavior in the 1990s. There is no disagreement on whether or not the gap exists, but Kauffman and Petrocik say that the change came not from women but from men.[8]

Kauffman and Petrocik analyze data from two presidential elections in the 1990s, but Janet Box-Steffensmeier and colleagues track poll data from 1979 to 2000 for a broader view of female preferences and voting. Using CBS and *New York Times* survey data, the authors show fluctuation of both male and female partisanship but a consistent and strong trend toward the Demo-cratic Party among women that began diverging in 1983 and either remained steady or increased over the ensuing seventeen years. Box-Steffensmeier and colleagues point out that as the nation turns in a more conservative ideologi-cal direction, the gender gap grows, which reinforces Kauffman and Petrocik's point that women vote more consistently than men with the Democrats and the gap emerges when men coalesce around the Republican Party.[9] Further, the evidence of gender-gap growth points to a general set of conditions that favor the Democratic Party, such as periods of economic decline.

In the realm of political knowledge, the story is not as clear. There is a com-mon perception that men are more knowledgeable about politics than women.[10] However, Jeffrey Mondak and Mary Anderson show that the gender knowledge gap is at least half an illusion, since men are more willing to guess on answers to poll questions, and thus their aggression makes it more likely they will get a correct answer by guessing.[11]

Women's voting is generally perceived as not being focused on policy issues. In a *New York Times Magazine* special report by Linda Hirshman on women's voting, examples abound of nonpolitical evaluations hypothetically being made by the female voter:

> The *Times* columnist Gail Collins briefly summed up the theories for Hillary's victory—"Do women Obama's age look at him and see the popular boy who never talked to them in high school?"

> Men are significantly more likely than women to be regular consumers of "hard news" (32 percent of men versus 22 percent of women), and to turn to the Internet, radio news, talk radio, newspapers, political comedy shows and political talk shows. Women, by contrast, are more likely to get their news from the morning news broadcasts and network

news programs. Although morning shows do offer news, they tend toward true crime, entertainment and lifestyle, and they regularly put a human-interest spin on government and foreign affairs.

The absence of women in journalism and on television news programs reduces the likelihood that women will form a significant part of the audience. Most hard-core news programs have hardly any women participants at all.

"Gender consciousness," far from helping women to organize themselves politically, has little power to generate political action, and . . . its influence has "waned over the last 30 years."

[Women] may not frame their decisions in terms of policy or party positions—not use legislative jargon—but they know what's in their family's interest.[12]

Hirshman relies heavily on quotes from Samuel Popkin, whose seminal work *The Reasoning Voter* provides some insight into views of the American voter generally and female voter specifically. Popkin views voters as looking for snippets of information to maximize their return on minimal information search investment.[13] Hirshman implies that women are looking for the personally relevant information specific to their gender. Politically speaking, those topics may be superficial, which leads to Hirshman's portrayal of women as politically underinformed. However, Popkin's main point is that all people look for information cues that help them get through their day-to-day lives more effectively. In a time when women are generally the primary caregivers for their children and work full-time, the pressure to find easily consumable and relevant information is significantly more pressing for women than for men. The conventional wisdom describing those who do not aggressively and constantly seek political information as underinformed, therefore, is rejected by Popkin. The low information rationality theory also makes more sense of the motherhood connection to political descriptions of women. If care for children is primary to a mother's life, then politics must by default be nothing better than second.

Women are not as distinctive as other groups when it comes to voting in presidential elections. Lewis-Beck and colleagues point out that union members as well as Jewish, Hispanic, and African American voters all show much more significant trends in Democratic voting. Women gave Democrats an advantage of between 7 and 9 percent in the 2000 and 2004 elections. However, African Americans voted 45 to 50 percent more often for Democrats than they did Republicans. Except for Catholics, women were the least divided in their 2000 and 2004 voting behavior. Women are also more independent when their group identification is considered.

The Pop Culture Gap

Men and women are treated so differently in popular culture that a colloquialism from popular relationship counselor Dr. John Gray has become an accepted truism: men are from Mars, women are from Venus. Gray's central point is that the two genders are so different from each other that it is fair to describe them as coming from separate planets. In describing communication about personal problems, for instance, Gray says that men share problems as a mechanism of seeking solutions to the problem, whereas women are looking for acknowledgment and support of their position.[14] The belief that men and women are so profoundly different as to defy commonality emerges in all forms of popular images of men and women.

Homer Simpson, Kevin James's Doug Heffernan in *The King of Queens*, and Tim Allen's Tim Taylor in *Home Improvement* are three obvious examples of the simplicity of male roles in sitcoms over the last twenty years. These characters were intended to be funny—but bumbling to the point of extremity. With the notable exception of Heffernan, all sitcom leading men are fathers. The bumbling and disconnectedness of the stereotypical father is present in the sitcom dad. When men are not funny on television, they are frequently evil. From Ian McShane's Al Swearingen on *Deadwood* to John Forsythe's Blake Carrington on *Dynasty*, numerous examples present the other pole of stereotypical male description in popular culture: power-mad and conniving, untrustworthy manipulators whose only goal was self-advancement. Presentations of men vary from incompetent to megalomaniacal but rarely land between the two poles.

Women have not been spared treatment as stereotypes in popular culture, either. The counterpart to the sitcom's bumbling husband is the saintly, all-forgiving wife. Leah Remini's Carrie Heffernan excused (and perhaps enabled) James's character to heights of idiocy while remaining steadfastly in love with him, just as Patricia Richardson's Jill Taylor did for Allen's Tim in *Home Improvement* a decade before. Gender roles were complementary but rarely complimentary.

Situation comedies of this sort present an excellent opportunity to examine gender role differences. Most sitcoms revolved around a traditional heterosexual married family, juxtaposing the stereotypical characterizations of men and women compounded by the dynamic of raising children. The true gap between men and women lies in the specific role of parent. Male characters in popular culture are breadwinners first and fathers second. Women are mothers first and only. Richardson's Jill Taylor on *Home Improvement* never worked a full-time job during the show's ten-year run. Only Leah Remini's Carrie Heffernan had full-time independent employment at a law firm, but, importantly, the Heffernans were also childless. Moreover, Jerry Stiller's Arthur Spooner introduced a caretaking role for Carrie; ironically, Stiller's character was Carrie's father. A subtle inference from *The King of Queens* was that men always need taking care of, and a woman must do the caretaking.

Men are often portrayed as outside the communitarian society with which women are stereotypically associated. Early westerns such as *The Searchers* and *High Noon* reflected a rugged frontier individualism. The legends of John Wayne, Alan Ladd, and Clint Eastwood, among many others, developed and expanded the idea of one man outside and against the traditional society. The concept of fatherhood as expressed in sitcoms like *The King of Queens* or *Home Improvement* is alien to these uncivilized drifters.

Men and women are represented in their parental roles, which adds new insight into the gender gap. Gender per se is not the defining element of the gap in these sitcoms, and the mother-father role difference might better explain the gap and the reason that female voters are depicted in politics as mothers while the treatment of men is much more varied. Men are not defined in popular culture by their fatherhood role as much as women are as mothers.

Male Voter Representation in Popular Culture

The description of the male voter is best captured in Paul Nathanson and Katherine Young's scathing critique, *Spreading Misandry*.[15] The authors assert that the male stereotypes presented in popular culture lead to a negative image of men as lesser contributors to society. Michael Douglas as William Foster in the 1993 film *Falling Down* is a prime example. Although the film is not a political movie per se, Douglas's character embodies the stereotypical depiction of men's outlook on the world and thus their political beliefs.

Douglas's character is a man on the edge of mental collapse. Divorced, unemployed, and feeling disrespected by society, Foster chooses to lash out at every person he encounters. Convenience store clerks, restaurant managers, road repair crews, and many others all suffer at Foster's hand. The vision of the American man is one with a hair-trigger temper who does not solve his problems peaceably or within the political methods that people typically use for resolution. In *Falling Down* the political man is angry, and he is ready to attack. Portrayals of men in politics, accordingly, are of people who only solve problems through violence or other antisocial behaviors. Men in popular culture tend to be mavericks, not members of a child-rearing community.

An alternative depiction of the male political citizen is the completely dis-engaged Bud Johnson of *Swing Vote*. Johnson, portrayed by Kevin Costner, has no political attitudes, interest, or information whatsoever. His daughter, Molly, treats him the same way the stereotypical sitcom wives treat their husbands: as doting and needed caretakers. Molly runs the household to the point that she tries to vote on her father's behalf. Once the plot device of *Swing Vote* emerges, that Molly's vote on Bud's unwilling behalf will determine the outcome of the next election, Bud becomes the focus of national attention. Both presidential nominees campaign to him alone, though his political ignorance is so great that the media and the candidates misinterpret his beliefs. Even in the movie's climactic scene, where the candidates debate for Costner's character, Bud John-son cannot develop his own questions: he asks the candidates questions that others sent him.

Previously, swing voters in American elections were connected to a politi-cal party. In 1980, the election-deciding demographic was termed "Reagan Democrats" for their decision to forsake Democratic Party loyalty on behalf of the Republican nominee.[16] Twelve years later, that same group was rechristened the "Clinton Republicans."[17] Both monikers were appropriate for times when party loyalty was still a significant factor in political life and elections. As the 1990s wore on, though, it became clear that the group had little party loyalty, and there was a better way to describe them. The "soccer mom," a much more specific term, came to describe female swing voters in the 1990s. The counter-part for the soccer mom was 2004's mythic "NASCAR dad."[18]

The Myth of the "NASCAR Dad"

For many years, male voters had no gender-specific description. By 2004, how-ever, that had changed. Democratic pollster Celinda Lake looked to men as the potential catalyst for her party to unseat incumbent president George W. Bush and coined the term "NASCAR dad" to describe the kind of voter she believed Democratic nominee John Kerry needed to attract.[19] A term like "NASCAR dad" oversimplifies any voter, but there are important elements of the concept that can help us understand the nature of media images about politics. The first and most important element that makes a NASCAR dad a unique political animal is the fact that there is no political content expressly in the term. A "Reagan Democrat" or "Clinton Republican" has two words: one a candidate's name and the other a political party. The individual identified as one has an inherently political agenda. Just as Bud Johnson showed in *Swing Vote,* the primary interest of the NASCAR dad has nothing to do with politics.

The NASCAR dad title also distances the voter more from politics by making the secondary role one of parenting and not politics. A NASCAR dad has two elements in his life: the sport he watches for entertainment and his children. No connection to or interest in politics is implied by the title. Substantively and in subtext, the NASCAR dad is a political prize with no political engagement.[20]

The fatal flaw in a NASCAR dad strategy for a candidate like Kerry is that the archetype of a NASCAR dad is anathema to his ideological leanings. NASCAR dads are culturally conservative and largely southern, which suggests that they are actually members of the Republican base. Instead of focusing on independent "swing" voters, Kerry's strategy was to try to win over members of the GOP base. The Kerry campaign was forced, in following the NASCAR dad strategy, to try to out-conservative the incumbent Bush administration. Even had Kerry successfully wooed NASCAR dads, since they lived in southern states, their numbers would not have been adequate to turn any state wins, and thus electoral votes, over to Kerry.

Our attention should then turn to the portrayal of women in popular culture. Are women treated as men in popular culture portrayals of the voter? Or are women simply ignored?

Female Voter Representation in Popular Culture

It is difficult to separate the individual woman from the traditional female role as mother in popular culture. There is little direct connection between women and political activity in popular culture. Amy Poehler's Leslie Knope in *Parks and Recreation* and Candice Bergen's title character in *Murphy Brown* stand as two of the few examples of leading female characters in programs with overtly political themes. Bergen's turn as Murphy Brown has been dissected in other venues, but Poehler's character is also highly political.[21] With a photo of Hillary Clinton on her desk, Poehler is a do-gooder local politico whose overeager demeanor betrays a serious ambition to rise to the top, as Poehler's efforts are mostly focused on rising up the political ladder.

In day-to-day citizen politics, the focus on women centers upon mother-hood as a symbol for political orientation. The most notable of the motherhood-centered political representations of women in popular culture is the soccer mom. The first noted use of the term was by Susan Casey, a former labor orga-nizer and campaign manager. Casey ran for Denver City Council in 1995 with the slogan "A Soccer Mom for City Council." Casey used the slogan to assure voters in her district that despite her high-powered background, she shared the values and perspectives of regular citizens.[22] The slogan was successful enough to get Casey elected. After her election, Casey's victory became an important touchstone for political strategists looking for the next demographic hot spot from which they would try to win votes.[23]

The Nonpolitical Politics of the Soccer Mom

The 1996 presidential election saw the soccer mom emerge as a national politi-cal image. Clinton and Dole strategists posited a new force in politics they identified as the soccer mom. The soccer mom was portrayed as a woman who administered the lives of her children with the same verve she had previously focused on her career. Motherhood has supplanted rising through the working ranks of a business as the top priority in her life. Soccer provided the former businesswoman the opportunity to engage her children in an activity free from gender separation and more accessible to a wider range of abilities. The soc-cer mom put her children and others into a minivan and chauffeured them to practice and games. Soccer moms were seen as noble individuals who put their children's recreation and development above all other things, but they needed support, and as the term became politicized, the soccer mom developed into the primary political identification of women at the time.[24]

The oracle status of the soccer mom in 1996 was not universally accepted, though. Patricia Schroeder, a longtime Democratic member of Congress from the same area that elected Susan Casey, called *soccer mom* "one of the most over-used terms in America." Like the "silent majority" or "Reagan Democrats" before, the "soccer mom" was a product of the moment. The common defini-tion of the soccer mom was narrower than the previously defined swing voter groups: soccer moms most often are white and married, have children under the age of eighteen, and work at least part-time outside of the home.

Prior to the soccer mom's emergence in Casey's campaign, though, there were few mentions of the term. In 1992 suburban married white women favored Bush over Clinton by a margin of 48 percent to 29 percent. The shift in support by 1996, then, cannot be solely explained by the presence of Bill Clinton on the ticket, though that analysis was common throughout the 1996 campaign cycle.[25]

The soccer mom meme persisted throughout the 1996 campaign. A rough computer scan of major American newspapers found just eight references linking soccer moms and politics before 1996, when the number suddenly jumped well past one hundred.[26] As the 1996 campaign progressed, women became the primary focus because of their different preferences in presidential nominee. Bill Clinton was favored greatly over Bob Dole, 49 percent to 39 percent.[27]

Prior to the 1996 contest, the difference between male and female voting was minor: the gap in gender voting, falling from 7 percent in 1984 to 4 percent in 1992, was not evident until 1996, when the difference became pronounced. Merged with the soccer mom theme, the stereotype of women looking to government for support in getting their children to practice and managing their days became accepted wisdom. Though the soccer mom was affluent, she was said to have a liberal attitude toward government support of education and welfare and to favor the charismatic and residually liberal candidate Clinton. With her help, he won handily over traditional conservative Dole. Journalistic accounts of the race did not address the fact that Clinton was not seen so favorably compared to George H. W. Bush, which significantly undermines the idea that Clinton was the draw for soccer moms.[28] Thus the term remained elusive and minimally helpful in predicting winners and losers in presidential elections.

The identity of the soccer mom is significant here, though, because politics is secondary to motherhood in the description of women as political participants. The soccer mom moniker is not inherently political and therefore not commensurate with political tags. Owing largely to a reemerging gender gap, however, the soccer mom picture persisted. In the 1996 presidential election, an eleven-point gender gap emerged on Election Day, according to the Center for American Women and Politics at Rutgers University.[29]

The soccer mom, politically speaking, has more in common with the previously established themes of 1980s "Reagan Democrats" and 1992's "Clinton Republicans." In those elections, the vital swing voters were defined not by gender but by party affiliation. The change in preferences cut across gender lines. With the continued decline of political parties and the Republican realignment of the South, however, Reagan's Democrats became Republicans, and Clinton's Republicans became Democrats. As party switchers realigned, the primary group left in the swing-voter category seemed to be women.[30] What separates the soccer mom from the Reagan Democrats, though, is specificity. "Reagan

Democrats" and "Clinton Republicans" are gender-neutral terms. The soccer mom identity by definition is gender-specific.

For the first time in American electoral history, the female voter was perceived publicly as being the swing voter. Women had a level of political power, at least in the public's view, that was unprecedented in history. The soccer mom phenomenon may, though, have simply been an artifact of the growing gender gap in politics. While women favored Republicans from Reagan to George H. W. Bush, in 1996 women turned toward the Democrats.[31]

Neil MacFarquhar points out a significant limitation to relying on the soccer mom image as a vote predictor: the soccer mom decided on her vote preference early in the campaign. Undecided women were not necessarily soccer moms. Democratic pollster Celinda Lake said in 1996, "There are more than twice as many Waitress Moms as Soccer Moms. . . . Right now they are voting Democratic, but many of them are undecided. . . . If you want to know the truth, it is now the Waitress Moms who are critical."[32] In the 1996 campaign, there was no certainty that the soccer mom would emerge as the swing vote.

From Soccer to Security to Hockey

The soccer mom concept persisted through the 2000 election, and the gender gap remained in double digits. The events of September 11, 2001, changed the circumstances of politics, but the gender-specific political theme lived on. The soccer mom, for whom politics was a secondary consideration to shuttling children to athletic events, morphed into the security mom, whose main concern was protecting her children from the possibility of terrorism. The security mom was likely the same woman as the soccer mom of eight years prior: a married white suburbanite with children under eighteen in the house, perhaps still driving the same minivan she drove in 1996.[33] The security mom was concerned about terrorism, and that had superseded the social services support that the soccer mom had supposedly wanted from government. Some reporters took to calling the domestic public opinion efforts a "two front war" of its own—an aggressive war for men, a reluctantly defensive war for women.[34]

The great problem with the security mom theme was that it was not robust enough. Kerry's support among women fluctuated during the 2004 campaign, enough to make the security mom an unreliable political predictor. Findings from National Election Studies data presented important countervailing evidence. Security moms were less supportive of social welfare spending than single women. However, their attitudes toward defense spending and military acts were similar. The security mom was not a distinct voting bloc.[35]

The security mom was as chimerical as the NASCAR dad: both segments of the population were base conservative voters, and the security mom theme quickly faded. A return to single-digit gender gaps followed, as the male-female voting difference in 2004 was 7 percent. The 2004 election did not turn on the security mom or the NASCAR dad. Despite an almost constant effort by political actors to define swing voters by gender since the soccer mom phenomenon of 1996, gender did not play the distinct role it had in subsequent elections.[36]

After three consecutive elections in which motherhood was a major media theme, other defining characteristics could have emerged as the swing voter definition in 2008. However, the inclusion of a woman as the Republican vice presidential nominee meant that motherhood would again be front and center in the 2008 campaign. Sarah Palin's children played hockey in Alaska, not soccer, and in an effort to reach out to the soccer mom demographic and hearken back to Susan Casey's run for Denver City Council, Palin termed herself a hockey mom. Although the term "hockey mom" was first used in a pickup-truck review in the *New York Times,* Palin brought the term national notoriety and extended the soccer mom theme into the 2008 cycle.[37]

Perhaps because of a marketing and societal backlash, the term "soccer mom" was out of vogue in 2008. Rather than have the term foisted upon her by the media, Palin referred to herself using a gender-specific political term. Palin, in an effort to project toughness and care, carefully crafted the image of the hockey mom as a "soccer mom on steroids"—more intense in her cheering and general demeanor than a soccer mom. Although the hockey mom meme emerged in 2008 with Palin's vice presidential bid, she had used the term previously while running for governor of Alaska two years before.[38]

Sarah Palin and the Brief Phenomenon of the Hockey Mom

The hockey mom descriptor became the omnipresent political definition for women through a combination of Palin's consistent references and the comedy of Tina Fey. Palin described the difference between hockey moms and pit bulls as being lipstick, inviting humorous assessments of the hockey mom.[39] Fey's gifted humor and her resemblance to Palin allowed her to skewer Palin's carefully crafted image in a series of skits on *Saturday Night Live (SNL).*

Fey made fun of Palin's background in beauty pageants and apparent lack of preparation for interviews with verve, and Palin became a national punch line. Thus the hockey mom image caused a backlash among the public that undermined Palin's electability. The gender gap, which some had theorized Palin's presence would shrink, did not. Polling throughout the 2008 campaign found that women viewed Palin more skeptically than men did.[40] Indeed, Palin's presence had no outward effect on the gender gap in 2008, as it remained at the same 7 percent as in 2004.[41]

The skits satirizing Palin on *SNL* encapsulated the public's perception of mom-centered political handles like "hockey mom" as nothing more than diversions from the real, important political topics involved in the campaigns. Most significantly, the skit portraying the vice presidential debate between Fey's Palin and Jason Sudeikis's Joe Biden stands out as a pop culture stereotype of the political woman. Palin appears out of her depth, more a hockey mom than a vice presidential contender. Disconnected from the politics of the real event, Fey's Palin introduces sideshows such as the "maverick" drinking game and tells the audience that her foreign policy experience consists of "being able to see Russia from my house." If Palin was a hockey mom thrust into national politics, then Fey's portrayal of her focused on the lack of preparedness that any typical citizen would exhibit when entering a serious political arena. Subsequent skits about Palin featuring Fey reinforced the image of Palin as out of her depth as a serious political candidate, as well. The result was beyond parody and a reinforcement of the pop culture theme that there is a significant disconnect between politics and women in America.

The *SNL* skit shows the stereotype of female political knowledge in sharp relief. The skit portrayed a disconnect between women, general speaking, and political knowledge. Using the 1996 Political Network Election Study, Jeanette Mendez and Tracy Osborn matched male-female dyads to compare their perceived levels of others' political knowledge. Regardless of respondent gender, participants perceived women's political knowledge to be lower than that of men. The skit thus reinforced the idea that women are poorly suited to political office because they are not as well informed or as smart as their male counterparts.[42]

Comparing the hockey mom image of 2008 with the soccer mom of previous elections leads to some telling conclusions about the popular conception of women as political entities. The hockey mom identity is most different from the soccer mom image in intensity and aggressiveness. Palin's comparison of a hockey mom to a pit bull inferred a tenacity and aggressiveness not attributed to the soccer mom.[43] Instantly, the hockey mom image in popular culture was closer to that of Hillary Clinton: a bare-knuckled political fighter. Aggressiveness was not a hallmark of the soccer mom: the image of a soccer mom was passive and introverted. To the soccer mom, family was first, and the soccer mom needed a hand from government to get through her myriad responsibilities. Palin's hockey mom was as likely to get into a fistfight as the hockey players she shuttled around in her SUV.

Palin's presence on the ticket with her hockey mom image is highly instructive for understanding how voters perceive female candidates. Women who run for political office suffer a double standard: they are expected to be tough military leaders while at the same time nurturing mother figures. That duality may have inspired the hockey mom strategy, as an attempt to show both toughness and motherhood. The McCain-Palin campaign strategy around the hockey mom theme was as destined to fail as the Kerry NASCAR dad strategy was. McCain's mantra on the campaign trail was that Barack Obama was not qualified or prepared enough to be commander in chief, but Palin's homespun ways and hockey mom persona led voters to question the qualifications of McCain's own running mate.

The vehicles associated with soccer and hockey moms tell much about their representation in popular culture. If the minivan was the identifying vehicle of the soccer mom, then the SUV became the mode of conveyance for hockey moms. The SUV itself is part of the popular hockey mom image of definition by negation: it is not a minivan. Like the soccer mom, hockey moms need to carry many children and their equipment, but they do not want to do so in a minivan, which has come to be seen as a stigma. The minivan tends to be regarded as a vehicle that envelops the driver in the image of being a parent. Singles and childless couples do not drive minivans; only parents do. As a result, much of the stigma about minivan driving comes from the perception that parenting is the first and only priority in the individual's life. The driver of the minivan is not a woman—she is a mom.[44]

The hockey mom, by contrast, is an SUV driver. SUVs have their own stigma, but it is a different stigma than that of the minivan. An SUV driver accepts a stigma that her vehicle is too large and aggressive, just as the hockey mom does. SUVs' gas mileage compares unfavorably with that of minivans and traditional cars, bringing a stigma of wastefulness to the driver. The hockey mom cares nothing about the stigma of driving one, though, because it is not a minivan. Bumper stickers and license-plate frames were sold during the 2008 election cycle emblazoned with the words "My hockey mom can beat up your soccer mom."[45]

The transition from soccer mom to hockey mom is as much a facet of changing times as it is of two distinct images of the American female voter. Political pundits and strategists looked for a new swing voter and by default assumed the new swing voter would be female. As times changed, however, so did the convenience of the soccer mom trend. With female voting more consistent across varying marriage and parental status, the importance of the female voter as a swing declined. Palin's emergence as a candidate forced the shift from one sport to another, but time caught up with a moniker that did not adequately explain voting behavior among women. The soccer mom as a political power center had been a myth, and the hockey mom experience exploded that mythology.

The Mom/Dad Gap

When we consider the political gender gap and its intersection with popular culture, it is clear that the two forces have combined to create a new distinction in politics. The gender gap has morphed into what I term the "mom/dad" gap. As popular culture describes women primarily as mother types, so will the gender gap display elements of parent-related causes. Susan Howell and Christine Day point to concerns central to motherhood as a driving force in the gender gap.[46] Bill Clinton's reelection in 1996, for example, is credited to the women's vote turning strongly in his favor. Howell and Day identify a series of issues they term "compassion" issues that women felt strongly about and helped determine their vote. Clinton was viewed as much more in tune with the female voter in areas such as abortion, child care, and education. The Republican nominee, Bob Dole, was more squarely focused on issues identified as "male" issues, such as gun control and the military. According to Howell and Day, those "compassion" issues define the gender gap and are one of the main determinants of female voting in presidential elections.

Compassion as an issue set is an important concept here. The term itself may identify stereotypical attitudes about male-female differences in issue relevance. Men view family care policy and social welfare as issues of compassion, whereas women may simply see those more as everyday issues in their lives. Popkin's work underscores the concept, showing that personal daily-life relevance trumps technical knowledge of politics or other significant campaign-relevant information. Relevance and the likelihood of encountering real-life examples of political issues moves those issues to the forefront of a voter's mind, so "compassion" may not accurately reflect the way women perceive those issues.[47]

The link between compassion issues and the popular culture vision of women as mothers makes perfect sense. As caretakers, women should be predisposed to favor candidates who support programs that provide care, such as Medicare, Medicaid, and Social Security, and social welfare programs such as unemployment insurance. But the reality is more complex and more focused on the individual family rather than the general idea of a village. Education for her children, not welfare for strangers, drives the female voter.[48] As Democrats tend to favor both education and social welfare programs, one can understand how the picture of why female voters favor Democrats would become distorted.

The advantage to Democrats also tends to follow individual candidates more than it does the party itself. Bill Clinton's reelection resulted in part from the largest voting gender gap since the phenomenon was first discovered. With a strong focus on compassion issues and the first presidential spouse that women could look to as a kindred spirit, the gender gap might also be renamed the "Clinton gap." While Bill Clinton was a candidate, the gender gap was significant. Without Bill Clinton, the gender gap was marginal.[49] Again, it is important to mention that women do not vote monolithically—the stereotypical view of the woman in popular culture is just as distorted as the stereotypical view of the political woman.

Despite the sense that 1980 marked the emergence of the gender gap and the rise of the political woman, the cultural references and our knowledge of societal changes suggest that the intersection of pop culture, the gender gap, and presidential politics truly revealed itself during Bill Clinton's time in national politics. A male candidate whom women saw as sympathetic and attuned to the issues important to them was one component; however, Clinton's wife was an equally important factor in the significance of Bill Clinton here.

Women had been in the workforce for generations, but prior to Hillary Rodham Clinton no prospective first lady had been. Hillary Clinton was an attorney, a strong woman in her own right who refused to shrink into the background and accept the traditional role of a first lady. The importance of Hillary Rodham Clinton as a symbol of the post–sexual revolution wife and mother was vital to understanding why Bill Clinton's candidacy was so deeply embraced by women.[50] Barack Obama's success can also be tied to similar sentiments among women, and not surprisingly both candidates' wives provided ample opportunity for the woman, be she a soccer mom, hockey mom, or security mom, to empathize with the wife and mother standing by, but not behind, her husband during his candidacy.

For three decades, the female voter has been mostly a Democratic faithful in presidential elections. While not the unified voting bloc that African Americans are, women are an important and pivotal voting bloc for Democratic candidates.

Democrats cannot fully rely on the female vote, however. Candidates who appeal to women on their preferred issues can win the female vote, as George W. Bush did in 2004 especially. The gender gap may have decreased in the past two presidential elections, but candidate appeal and issue preferences explain variations in the gender gap more than they mirror trends in gap decline.

Empathy is an important concept to understand when we examine the role of the female voters in American politics today. Most of the elements that identify the modern female voter relate to their personal lives and needs. Whether seen as a predilection toward male candidates with strong spouses or a preference for "compassion" issues, the female voter is very much wrapped up in her role as a mother. Caretaking is the dominant theme in popular culture's depiction of women, whether as characters or as voters. Women, perhaps drawn to male candidates with strong spouses because of the few depictions of men in popular culture comfortable with strong women, respond to candidates who thwart stereotypes in the midst of such images.

Politics and popular culture intersect at a dangerous place. The simplification of themes into pop culture entertainment may make political information more accessible to a mass audience, but along with that simplification comes a corresponding absence of important information. The simpler we make political explanations, the more causal factors we lose. The term "soccer mom" may have been a convenient way to simplify the concept of a swing voter, but soccer moms and their extensions were not necessarily the pivotal voting bloc they were made out to be, especially in the 1996 elections. A gender gap has existed for more than five presidential election cycles, and motherhood does not cause a woman's vote to deviate so significantly from those of other women to identify them as a distinct political entity.

Motherhood, though, takes cultural images of women in a very different direction than the soccer mom as swing voter concept: a nonpolitical direction. The images of soccer moms in popular culture are nonpolitical in the extreme. Motherhood is the primary definition of the soccer mom, and politics is squeezed out as a by-product. No direct images of women as voters exist in American popular culture.[51] Women are represented in popular culture as mothers first, creating a false image of motherhood driving their political decisions by definition. Whether the images are of minivan-driving soccer moms or SUV-piloting hockey moms, the image of motherhood overshadows any political content or vision of the American woman in popular culture.

Notes

1. See, for example, Bernard Berelson, Paul F. Lazarsfeld, and William N. McPhee, *Voting: A Study of Opinion Formation in a Presidential Campaign* (New York: Macmillan, 1954); and Angus Campbell et al., *The American Voter* (Chicago: University of Chicago Press, 1960).

2. Jeff Manza and Clem Brooks, "The Gender Gap in U.S. Presidential Elections: When? Why? Implications?" *American Journal of Sociology* 103, no. 5 (1998): 1235–66.

3. Michael S. Lewis-Beck et al., *The American Voter Revisited* (Ann Arbor: University of Michigan Press, 2007).

4. Carol Mueller, *The Politics of the Gender Gap: The Social Construction of Political Influence* (Thousand Oaks, CA: Sage, 1988).

5. Valerie R. O'Regan, Stephen J. Stambough, and Gregory R. Thorson, "Understanding the Changing Dynamics of the Gender Gap in American Presidential Elections, 1952–2004," paper presented at the Annual Meeting of the American Political Science Association, Washington, DC, 2005.

6. Karen M. Kaufmann and John R. Petrocik, "The Changing Politics of American Men: Understanding the Sources of the Gender Gap," *American Journal of Political Science* 43, no. 3 (1999): 864–87.

7. Margaret C. Trevor, "Political Socialization, Party Identification, and the Gender Gap," *Public Opinion Quarterly* 63, no. 1 (1999): 62–89.

8. Kaufmann and Petrocik, "Changing Politics."

9. Janet Box-Steffensmeier, Suzanna De Boef, and Tse-Min Lin, "The Dynamics of the Partisan Gender Gap," *American Political Science Review* 98, no. 3 (2004): 515–28.

10. Michael X. Delli Carpini and Scott Keeter, *What Americans Know about Politics and Why It Matters* (New Haven, CT: Yale University Press, 1996).

11. Jeffrey J. Mondak and Mary R. Anderson, "The Knowledge Gap: A Reexamination of Gender-Based Differences in Political Knowledge," *Journal of Politics* 66, no. 2 (2004): 492–512.

12. Linda Hirshman, "16 Ways of Looking at a Female Voter," *New York Times*, February 3, 2008.

13. Samuel L. Popkin, *The Reasoning Voter: Communication and Persuasion in Presidential Campaigns* (Chicago: University of Chicago Press, 1991).

14. John Gray, *Men Are from Mars, Women Are from Venus: A Practical Guide for Improving Communication and Getting What You Want in Your Relationships* (New York: HarperCollins, 1992).

15. Paul Nathanson and Katherine Young, *Spreading Misandry: The Teaching of Contempt for Men in Popular Culture* (Toronto: McGill-Queen's University Press, 2006).

16. Stanley Greenberg, *Middle Class Dreams: The Politics and Power of the New American Majority* (New York: Times Books, 1996).

17. Lewis-Beck et al., *American Voter Revisited.*

18. Jeff MacGregor, "The New Electoral Sex Symbol: NASCAR Dad," *New York Times,* January 18, 2004.

19. Ibid.

20. Doug Lesmerises, "NASCAR Dads Downplay Their Label," *USA Today,* September 27, 2004.

21. Lilly J. Goren, ed., *You've Come a Long Way Baby: Women, Politics, and Popular Culture* (Lexington: University Press of Kentucky, 2009).

22. Fawn Germer, "Casey, Himmelman Capture Council Seats," *Rocky Mountain News,* June 7, 1995.

23. Philip Klinker, "Deflating the 'Security Moms' Angle," *Newsday,* October 5, 2004.

24. Susan J. Carroll and Richard L. Fox, eds., *Gender and Elections: Shaping the Future of American Politics* (New York: Cambridge University Press, 2006).

25. Neil MacFarquhar, "Don't Forget Soccer Dads—What's a Soccer Mom Anyway?" *New York Times,* October 20, 1996.

26. Ibid.

27. Trevor, "Political Socialization."

28. Debbie Walsh, "Gender Gap in the 2000 Elections" (New Brunswick, NJ: Center for American Women and Politics, 2000).

29. "The Gender Gap: Voting Choices in Presidential Elections," Center for American Women in Politics, New Brunswick, NJ, 2009.

30. Box-Steffensmeier, De Boef, and Lin, "Dynamics."

31. Ibid.

32. MacFarquhar, "Don't Forget."

33. Carroll and Fox, *Gender and Elections.*

34. Joe Klein, "How Soccer Moms Became Security Moms," *Time,* February 10, 2003, http://www.time.com/time/columnist/klein/article/0,9565,421149,00.html.

35. Laurel Elder and Steven Greene, "The Myth of 'Security Moms' and 'NASCAR Dads': Parenthood, Political Stereotypes, and the 2004 Election," *Social Science Quarterly* 88, no. 1 (2007): 1–19.

36. Richard Morin and Dan Balz, "'Security Mom' Bloc Proves Hard to Find," *Washington Post,* October 1, 2004.

37. James G. Cobb, "Behind the Wheel / Chevrolet Silverado: The Cover Is Familiar but the Book Is All New," *New York Times,* May 30, 1999.

38. Vikas Bajaj, "The 2006 Elections: State by State; West," *New York Times,* November 9, 2006.

39. Polly Ingraham, "Hockey Moms Are More Than Pitbulls with Lipstick." National Public Radio, October 1, 2008, http://www.npr.org/templates/story/story.php?storyId=95251615.

40. Nate Silver, "Women View Palin More Skeptically Than Men," *FiveThirtyEight: Politics Done Right,* August 30, 2008, http://www.fivethirtyeight.com/2008/08/women-more-skeptical-of-palin-than-men.html.

41. "The Gender Gap."

42. Jeanette Morehouse Mendez and Tracy Osborn, "Gender and the Perception of Knowledge in Political Discussion," *Political Research Quarterly* 63, no. 2 (2010): 269–79.

43. Andrea Gordon, "Sarah Palin: Defining 'Hockey Mom,'" *The Star,* September 8, 2008, http://www.thestar.com/living/article/492414.

44. Amy Williamson, "Minivan Stigma," trianglemom2mom, August 20, 2008, http://www.trianglemom2mom.com/content/minivan-stigma.

45. Cobb, "Behind the Wheel."

46. Susan E. Howell and Christine L. Day, "Complexities of the Gender Gap," *Journal of Politics* 62, no. 3 (2000): 858–74.

47. Samuel Popkin, *The Reasoning Voter: Communication and Persuasion in Presidential Campaigns* (Chicago: University of Chicago Press, 1991).

48. Howell and Day, "Complexities."

49. Carroll and Fox, *Gender and Elections.*

50. Greenberg, *Middle Class Dreams.*

51. Alex Weprin, "TLC Learns the Secret Life of the Soccer Mom," *Broadcasting and Cable,* February 15, 2008, http://www.broadcastingcable.com/article/112475-TLC_Learns_The_Secret_Life_of_a_Soccer_Mom.php.

Part II

HOLLYWOOD'S INFLUENCE ON PRESIDENTIAL POLITICS

5

FACT OR FICTION

The Reality of Race and Gender in Reaching the White
House

Lilly J. Goren

> I had met far more discrimination because I am a woman than because
> I am black.
>
> —Shirley Chisholm

In 2008, we watched as an African American man first won the presidential
nomination of one of the two major parties and then, in November, was elected
to the American presidency. Former president George W. Bush noted, the
day after the 2008 election, that "it will be a stirring sight to watch President
Obama, his wife, Michelle, and their beautiful girls step through the doors of
the White House. I know millions of Americans will be overcome with pride at
this inspiring moment that so many have awaited so long."[1] For a president not
regularly known for his eloquence, this statement appropriately encapsulated the
emotions of many Americans, whether or not they were supporters of Barack
Obama. Acknowledging the stirring sight of America's first minority president
coming through the doors of the White House with his family, a house built by
slaves from whom his wife and children are descended, puts the promise of the
presidency (and the ideal of the American experiment) in stark relief.

Just after the election, President Bush's political advisor Karl Rove suggested that it was Bill Cosby's *The Cosby Show,* a hit television show that aired
from 1984 to 1992, that really paved the way for the election of Barack Obama,
since it presented a "normal" African American nuclear family and Americans
became more comfortable, according to Rove, with African Americans within
society and holding positions of leadership. This assertion, referred to as "the

Huxtable effect," was a misinterpretation of a theory proposed by cultural scholar Alisa Valdes-Rodriguez, who noted in discussing this idea about *The Cosby Show* "that the social norms of a population are generally formed through its popular culture."² She also explained the political and cultural theory in terms of the foundation that must be laid for social change to take root and grow: "This pattern of political change echoing cultural change happens across the world, in every culture. It adheres to the concept in social sciences that in order for the status quo to actually change in a society, many sectors of the public must coalesce around that change. Popular culture and entertainment tend to be the most effective tools for changing public perception."³ Popular culture and entertainment do provide effective and broad-reaching tools for changing the way a society conceives of ideas, individuals, groups, and culture. Numerous examples can be identified in this regard, as we have seen dramatic shifts in public attitudes in the United States toward gays and lesbians as positive presentations of gay and lesbian characters in movies and on television have been integrated into mainstream entertainment through such presentations.

There is much to Valdes-Rodriguez's analysis—especially of the way African Americans came to be presented through the 1980s and 1990s in popular culture. The Huxtable effect, as presented by Valdes-Rodriguez, delineates one side of the equation of "normalizing" African Americans within American society through the multiple avenues where African Americans were integrated into mainstream culture and acknowledged in such capacities over the past thirty years. But there has been a particular and oddly interesting corresponding experience among fictional presentations of the American president, who was first presented as a black man in the 1933 film *Rufus Jones for President*. The reason this experience, in the presentation of African American (or other minority male) presidents, is extremely useful is that fictional female presidents have been experiencing the same trajectory as the fictional African American presidents, but with a lag time of about thirty years. This may indicate differing levels of readiness on the part of the American populace with regard to the election of a female president.

In visual fiction, African American and Hispanic American men have been *elected* to the presidency for the past fifteen years, but in fiction, women have, until only very recently on *24*, ascended to the presidency through other turns of events that—almost accidentally—landed a woman in the Oval Office. I found this conclusion, based on an exploration of who had played the president and how they had achieved that office in filmic and televisual presentations, quite curious. Oddly enough, before minority men were *elected* to the fictional presidency, they too had ascended to that highest office through other means.

This chapter examines the way in which our actual political landscape may have been more prepared for the success of Barack Obama in 2008 than for that of Hillary Clinton. There may also be a telescoping of these preparations, suggesting that the cultural shifts necessary to normalize our understanding of a female president may prompt this reality more quickly than the time it took to prepare the electorate for a black president.[4]

Valdes-Rodriguez explains, referencing Harold Cruse's work in *The Crisis of the Negro Intellectual,* "that many social scientists agree that political movements of sweeping scope must be rooted in prior cultural movements, in order to prime the public for the change."[5] In an effort to explore the nation's receptivity to the prospect of a nonmale or nonwhite president, Valdes-Rodriguez's analysis provides an avenue into this discussion. She suggests that in order to move to accept a "new norm," some foundation must be laid that allows for some interaction with such ideas. The movement of African Americans from very little exposure in popular culture, in very particular roles ("mainstream movies have featured blacks in stereotypical roles such as jokers, minstrels, sidekicks, and villains") to much more mainstream positions (middle-class, nuclear family, educated, "normal") primed the public, according to Valdes-Rodriguez.[6] But it was not merely *The Cosby Show* that achieved this but a general shift throughout popular culture, with the rising fame and "bankability" of stars like Will Smith and Denzel Washington who could open movies, the iconic presence of Oprah Winfrey, who changed the world of publishing and daytime television, and other popular celebrities including Halle Berry, Chris Rock, Bernie Mac, Don Cheadle, and Blair Underwood.

Part of what was at work over the past twenty years is the evolution of the popular view of African Americans as they have been presented throughout American culture. This shift was neither quick nor simple. Nicholas Winter notes that "race and gender are two particularly important stratification systems in contemporary America. Both define appropriate relationships among individuals and between individuals and groups, and both play important roles in structuring society, culture, and politics both today and throughout American (and human) history."[7] This is the case in both our understanding of the position of African Americans within society and our understanding of the position of women within our society.

While there has been a more or less linear shift in the cultural position of African Americans, there has been a more contested, far less linear shift in the cultural position of women (white or otherwise) in American society. Though Julia Roberts and Sandra Bullock can open movies as well as George Clooney or Matt Damon, most of the films that Roberts and Bullock headline reinforce traditional female roles—so while the stars have broken out of traditional confines, the ideas that are presented only reify societal conceptions of gender roles. When it comes to the presidency, which, by its nature is a position defined by masculine attributes—especially the role of commander in chief—this contested cultural position of women is relevant to what we have seen over the past twenty years in fictional presentations of the commander in chief.

Morgan Freeman in the Oval Office

A decade before the election of Barack Obama to the White House, America saw another black man as president in movie theaters. And while he may have been elected in the usual manner in the film, through a campaign and a November election, we, the actual voters, did not elect him. In 1998, Morgan Freeman was president of a fictional United States in the film *Deep Impact.* The oddest part about Freeman's presence in the Oval Office that year was that it was met with little or no comment or controversy, though the film came out during a period of great comment and controversy surrounding the actual president of the United States at the time, Bill Clinton.

Deep Impact was the center of considerable controversy, since it was made and released in close proximity to another movie on exactly the same subject with almost exactly the same plot, *Armageddon.* They had similarly star-studded casts and high production budgets.[8] Both films presented the tale of a threat to earth as a monstrous asteroid hurtles toward the planet—with a high likelihood of impacting the United States. Of course, if there is an asteroid heading toward the United States, there has to be some focus on the president of the United States and how he (in both films the president is male) responds to the threat, preparing the citizens of the country to contend with the impending danger. At the time, much was written about the fact that two movies with more or less the same plotline had been given the green light by competing studios and were coming out within weeks of each other and both had big-name casts and were very expensive.[9] A great deal was said in the mainstream media about *Deep Impact* and *Armageddon* before the films even opened. Yet little was said about the Oval Office being filled by Morgan Freeman in *Deep Impact* instead of by one of the white actors usually chosen to play a movie president.

The previous spring and summer (1997) had seen the release of a number of overtly "political" movies turning on the institution of the presidency. In *Primary Colors,* John Travolta played a candidate for president of the United States.

Wag the Dog cast Michael Belson as the president, and *Air Force One* had Harrison Ford as a president who is kidnapped. All these films were major releases, with plenty of publicity. They did well at the box office and received fairly good reviews.[10] The American presidency had a rather high profile in films in the late 1990s.[11] *Deep Impact* and *Air Force One* both broke out of the usual mode just a little in the choice of actors who portrayed, respectively, the president and the vice president. Morgan Freeman played President Tom Beck in *Deep Impact*; Glenn Close played Vice President Kathryn Bennett in *Air Force One,* and she nominally takes over for the president when he and his family are kidnapped.[12] Thus, in very short order in the late 1990s, we have an elected African American president as portrayed by Morgan Freeman and a quasi-constitutionally elevated female president as portrayed by Glenn Close. What does this indicate with regard to fictional presentations that become embedded parts of our popular culture? And what does it suggest about our current political landscape, where we have elected an African American man president of the United States while in the same election cycle we have the strongest showing yet by a woman running for a major-party nomination and the second woman to be tapped as the vice presidential nominee? Over the past ten or twelve years, we have had more experiences—in fiction—with other minority and female candidates. We have also had more actual experiences with minority and female candidates, with the brief candidacy of Elizabeth "Liddy" Dole (2000), the more extensive but no more successful candidacy of Al Sharpton (2004), the Democratic primary battle between Hillary Clinton and Barack Obama for the 2008 nomination, and Sarah Palin's nomination for the vice presidential slot on the Republican ticket in 2008. In 2012 both Herman Cain and Michele Bachmann ran for the GOP presidential nomination, and both of them had periods of high popularity during the primary election cycle before they each bowed out for different reasons.

African Americans and Women in the White House

One of the underlying questions that dogged both Barack Obama and Hillary Clinton as they were running for the Democratic nomination (and as it became clear that one or the other of them would ultimately be the Democratic standard-bearer) was whether the country was ready for either an African American president or a female president. The country's preparedness for such a shift implies the ability of the electorate at large to overcome long-standing prejudices and to judge individuals less by their gender or race and more on the quality of their character and the substance of their policy proposals. As we saw over the course of the 2008 election cycle, as Hillary Clinton and Barack Obama emerged as formal candidates for the Democratic nomination for president, and then as Obama ran for president and Sarah Palin was chosen to be the Republican vice presidential nominee, the markings of the minority status of these candidates were discussed, parsed, polled, analyzed, and debated, at the same time that their qualities as candidates, politicians, elected officials, and policy makers were also discussed, parsed, polled, analyzed, and debated.[13]

Over the course of the election cycle, one could read reams of articles discussing Barack Obama's blackness and whether he was actually "black enough."[14] At the same time, there were extensive discussions about Hillary Clinton and the women's vote. In the early days of the Democratic primary, there was the controversy initially voiced by the late Elizabeth Edwards, John Edwards's former wife, with regard to which candidate was best on women's issues, Hillary Clinton or John Edwards.[15] During the general election, much attention was paid to Sarah Palin's clothing choices, the cost of her wardrobe, and her qualities a mother, as well as whether or not she should be considered a feminist and whether she considered herself a feminist. White male candidates are generally not asked these kinds of questions, and the media do not spend much time critiquing men on their fathering skills or whether they are white enough.

The reality of minorities and women running for the highest office in American politics is definitely having an effect on how voters think about the office and who should inhabit that office. Over the years, polls have asked both specific questions about particular candidates ("Would you vote for Hillary Clinton?" "Would you vote for Elizabeth Dole?" "Would you vote for Barack Obama?") and also more general questions about voters' positions on minority or female candidates ("Would you vote for an African American for president?" "Would you vote for a woman for president?"). The polls have produced some interesting data in response to these questions. *Newsweek* polls on this topic—a year before Barack Obama became the Democratic nominee—showed that more than 90 percent of those asked said they would vote for an African American or black if that was their party's nominee for president (as long as this person was suitably qualified for the position). About 85 percent said the same about a woman as the party's nominee. When asked if the country was ready for its first African American or female president, the majority of respondents answered in the affirmative, 58 percent indicating the country was ready for a female president and 59 percent indicating it was ready for an African American president.[16] This is an interesting perception and reality distinction: a large majority of voters said that they were willing to support and vote for a woman or a minority for the White House, but fewer expected that their fellow citizens were ready for this potential change from the current norm.

Thus there is a kind of disjuncture between perception and reality according to voters—they are willing to vote for a woman or an African American, but they sense that not everyone else is open to such a candidate—and these juxtaposed conclusions prompt a consideration of the fictional occupants of the White House. As those who study culture in order to understand its role in society note, "Representation shapes what we know."[17] Cultural studies critics go even further, explaining that fictional representations of the president and the presidency in both television and film directly affect our understanding of this preeminent position and those who occupy it or campaign to occupy it.[18] At the same time, campaigns and the subsequent presentation of the president are organized, framed, and presented by the many staff members who serve the candidate or the president.[19] Thus the presidency is as distant from most individuals as are films and television shows. We all know that we vote for the president, but not many of us can readily say that we have met or know the person who is the president. Television shows and movies that feature the president may well be "reflecting and echoing the 'real' presidential administrations" at the same time that they may be "shaping our perceptions" of the presidential administrations.[20]

Terry Christensen and Peter J. Haas explain the important role of political movies within a broad cultural conversation, noting in their book *Projecting Politics* that "political movies have debated the great issues of the day as the nation debated them, sometimes ahead of the public and sometimes lagging behind, sometimes dissenting and sometimes reinforcing."[21] They further note that most political films are fundamentally conservative in disposition, because "they reinforce faith in the [political] system."[22] Like many other cultural critics, they also note that the studios that produce films and television shows expect a return on their investment, and this often results in films and television shows that have wide appeal, that entertain, and that generally do not make us feel uncomfortable. As a result, there have been many traditional white men in fictional oval offices.[23] For every groundbreaking Morgan Freeman, Jimmy Smits, or Geena Davis in the fictional West Wing, there are quite a few Gene Hackmans, Martin Sheens, and James Cromwells cast and recast as president of the United States.

It is significant that Hollywood decided to elect minorities and women to the presidency some time before reality moved in that direction. In the cases of *Deep Impact, Air Force One, 24, Commander in Chief,* and the remake of

Battlestar Galactica, the cautious studios and networks that produced them were willing to venture into rather unconventional waters by casting realistic, highly visible actors in believable parts that might otherwise have been rather unbelievable. What is most fascinating with regard to Morgan Freeman's turn as the president is that there was little attention paid to the groundbreaking role that he had taken on in *Deep Impact.*[24]

Minority Men in the White House

There have been other African Americans cast as senators, members of Congress, even cabinet members, but in *Deep Impact,* playing a particularly high-profile role in a high-profile movie, Morgan Freeman made a lot of sense as an individual with sufficient gravitas to fill out the role of president, especially given the crisis situation portrayed in the movie. Freeman has a nuanced voice—both deep and quiet as necessary—and a solemn demeanor for playing such roles. As President Beck, Freeman responds to the situation as the public hopes and expects the president to respond—with "decision, activity, secrecy and dispatch."[25] President Beck is serious; he understands the complexity and tragedy of the situation that he and his country face. He makes decisions and takes on the burden of the deaths of millions of his citizens. This, ultimately, is what most Americans require from a president: an individual who can accept responsibility for the difficult decisions that must be made in the Oval Office and who will accept the burden of sacrificing American lives if such a sacrifice is required for the greater good of the country.

Since Morgan Freeman's turn in the Oval Office, a few more African Americans have moved into the White House—Chris Rock in *Head of State* in 2003 and, prominently, on television, Dennis Haysbert and subsequently D. B. Woodside on *24.* Blair Underwood (as a Cuban American) took on the presidency in the television series *The Event. The West Wing* concluded with the election of the first Hispanic American to the White House in Jimmy Smits's character Matt Santos.[26]

Chris Rock's role as president in *Head of State* was a kind of hybrid in terms of his election. Rock's character, Mays Gilliam, was an elected alderman in Washington, DC, when he was tapped by leaders of the Democratic Party to run for president because the previous candidate had suddenly died in a plane crash. Gilliam was supposed to act as a kind of place keeper, running and losing the election and opening the path for the Democratic vice presidential candidate to become the nominee in the next presidential election cycle. In this capacity, Rock's Gilliam becomes the presidential nominee not through the usual primary process but through a more "old school" means, being picked by the party elite—but in this case for the sole purpose of losing the general election. Yet he becomes a viable candidate for the presidency because he is willing to "speak truth to power," not unlike Warren Beatty's character Senator Jay Billington Bulworth in *Bulworth* (1997), or Eddie Murphy's character Congressman Thomas Jefferson Johnson in *The Distinguished Gentleman* (1992). *Head of State* is presented as a comedy and pursues its comic aspirations, perhaps more than its satirical potential. And while Chris Rock may not generally look "presidential," he has a passing physical resemblance to Barack Obama, who may not look like a casting director's ideal of a presidential candidate—African American or otherwise—but who has carried himself both during the campaign and since becoming president with the gravitas that is a key dimension of the office.[27]

Dennis Haysbert's turn as first Senator David Palmer and then President David Palmer put an African American in the White House in the highly visible hit television show *24*. Haysbert's Palmer was, in every way, the kind of symbolic president that most Americans long to see inhabit the White House. Palmer had the correct mix of stately good looks, virtue, truthfulness, strength, intelligence, humility, and resolve. He was appropriately serious and has a deep baritone voice, conveying responsibility and gravitas. Haysbert's Palmer is presented as a heroic figure in the White House—not unlike his Caucasian counterparts, specifically Martin Sheen's Jed Bartlet. Viewers come to know President Palmer as a man who can and will sacrifice his personal life and happiness (and even that of his family as well) for the good of the country or for what he deems right—he readily files for divorce from his wife when he comes to distrust her actions and sees that those actions may have jeopardized the safety and security of the country.

The idea of a black man as president within the context of the gritty realism that the show conveys is not outlandish. And although there are certainly aspects of Fox's *24* that are outlandish and perhaps unbelievable, it is a scripted television show more grounded in reality than many such dramas. *24* and its main protagonist, Jack Bauer (played by Kiefer Sutherland), have made their way into our cultural vernacular, with presidential candidates readily demanding that they would be "looking for Jack Bauer" in response to questions about using torture techniques to get information from possible terrorist suspects.[28] Haysbert portrays President Palmer as the right man for the job at that moment; he has the necessary resolve to withstand grueling national campaigns and to take on evil terrorists.[29]

The presidents portrayed by Morgan Freeman, Chris Rock, Dennis Haysbert,

D. B. Woodside, Tommy "Tiny" Lister (in *The Fifth Element*), Terry Crews (in *Idiocracy*),[30] and Danny Glover (in *2012*) are elected to the White House by the normal process. They have not ascended to the position through succession or any other anomalous route. *The West Wing*'s Matt Santos is also elected to the White House through a fairly normal electoral process.[31] All these characters, we assume, have been successful in persuading the voters that they are the right person for the job. They have the requisite capabilities, and they have suc-ceeded through both the primary process and the general election. Thus, by the early twenty-first century, African American men were considered viable for fictional White Houses—without the need to explain how they arrived there or for peculiar circumstances to have landed them there.[32] More than twenty years earlier, this was not the case.

In 1972, Joseph Sargent directed the film *The Man*, originally created for television, but since the cast was quite well known, the film was released in the-aters around the country. This film, with a script written by Rod Serling, taken from a novel by Irving Wallace, was about the accidental landing of an African American man (in this case, a young James Earl Jones) in the Oval Office.[33] In this fictional portrayal, Jones's character is senate president pro tempore Douglass Dilman, a former university professor who ascends to the Oval Office because of the death of the president and the Speaker of the House of Representatives at a summit in Germany when the ceiling of the castle at which they were staying collapses upon them.[34] The vice president declines to take the position of presi-dent because of his declining health as the result of a stroke.[35] In this way, Jones's Dilman becomes an *accidental* president, happening into the office not because he was elected to it but because of an odd and unexpected turn of events. Those around him view him as a place keeper, not as a "real" president. This is a much different perception than we have of Freeman's Beck, Haysbert's Palmer, or even Rock's Gilliam (who was supposed to be a place keeper, but not in the White House). Of course, Kevin Kline plays a Caucasian version of a place-keeper presi-dent in *Dave,* pretending to be the president either until the president recovers from the massive stroke he has suffered or until those in power figure out how best to replace the president. *Dave* is more a romantic comedy than a political satire, and the satirical dimension comes out of the attempt by Dave and his Jewish accountant friend, Charles Grodin's character Murray Blum, to balance the federal budget over pizza at night in the West Wing. Dave, in his stand-in role as the president, attracts people to him, including the actual president's wife (Sigourney Weaver), the vice president (Ben Kingsley), and the American public. This is not the case in *The Man,* where the idea of an African American in the

Oval Office—at the height of the Cold War, when the United States was deeply involved in Vietnam and there was great domestic unrest around the issues of the war and equal rights for women and minorities—is depicted as scary and unpredictable, and Dilman's loyalty to the country, his party, the office, and his race are all called into question.[36]

Women in the White House

Douglass Dilman would have been able to relate to the plight of fictional female presidents, since they have achieved that office much as he did, accidentally. Women, as they move into the fictional Oval Office, have not quite been given an equal chance to prove themselves in the way that minority men have, through the primary and general election process—at least thus far. One of the first opportunities for Americans to imagine a female president was in the 1964 film *Kisses for My President,* starring Fred MacMurray and Polly Bergen. Bergen had the lead role as President Leslie Harrison McCloud (an interestingly androgynous name), and MacMurray plays "first gentleman" Thad McCloud. Most of the film's comedy stems from the peculiar situations that the first gentleman finds himself in, given the overtly feminine dimensions that have traditionally characterized the role of first lady. Interestingly, President McCloud, until the twist at the end when she discovers that she is pregnant and resigns the presidency, is portrayed as a strong and able president. She is elected to the office, which is novel in relation to the subsequent experiences of fictional females moving into the White House since second-wave feminism has advocated for equal rights. The central focus of much of the movie is the awkward situations in which First Gentleman McCloud finds himself and the comedic twists and turns he faces as he tries to fit into what is clearly presented as a woman's place. Just for good measure, there is a rival woman worked into the plot, an old flame of Thad's, herself a career woman, who tries to entice Thad back into her arms by offering him a position in her company. From our third-wave perspective, it is difficult to view this film as anything other than absurd, with its broad humor based on inappropriate gender expectations of how a man might occupy the position not of president but of spouse to the president. What is interesting, of course, is that the two primary female characters are presented as smart, able, and respected career women inhabiting strong and masculine-defined positions (president of the United States and CEO of a multinational corporation).

There were very few fictional women in the presidency between Polly Bergen's President McCloud in 1964 and Glenn Close's Vice President Kathryn Bennett in 1997's *Air Force One*. One that should be noted is President Julia Mansfield, played by Patty Duke, in *Hail to the Chief*, which was initially broadcast in April 1985 and canceled after seven episodes. *Hail to the Chief* was a situation comedy very much along the lines of other half-hour sitcoms of the time like *Soap*. President Mansfield is one step more "liberated" than President McCloud, as much of the show's plot is about how Mansfield is juggling her career and her family. Since this was a political comedy in the 1980s, there were issues around "family values" and the fact that Mansfield's husband, the first gentleman, is having an affair and her son's girlfriend becomes pregnant. There was also a Jerry Falwell–like character as Mansfield's conservative nemesis. This sitcom was really just a blip on the screen of women in the Oval Office, since it lasted less than two months on the air; little has ever been written about it, nor is it often noted in analyses of the idea of women as president.

Most of the women who have made it into the Hollywood White House have made their way there not through election but through ascension—one exception being Cherry Jones's character, President Allison Taylor, who was in the White House on *24* during its seventh and eighth seasons (2009–2010). Aside from the very recent portrayal by Jones on *24*, women have been elected as vice president, as were Glenn Close in *Air Force One* (1997) and Geena Davis on television's *Commander in Chief*, or appointed to the vice presidency, as was Joan Allen's character in *The Contender* (2000). Glenn Close's Kathryn Bennett never actually ascended to the presidency, since she refused to sign the required documents to comply with the Twenty-Fifth Amendment and make her position as president official. Thus she was not even an official placeholder president. Joan Allen's Senator Laine Hanson becomes the vice president, and because of the popularity and positive feelings toward the sitting president, Jeff Bridges's President Jackson Evans, the discussed assumption is that she will be the Democratic Party's next presidential nominee. All the indications in *The Contender* are that she will easily sweep into the White House following on the coattails of Bridges's popular President Evans. Of course, we do not know that this happens, but she does become vice president after a most extraordinary and unusual joint congressional session, where the president goes to the well of the House of Representatives and lectures (or badgers) the entire Congress on their duty and their need to "do the right thing."[37]

Like African American presidents, female presidents have also been presented in science fiction—but only as accidental presidents.[38] In 2003, Syfy produced a "reimagined" version of the late-1970s television series *Battlestar Galactica*. There was much controversy about how the show would be reimagined, and fans of the original series were quite concerned about the connection between the new show and the original show, the graphic novels, and the literary novels that have traced the story of *Battlestar Galactica*. But one of the key events that takes place in the inaugural episode is the swearing in of Laura Roslin, who had been the secretary of education under President Adar, the president of the Twelve Colonies. We know little about her except that she has cancer and had been sent to the decommissioning of the *Galactica* as a representative of the presidential administration. When the Cylons attack the multiple planets and spacecraft with the many other members of the cabinet, including President Adar, Roslin is forty-second in the line of succession. She is quickly sworn in and takes command. Her authority is almost immediately challenged by Admiral Adama, who is in command of the *Galactica*, when he yells at his son, who is on board the spacecraft with President Roslin, to ignore her orders, calling her a "kindergarten teacher." Mary McDonnell, who played President Roslin, explains her own thinking about Laura Roslin as president: "This was a woman who hadn't a clear political ambition. This made her very different from the women in power that we see on TV. Her story was one of a woman grappling with untapped, literally unrecognized, qualities classically male, in order to achieve one paramount goal—the survival of the Human Race."[39] Although Roslin becomes president accidentally—never really aspiring to such a position, as have other fictional female politicians—she subsequently runs for and loses her campaign for election to the office. Oddly, she is ultimately reinstalled as president but, again, not through the usual electoral process. And all of this is in a science fiction fantasy, though in real time it was written and produced more or less in tandem with *24*, where we saw, as noted, two elected African American presidents and, finally, the election of a female president. *Battlestar Galactica* ran from 2003 to 2010; *24* ran from 2001 to 2010.

In the midst of this same time period, in the fall of 2006, Americans were told that there would be a woman in the White House weekly, on ABC's television show *Commander in Chief*. Similar to *Hail to the Chief* in 1985, however, *Commander in Chief* did not last very long, and ABC ultimately canceled the series without showing all of the episodes.[40] In the episodes that aired, Geena Davis's Mackenzie Allen also gets the job because she is vice president when the president dies, though not before he tells her that he wants her to step aside so a real party loyalist (and perhaps a "real man"?) can become president instead. She had been selected for the vice presidency, she is told, for balance and for the sake of novelty (she is an independent and was recruited onto the Republican ticket, and she is a woman). But production and scheduling complications led to the demise of Geena Davis's run as the first female, independent president.[41] The cancellation also meant the loss of an opportunity to truly get into the complexity and reality (as much as network, scripted television confronts reality) of what such a person in such a position might mean, how it might work, and what kind of gender-based opposition might be faced by a female president.

24's casting of Cherry Jones as President Taylor followed that show's initial tendency to break from the norm, as seen in Dennis Haysbert's casting as the likely president in the first season. While Haysbert's David Palmer was not president during the first season, the show's producers and writers gambled by structuring the prospect of having an elected black president for the second season if the show was a success and was picked up for another season. Jones's President Taylor faced some of the complications that were expected to come up for Davis's President Allen on *Commander in Chief*—President Allen on *Commander in Chief* often had to square off against members of the Republican-elected establishment (including her own daughter) who doubted her because she was not a member of the Republican Party. Jones's President Taylor, though facing some of the expected criticisms and doubts that have been directed at actual candidates like Hillary Clinton, Sarah Palin, and Michele Bachmann, did not have to contend with the issues of party loyalty and policy advocacy that President Allen faced from Speaker of the House Templeton (who had also expected to become president when the elected president fell fatally ill). This presentation of the fictional Oval Office also reifies the gendered nature of the office, casting the relationship of president and vice president (successor) in the context of a traditional marriage, with the woman as subordinate, in the vice presidency, and thus her path to power and her use of power as coming only with the death of the male (husband/president). Commenting on the novelty of the choice of a female president for *24*, Jones noted that the writers and producers "had few options left, having had two African American male presidents and three or four older white guys, I think they realized that, if they had a prayer of staying cutting edge, they had to go with a gal."[42] Jones's character on *24* is supposed to be the first female president, and she comes to that job via the U.S. Senate, just as David Palmer came to his position as president on *24* from his California senate seat. This path to the presidency is unusual, since the vast majority of recent presidents have come out of governors' mansions (with the recent exception of Barack Obama), places not particularly populated by either women or African Americans (there have been more female senators than female governors, and about equal numbers—extremely few—of African American governors and senators).[43]

Reality versus Fiction

Although there have been more women in elected and appointed positions of power than minority men over the years, there have been more fictional minority men elected to the Oval Office than women. Certainly the reality of the late Geraldine Ferraro's run for vice president on the Democratic ticket in 1984 opened up the option of the fictional role of women as vice president or president, as *Hail to the Chief* briefly highlighted in 1985. Four years later, in 1988, Reverend Jesse Jackson ran a legitimate but ultimately unsuccessful campaign for the Democratic nomination for president.

Of course, white men still dominate Hollywood's West Wing, even if they don't currently inhabit the actual Oval Office, but there seems to be an opening for more diversity in the presidency. This both reflects and refracts reality. Surveying the field of television shows as well as films that include the president or presidential appointees in the post-Reagan era (George H. W. Bush, Bill Clinton, George W. Bush, Barack Obama) indicates that there have been some openings made in the direction of more openness to women and minorities in positions of power.

As Americans look at the presidency, it has become more "normal" to see diversity among cabinet secretaries and presidential advisors than at any time in our past. Does this mean that the first female president is just around the corner? Perhaps. The majority of the electorate voted for an African American president in 2008. Generally those who consider running for president have held significant political positions in the past, positions that will provide them with experience that can be used to persuade the public that they can do the most important job in the world, to be president of the United States. The fact that women are now regularly serving in powerful cabinet-level positions carries symbolic significance, as, finally, women have moved to positions adjacent to the very apex of political power in the United States.

Symbolism and the White House: What the Public Can Handle

Women and minorities are still far from fully integrated into the presidential politics we see on television and in movie theaters. The ideas that are suggested to us as consumers of culture are often just reflections of what we are willing to tolerate, what does not push us too much with regard to our comfort zones. Most presidents in films and television shows are still white, generally Christian, and fairly traditional—though, as discussed throughout this chapter, there are a growing number of exceptions.[44] Movie studios and television producers have the capacity to break down prejudices and fears in fiction, and they have done that to some extent already.

It is the symbolic nature of the presidency itself that attracts our attention as citizens and as voters—and we pay attention to how that office is portrayed because we, as Americans, have spent more than two hundred years attaching all kinds of desires, hopes, demands, and requirements to the office of the president. Scholars of the presidency regularly try to interpret and analyze what the American people want from the president, both the office and the person. It is reasonable to examine who has held the office in fiction as well as in fact, since our fictions are reflective of some of our desires and may, on rare occasions, help us to form or explore certain desires. Thus the fiction of women and, until recently, minorities holding the office of president has real significance. There is a connection between what is consumed and (more or less) accepted culturally in terms of diversity in the White House and what happens every four years in the United States. The fiction suggests that an African American or Hispanic male president might be more acceptable to Americans than a female president. The recent fictional African American and Hispanic presidents have all attained that position through the normal election process but not the fictional women in the Oval Office.

Women have made more inroads into actual higher office than have minority men, though minority men have been more successful and realistically portrayed in fictional higher office than women—and their position as president has been far less contested in recent presentations, their hold on power presented as legitimate. But competing historical precedents may also be relevant in this context. African American men have been, officially, full voting citizens (and officeholders) in the United States much longer than have women. African American men were given full citizenship rights following the Civil War, while women (of all colors) had to wait another fifty years before they could vote and be considered full citizens of the United States. Following the Civil War, African Americans were elected to public office, including the U.S. House and Senate. This did not generally happen for women until late in the twentieth century. Most earlier women in Congress were appointed after their husband had died in office. As in the movies and on television, women most often attained public office by accident as opposed to achieving their position through the electoral process. Often these appointed wives served merely as place keepers until the next election, when a "real" candidate could be elected.[45] Fictional female presidents have generally attained that position because of the death or incapacity of the president, which draws more on historical precedent than on the current state of affairs, where women run for and win public office in their own right, having little or nothing to do with their husband. Hillary Rodham Clinton and Jean Carnahan are a kind of hybrid in this regard. Clinton certainly would have gone quite far politically on her own—without her president husband—but she does enjoy more name recognition because of her position as first lady during the Clinton administration. Jean Carnahan (D-MO) was appointed after her husband's death to fill the position that he had won, posthumously, to represent the state of Missouri in the U.S. Senate. Carnahan hardly operated as a place keeper during her tenure in the Senate and ran for the seat in her own right in 2002, losing in a tight race to Jim Talent (R-MO).

This provides an interesting juxtaposition, especially given the general operating impetus of most organized interest groups who would like to see their candidates in elected office. For the past thirty years, the operating strategy has been to establish a pipeline of individuals who are cultivated and elected to lower-level positions so that they will be ready when there is an opening for higher elected office. This is certainly the way many women's groups have operated—as well as many evangelical Christian groups—and they have all had much success in moving individuals with particular policy interests into higher and higher office.

In this way women have had some success in being elected to important political positions. Throughout U.S. history, there have been thirty-five female governors (many of the initial female governors were filling in in one capacity or another), while there have been only eight African American governors; there is currently one African American governor, and six female governors, and the governor's office has been the most successful jumping-off point for election to the White House for the past forty years.[46] There are seventeen women in the U.S. Senate (including four pairs of female senators: both senators from California, from Maine, from New Hampshire, and from Washington State are female); there are no African American members of the Senate at this point.[47] Given the current crop of officeholders, women seem much better poised to be elected to the White House than do minority men—this was also the case when Barack Obama was elected.

Certainly some significance can be attached to the fact that there have been women and minorities cast in the fictional role of president of the United States. The Hollywood tastemakers (if there really are such things) are generally supportive of actually electing women and minorities to public office. Many actors, producers, directors, and creative agents regularly donate money to campaigns and causes and work to help elect candidates they support, especially by campaigning with those candidates.[48] Certainly the personal political tendencies of these writers, directors, producers, and actors open them up to the possibility of and even advocacy for minorities and women to be realistic contenders for the White House. At the same time, those who work in the entertainment industry understand that the industry is based on the bottom line, and that means making money with a product that will be consumed by the public. This requires entertainment industry executives to try to gauge what is acceptable to the public (serious and realistic African Americans elected to the presidency, perhaps based on a Colin Powell–like ideal) and what is too much for the public to accept (which the film and television industry seems to think is the actual election of a woman to the White House, as opposed to the unexpected outcome of finding a woman suddenly in power in the Oval Office).

The reality of how race and gender are perceived by voters during an actual election cycle is not simple—and remains an ongoing consideration. The controversy over Barack Obama's birth certificate, which has continued long after his election to the presidency, indicates that the idea of an African American president is not a fully accepted concept. Marie Wilson, president of the White House Project, suggests that gender acceptance has become "more normal in leadership" as more women hold elected office.[49] At the same time, the presidency is the most patriarchal of patriarchal institutions, and on some level, a female in that office may seem a more foreign idea than the office being filled by a man of color. Fictional presidents are just that, fictional, but they may have laid out some guideposts for understanding the cultural responses to women and minorities as these novel candidates pursue the White House.

Notes

Epigraph: Shirley Chisholm served as a member of Congress representing New York's Twelfth Congressional District from 1969 to 1983 and, in 1972, became the first African American candidate to run for president (and only the female woman candidate, after Republican Margaret Chase Smith ran in the 1964 primary for her party).

1. George W. Bush, Remarks by the President, November 5, 2008, Rose Garden, the White House, Washington, DC.

2. Alisa Valdes-Rodriguez, "The AP and CNN Get 'The Huxtable Effect' All Wrong," *AlterNet*, November 13, 2008, http://www.alternet.org/blogs/mediaculture/106999/.

3. Ibid.

4. This telescoping of social change is not just apparent in regard to the shift in fictional female presidents. The swiftness with which gays and lesbians have been "normalized" to a large extent within American society and culture is dramatically different (and faster) than for other groups who have traveled through social and legal movements to achieve equality within American society. This is not to say that gays and lesbians are not still—especially legally—discriminated against, but the move toward full equality and acceptance has been remarkably quick. It should also be noted that in the 2012 election season, the presence of both Representative Michele Bachmann (R-MN) and Herman Cain as real and viable candidates, at least for a time, contributes to the normalization and regularization of women and African American men competing for the presidential nomination.

5. Valdes-Rodriguez, "The AP and CNN."

6. Terry Christensen and Peter J. Haas, *Projecting Politics: Political Messages in American Films* (New York: M. E. Sharpe, 2005), 247.

7. Nicholas J. G. Winter, *Dangerous Frames: How Ideas about Race and Gender Shape Public Opinion* (Chicago: University of Chicago Press, 2008), 3.

8. *Deep Impact* starred Téa Leoni, Robert Duvall, Blair Underwood, Elijah Wood, Vanessa Redgrave, Maximilian Schell, and James Cromwell. *Armageddon* starred Ben Affleck, Liv Tyler, Bruce Willis, Billy Bob Thornton, Steve Buscemi, Owen Wilson, and Michael Clarke Duncan. The estimated cost for *Deep Impact* was $75 million. The estimated cost for *Armageddon* was $140 million. *Deep Impact* opened the weekend of May 10, 1998, and *Armageddon* opened the July 4 weekend in 1998.

9. The costs of the films were so high not only because they had expensive cast members to pay but also because there were quite a lot of special effects involved.

10. In 1998, Warren Beatty followed as a U.S. senator (from California) in *Bulworth,* a political satire about the capture of political institutions by special interests, the disdain of major parties for African Americans, and the disregard of issues relevant to minorities.

11. See Joseph Uscinski, "Presidential Cinema: Which Presidents Make It to the Silver Screen," *White House Studies* 10, no. 3 (2010): 197–209.

12. She never signs the documents, which were signed by the majority of the cabinet, to make her constitutionally the acting president while the president is incapacitated in accordance with the Twenty-Fifth Amendment. She and the secretary of defense spar over who has the final say with regard to military decisions during the initial absence of the president. They call for copies of the Constitution and for the attorney general to comment on which of them ultimately has the authority to make national security and military decisions, even without the formal transfer of power to the vice president.

13. Governor Bill Richardson should also be included as a viable minority candidate, but his campaign ultimately had little traction and never really made

much progress. The Obama administration considered Richardson for a cabinet appointment during the transition period, but because of some questions about political deals, he withdrew his name from consideration for secretary of commerce.

14. This issue keeps popping up in various forms and with a variety of dimensions. Stanley Crouch raised it in an editorial in the *New York Daily News* in November 2006. It again came up in February 2007, when the controversy focused on whether Obama could really claim the mantel of truly being an "African American" because his ancestors had not been slaves in the United States. In August 2007 the debate flared again, when the issue was not even the factual nature of Obama's blackness but a much more amorphous question about the reception of African Americans by white Americans. Obama himself noted this to an audience of African Americans at the National Association of Black Journalists convention, explaining, "We're still locked into the notion that somehow if you appeal to white folks then there must be something wrong" (August 10, 2007, Miami, Florida). This is not the issue of ancestry or depth of skin color, but the continued current (undercurrent or overt current) of racial prejudice—in both directions—that still characterizes life in the United States. Cornel West raised the issue of Obama's blackness again in remarks he made on *The Ed Show* (MSNBC) on May 18, 2011.

15. Elizabeth Edwards, "The Salon Interview: Elizabeth Edwards," by Joan Walsh, *Salon,* July 17, 2007, http://www.salon.com/2007/07/17/elizabeth_edwards_5/.

16. Brian Braiker, "*Newsweek* Poll: Americans Ready to Elect a Black President," July 6, 2007, http://www.prnewswire.com/news-releases/newsweek-poll-americans-ready-to-elect-a-black-president-52709272.html.

17. Beth Berila, "Savvy Women, Old Boys' School Politics, and the West Wing," in *Geek Chic: Smart Women in Popular Culture,* ed. Sherrie A. Inness (New York: Palgrave Macmillan, 2007), 155.

18. Ibid. See also Linda Horwitz and Holly Swyers, "Why Are All the Presidents Men? Televisual Presidents and Patriarchy," in *You've Come a Long Way Baby: Women, Politics, and Popular Culture,* ed. Lilly J. Goren (Lexington: University Press of Kentucky, 2009), 115–34.

19. Berila, "Savvy Women," 155.

20. Ibid.

21. Christensen and Haas, *Projecting Politics,* 278.

22. Ibid., 281.

23. As he has grown older, Gene Hackman has apparently also become more serious as a political contender, having played the president twice, as President Monroe Cole in *Welcome to Mooseport* and President Allen Richmond in *Absolute Power.* He played Senator Kevin Keeley in *The Birdcage* and Secretary of Defense David Brice in *No Way Out.* Another regular recruit into political roles is James Cromwell, playing President Robert Fowler in *The Sum of All Fears,* President D. Wire Newman in an episode of *The West Wing,* and actual President George H. W.

Bush in *W.* Harrison Ford took his turn as President James Marshall in *Air Force One.* Michael Douglas starred as President Andy Sheppard in *The American President* and played Judge Robert Wakefield, the newly appointed U.S. "drug czar" in *Traffic.* Martin Sheen, who played chief of staff A. J. MacInerney to Michael Douglas's Andy Sheppard in *The American President,* was elected to the White House twice on *The West Wing.* Jeff Bridges was nominated for an Academy Award for his role as President Jackson Evans in *The Contender.* Bill Pullman helped save the planet from aliens as the former jet pilot cum president Thomas J. Whitmore in *Independence Day.* John Travolta may or may not have become President Jack Stanton in *Primary Colors;* we do not know because the film ends before the general election. Roy Scheider was POTUS not once but twice in 1997, in both *Executive Target* and *The Peacekeeper.* Kevin Kline had a different double ascendance to the presidency, replacing, as a body double, the real president he also played as suffering from a massive stroke in *Dave.* There have been British actors tapped to play the president as well, including Sir Anthony Hopkins as Richard Nixon in *Nixon,* and Sir Ben Kingsley played Vice President Nance in *Dave.* Frank Langella played Nixon in *Frost/Nixon,* and Josh Brolin played George W. Bush in Oliver Stone's biopic, *W.* These are just a small sampling of some of the white actors who have played the president in some of the bigger budget, often more serious films in recent decades.

24. Morgan Freeman has gone on to play God in *Bruce Almighty.* But since there isn't a two-hundred-year precedent as to what God looks like up to this point, perhaps there may be a bit more latitude with the casting of God in unexpected ways. (Alanis Morissette played God in *Dogma.*) Women and minorities have been cast in this unknowable role more easily because God's personification is just that, unknowable.

25. *Federalist Paper* 70, discussing how the single executive should be able to act, especially with regard to matters of national security and crisis. Alexander Hamilton explains in this *Federalist Paper,* "That unity is conducive to energy will not be disputed. Decision, activity, secrecy, and dispatch will generally characterize the proceedings of one man in a much more eminent degree than the proceedings of any greater number; and in proportion as the number is increased, these qualities will be diminished."

26. Alan Alda did not make a successful return to the White House on *The West Wing,* though he had served as the president in the mid-1990s in *Canadian Bacon.* Alda is not a stranger to casting directors' ideal for political office. He has served as a senator in film (*The Seduction of Joe Tynan, The Aviator*) and a national security advisor (*Murder at 1600*), and his run on *The West Wing* cast him as Senator Arnold Vinick, a moderate Republican senator from California who would become secretary of state in the new Santos administration. Alda seems to convey a particular political character or gravitas. At the same time, Alda himself has been seen as "political"—especially in a liberal vein—since his days on television's *M*A*S*H.*

27. President Obama's voice is a bit deeper than Rock's, and he is much taller—and Obama certainly had the proper pedigree in many respects compared with past presidents and candidates. Obama physically resembles Chris Rock more than he does Dennis Haysbert or Morgan Freeman (or James Earl Jones), and he characterized himself as a young person as "the skinny kid with the funny name."

28. Transcript of debate (May 15, 2007, South Carolina), http://www.cfr.org/publication/13338/.

29. In season 6 of *24*, David Palmer's brother Wayne Palmer is the president and presides over the office much as his brother, with resolve and steely determination, though he is subsequently injured in a terrorist attack and there are fissures within his cabinet about what approach should be taken toward terrorists. In this context, we have seen two strong, intelligent, believable African American presidents on *24*.

30. Lister and Crews play presidents elected far in the future, and the suggestion is that although they do get elected through the "normal" election process, the dystopian quality of life on earth and in the United States at that point more easily allows for the election of minority men to the White House.

31. While Santos wins the general election after a normal campaign season, he only gets the Democratic nomination as the result of a brokered convention, which has not occurred in recent history.

32. There has been discussion about the fact that often African American presidents only occur in science fiction films, suggesting that the conception of such a turn of events remains something of a fantasy or still only likely to happen in the distant future. See also Justin S. Vaughn, "Barack Obama's Black Presidential Predecessors: The Myth of Pop Culture Predestination," *White House Studies* 10, no. 3 (2010): 243–58; Troy Patterson, "Black Presidents: A Pop-Cultural Survey," *Slate*, October 24, 2008, http://www.slate.com/id/2202810/.

33. James Earl Jones went on to play Admiral James Greer, a national security advisor, in a number of the film versions of other Tom Clancy books.

34. Interestingly enough, our current African American president also used to be a university professor. One of the few career avenues open to African Americans since the Civil War has been the opportunity to move into the mainstream via education—university education (at traditional black colleges before many white institutions broadly accepted minorities) and the capacity to earn a doctorate conferred status and position and, to a degree, was respected within white communities.

35. The discussion here references the film version of *The Man*. Although they are very similar, some small differences exist between the book and film versions. For example, in the book, the vice president does not decline taking office because of poor health but had actually passed away a short time before the accident that killed the president and Speaker of the House of Representatives.

36. Dilman's former position as a college professor (and essentially back-bencher in the Senate) also softens his image. As opposed to delineating his character as

a tough litigator or businessman, he is sketched as a thoughtful, erudite, but still "elite" academic.

37. We do not actually see her become vice president, which is interesting, because while we, as an audience, are asked to imagine Senator Hanson as the vice president, we do not see her in this position—it is never overtly presented to the audience as an image. We are given the framework to consider a woman in this role, but we are not presented with the actuality.

38. At the same time, cultural critic Ron Mwangaguhunga points out that in the "history of the United States there has never been anything but a constant succession of white male presidents," and thus in 2003 he predicted that "America probably has to break a few more social barriers before a black president could be elected." Although there have been filmic portrayals of African American presidents, he suggests that they have not been in "serious" films, instead relegated to either comedic visions of the White House, with examples such as Chris Rock as president in *Head of State,* or science fiction films such as *Deep Impact* or *The Fifth Element.* Film studies scholars and critics suggest that science fiction as a genre is, in fact, quite serious and often more political than other genres and would discount Mwangaguhunga's discounting of the African American presidents in *Deep Impact* and *The Fifth Element.* Mwangaguhunga's thesis is that, given the pipeline of those who had been elected to and held public office, it is much more likely that a woman would make it to the White House before an African American man. See Ron Mwangaguhunga, "The First Black President?" *Global Black News,* July 15, 2003.

39. Kate O'Hare, "President Roslin—Q&A with *Battlestar Galactica's* Mary McDonnell," Zap2it.com, February 23, 2009, http://blog.zap2it.com/kate_ohare/2009/02/president-roslin-speaks-qa-with-battlestar-galacticas-mary-mcdonnell.html.

40. The production of *Commander in Chief* ran into some of its own problems, with a number of changes in writers and the directors of the show. Although there was much hype and publicity for *Commander in Chief* before it began and it initially received very good reviews and brought in some of the best ratings for a new television show, ABC seemed to doubt its viability, particularly as the production problems persisted, eventually losing faith in the show and canceling it. This was an interesting backstory, given that a similar situation plagued *The West Wing* under the writing and direction of creator Aaron Sorkin. Sorkin was notorious for rewriting the scripts for the shows, ballooning budgets because of the need to reshoot segments of the show, and for being late with completed drafts of the script. At the same time, NBC was willing to stand behind *The West Wing* more consistently than ABC was willing to support the continued production of *Commander in Chief.* Melissa Crawley's analysis of Sorkin's philosophical inclinations toward the American presidency includes a more in-depth discussion of the causes and consequences of his removal from the show. See Melissa Crawley, *Mr. Sorkin Goes*

to Washington: Shaping the President on Television's "The West Wing" (Jefferson, NC: McFarland, 2006).

41. An interesting offhand comment was made by one of the reviewers with regard to *Commander in Chief* and the height of the main characters: Geena Davis, Kyle Secor, and Donald Sutherland are all over six feet tall; thus Davis's President Allen was in no way diminutive or delicate, especially in her interactions with her primary antagonist, Donald Sutherland's Speaker Nathan Templeton.

42. Nancy Mills, "Actress Cherry Jones: No Doubt, She's in Charge as the New President on *24*," *Reading Eagle*, January 11, 2009, http://readingeagle.com/article.aspx?id=120718.

43. This is yet another interesting twist on what we can realistically imagine because we are already familiar with this reality—women as senators—as opposed to presenting the audience with a picture of a woman as a governor ascending to the presidency. The centerpiece of this particular gloss—for both African American men (Douglas Dilman was a professor-senator, Barack Obama was a professor-senator) and for women (Hillary Clinton was a senator, as was Liddy Dole; Shirley Chisholm was a House member, as was Geraldine Ferraro, but Sarah Palin was a governor)—is that when an elected representative is 1 of 100 or 1 of 435, he or she is much less threatening and can be checked by others. When one is an executive, on the other hand, as either a governor or president, the power that one has is potentially more extensive and is often characterized in more masculine terms as well, and it can only be checked by another branch of government, not by colleagues within the same branch.

44. One of the interesting critiques of former governor Mitt Romney as he has been running for the GOP nomination is that he looks and acts too much like a Hollywood *idea* of a president as opposed to the reality of the individuals who have, of late, run for and been elected to the White House.

45. The character played by Chris Rock in *Head of State*, Mays Gilliam, is a placeholder candidate.

46. Of the last six individuals elected to the presidency, only two had never been elected governor of a state: George H. W. Bush and Barack Obama, and the elder Bush was elected president from the vice presidency.

47. Election to the White House from the Senate used to be a common path, but, as mentioned in the previous note, the governor's office has been a better bet for actually getting elected to the White House, at least in recent years.

48. Most of the actors from NBC's *The West Wing* toured the country as a group during the 2000 election, campaigning for Al Gore and the Democrats. This is only one of many examples of such support and campaign assistance.

49. Quoted in Benjamin Wallace-Wells, "Is America Too Racist for Barack? Too Sexist for Hillary?" *Washington Post*, November 12, 2006.

6

GENDERING THE PRESIDENCY WITHOUT GENDER IN THE PRESIDENCY

Joseph E. Uscinski

In recent years, a series of polls have found that majorities of voters at least claim to be willing to vote for a female presidential candidate. For example, a poll of registered voters conducted by the Siena College Research Institute found that 81 percent of voters would vote for a woman for president. And prior to Hillary Clinton's primary campaign of 2008, polls found that about 60 percent of voters said they expected a woman to be the Democrats' nominee for president in 2008.[1] These numbers show a significant increase in recent decades in the public's perception of females' ability to campaign for and serve in the upper echelons of American power. For example, polls taken in the late 1960s showed that only half of voters would support a well-qualified female presidential candidate.[2]

These changing poll numbers and the recent presidential candidacy of Hillary Clinton suggest that America is in fact ready for a female president. With this said, however, these anecdotal considerations can be deceptive. First, Hillary Clinton lost the nomination race to a male candidate amid gendered treatment and a series of misogynistic attacks from both her opponent and the media.[3] This misogynistic environment fit well with historical treatment of female candidates.[4] Second, the observed increase of acceptance of female presidential candidates seen in polls might not indicate more willingness to elect women; it may simply indicate the public's greater willingness to hide their long-held misogynistic attitudes in a society that no longer views such overt attitudes as openly acceptable.[5]

Furthermore, and perhaps most telling, poll respondents, when asked about how a woman might fare in certain aspects of the presidency, 75 percent said that a female president would perform worse than a male candidate in the area of foreign policy (perhaps the one policy area where the president has the most autonomous control).[6] Based on this, the question researchers might then ask is, given that a female has never served as president and, thus, females have no track record indicating how they would perform in the White House, how can the public have such decidedly negative views about how they would perform?

There are perhaps many answers to this question; however, most answers likely trace back to socialization processes that occur in a society that has traditionally harbored views that favor the leadership of males over that of females.[7] In American society, notions of gender are engrained in early socialization processes and reinforced throughout life. Thus citizens can have a seemingly fully developed notion of how well a female would perform as president without ever seeing a female perform as president.

In this chapter, I focus on one of the agents that act to reinforce and catalyze gendered stereotypes: popular cinema. I argue that portrayals of female characters in popular cinema, regardless of whether those characters hold high office or not, perpetuate gendered stereotypes and propagate the notion that women are "unsafe" choices to hold high office.

Popular Cinema and Politics

Popular culture has an important nexus with politics—it reflects, reinforces, and affects public opinions about a great variety of issues. This gives popular culture a vastly important role in democracies, because it is public opinion that drives the election and policy-making processes. By understanding the messages embedded within popular culture, we can understand the sociological forces that affect government, governance, and policy outcomes. In keeping with the theme of this volume, there is much to be learned about popular notions of gender from popular culture. There are of course many movies, television shows, and musical artists who wade into explicit political debates within their work. These statements within popular culture often represent the opinions of purveyors (whose attitudes are quite distinct from those of society in general and therefore somewhat unrepresentative). While such statements are important and fascinating in their own right, we are limited in what we can learn about society in general from such *explicit* popular takes on specific issues. On the other hand, almost all facets of popular culture portray something to do with gender, whether the particular movie, television show, or song is intended to address gender issues or not. For example, one cannot make a movie containing a love story without at least unintentionally portraying the power relations between the two genders and the role of the two genders within society and politics.[8] Thus, while the portrayal of gender is often not used to make explicit or topical political statements, statements about gender are nonetheless made. And the audience, uninhibited by the commonplaceness of such portrayals, is receptive to such messages.

For instance, there are many films that feature a "damsel in distress" who must be rescued by a strong masculine male hero. In these cases, portrayals of gender often rely on ingrained stereotypes that fly under the radar and are not necessarily intended by the producer. Thus gender presents a fascinating vantage point from which to view not only how popular culture producers view the role of women in politics but also how society as a whole views the role of women in politics. While images of gender are present in all facets of popular culture, I focus narrowly on popular films rather than other facets of popular culture such as television programs, soft news, music, novels, art, plays, or minor independent films.

While other chapters in this volume address the explicit messages that come from portrayals of male or female politicians, it is perhaps most interesting to note that cultural outlets rarely portray female characters as holding high political office, especially the presidency, or wielding substantial power. Thus our understanding of how women are portrayed in presidential roles is plagued by the fact that so few films are made featuring women in such roles. With this said, a lack of female presidents in films does not necessarily indicate that gender has not been addressed in a political way by film, nor does it indicate that films have not expressed, or conversely affected, the public's views about female leadership. Let's briefly review what scholars currently know about the portrayal of female leadership in popular cinema.

POLITICAL LEADERS ARE MASCULINE LEADERS

Popular cinema portrays leadership characteristics as uniquely masculine in nature. For instance, politicians are often portrayed as warriors or action heroes. In examining portrayals of presidential characters in film, Caroline Heldman writes: "The typical hyper-masculine portrayal of 'warrior' presidents frames presidential politics as a masculine pursuit. The most notable examples are Harrison Ford's character in *Air Force One,* who personally foils a terrorist attempt, and Bill Pullman's character in *Independence Day,* who uses his fighter pilot skills to save the world. Manly leadership is often taken to the extreme in movies portraying the president, giving a platform for the performance of hypermasculinity that has become a major staple in contemporary political rhetoric."[9] Heldman's critique is not unlike those of others who have observed the portrayal of politicians in film. For example, Phil Melling, commenting on cinematic portrayals of the presidency, writes, "Heroic leadership skills are integral to the presidency."[10] In some portrayals, it is not that Hollywood has masculinized the presidency but that Hollywood has *overmasculinized* the presidency. Single-handedly foiling terrorist plots from twenty thousand feet and pushing back alien invaders from a fighter jet set a standard that is unattainable by men as well as women. But, given that the fictional presidents that do accomplish these ridiculous feats are men, such movies suggest that such an ideal is better suited for men and never for a woman. It is therefore not surprising that this has led to both the portrayal in film and the normalized belief that women are "interlopers in the world of politics" and do not belong.[11]

WOMEN ARE RARELY CAST AS U.S. PRESIDENTS

Several studies surveying presidential cinema show that the number of films that include a woman portraying a president can be counted on one hand.[12] Many gender scholars have observed that presidential characters are rarely female, and if the president is, she has inherited the position by accident.[13] The critique is that popular films have not allowed the idea of a female president to enter the American psyche because they have rarely presented one on screen for the audience to imagine. As Heldman writes, this "naturalizes the notion that the presidency is for men only."[14]

We can deduce from the small number of films made featuring high-powered woman politicians that Hollywood does not view women as realistic, believable, or attractive political characters. Some might argue that the lack of women leaders in society has led to a lack of female leadership in popular culture; in this case popular culture only reflects reality. This is a difficult argument to support given that popular culture stretches well beyond reality in most of its offerings. For instance, people rarely fly to the stars, emerge from the dead as zombies, or become possessed by the devil; however, popular movies depict these events rather often. I would argue that the absence of women holding power seems to reflect not political realities but ingrained cultural stereotypes about who should hold power and who should not. Female movie characters fly to the moon, journey to the center of the earth, and communicate with aliens; however, they never win a presidential election.

WOMEN ENTER POLITICS IN SUPPORTING ROLES

The fact that few films feature female presidents does not mean that women never hold office or power in popular film. Women have served as vice president in films such as *The Contender* and *Air Force One* and as governor in films such as *Black Sheep*. However, these are less powerful and less stereotypically masculine offices. From the few films that feature women even in these less prominent political roles, we can again infer not only that Hollywood engenders typical gender roles and stereotypes but also that Hollywood views women as competent for supporting roles in political decision making. As Heldman comments, "Women in popular culture have rarely been shown in the vice presidential role, including Joan Allen as Senator Laine Hanson in *The Contender* (2000); Glenn Close as the vice president in *Air Force One;* and the second Brady Bunch Movie, in which President Mike Brady appoints his wife vice president. The American public is more comfortable with a woman in the vice presidential rather than presidential role, and popular culture reflects this in allowing a few female characters to serve as the second in command."[15] Thus scholars have observed over time that (1) the presidency is portrayed as a masculine position, (2) Hollywood rarely features a female presidential character, and (3) females are portrayed in politics mostly in subordinate positions. However, I would not dismiss the medium as a portal for understanding perceptions of the ability or suitability of females to serve as president simply because women rarely serve as president in popular movies. I claim the opposite: popular movies make strong statements about the ability of women to serve in the presidency even without portraying women in the presidency. Gender is a powerful trait that carries many stereotypes with it: one cannot enter into a conversation with a doctor, cashier, or pauper without noticing the person's gender.[16] The differences in the portrayal of the two genders signal the popular notions about gender. It is these notions that color the way citizens view the suitability of each gender for particular societal functions, including serving as the president. Thus, even without explicitly portraying female presidents, films can make many statements about the suitability of women for the job. This can in turn affect how citizens view women's political competence.

Hollywood's Messages on Gender and Leadership

This chapter examines four major themes regarding women that have run through popular films during the last few decades: (1) a fear of femininity, (2) a fear of feminine power, (3) the subordination of women in American society, and (4) a gendered view of leadership. I discuss each of these themes with an eye toward their statements about the suitability of females to hold office. As there are many portrayals of women in relation to power, the messages are often mixed and present both positive and negative frames of female leadership.

A FEAR OF FEMININITY

Gender is a master status; every interaction is affected by the gender of the participants in that interaction.[17] Therefore, when choosing political leaders, voters cannot separate a candidate's gender from the candidate; they are inextricably intertwined.[18] The view citizens have of each gender colors the perceptions each citizen has of candidates.[19] If a woman is to become president, not only must citizens view her as competent, but they must also view her gender as competent to serve as president as well.

Popular films have presented a mixed set of views regarding femininity. One such view stems from fear of the feminine: reproduction and motherhood. Let's begin with a look at Hollywood's portrayal of reproduction. The film *Knocked Up* presents a somewhat derogatory view of motherhood in its very title. The film portrays its leading female character as a woman who experiences motherhood because of drunkenness and promiscuity. Her pregnancy becomes a hindrance to achieving her personal and professional goals and limits her in her career. The father of her unborn child, meanwhile, is able to pursue his life unhindered, despite his lack of talent and ambition. Despite the reconciliation of the mother and father of the child at the end of the movie, the audience is left with the sense that maternity, one integral part of femininity, is a debilitating characteristic. Thus, the woman's struggles throughout the film stem from her gender and suggest that being a woman is at best a professional disadvantage.

The film *Juno* picks up on this point. In this film, a teenager becomes pregnant and puts the baby up for adoption to a thirtysomething married couple. Juno, the female teenager in the film, is advised to give the baby up for adoption so that she can pursue a college degree and a career unhindered. Juno is essentially asked to give up her gender, in this case her motherhood, in order to be successful, while the father of the child does not have to face any such choices. The adopting couple separates because the father does not want the burden of child rearing and would prefer to remain free to pursue his interests and his career. Thus the viewers see a depiction of an integral part of femininity, motherhood, as a disability.

Beyond pregnancy, the resultant child and the act of childbearing are occasionally shown by Hollywood not only to restrict rational thought and competent action but also to have an evil connotation. The Roman Polanski film *Rosemary's Baby* began a string of movies that portrayed childbirth as the mechanism for evil to enter the world. In this movie Rosemary Woodhouse becomes mother to the Antichrist and chooses to raise him. This theme suggests that mothers have a lapse of cognitive judgment when it comes to balancing the needs of society against the needs of their young. Certainly, if a woman cannot be trusted to thwart the evil spawned from within her, how could a woman be trusted to lead a nation? The theme of motherhood as an evil trait is echoed in the horror film *Friday the 13th:* Pamela Voorhees stalks and kills a group of camp counselors as revenge for the accidental drowning of her son, Jason. Jason, of course, goes on to brutally murder scores of innocent victims throughout a dozen more films.

The idea that children are evil was carried further, especially in the 1970s and 1980s, with films such as *Children of the Corn, The Omen, The Other,* and *Pet Sematary.* In these films children, as a result of child rearing by females, often turn on their parents and society in general with an unmatched destructive power. In *Children of the Corn* for instance, the children kill off the entire town. It goes without saying that child rearing and children are closely linked to women, for both biological and societal reasons. And press coverage of women presidential candidates inordinately focuses on their relationships with their children and their ability to raise those children while in office. Male candidates, on the other hand, receive little coverage in that way.[20]

In short, Hollywood has at times taken a rather skeptical view of motherhood. And given that women are by their very nature associated with childbirth and child rearing, it is difficult for the public to separate those gender traits from an individual candidate or leader; furthermore, news coverage of female candidates avoids letting the public separate those candidates from such gendered traits. Given the unusually dark nature of the portrayals mentioned here, it comes as little surprise that women face an uphill battle when running for high office.

A FEAR OF FEMININE POWER

Given Hollywood's portrayal of motherhood, it is not surprising to find that popular movies also present a narrative suggesting that female power is dangerous and should be feared. As previously discussed, Hollywood films portray femininity as unsuitable for high office. Hollywood appears to present this portrayal of femininity with power (either personal, professional, or political) to suggest that as women increase their power, there is more to fear.

All movies strive for tension, often between a good force and an opposing, sometimes villainous force. It is not surprising that movies have female villains.

It is surprising, however, that the likelihood of a female character becoming dark or villainous is closely tied to her relative power within a film. This power can come in the form of sexual liberation or protections against harassment in the workplace. Perhaps the most notorious film depicting this narrative is *Fatal Attraction*, starring Glenn Close as a jilted lover who becomes psychotic and murderous. Frequently commented on, this film shows a darker side to female sexual liberation and power that perhaps was a response to the feminist movement of the 1960s and 1970s. This theme is echoed in the films *Disclosure* and *Swimfan*, which show how feminine sexuality can be harmful and dangerous. *Disclosure* features Demi Moore as a female business executive who has used trickery, treachery, and her overbearing sexuality to make her way to the top. Moore forces her male subordinate, played by Michael Douglas, into a sexual encounter, forcing him to pursue sexual harassment charges against her. In *Swimfan*, male swimmer Ben Cronin is a successful swimmer in a happy relationship. However, Ben encounters Madison Bell, a female fan of his. Madison seduces Ben and then stalks him and attempts to ruin his life. In both *Swimfan* and *Disclosure*, the audience is told that female sexuality is a weapon that can destroy the lives of good people.

Hollywood has also displayed this theme with female characters who hold professional or political power. *The Devil Wears Prada* centers on Miranda Priestly, a female magazine editor. As viewers are brought into the professional world of Miranda, they find a person who is ruthless, bitter, and cruel. Hence, the devil in the title is a woman. Miranda's portrayal is in contrast to her male competitors in the film, who are portrayed more sympathetically. Although this film is based loosely on a true story, it was likely produced because it matches Hollywood's narratives. This portrayal of females who attain power is echoed in the film *Black Sheep*, in which a female governor uses election fraud and dirty tricks to stay in office, and also in the classic Disney film *101 Dalmatians*, in which Cruella De Vil attempts to use her wealth to slaughter puppies to make a fur coat.

Beyond the films where women are essentially out of political power, films show that women within the power structure can be the most dangerous. As Heldman points out, "One poignant example is the 2004 remake of *The Manchurian Candidate*, in which Meryl Streep plays an incestuous, maniacal mother who attempts to gain the White House by brainwashing her son and getting him elected to the presidency. The movie is sprinkled with thoughtful comments about women being barred from the Oval Office, but the lengths Streep's character goes to in attempting to gain presidential power overshadow them.

The message is that women have been barred from the presidency, but that is acceptable because they cannot handle the job."[21] This seems to have created a strange but well-recognized catch-22 for female leaders. If female characters stay out of power, then it sends the message that women are not meant for power. If female characters have power, these characters then send the message that women are not meant for power either.

THE SUBORDINATION OF WOMEN IN AMERICAN SOCIETY

Hollywood films do not always portray femininity and female power as overtly negative. Certainly there are many films with positive female characters. But many of these female characters are portrayed as appendages to male characters. A series of recent films touches on this theme. In the recent Batman movies *Batman Begins* and *The Dark Knight,* Rachel Dawes is an assistant district attorney whose mission is to fight crime. On one hand, she is competent, bright, and well intentioned. She is a character that women can aspire to emulate. On the other hand, she works for her superior, the district attorney, Harvey Dent, with whom she happens to be in a sexual relationship. In this sense, Rachael's power is comforting and welcomed in the movie partially because she is subordinate to and linked with a more powerful male leader.

This theme is echoed in *The Distinguished Gentleman,* a comedic version of *Mr. Smith Goes to Washington.* In this film, the most knowledgeable and sincere person in the film is a woman, Celia Kirby, who lobbies the con-artist politician played by Eddie Murphy for legislative reforms. However, Celia holds no true political power and has to rely on Murphy's sexual interest in her to affect policy. In other films, such as *The American President* and *Get Smart,* women occupy similar subordinate positions to men despite their superior or equal ability. For example, in *The American President,* Annette Bening's character is supposedly a powerful lobbyist, but she can only get her policies considered by the president by sleeping with him and then threatening to leave him.

A Knight's Tale also echoes this theme. Despite the aptitude of Jocelyn, a noblewoman, and Kate, an innovative female blacksmith, neither is able to exist without reliance on a male. Jocelyn's existence in the film revolves around the two knights who are pursuing a sexual relationship with her. Kate, despite being a blacksmith, is unable to travel and pursue her business on her own without men to accompany her and endorse her work. So rather than being able to pursue their ends on their own, female characters are often portrayed as dependent on men for their success. This theme is also echoed by the rare films that present females characters in power roles in American politics. For instance, the female protagonist vice presidential candidate in *The Contender* shows her ability to serve the hypermasculine president played by Jeff Bridges. In *Air Force One,* the female vice president played by Glenn Close is lauded for her refusal to take presidential power from the president even though he has been kidnapped by Russian terrorists and forced to make foreign policy decisions under threat of violence. Thus, while Hollywood depicts women as competent, they are not depicted in a way that would indicate they could handle an office such as the presidency on their own.

A GENDERED VIEW OF LEADERSHIP

As noted earlier, females are rarely portrayed in positions as powerful as that of the American presidency. For instance, films such as *Air Force One* and *Independence Day* depict courage, decisiveness, and strength on the part of male leaders; these leaders are shown for their actions and not for their physical sexuality. However, when females are portrayed in such positions, they are not portrayed with the same vigorous leadership traits, and they are portrayed with far more overt sexuality.

For example, George Lucas's *Star Wars* series features two female characters as political leaders who have many of the "action-hero" traits of typical male characters. Princess Leia, featured in the original *Star Wars* trilogy, is a rebel political leader with significant political power and military prowess. Offsetting these leadership traits, she is also portrayed as a damsel in distress, needing rescue by her male counterparts. In the original movie, *A New Hope,* Leia is captured by the Empire and locked in a prison cell. She is rescued from this predicament by males and resumes her leadership by finding a way to escape down a trash chute. However, despite her daring, Leia's sexuality is immediately referenced when one of the males, Han Solo, exclaims, "Either I'm gonna kill her or I'm beginning to like her." Leia's sexuality is again referenced in 1983's *Return of the Jedi.* While she attempts to rescue her male counterpart from imprisonment, she fails and is forced to wear a skimpy gold bikini.

Despite the advances of women in society between the 1980s and 2000s, the *Star Wars* series continued to portray female leadership in an overly sexualized manner. In the newer *Star Wars* films, Padme, played by Natalie Portman, is a strong-willed queen. Despite her political leadership and considerable clout, and despite her ability to fight off robot attackers with a gun, she is depicted as a sexual object. She is shown in outfits with her midriff bare, and her main contribution to the plot is her pregnancy. Beyond these portrayals, when Hollywood does not advertise the overt sexuality of women in leadership roles, it is clear that females are there as novelties of their gender. For example, as Barbara Morris argues:

> *The Contender* examines the foray of a woman into executive politics. After a parade of gender-based accusations, trials, and tribulations, a female senator is finally confirmed as vice president to replace an elected vice president who died. The climax of the movie comes when the president calls a special session of Congress and gives a forceful speech decrying the egregious confirmation process and those who opposed a nominee based on gender. He claims emphatically that a woman executive is "an idea whose time has come." Yet as the president descends from the podium, he hugs his chief of staff and whispers, "how is that for a swansong?" Thus, we are left with the bittersweet taste of celebrating the first woman national leader, while acknowledging that it was nothing more than a symbolic gesture to secure the legacy of a soon-to-depart president.[22]

Females have made much advancement in recent decades; however, the same stereotypes seem to prevail over time. Even when females assume a leadership or action-hero role similar to male leaders, their sexuality takes precedence. Thus the audience is shown that female leaders are feminine first and leaders second. Citizens generally do not like to see the president in such sexually compromising positions but find it far more acceptable for a male leader than for a female leader. Thus these films depict females as incompatible with the presidency.

Gender is an important part of one's being: it colors all aspects of a person. Thus the way voters view candidates is affected by how they view the gender of the candidates. If being female is viewed as incompatible with being president or having independent leadership traits, then voters will not support a female candidate regardless of that candidate's personal talent.

This chapter provides some indication of how females are treated in popular film portrayals. I have shown that films present some misgivings about femininity. These film portrayals of females appear to stem from stereotypes. Females are rarely in positions of true independent power, and when they are, they are often depicted in an overtly sexual way or as reliant on males. Given these pervasive messages, it is little wonder that a female has not won the presidency.

For the first time in decades, gender became a hot topic in 2008 during the Democratic nomination process because of the media's treatment of Hillary

Clinton. For instance, Katie Couric commented, "Like her or not, one of the great lessons of that campaign is the continued—and accepted—role of sexism in American life, particularly in the media." Entering the 2008 general election, gender again entered the public discourse because of the media's treatment of Republican vice presidential candidate Sarah Palin. The media paid great attention to Palin's dress, her home life, and her ability to care for her handicapped child. Neither of these experienced and qualified women was treated the way a man would have been. And unfortunately, this tradition has carried forward into the 2012 election cycle with highly gendered coverage of Republican contender Michelle Bachman. This is likely because ingrained stereotypes about the role of women are still pervasive and continue to be accepted in both our hard news and popular culture.

Notes

1. "Poll: Majority Ready for Woman President," *USA Today,* February 22, 2005.

2. Andrew Kohut, "Are Americans Ready to Elect a Female President? Past Statewide Elections Suggest Gender Is Not an Obstacle—at Least for Democratic Candidates," Pew Research Center Publications, 2007, http://pewresearch.org/pubs/474/female-president.

3. Joseph Uscinski and Lilly Goren, "What's in a Name? Coverage of Senator Hillary Clinton during the 2008 Democratic Primary," *Political Research Quarterly* 64, no. 4 (2011): 938–49; Susan J. Carroll, "Reflections on Gender and Hillary Clinton's Presidential Campaign: The Good, the Bad, and the Misogynic," *Politics and Gender* 5 (2011): 1–20; Diana Carlin and Kelly Winfrey, "Have You Come a Long Way, Baby? Hillary Clinton, Sarah Palin, and Sexism in 2008 Campaign Coverage," *Communication Studies* 60 (2009): 326–43; "Air America Host Randi Rhodes Suspended for Calling Hillary a 'Big F*cking Whore,' *Huffington Post,* April 3, 2008, http://www.huffingtonpost.com/2008/04/03/air-america-host-randi-rh_n_94863.html.

4. Dianne Bystrom, "Advertising, Web Sites, and Media Coverage: Gender and Communication along the Campaign Trail," in *Gender and Elections: Shaping the Future of American Politics,* 2nd ed., ed. Susan J. Carroll and Richard L. Fox (Cambridge: Cambridge University Press, 2010), 239–62.

5. Adam Berinsky, "The Two Faces of Public Opinion," *American Journal of Political Science* 43, no. 4 (1999): 1209–30; "Americans' Support for a Female President Is Significantly Exaggerated, Researchers Say," *Physorg,* January 22, 2007, http://www.physorg.com/news88699539.html.

6. "Poll: Majority Ready."

7. Alice H. Eagly, Mona G. Makhinjani, and Bruce G. Klonsky, "Gender and

the Evaluation of Leaders: A Meta-Analysis," *Psychological Bulletin* 111 (1992): 3–22; Alice H. Eagly and Steven J. Karau, "Role Congruity Theory of Prejudice toward Female Leaders," *Psychological Review* 109, no. 3 (2002): 573–98; Rae Lesser Blumberg, "A General Theory of Gender Stratification," *Sociological Theory* 2 (1984): 23–101; Mahzarin Banaji and Anthony G. Greenwald, "Implicit Stereotyping and Prejudice," in *The Psychology of Prejudice*, 7th ed., ed. Mark P. Zanna and James M. Olson (Hillsdale, NJ: Lawrence Erlbaum Associates, 1994), 55–76.

8. Laurie Naranch, "Smart, Funny, and Romantic? Femininity and Feminist Gestures in Chick Flicks," in *You've Come a Long Way Baby: Women, Politics, and Popular Culture*, ed. Lilly J. Goren (Lexington: University Press of Kentucky, 2009), 35–52.

9. Caroline Heldman, "Cultural Barriers to a Female President in the United States," in *Rethinking Madam President: Are We Ready for a Woman in the White House?*, ed. Lori Cox Han and Caroline Heldman (Boulder, CO: Lynne Rienner, 2007), 32.

10. Phil Melling, "The Adversarial Imagination," in *American Film and Politics from Reagan to Bush Jr.*, ed. Phillip John Davies and Paul Wells (Manchester: Manchester University Press, 2002), 189.

11. Heldman, "Cultural Barriers," 33.

12. Joseph Uscinski, "The Timing of Presidential Cinema," *Social Science Quarterly* 90, no. 3 (2009): 687–702; Peter C. Rollins and John E. O'Connor, eds., *Hollywood's White House: The American Presidency in Film and History* (Lexington: University Press of Kentucky, 2003).

13. Lori Cox Han and Caroline Heldman, eds., *Rethinking Madam President: Are We Ready for a Woman in the White House?* (Boulder, CO: Lynne Rienner, 2007).

14. Heldman "Cultural Barriers," 32.

15. Ibid.

16. Martha Foschi, "Status Characteristics, Standards, and Attributions," in *Sociological Theories in Progress: New Formulations*, ed. Joseph Berger, Morris Zelditch, and Bo Anderson (Newbury Park, CA: Sage, 1989), 58–72; Martha Foschi, Larissa Lai, and Kirsten Sigerson, "Gender and Double Standards in the Assessment of Job Applicants," *Social Psychology Quarterly* 57, no. 4 (1994): 326–39.

17. Kay Deaux and Marianne Lafrance, "Gender," in *The Handbook of Social Psychology*, ed. Susan T. Fiske, Daniel T. Gilbert, and Gardner Lindzey (New York: McGraw Hill, 1998), 788–827.

18. Donelson R. Forsyth, Michele M. Heiney, and Sandra S. Wright, "Biases in Appraisals of Women Leaders," *Group Dynamics: Theory, Research, and Practice* 1 (1997): 98–103; Susan Faludi, *Backlash: The Undeclared War against American Women* (New York: Anchor, 1992).

19. Laurie E. Eckstrand and William A. Eckert, "The Impact of Candidate's Sex on Voter Choice," *Western Political Quarterly* 34 (1981): 78–87.

20. Carroll, "Reflections on Gender."

21. Heldman, "Cultural Barriers," 33.

22. Barbara Morris, review of *Anticipating Madam President*, ed. Robert P. Watson and Ann Gordon, *Presidential Studies Quarterly* 33, no. 4 (2003): 943.

7

IT'S A MAN'S WORLD

Masculinity in Pop Culture Portrayals of the President

Justin S. Vaughn and Stacy Michaelson

Late in the evening of May 1, 2011, President Barack Obama called a press conference that would ultimately mark the end of a significant chapter in the history of the United States and, especially, the nation's engagement in the global war on terror. The subject of the event was the president's surprise announcement that, only several hours earlier, American special forces had, under Obama's authorization, stormed a compound near Abbottabad, Pakistan and, after a firefight, killed Osama bin Laden, founding leader of the terrorist organization Al Qaeda and the central figure responsible for the infamous September 11, 2001, attacks.[1] As the president departed the East Room at the conclusion of his statement, near midnight eastern daylight time, journalists and pundits across America and around the globe rushed to chronicle the historical development. In the days that followed, coverage of the mission and its outcome was complemented by countless process stories, with pieces reporting dimensions of the story that included the impromptu public celebrations outside the White House gates, quibbles over which political leaders had given or received the proper amounts of credit for the mission's success, implications for Al Qaeda as well as American national security policy, and a host of other issues.

As the media clamored for background on the decision making and planning behind the mission, the White House responded by releasing selected information. In the absence of a photograph of bin Laden's corpse, which the president argued would be inappropriate and offensive to much of the Muslim world, the world's eyes instead became riveted on another photograph. Referred to by CNN as both a "photo for the ages" and potentially the "defining image of Barack Obama's presidency," the image simply identified as P05011PS-0210 on the White House's flickr photostream almost immediately reoriented the visual politics of Obama's presidency.[2] The shot, captured by White House photographer Pete Souza, was accompanied by a caption that stated innocuously enough, "President Barack Obama and Vice President Joe Biden, along with members of the national security team, receive an update on the mission against Osama bin Laden in the Situation Room of the White House, May 1, 2011."[3] The understated nature of the caption, compared to the powerful visual rhetoric of the photograph itself, fails to communicate the full meaning of the image, which included not only the president but more than a dozen other high-ranking members of the Obama administration, including Vice President Joe Biden, Secretary of Defense Robert Gates, and several important military officials and civilian members of the president's national security team. The range of expressions on the faces of the individuals, particularly the president's, is a study in seriousness and tension, but other than the chief executive, the response most frequently commented upon was that of Secretary of State Hillary Clinton. Unlike the rest of the individuals in the picture—who, save the African American president and female director for counterterrorism Audrey Tomason, were all white males—Clinton's expression displayed visible emotion, something akin to anxiety or even fear, her right hand covering her mouth as she viewed something beyond the photo's edge.

This imbalance did not escape the attention of the press, as early reports of the photograph drew attention to Clinton's expression first as a testament to the severity of the situation and, later, in comparison to Obama's own steely glare. Within a few days, Clinton responded to the commentary, stating that she was unsure what she might have been watching at the precise moment that the photo was taken, but offering as a potential explanation: "I am somewhat sheepishly concerned that it was my preventing one of my early spring allergic coughs. So, it may have no great meaning whatsoever."[4] The response to Clinton's reaction was mixed, from disbelief to disappointment that the secretary of state felt the need to explain her expression. In an editorial for the *Rochester Democrat and Chronicle,* Jane Sutter lamented the attention paid to the matter, arguing, "It's just a photo. Move on." However, in Sutter's own editorial, she offered, perhaps unintentionally, two reasons this development was not insignificant. First, Sutter offers in the form of a rhetorical question the suggestion that the difference between Clinton's expression and those of the rest of the individuals in the room may be because "she's female and thus more emotional"; this is followed by an expression of wonderment over whether the White House would have released the image if it had not been Clinton but Secretary Gates, Vice President Biden, or President Obama with his hand over his mouth.[5] Both of these comments hinge on the notion that the photograph and the expectations that everyone involved—the decision makers in the room, the members of the press covering the issue, the audience consuming the image in newspapers and online—seems to share about the nature of the presidency are significantly gendered.[6]

In other words, it seems that this quickly iconic photograph serves not only as a window into one of the most secure rooms in the nation at one of the most important moments in recent history but also as a rhetorical tool that reinforces ongoing gendered notions of the American presidency. By enhancing the president's masculinity (and calling attention to the femininity of the most powerful female member of the government), image P05011PS-0210 becomes the latest in a long line of images that certify the patriarchal nature of the chief executive.

In this chapter we reflect on this nature and advance the argument that one need not only examine photographs and other ephemera of presidential history in seeking out other examples. Instead, we contend that popular cultural images of the presidency, including those that provide fictional depictions of the institution, provide an ongoing gendering of the office that continues to serve as an informal yet still unbreached barrier between women and presidential leadership. This chapter is predicated upon the notion that the way popular culture portrays political leadership matters in two important ways: it both reflects contemporary political reality and shapes public understanding and expectations about politics. In an exhaustive account of presidential portrayals in popular culture dating from the founding of the Republic to the current historical moment, Jeff Smith has made the case that "imaginings of presidents, like imaginings of the nation itself, are not just significant artifacts of America's cultural history, and not just reflections of the conflicting fears, hopes, and beliefs of its people(s)—though they are very importantly those things too. But beyond reflecting, they also *participate* in the ongoing 'fiction' that is America. They are grounds of its existence, one layer of the soil out of which the nation has grown. The stories that Americans tell and have told about presidents are part of what makes America the nation that it is."[7] Smith's analysis and argument reflect the realities of the burgeoning nexus between contemporary pop culture and the transmission of historical and political understandings of the American presidency. Trevor and Shawn J. Parry-Giles have noted the increasing availability of fictional portrayals of the presidency in a variety of cultural forms, commenting that this proliferation not only reflects cultural preoccupation with the institution but also provides an ongoing commentary on its nature. More important, they argue that these portrayals offer what they call

presidentiality, "a discourse that demarcates the cultural and ideological meaning of the presidency for the general public."[8] In other words, communicating
presidentiality means to communicate the appropriateness of an individual,
a situation, or institutional trappings and vestiges for entrance and occupation of the Oval Office. Whereas the president may be granted his powers and
privilege from Article 2 of the U.S. Constitution, legitimacy comes from a vast
array of sources—historical, political, and cultural—all of which combine and
conspire either to confirm or invalidate the fit between reality and the public's
imagination. We focus on the cultural component of this mixture because, as
Justin Vaughn and Lilly Goren have noted, "Fictional portrayals of American
presidents are increasingly important in shaping the way Americans know and
learn the institution of the presidency."[9] Furthermore, empirical analyses demonstrate that popular cultural representations of the presidency directly affect
individual-level perceptions of the institution.[10]

Moreover, contemporary portrayals of the presidency continue to reinforce
conventional gender dynamics with respect to power, politics, and presidentiality. Nichola Gutgold contends that seeing women cast in presidential roles
could serve to desensitize the press and American public to the novelty of the
idea in reality, and Eleanor Clift and Tom Brazaitis have suggested that recent
popular cultural portrayals have moved us closer to this dream of many becoming a reality for all Americans.[11] This observation is not a new one to scholars
of the presidency, nor is it an unstudied one. Indeed, a sizable literature has
emerged, based on the work of leading scholars in several disciplines, which
seeks to disentangle and explain the connections between popular culture,
gender politics, and the presidency. Of these, three contributions stand out and
merit discussion here.[12]

In 2006, Trevor and Shawn J. Parry-Giles published a book-length analysis
of the popular NBC political drama *The West Wing*. Their central purpose in this
book, *The Prime-Time Presidency: "The West Wing" and U.S. Nationalism*, was to
examine presidentiality as put forward in the program, a popular culture artifact
they took seriously as "meaningful discourse about presidential leadership and
identity" with the "capacity to offer a meaningful and powerful rhetoric concerning
the U.S. presidency."[13] As a program, *The West Wing* offered, in the words of Lane
Crothers, "an idealized, compressed vision of the workings of American democracy," one that—with respect to gender—portrayed women in powerful positions
(e.g., press secretary, national security advisor, surgeon general) who "fight as
effectively and as passionately for their causes as do their male counterparts."[14]

The West Wing also, according to Parry-Giles and Parry-Giles, reflected the ideological contestations of American nationalism, offering portrayals that were at once complex and multifaceted yet still ingrained with reinforced hegemonic considerations of the role gender (as well as race and militarism) plays in identifying not only what the presidency means but also what America as a powerful political idea means. As a result, while Parry-Giles and Parry-Giles lauded the inclusion of women cast as influential characters in *The West Wing*, they also realized the numerous ways traditional gender roles were reinforced, identifying sources of patriarchy in both the fictional president's family and the president's office. As they note:

> In the end, true romance imbued with passion, respect, and commitment is reserved for the president, the embodiment of the nation; love of the president, and thus the nation, must transcend other competing romances. Within this sexualized context the women of the West Wing are filled with power and influence yet delegitimized as political actors. Women's issues are also construed as falling outside the scope of the male political context, reifying men's control over the nation-state, marginalizing women on [*The West Wing*], and reinscribing the mythos of presidency as the key ideological site of U.S. nationalism. In the end, the president represents the father to whom all commit, evidencing the lasting, loving, and loyal relationship between citizens and their president and, by extension, the nation.[15]

Parry-Giles and Parry-Giles go on to detail numerous instances of female characters, especially Press Secretary C. J. Cregg and feminist activist Amy Gardner, being portrayed as inappropriately emotional; frequently incompetent; primarily concerned with secondary, gender-related issues; and subject to routine narrative and dialogue developments that serve either to sexualize them in a way most male characters are not or to reinforce more traditionally feminine characteristics such as maternal instinct. Ultimately, even the few powerful recurring female characters on the program find their strength undercut not by disdainful male scheming but by their own mistakes and inability to focus on serious policy matters rather than frivolous romantic notions.

A second important scholarly take on the subject of Hollywood's portrayal of women and the presidency concerns not the patriarchal Bartlet administration in *The West Wing* but rather an alternative posturing of a White House led by a female president. In an essay included in the volume *Rethinking Madam President: Are We Ready for a Woman in the White House*, Caroline Heldman investigates the cultural barriers that continue to stand between aspiring female politicians and the Oval Office by offering a deep analysis of ABC's *Commander in Chief,* a 2005 series in which the president, Mackenzie Allen, is portrayed by Geena Davis.[16] Although this was not the first time a woman had been cast in the role of America's chief executive, it is one of the most noteworthy and extensive instances (even though the program lasted only a single season before the network canceled its contract).[17]

Heldman's analysis of *Commander in Chief* ultimately concludes that "popular culture furthers stereotypes that act as barriers for women seeking the White House."[18] These stereotypes include portraying the president as equally active in the domestic realm as in the professional, a woman less focused on ambition and partisan confrontation than on success on the same secondary policy issues put forward by women in *The West Wing.* Perhaps still more damaging to the likelihood that *Commander in Chief*'s President Allen could be taken seriously was the overt sexualization of Davis's character, something owing as much to sexist coverage by entertainment journalists as to decisions by screenwriters and producers. According to Heldman, "President Allen's sexual image carried with it the damaging side effect of diminishing her status as a possessor of knowledge, making her character's position as the most powerful political leader in the country implausible. Additionally, as a sexualized, feminine being without military experience, President Allen was not a citizen-soldier. She lacked many of the informal credentials required for the presidency that are difficult, if not impossible, for women to acquire."[19]

Finally, an essay by Linda Horwitz and Holly Swyers engages both NBC's *The West Wing* and ABC's *Commander in Chief,* along with cable channel Syfy's science fiction allegory *Battlestar Galactica.* Included in a volume about popular culture and gender politics, Horwitz and Swyers's chapter argues that the way television has heretofore portrayed female leadership in the White House prohibits positive imagination of a female president.[20] To support their argument, their analysis positions *The West Wing* as a presentation of legitimacy against the illegitimate (and female) presidents of both *Commander in Chief* and *Battlestar Galactica.*

Throughout their essay, Horwitz and Swyers contrast the accepted patriarchal basis (and its concomitant bestowal of presidentiality) of *The West Wing*'s President Bartlet's authority with the accidental and tragic rise to power of *Commander in Chief*'s President Allen (who becomes president when the sitting president dies from a stroke, despite his deathbed request for her to resign, which Mackenzie interprets as a request directly related to her gender) and *Battlestar*

Galactica's President Laura Roslin (who became president when a massive attack led to the demise of the forty-two officials ahead of then–secretary of education Roslin in the official line of succession).[21] Moving on from the observation that contemporary portrayals of female presidential leadership seem to suggest that women must inherit the presidency rather than legitimately win it in a democratic election, Horwitz and Swyers further note the consistent message in both *Commander in Chief* and *Battlestar Galactica* that "a female president is viable only when she is backed by men," further cementing the cultural notion that men are the legitimate leaders. According to Horwitz and Swyers, "This is most evident because the women who occupy the office in *Commander in Chief* and *Battlestar Galactica* are presented *not* as bumbling incompetents but as legally qualified individuals with appropriate credentials and decision-making abilities. Despite these qualities, they are depicted as being unable to lead on their own; instead, they must either suffer the undermining efforts of those around them or rely on masculine support to prop up their presidencies."[22] Ultimately, Horwitz and Swyers contend that both types of fictional depictions—legitimate male presidents and illegitimate female presidents—come together to reinforce the masculinist basis of the presidency. Combined with the paucity of female presidential portrayals, also noted by Heldman, the current population of popular culture artifacts indicates to Horwitz and Swyers that the nation is not ready for female presidential leadership.

In this chapter, we build on the work done by Parry-Giles and Parry-Giles, Heldman, and Horwitz and Swyers, continuing their methodological approach of discerning patterns of gendering in fictional portrayals of the American presidency. Basing our decisions on insights garnered from their informative analyses, we have identified several characteristics of masculinity that merit further analysis. By incorporating a larger survey of presidential portrayals into our analysis, we can cover deeper and wider data terrain. Further, we are able to enlarge the scope of our study to account for many more popular culture artifacts than have been heretofore examined in a single analysis. In this way, our methodological approach is more similar to Lilly Goren's chapter in this volume in its utilization of numerous popular culture artifacts to discover cultural patterns rather than deep analysis in only a very small number of artifacts. However, it must be noted that where Goren moves chronologically in her analysis across artifacts featuring portrayals of two different kinds of nontraditional presidents (female presidents and African American presidents), we survey a broad range of artifacts to examine cultural patterns across multiple dimensions of masculinity. In the sections that follow, we identify our conceptual underpinnings, describe our categories, and analyze the ways in which masculinism has been performed in the popular cultural treatments of the American presidency.

The Masculinity of the American Presidency

We base our understanding and usage of the term *masculinity* on Georgia Duerst-Lahti's conceptualization of masculinism. According to Duerst-Lahti, the masculine impulses so evident in our political institutions and practices are the function of an ideology that assumes it appropriate that men should wield power. As Duerst-Lahti notes, "Like all political ideologies, masculinism makes judgments about human nature and its potential and problems, allocates power and resources according to those judgments, and devises a plan to implement that judgment. . . . In this case, masculinism determined that men had the potential to govern, regardless of other political beliefs, and so power was allocated to them and institutions were established accordingly."[23] Further, as Patricia Sykes has noted, the institution of the presidency is predominantly masculinist in that it "privileges conventional masculine attributes of strength, determination, and decisiveness."[24] Or, as Karrin Vasby Anderson puts it, the institution's masculinity constitutes a "hegemonic cultural force," one that has coded the institution with masculinist meaning.[25] Indeed, as Suzanne Daughton has noted, "First and foremost, the president is the national patriarch: the paradigmatic American man."[26]

Sykes notes that the masculinist dimensions of the presidency as an institution are ever in flux and that factors such as developments in historical time and political time can cause changing contexts for gendered presidential leadership, even as the dominant pattern remains significantly patriarchal. In other research, Duerst-Lahti demonstrates the ways masculinism defines not only the institution of the presidency but also the electoral processes through which candidates challenge one another for the office. She notes that masculinity has "always been in play in presidential campaigns," even if not always noticed by American voters, and shows the extent to which the entire 2004 election and the early portions of the 2008 election, like all previous presidential contests since the founding, "dripped with projections of masculinity."[27] Similarly, Meredith Conroy has identified political parties' role in advancing these masculinist expectations not only by reinforcing the primacy of male candidates but particularly by supporting more masculine women in more desirable races over more feminine women. According to Conroy, this pattern "suggests that feminine traits and behaviors, such as caring and collaboration, have little place

in national politics," ultimately serving to reinforce rather than refashion masculinist norms. The effect of such reinforcements is to make ever less likely the
public's imagination of a female president. In the sections that follow, we build
upon these observations by arguing that in addition to the political and historical dynamics identified by Sykes, cultural explanations also serve to revise and
reinforce gender-based expectations.[28]

How Hollywood Reinforces the Masculinity Theme

In this section, we assess Hollywood's reinforcement of masculinist impulses in
contemporary portrayals of the American presidency. To maximize the scope
of our engagement with the concept of masculinity, we identify and evaluate
the presence of four distinct dimensions of masculinity in these popular cultural portrayals. These categories include aggression and physicality, technical
expertise, unilateral versus collaborative approaches to leadership, and the role
of family and sexuality. Each dimension will be discussed in turn, in terms of
both its conceptual underpinnings and the way it has been expressed in popular culture.

AGGRESSION AND PHYSICALITY

The first category under analysis, *aggression and physicality,* incorporates both
psychological and physiological orientations consistent with what John Orman
has referred to as the "macho" presidential style.[29] According to Orman, this style
(and its corresponding myth of masculinity) is embodied in seven components,
requiring presidents who are competitive in political life; sports-minded and
athletic; decisive, never wavering or uncertain; unemotional, never revealing
true emotions or feelings; strong and aggressive, not weak or passive; powerful; and a "real man," never "feminine."[30] Orman, who acknowledges that "all
presidents do not fulfill all the demands of the macho myth," goes on to evaluate
the presidencies of Jimmy Carter and Ronald Reagan, locating the seeds of the
former's failure and the latter's success in the extent to which each man projected
an image consistent (or, in Carter's case, inconsistent) with the macho expectations of the national political culture. These expectations influence not only the
performances of actual presidential administrations but also how the idea of the
presidency itself is performed within the broader popular culture. Mary Stuckey
and Greg Smith have discussed the particularly aggressive (and protective) version of heroic presidents portrayed by Hollywood, noting that these presidents
"exercise power through physical force rather than strategic acumen or moral

suasion."[31] This is particularly the case in films that depict presidents directly involved in violent crises, such as war or other national security emergencies, for as Geoff Martin and Erin Steuter have noted, "War and militarism are the masculine activities of a patriarchal society."[32]

Perhaps the most noteworthy example of popular culture's reinforcement of this dimension of the norm of presidential masculinity can be found in the 1997 feature film *Air Force One*. This movie—directed by Wolfgang Peterson and starring Harrison Ford as President James Marshall—focuses on the heroic struggle of an American president to wage a solitary battle against terrorists who have hijacked the president's plane (i.e., *Air Force One*) in an effort to extort the release of terrorist leader and deposed ruler of Kazakhstan general Ivan Radek (played by Jürgen Prochnow). The film is perhaps most famous for a line delivered by Marshall—"Get off my plane!"—when he literally throws the terrorist ringleader (played by Gary Oldman) off the aircraft's rear parachute deck; however, repeated events and developments in the narrative reinforce the centrality of Marshall's machismo to his credibility as president. It should be noted that Marshall is a former Medal of Honor recipient, a fact that Crothers has argued marks his character as more courageous and noble than the typical citizen/filmgoer.[33] Throughout the film, Marshall lives up to this image, refusing to leave the plane on an escape pod; stalking the lower compartments of the plane killing multiple terrorists by hand; attempting to fly the plane; demanding his wife, child, and wounded agents be rescued before him; and then finally escaping via a zip line attached to an Air Force MC-130 cargo plane when the crash of *Air Force One* becomes imminent.

Clearly, the version of presidentiality suggested in *Air Force One* is characterized by strength, aggression, certitude, and power and thus serves to reinforce masculinized conceptions of the executive institution. Not all films present this kind of macho portrayal; however, those that take an opposite stand usually do so in a manner that actually delegitimizes the less macho presidential character.[34] For example, in the 1972 film *The Man*, numerous situations serve to undermine the manliness of the presidential character, Douglass Dilman.[35] Dilman, who is played by James Earl Jones and initially appears as the president pro tempore of the U.S. Senate, is an African American and becomes president not because of the will of the people but because the sitting president and Speaker of the House are killed in an accident abroad and the vice president is too infirm to take office. Throughout the film, the conflict between Dilman's race and traditional racial conceptions of presidentiality is a central point of the film's narrative, making it thematically consistent with most other films that portray the prospect of a black president.[36] However, beyond the obvious racial tensions, much of Dilman's struggle as president concerns whether he is considered by his allies and foes alike to be a man at all. Jeff Smith has discussed this subject, commenting on what Dilman sees as his problem: "To whites, he is 'a black man, meaning a half man,' as he tells his lawyer and confidant Nat Abrahams."[37] Further, Smith notes that, just as President Marshall in *Air Force One* consistently performs macho actions, President Dilman in *The Man* repeatedly shows physical distress. According to Smith, "Dilman's worries are registered bodily; he takes office feeling 'almost physically ill' and wakes up on his first morning as president with a headache. And his first outing on the presidential yacht makes him seasick, a condition he tells Abrahams is symbolic of his inborn inadequacy."[38] Indeed, in one scene, Dilman begins to cry when attempting to refer to himself as "Mr. President." Where Harrison Ford's President Marshall exudes macho qualities as he powerfully fulfills the expectations of the presidency, James Earl Jones communicates President Dilman's lack of preparation and gravitas for the office by emphasizing not his physical strength but his weakness, anxiety, and fear.

In this respect, *The Man* has more in common with another film, the 1964 feature *Kisses for My President*, which portrays Polly Bergen as the nation's first female leader, President Leslie McCloud. Though *The Man* is a dramatic portrayal of an accidental black president while *Kisses for My President* is a comedic take on a democratically elected female president, both show nontraditional chief executives facing physical limitations that prohibit their complete discharge of the office's powers and responsibilities. Rather than being seasick and emotional like Jones's President Dilman, Bergen's President McCloud ultimately loses her battle to prove she is not too feminine in the way she handles the realpolitik of foreign policy when she becomes pregnant and decides to resign, a development revealed by her fainting. The gender-based challenge to traditional notions of presidentiality is underscored during the film by the presence of a visiting South American head of state who oozes machismo, spending his time attempting to woo McCloud romantically, and pursuing stereotypically hypermasculine interests such as sports cars, speedboats, exotic dancers, and bar fights. At the same time, McCloud's own son exhibits macho tendencies at school, and her daughter is dating a cad with his own hypermasculinist inclinations.

Taken together, these three films demonstrate the broader pattern found in Hollywood treatments of presidential masculinity. The conclusion viewers are left with is that the legitimate and laudable president is one who is physically powerful and courageous; chief executives who are weak, timid, or—in these cases, at least—demographically nontraditional are neither appropriate for the highest office in the land nor likely to wield its powers adequately. Whether the linkage between how masculine a presidential character is and how wisely, as opposed to powerfully, he occupies the Oval Office exists, however, is the question we engage in the next section of this chapter.

EXPERTISE AND WISDOM

A second trait of portrayed presidential masculinity, expertise, concerns the common narrative trope that relates to the ability (or lack thereof) of leaders to display or affirm their own expertise about complex phenomena or in difficult situations. Psychologists have long recognized this trait as masculine, and gender scholars have written about the difficulties female leaders have when adopting similar attitudinal or rhetorical approaches.[39] Further, in Warren Rochelle's essay on literary portrayals of fictional presidents, he argues that a central component of the mythos of the American presidency is the consideration of the president as a wise man, or sage. According to Rochelle, this is because "as president, he is privy to knowledge necessary to run the country that lesser man cannot know."[40] Popular cultural portrayals of the presidency reinforce the masculinist notion that, like aggressiveness and physicality, legitimate presidents possess this trait and illegitimate presidents do not.

Examples of fictional presidential wisdom abound, from the military prowess of President Marshall in *Air Force One* to the intellectual heavyweights that have occupied Aaron Sorkin's vision of the Oval Office in both *The American President* and *The West Wing*.[41] While some of the brilliance portrayed in Hollywood approaches to the presidency may be over the top—a 2008 editorial in the *New York Times* asked if the notion of an economics Nobel laureate sitting in the Oval Office could ever rise above the level of fantasy—the idea of presidential competence courses through the culture.[42] Even more prevalent, however, is the converse: the portrayal of an unacceptable president as one who is foolish or incompetent. According to Lane Crothers, "Incompetent presidents are by definition incompetent because their efforts fail. They face crisis or challenge like heroic presidents do, but simply cannot make things happen that will save the day. They may be selfless in their motives, but motives cannot substitute for outcomes."[43]

The importance of competence as a masculinist characteristic of the presidency is underscored in a particular—and perhaps peculiar—way in the 2006 film *Idiocracy*. In this science fiction comedy, the central premise is that as a reproduction gap grows between the intelligent and unintelligent groups in society (with intelligent individuals having fewer children), several centuries of this pattern leave the world in a decayed and ludicrous state. In the film, two modern-day humans—one female prostitute and one exceedingly mediocre male soldier—are subjected to a top-secret hibernation project that goes awry. Waking up five hundred years in the future, Rita (played by Maya Rudolph) and Joe (played by Luke Wilson) are confronted by a society characterized by filth, vulgarity, corporate advertising, and stupidity. Eventually, Joe is arrested and subjected to an IQ test that shows he is the smartest man on the planet. He becomes a ranking member of the government, then led by President Camacho (played by Terry Crews), a charismatic leader better known for his previous stints in pornography and professional wrestling than for his intellect. Eventually, it is revealed that the planet's central challenge is the inability to grow crops, caused by the widespread use of a Gatorade-like product for watering. Joe solves the problem and is rewarded with first the vice presidency and later the presidency. Comedy aside, the central message of the film reinforces the notion that wisdom, a central masculinist trait, is a requisite for successful presidential leadership.[44]

In addition to the portrayal of President Camacho in *Idiocracy,* Jack Nicholson's portrayal of President James Dale in another science fiction comedy, *Mars Attacks!,* reinforces the need for expertise and wisdom in the Oval Office. In this movie, Earth is faced with imminent attack from Martian spacecraft. Seeking a diplomatic opening, Dale arranges to meet a Martian delegation in Nevada. Time after time, Dale continues to seek a diplomatic solution to the growing Martian problem, despite overwhelming evidence that the Martians are not visiting the planet for anything other than hostile reasons. Ultimately, Dale's inability to understand the threat posed by the Martians leads not only to his own death but to the destruction of the U.S. Congress, numerous world heritage sites, and countless human lives.

In a less absurd example, the ABC series *Commander in Chief* features a female vice president (Mackenzie Allen, played by Geena Davis) who left a successful career in academia for a spot as an independent on a presidential ticket before eventually becoming president when her predecessor suffers an aneurysm and dies. Despite Allen's demonstrable intellectual credentials and occasional moments of policy expertise, as the series evolves the narrative increasingly features Allen stepping back and looking to male experts for assistance. In an article on nontraditional presidential characters in *Newsweek,* series creator Rod Lurie (who was fired from the show after seven episodes) notes, "She was always turning to her husband or to a man for advice or approval, so the show was beginning to become not about why we should have a female president, but why we should not have one."[45]

DECISIVENESS AND AUTHORITY

One need not have a long political memory to recall the rhetoric during the 2004 campaign surrounding John Kerry's "flip-flopping" on the war in Iraq. For Anna Fahey, this was part of a broader strategy by the Republican Party to feminize Kerry. In part, this was accomplished by playing up Kerry's perceived "Frenchness," associating him with a country that at the time was considered weak and submissive in the popular mind. This view of France was shaped largely by that nation's disagreement with the (hypermasculine) unilateral approach of the Bush Doctrine.[46] The political calculations behind these attacks were far from arbitrary, but rather quite strategic, for just as one must appear wise as a masculinist prerequisite for the presidency, so too must one seem able and willing to act with authority when the moment demands.

In studies on gender stereotypes, men are found to be perceived as more "decisive," "experienced," and "assertive" than women.[47] A presumed proclivity of males for rational decision making is the basis for the now age-old skepticism about a female president having access to "the button." In fact, this historical social concern over a woman's decision-making ability is really twofold, encompassing not only the question "Will she make a rational decision?" but also "Will she make the right decision should the occasion actually call for the use of force?" It is this same gendered schema that fed the response to image P05011PS-0210 discussed in the introduction of this chapter. In this section, we show that films and television programs reinforce this masculinist dimension of the presidency, although there are some promising signs for female presidents.

The 1999 film *Deterrence* was perhaps a strange foreshadowing of things to come. Released in the United States just eighteen months before September 11, 2001, the film stars Kevin Pollak as vice president–cum–president Walter Emerson, who makes a unilateral decision to respond on a grand scale to an Iraqi invasion of Kuwait. Possessing inside information about the existence of nuclear weapons in Iraq's possession, Emerson makes a calculated risk and orders a nuclear bomb dropped on Baghdad after the leader of Iraq refuses to withdraw his troops from Kuwait. He does this all while stranded in a Colorado diner in the middle of a blizzard. Throughout the film, Emerson is decisive and authoritative to a nearly hypermasculine degree, to the point that those civilians present at the diner begin to question his sanity. He frequently dismisses the recommendations of National Security Advisor Gayle Redford (played by Sheryl Lee Ralph), most notably in the following exchange:

Pollak (as President Emerson): Our strategy is to roll the dice that he'll comply.

Ralph (as Gayle Redford): With all due respect to your Vegas metaphor, sir, nuclear warfare is not about gambling; it's about certainty— strategic certainty, moral certainty.

Pollak (as Emerson): Do I seem uncertain to you, Gayle?

Also notable is Emerson's refusal to negotiate with the Iraqis. He speaks to Iraqi leaders on multiple occasions in the film but always stands firm on his demand that they vacate Kuwait, even as his staff urges him to accept locked-in oil prices as a win. But Emerson will have none of it. After all, he is out to prove a point; after announcing the withdrawal of his reelection bid, Emerson responds to his staff's questions about his motivation by explaining, "There's a big difference between strategy and tactics. When China backs down, was it all for nothing?"

Compared with President Emerson, President Allen of *Commander in Chief* is both far more reluctant to use extreme force and more willing to consult and negotiate. Allen's lack of military experience is an obstacle, but she takes great care to consult with Joint Chiefs. Nonetheless, although she is willing to seek advice, she too has an idea of how things should be done. In the episode "No Nukes Is Good Nukes," Allen must decide how to deal with a nuclear submarine that has gotten stuck in North Korean waters. First, Allen must assert herself with the military, as she had not been briefed on the presence of any vessels near North Korea (the order was enacted by her predecessor). Then she must choose whether to leave the submarine where it is as a matter of national security— knowing the crew will die—or risk a rescue operation that may threaten the stability of the region. Against the advice of many in the Defense circle—as well as the Speaker of the House, who would have been president had Allen stepped down as requested by President Teddy Bridges on his deathbed—she chooses to negotiate with the North Koreans after they become aware of the submarine. In the end, the mission is successful, and Allen seems to have proven herself with the military. Although ultimately the outcome is successful, Allen's willingness to consult and negotiate strikes a far different chord than the approach taken in *Deterrence* by Emerson.

Allen is more successful in this situation than Vice President Kathryn Bennett, played by Glenn Close, in *Air Force One*. Although the film's audience knows the president is hidden away on board *Air Force One*, waging a secret insurgency against the Russian nationalist terrorists, the president's whereabouts are unknown to members of his administration for a considerable part of the film. Faced with a president who is clearly indisposed, possibly even dead, Vice President Bennett must decide how to handle the situation in his absence. Bennett is inclined to negotiate the release of the prisoner demanded by the terrorists, making the assumption that U.S. forces could recapture him again, but faces challenges from both the terrorist leader Ivan Korshunov (played by Gary Oldman) and Secretary of Defense Walter Dean (played by Dean Stockwell). Key examples include:

> Oldman (as Ivan Korshunov): I'm sure you can't wait for [the President] to get back to making the decisions, so you can stop sweating through that silk blouse of yours.

> Stockwell (as Secretary Dean): If you could try and relax Kathryn, I'm in charge here.

> Stockwell (as Dean): It's not her decision. . . . This is a military situation; I'm the Secretary of Defense. Check your regs. In the absence of the president, the buck stops here.

After talking with the Russian president, Bennett gives Dean the OK to begin looking at other options, but when contact is finally made with President Marshall, she once again seems reluctant to risk the lives of those on board the plane. The president insists that the prisoner cannot be released, though he later agrees to the release when his daughter is held at gunpoint. When the secretary of defense asks Bennett to align with the cabinet in declaring the president under duress and unable to perform the job, she refuses. While Vice President Bennett's decision is clearly not wrong in the context of the film—she is validated by the president's ability to defeat the terrorists—it cannot be said that she makes as strategic or political a decision as the men in the room; ultimately her choice is to follow the president's lead.

As in other categories discussed in this chapter, some of the best examples of men failing to exhibit sufficient decisiveness occur in comedies. One of the most iconic examples is the 1964 Stanley Kubrick cult classic *Dr. Strangelove or: How I Learned to Stop Worrying and Love the Bomb*. In the film, a crazed brigadier general, Jack Ripper, calls for a nuclear attack on the Soviet Union unbeknownst to President Merkin Muffley. Not only are the bombs launched without the president's approval, but he is unable to call off the attack, with communication to Ripper's base cut off. Muffley deals with a collection of Joint

Chiefs who cannot do anything, and he resorts to communicating with the Soviets against the advice of the chair of the Joint Chiefs. It is revealed that the Soviets have created a doomsday device that will be detonated should the bomb raid be completed. Muffley gives away national security secrets to the Soviets in an effort to stop the bombs from being deployed, but in the end there is a single plane that does not get the message to abort the mission, and the doomsday device goes off. This dark comedy, a commentary on the global politics of the time, in part finds its subversive humor in the president's impotence with regard to his own military and his inability to solve the problem even after seeking help from the Soviets.

Each of the aforementioned films and television shows plays out stereotypical beliefs about gender and decisiveness. Masculine President Emerson is willing to resolutely make the difficult decision to drop a nuclear bomb for the sake of the United States' legitimacy in the future, while the female leaders—President Allen and Vice President Bennett—err on the side of negotiation and to prevent the loss of even one life; male yet unmasculine President Muffley is utterly unable to control the situation.

Worthy of particular note, though, is the fact that President Allen's tendency toward negotiation ultimately earns her the respect of the military and serves to legitimize her position as commander in chief. If we look at the timing of the show—2005—it is the only post–September 11 example discussed here; it was also made shortly after the 2004 election, in which the debate over Bush's unilateral actions in the Middle East had played a central role. The literature on sex stereotypes of candidates indicates that women can have an advantage in election years when the political climate is ripe for change.[48] It is plausible that President Allen met more legitimate success in her choice to negotiate than did Vice President Bennett in part because a large portion of the electorate (and viewing public) had expressed a desire for more multilateral decision making by the Bush administration that was currently in office. It is also possible then to postulate that while it is likely that fictional portrayals of the presidency will continue to rely on gendered stereotypes about men's and women's decision-making ability, traditionally feminine characteristics may be able to make inroads and to be viewed with greater acceptance under certain political conditions.

FAMILY AND SEXUALITY

Despite how easy the Obamas may make it look, conventional wisdom would tell us that raising a family in the White House cannot be easy; how can one have an adequate private life while filling such a public role? Indeed, academic research tells us that women are likely to face more obstacles than men in trying to effectively balance such a dual existence. Jennifer Lawless and Richard Fox have found that among eligible candidates, women are twice as likely as men to be single, twice as likely to be separated or divorced, and nearly 20 percent less likely than men to have children.[49] Women are also more likely to assume the majority of household and child care responsibilities.[50] On top of the practical realities of having a family while holding office, there is also the matter of public perception, shaped by larger social issues. With domesticity dominating our public narrative of family life, women are seen as primarily responsible for the private spheres while men handle the public spheres, and this divide has in part come to shape our expectations of gender.[51] For example, in an extensive study by Kathleen Dolan, it is clear that candidates are evaluated in part based on inferences drawn from their gender.[52] Further, as is the case regarding portrayals of presidential physical aggressiveness, wisdom, and decisiveness, our analysis of the ways in which Hollywood portrays presidential family and private lives reinforces masculine norms at the expense of feminine possibilities.

The blurring of the line between the public and private spheres is a central theme in the 1995 film *The American President*. Written by *The West Wing* creator Aaron Sorkin, the film is similar to Sorkin's later television series in its focus on the day-to-day politics of the presidency and life in the nation's capital. The film, which features Michael Douglas as President Andrew Shepherd, does not revolve around the president's physical prowess or military acuity; rather, the presidential ideal is found in the morality of Shepherd's choices as he navigates the battles waged every day in Washington. Ultimately, however, the film is a love story, and the president faces challenges as a widowed father who falls for environmental lobbyist Sydney Wade, played by Annette Bening.

It becomes clear in the film that the president's personal life has been closely linked with his political success. In a rather heated moment, the president and his chief of staff (Martin Sheen's A. J. MacInerney) share the following exchange:

Douglas (as President Shepherd): If Mary hadn't died . . . would we have won three years ago?
Sheen (as A. J. MacInerney): Would we have won?
Douglas (as Shepherd): If we'd had to go through a character debate three years ago, would we have won?
Sheen (as MacInerney): I don't know. But I would have liked that campaign. If my friend Andy Shepherd had shown up, I would have liked that campaign.

It seems that Shepherd's role during the campaign not only as candidate but also as devoted father and husband taking care of a sick wife helped shape his public image as a good man. Although for many the idea of being both a single parent and leader of the free world would be unfathomable, the idea put forward in the script is that it seems to have endeared President Shepherd to voters. Though the film fails to portray the president engaged in the day-to-day care of his daughter, it is assumed that he has managed to raise a well-adjusted daughter who is mature enough to accept her father's beginning to date again.

It is this more intimate aspect of the president's personal life that begins to challenge his image as the wholesome family man. As Shepherd and Wade grow closer, the public sees the relationship as increasingly problematic, evidenced by the press response when she first spends the night at the White House. The concern seems less over the president's dating than whom he is dating and under what circumstances. Shepherd had been considered an upstanding single father who is now spending illicit evenings with a player in the political game; he is sleeping with the enemy out of wedlock. Although the president receives criticism and suffers public opinion fallout for his perceived poor decisions, it is Wade who takes the brunt of the personal attacks. Ultimately, the president plays the hero by defending Wade's honor at a climactic press conference, albeit one in which he publicly legitimizes, even as he disagrees with the sentiment, the idea of Wade as a whore.

Unlike the relationship between President Shepherd and his daughter in *The American President*, the family dynamic in the television series *Commander in Chief* is more challenging for President Mackenzie Allen. The show portrays President Allen striving to be both a good president and a good mother; she puts in long days and still tries to make it home for dinner at night. Although her commitment to being a good mother is laudable, it is clear that she struggles with the work/family balance more than President Shepherd; the focus on this balance is also of greater concern to the narrative in *Commander in Chief* than it is in *The American President*. Throughout *Commander in Chief*'s run, Allen is bothered by coming home after her younger daughter has gone to bed, and she struggles to deal with her elder daughter's very vocal displeasure over the upheaval of their family. In short, she does not find it as easy to blend her two worlds as does President Shepherd, and the film serves to highlight commonly held claims about why women might find it easier to run for office after their children (if they have any) are grown.

Although *Commander in Chief* received much criticism for the overt sexuality of President Allen, the character's sexuality is rarely portrayed as an obstacle to her political efficacy. In fact, the few brief instances of intimate alone time between the president and her husband are inevitably interrupted by sleep or other duties. This is not entirely unlike the struggle faced by President Leslie McCloud in *Kisses for My President.* If anything, it seems Allen's lack of time for sex (if not her sex appeal) is a further example of the difficulty she faces in trying to balance her personal and political lives.

On the opposite end of the sexuality spectrum from Mackenzie Allen, whose waning love life exemplifies a woman's struggle with balancing family and work life, is Laine Hanson in the 2000 film *The Contender.* Both women are portrayed as sexual beings, but where Allen is "failing" in her role as wife because her role as president makes her too tired for sex, Hanson is portrayed as sexually enthusiastic, both by showing her engaged in sexual activity and also through the false scandal that makes up the central plotline of the film. Played by Joan Allen, Senator Laine Hanson first appears on screen having sex with her husband when she is interrupted by a call from the president. She becomes the vice presidential nominee, and the bulk of the film concerns her tumultuous path through senate confirmation. When photos of a sexual orgy—allegedly involving a college-aged Hanson—are leaked to the press, she refuses to acknowledge (and therefore legitimize) the questions about her sex life that have become water-cooler conversation. Though the sexual acts in question took place decades in the past, the public—and the Washington-based political class, including the president who nominated her—still seem to feel they have bearing on Hanson's qualifications as a potential vice president. Indeed, one gets the sense that, for many in the film, her success hinges on denying that she is the woman in the photos. Though she tries mightily to argue otherwise, the question seems to hinge not on whether her college sexual activities have relevance but whether the claims about her sexual activity are true. Unlike the concern raised over President Shepherd's sex life in *The American President,* which focused mostly on the president's ability to do his job while sleeping with a lobbyist, Hanson receives treatment far more similar to Sydney Wade's; she is criticized for her sexuality itself.

For both Laine Hanson and Mackenzie Allen, much of their struggle is tied to a failure, in some respects, to adhere to socially normed gender roles. This is played out on the male side of the spectrum in both *Commander in Chief* and *Kisses for My President,* in which the husbands of the female presidents struggle with their role as "first spouse." Rod Calloway in *Commander in Chief* must deal with having less of a role in policy than he is used to (he takes a bit of a blow when his wife does not name him her chief of staff), and Thad McCloud in *Kisses for My President* goes from business executive to stay-at-home dad wandering the White House with little to do. Both examples employ the gag of husbands being asked to select the menu for an upcoming state dinner, reinforcing the notion that when a woman serves as one of Hollywood's presidents, there is potential for crisis, but when a man in the White House is asked to fill a traditionally female role, it is funny.

The cultural phenomenon of Madam Presidents on the big and small screens remains a curious one. Even as more fictional female chief executives find their ways into the nation's movie theaters and living rooms, the portrayals themselves seem to reinforce masculinist notions of power and political leadership. Indeed, as the analyses in this chapter demonstrate, Hollywood's portrayal of presidential leadership is masculinized across a range of characteristics in ways that show successful presidents in possession of masculinist virtues and unsuccessful, even dangerously flawed presidents as feminized, whether in gender or in attribute. In this way, Hollywood screenwriters frequently wield femininity like a weapon, reinforcing the cultural presumption of the inappropriateness of female presidents and using it to show weakness of feminine male presidents.

Thus as the likelihood that we may one day see the first female president inaugurated into the nation's highest office increases, this eventuality may be brought about as much by female politicians successfully embracing masculinist characteristics as by the American public becoming reconciled to new ways of imagining the presidency. It would seem that the two women who came closest to the presidency in 2008 agree with this expectation, considering Hillary Clinton's attempt to outmasculine Barack Obama during their Democratic primary battle with the "3:00 A.M." advertisement and Sarah Palin's range of messages that suggest an alternative portrayal of female power that is ferocious more than feminine. At the same time, perhaps Nichola Gutgold's observation that more women in the political pipeline equals greater cultural acceptance of nonmasculinist images of leadership will ultimately prove wisest of all.[53] Whether one of these women ultimately ascends to the presidency remains to be seen, but if one does, it will have been by engaging and either beating back or aligning themselves with the masculinist expectations of presidential leadership imparted by Hollywood.

Notes

1. Barack Obama, Remarks by the President on Osama Bin Laden, East Room, White House, May 2, 2011, http://www.whitehouse.gov/the-press-office/2011/05/02/remarks-president-osama-bin-laden.

2. The White House flickr photostream is available at http://www.flickr.com/photos/whitehouse/.

3. The image and corresponding caption are available at http://www.flickr.com/photos/whitehouse/5680724572/in/photostream.

4. Huma Khan, "Hillary Clinton Explains Famous Osama bin Laden Raid Photo," ABC News, May 5, 2011, http://blogs.abcnews.com/politicalpunch/2011/05/hillary-clinton-explains-infamous-osama-bin-laden-raid-photo.html.

5. Jane Sutter, "Too Much Drama over Clinton's Expression," *Rochester Democrat and Chronicle,* May 6, 2011.

6. In an interesting twist to this debate, an article in the *Huffington Post* on May 9, 2011, reported that Secretary of State Clinton, along with Director for Counterterrorism Tomason, were photoshopped out of a version of the photo published in the Brooklyn-based Hasidic Jewish newspaper *Der Tzitung,* reportedly because reproducing photographs of women violates the paper's modesty guidelines. See "Hillary Clinton Removed from Situation Room Photo by *Der Tzitung,* Hasidic Newspaper," *Huffington Post,* May 9, 2011, http://www.huffingtonpost.com/2011/05/09/hillary-clinton-der-tzitung-removed-situation-room_n_859254.html.

7. Jeff Smith, *The Presidents We Imagine: Two Centuries of White House Fictions on the Page, on the Stage, Onscreen, and Online* (Madison: University of Wisconsin Press, 2009), 9.

8. Trevor Parry-Giles and Shawn J. Parry-Giles, *The Prime-Time Presidency: "The West Wing" and U.S. Nationalism* (Urbana: University of Illinois Press, 2006), 1–2.

9. Justin S. Vaughn and Lilly J. Goren, "Presenting Presidents: How American Presidents Are Portrayed and Why It Matters," *White House Studies* 10 (2010): vii.

10. R. Lance Holbert et al., "*The West Wing* as Endorsement of the U.S. Presidency: Expanding the Bounds of Priming in Political Communication," *Journal of Communication* 53 (2003): 427–43.

11. Nichola D. Gutgold, *Paving the Way for Madam President* (Lanham, MD: Lexington Books, 2006), 13; Eleanor Clift and Tom Brazaitis, *Madam President: Women Blazing the Leadership Trail* (New York: Routledge, 2003), vii.

12. See also Mary E. Stuckey, "Rethinking the Rhetorical Presidency and Presidential Rhetoric," *Review of Communication* 10 (2010): 43–45.

13. Parry-Giles and Parry-Giles, *Prime-Time Presidency* 5, 14.

14. Lane Crothers, *Globalization and American Popular Culture* (Lanham, MD: Rowman and Littlefield, 2007), 83. See also Christina Lane, "The White House Culture of Gender and Race in *The West Wing*: Insights from the Margins," in *"The West Wing": The American Presidency as Television Drama,* ed. Peter C. Rollins and John E. O'Connor (Syracuse, NY: Syracuse University Press, 2003), 32–41.

15. Parry-Giles and Parry-Giles, *Prime-Time Presidency,* 58.

16. Caroline Heldman, "Cultural Barriers to a Female President in the United States," in *Rethinking Madam President: Are We Ready for a Woman in the White*

House?, ed. Lori Cox Han and Caroline Heldman (Boulder, CO: Lynne Rienner, 2007), 17–42.

17. Lilly Goren's chapter in this volume has an excellent rundown of popular culture artifacts that feature female presidents.

18. Heldman, "Cultural Barriers," 18.

19. Ibid., 37.

20. Linda Horwitz and Holly Swyers, "Why Are All the Presidents Men? Televisual Presidents and Patriarchy," in *You've Come a Long Way Baby: Women, Politics, and Popular Culture,* ed. Lilly J. Goren (Lexington: University Press of Kentucky, 2009), 115–34.

21. Although *Battlestar Galactica* is a science fiction series based on the fortunes of approximately fifty thousand survivors of a democratic empire called Kobol, many factors make clear the allegorical linkages between Kobol and the contemporary United States. Horwitz and Swyers discuss this in greater detail, but the basic contours of the linkage include a shared foundational myth about thirteen colonies, various American-style democratic institutions and practices, and a range of topical thematic linkages in the story line of various episodes that parallel American engagement in the global war on terror with the Kobol refugees' interaction with their Cylon attackers.

22. Horwitz and Swyers, "Why Are All the Presidents Men?" 125.

23. Georgia Duerst-Lahti, "Governing Institutions, Ideologies, and Gender: Toward the Possibility of Equal Political Representation," *Sex Roles* 47 (2002): 373. See also: Kenneth R. Hoover, *Ideology and Political Life,* 2nd ed. (Belmont, CA: Wadsworth, 1994); and Virginia Sapiro, "Gender Politics, Gendered Politics: The State of the Field," in *Political Science: Looking to the Future,* ed. William J. Crotty (Evanston, IL: Northwestern University Press, 1991), 165–88.

24. Patricia Lee Sykes, "Gender in the 2008 Presidential Election: Two Types of Time Collide," *PS: Political Science & Politics* 41 (2008): 761.

25. Karrin Vasby Anderson, "Bros before Hos: The Burden of Racism and Misogyny in the 2008 Presidential Campaign," paper presented at the Rhetoric, Politics, and the Obama Phenomenon Conference, Texas A&M University, March 4–7, 2010.

26. Suzanne Daughton, "Women's Issues, Women's Place: Gender-Related Problems in Presidential Campaigns," *Communication Quarterly* 42 (1994): 114.

27. Georgia Duerst-Lahti, "Masculinity on the Campaign Trail," in *Rethinking Madam President: Are We Ready for a Woman in the White House?,* ed. Lori Cox Han and Caroline Heldman (Boulder, CO: Lynne Rienner, 2007), 88, 87. See also Susan J. Carroll and Richard L. Fox, eds., *Gender and Elections: Shaping the Future of American Politics* (New York: Cambridge University Press, 2006); and Mark E. Kann, *A Republic of Men: The American Founders, Gendered Languages, and Patriarchal Politics* (New York: New York University Press, 1998).

28. Meredith Conroy, "Political Parties: Advancing a Masculine Ideal," in

Rethinking Madam President: Are We Ready for a Woman in the White House?, ed. Lori Cox Han and Caroline Heldman (Boulder, CO: Lynne Rienner), 142–43.

29. John Orman *Comparing Presidential Behavior: Carter, Reagan, and the Macho Presidential Style* (Westport, CT: Greenwood, 1987).

30. Ibid., 7–8.

31. Mary Stuckey and Greg M. Smith, "The Presidency and Popular Culture," in *The Presidency, the Public, and the Parties,* 3rd ed. (Washington, DC: CQ Press, 2008), 215.

32. Geoff Martin and Erin Steuter, *Pop Culture Goes to War: Enlisting and Resisting Militarism in the War on Terror* (Lanham, MD: Lexington Books, 2010), 20.

33. Lane Crothers, "'Get Off My Plane!': Presidents and the Movies," *White House Studies* 10 (2011): 229–42.

34. See also Bruce E. Altschuler, "From Hero to Anti-Hero: The Transformation of the American Presidency on Stage," *White House Studies* 10 (2011): 211–28.

35. This film was based on the 1964 novel of the same name by Irving Wallace.

36. Justin S. Vaughn, "Barack Obama's Black Presidential Predecessors: The Myth of Pop Culture Predestination," *White House Studies* 10 (2011): 243–58.

37. Smith, *Presidents We Imagine,* 185.

38. Ibid.

39. Kathleen Hall Jamieson, *Beyond the Double Bind* (New York: Oxford University Press, 1995).

40. Warren G. Rochelle, "The Literary Presidency," *Presidential Studies Quarterly* 29, no. 2 (1999): 410.

41. For a compelling discussion of how intellect is both a fundamental and energizing component of Sorkin's version of the presidency, see Melissa Crawley, *Mr. Sorkin Goes to Washington: Shaping the President on Television's "The West Wing"* (Jefferson, NC: McFarland, 2006), 181–87.

42. "Could an Economist Ever Be Elected President?" *New York Times,* September 25, 2008.

43. Crothers, "Get Off My Plane!" 235. See also Stuckey and Smith, "Presidency and Popular Culture," 217–19.

44. It also bears mention that Joe is a white male and President Camacho is a man of color, continuing the trend noted in the first section of this analysis that demographically nontraditional figures are more likely to be portrayed in illegitimate ways.

45. Joshua Alston, "Diversity Training," *Newsweek,* February 2, 2008, http://www.newsweek.com/2008/02/02/diversity-training.html.

46. Anna Cornelia Fahey, "French and Feminine: Hegemonic Masculinity and the Emasculation of John Kerry in the 2004 President Race," *Critical Studies in Media Communication* 24 (2007): 132–50.

47. Kathleen A. Dolan, *Voting for Women: How the Public Evaluates Women Candidates* (Boulder, CO: Westview, 2004).

48. Kim Fridkin Kahn, *The Political Consequences of Being a Woman: How Stereotypes Influence the Conduct and Consequences of Political Campaigns* (New York: Columbia University Press, 1996). See also Elizabeth Adell Cook, Sue Thomas, and Clyde Wilcox, *The Year of the Woman: Myths and Realities* (Boulder, CO: Westview, 1994).

49. Jennifer L. Lawless and Richard L. Fox, *It Takes a Candidate: Why Women Don't Run for Office* (New York: Cambridge University Press, 2005), 61.

50. Ibid.

51. Joan Williams, *Unbending Gender: Why Family and Work Conflict and What to Do about It* (New York: Oxford University Press, 2000), 1–3, 48–50.

52. Dolan, *Voting for Women*, 5–10, 82.

53. Gutgold, *Paving the Way*, 163–64.

Part III

"ALL THE NEWS THAT'S FIT TO PRINT"?

Alternative Avenues for Political Information

8

SITTING WITH OPRAH, DANCING WITH ELLEN

Presidents, Daytime Television, and Soft News

José D. Villalobos

On July 29, 2010, President Barack Obama took to the air on *The View* to talk politics, policy, and family. Pundits billed the visit as the first time a sitting U.S. president appeared on a daytime television program, calling it a crowning moment for *The View*.[1] The telecast drew about 6.7 million viewers, the highest rating ever for the show.[2] The episode also garnered "the largest number of women viewers in 17 months with 516,000 in the 18–34 age group and 1.3 million females tuning in aged 18–49."[3] At a time when the president was gearing up for the midterm elections while still trying to recover some of the spark and popularity he had heralded to clinch his 2008 election victory, Obama's interview with the famous hostesses placed the commander in chief under a new spotlight in previously uncharted territory.

As Obama took to the air, much speculation swirled over the appearance—whether it was appropriate, what the topics of conversation would be, and how it might affect the president's standing, particularly among women.[4] Critics varied widely in their views. Governor Ed Rendell (D-PA) publicly warned Obama that appearing on *The View* would be beneath the dignity of the office of the presidency and comparable to appearing on *The Jerry Springer Show*.[5] Rosie O'Donnell and Sarah Palin made similar complaints from the far left and right, respectively.[6] At the same time, other news sources and prominent bloggers touted the president's renewed efforts to reach women viewers and try new venues with headlines such as "I Am Glad We Have a Media Accessible President" and "Obama Goes to Where the Women Are."[7]

163

During the interview itself, Obama split his time between serious political conversation and answering more personal questions related to family and American pop culture. On the one hand, the president energetically addressed and answered questions about how his administration had been dealing with unemployment, the overall state of the economy, and the war in Afghanistan since his taking office.[8] Otherwise, Obama let the panelists quiz him about his daughters, the songs on his iPod, and his Blackberry phone, as well as some more gossip-oriented pop culture questions, including whether Obama was aware of actress Lindsay Lohan's legal problems and how familiar he was with the reality television star known as Snooki.[9] As the episode unfolded, viewers were thus simultaneously exposed to strong doses of policy substance as well as casual entertainment fluff for the curiously minded.

In the aftermath of the episode, critics reengaged in debate over whether the president's visit was appropriate and how, if at all, it may have changed people's perceptions about the president. Did Obama win over some of the soccer moms so critical for the midterm elections and his own political future? Did he strike the right balance in connecting on a personal level with the American public while taking on serious issues? Otherwise, did his appearance on a daytime show somehow damage the prestige of the presidency?

Certainly, Obama's daytime show appearance received a great deal of attention, with untold numbers of Internet downloads to accompany the historic television ratings. Looking at the polling outcomes around his visit, Obama's job approval rating appeared to increase only between one to two percentage points the week after the event, a far cry from what pundits would consider a significant bounce in popularity, particularly considering the numerous other factors known to influence such numbers.[10] However, whether and to what extent Obama succeeded in getting his message out and endearing himself to female voters remains an open question that merits further scholarly inquiry. To address these considerations, I begin by putting Obama's visit to *The View* in historical context with respect to previous presidential candidate appearances on daytime and other types of talk shows (e.g., prime-time and late-night programming). I then delve into the research that examines people's potential for integrating political knowledge as well as more recent work on whether presidential appearances on soft news programming may influence voter knowledge and political behavior. With particular reference to daytime television, I further consider whether and to what extent presidents may employ such venues for effectively reaching out to the female demographic and, more broadly, affecting the public discourse.

A Look Back: Political Candidates Taking to the Airwaves

Presidential candidates and presidents themselves have increasingly turned to various outlets of nighttime entertainment, "soft" news, and, more recently, daytime television as a platform for their political messages.[11] Such shows are touted for their potential to reach broader audiences and are said to help "humanize" political figures that otherwise appear separated from everyday life. To illustrate, I briefly touch on a few noteworthy examples across the decades, putting in context the growing tendency by presidential candidates and commanders in chief to take to the airwaves, often with a little sense of humor and a lot at stake.

On September 16, 1968, presidential candidate Richard Nixon appeared very briefly on NBC's *Rowan and Martin's Laugh-In,* uttering Judy Carne's famous line "Sock it to me!"[12] The appearance was made possible in part through Nixon's friendship with one of the show's writers, Paul Keyes, who coached the candidate through six takes and captured what was arguably Nixon's most humanizing moment during the 1968 presidential campaign. Ahead of the appearance, however, some of Nixon's advisors expressed serious concerns about how the American public would react to such a comedic exploit. In the end it was decided that, rather than relay the famous words with an exclamation, Nixon would instead deliver the line as an incredulous question—"Sock it to *me*?"—and thereby avoid getting doused by any liquid or dropped through a trap door as was typical for most guests. The appearance made headlines and was generally well received, seeming to strike a balance between comedy and appropriateness. It was a rare show of media savvy by a man who would develop great disdain for the industry.

Years later, in 1984, Jesse Jackson was much more daring when he hosted a full episode of *Saturday Night Live* (*SNL*) while also running as a Democratic presidential candidate.[13] During the episode, Jackson did a number of impressions, including one of then vice president George H. W. Bush. He also openly criticized NBC for not having enough minority workers on staff. Not long after the show's airing, NBC reported it had received "about 300 calls—three times the normal number of phone calls—many complaining that the show was in bad taste and not funny."[14] Despite the criticism, the national exposure significantly raised Jackson's visibility, aiding his battle for attention against Democratic front-runners Gary Hart and Walter Mondale. Garnering such attention was essential to Jackson's campaign efforts, particularly because he was seen as more of a beltway outsider and was at that point only the second African American (following Shirley Chisholm) to take on a nationwide campaign for president. Though some pundits had written him off early as a fringe candidate, Jackson surprised many when he went on to finish third in the primary battle. His impressive finish also helped set the foundation for a very competitive 1988 Democratic primary bid against Michael Dukakis.

Perhaps most memorably, Bill Clinton famously appeared on *The Arsenio Hall Show* in June 1992 to play "Heartbreak Hotel" on the saxophone before going on to win the 1992 presidential election.[15] Clinton's display of musical talent and charismatic character came at a very opportune time; he had just captured the Democratic nomination but was trailing in the polls behind President George H. W. Bush and Ross Perot in the general election campaign. Clinton's key advisors—including Paul Begala, James Carville, and Dee Dee Myers—all insisted on the appearance, debating instead over what outfit would suit the candidate best. After a short huddle, it was decided that Clinton would wear Begala's sunglasses and a jazzy tie, creating a more "hip" image of Clinton that would stick in the minds of voters. Pundits later claimed that the performance helped set the momentum for Clinton's famous June 1992 rebound in the polls that turned his campaign around and galvanized his reputation as the election's "Comeback Kid."[16]

Since such earlier appearances, presidential candidate visits to entertainment talk shows have been on the rise. Particularly since the 1990s and into the new century, appearances on prime-time and late-night television have become common, with many presidential candidates and some sitting presidents seeking out not only nighttime entertainment shows but also soft news venues that allow for both humanizing comedy and political campaign messages to transpire. Long-serving senator John McCain, for instance, has appeared on *The Daily Show with Jon Stewart* more than a dozen times and was the first sitting U.S. senator to host *SNL* in 2002.[17] Moving beyond prime-time and late-night shows, political figures and their advisors also began to expand and exploit the potential for positive exposure and visibility afforded by daytime talk shows, which have also evolved to include more air time for political discussion and debate.

From Prime Time to Daytime

Although daytime television has not always been a force of politics and campaigns, it has long delivered "some of the most progressive television in the nation."[18] Compared to their nighttime counterparts, daytime shows of all stripes were ahead of their time in beginning to employ female central characters and address issues central to women and other minorities. Early on, soap operas like *All My Children* and talk shows such as *Donahue* took on issues like sexism, machismo, and abortion; addressed the need for greater female equality and assertiveness; and provided a springboard for pushing the acceptance of diversity in sexual orientation, race, and ethnicity into the mainstream.[19]

Between the 1970s and the 1990s, public affairs slowly began to take hold in daytime television. Thereafter, from the mid-1990s onward, Oprah Winfrey received praise from many critics for abandoning a "tabloid television" platform in order to transition herself—and her audience—into a more sophisticated arena filled with progressive conversations about public affairs, as well as a hefty Rolodex of guests concerned with the betterment of society and healthy living.[20] Political candidates responded (and contributed) to the trend by increasingly seeking daytime television spots to take advantage of the new opportunities for political discourse.

By the time the 2000 election kicked off, all the major presidential candidates—Al Gore, George W. Bush, and Ralph Nader—wasted no time in paying numerous visits to various daytime television shows. Among their numerous visits, Bush and Gore both sought out a slot with the star of daytime television, Oprah Winfrey, while Nader taped an episode with Queen Latifah that focused on getting out the youth vote.[21] All three appearances received positive reviews and garnered notable television ratings. By then, appearances by presidential candidates on daytime television had become a mainstream practice.

DAYTIME HOSTS: HUGE RATINGS AND BIGGER MEGAPHONES

To many observers, it is not surprising to see the increased efforts by presidential figures to make soft news appearances, particularly since they often garner larger audiences than do more traditional venues.[22] What should not be overlooked, however, is the extent to which daytime talk show hosts have actively and increasingly sought out presidential candidates as well, particularly given the tendency of such guests to be ratings winners. As Jennifer Parker puts it, "Booking an interview with a leading presidential candidate can be as much of a score as booking a Hollywood star—and the presidential candidates are more than happy to oblige."[23]

Beyond the incentive for ratings, bringing presidential candidates onto their shows also gives daytime talk show hosts an opportunity to take part in and shape public debates themselves. To date, Oprah Winfrey is arguably the standard-bearer when it comes to daytime television hosts taking on and engaging in public discourse over policy and politics.[24] As Rebecca Traister puts it, "For decades daytime has been the home of culture-changing Oprah Winfrey, who made blackness, and black womanhood, not only visible in the lily-white mainstream media—not only acceptable, not only likable—but also deeply and powerfully relatable. Were it not for Oprah Winfrey, we might not have Barack Obama as our Democratic candidate for president, both because of her early endorsement of his candidacy and also because of her presence and power in American culture."[25]

Indeed, pundits and scholars have pointed to the major role that Oprah Winfrey played in determining the outcome in the lengthy Democratic primary battle between Barack Obama and Hillary Clinton.[26] By most accounts, Winfrey's endorsement of Obama appeared to improve the candidate's credibility among key voting blocs at the height of his primary election battle against then senator Clinton. Observers found interesting the implicit choice Winfrey made between her gender and her race and how it affected the choices made by her viewers, particularly African American female viewers split between choosing either the first female or first African American male to lead the Democratic ticket.[27] Winfrey also took some ratings hits from viewers who disagreed with her choice, as well as some hard questions about her loyalty to the women's movement.[28] Thereafter, Winfrey became a bit more careful and cautious in her approach to politics, often passing on the opportunity for major political interviews and focusing instead on addressing topics related to societal needs. Most recently, Winfrey started the Oprah Winfrey Network (OWN), along with a new show entitled *Oprah's Lifeclass,* which she uses as a platform for addressing a range of personal challenges facing many Americans.[29]

Oprah Winfrey has also inspired other female hosts to take on the major political candidates and issues of the day. For instance, despite being relatively new to the scene, Ellen DeGeneres has already had numerous political guests, including Barack Obama (who famously danced with her), Hillary Clinton, and John McCain. Aside from DeGeneres, many cite the star-studded panel from *The View* not only for their ability to interview the big names, but also for holding daily substantive debates over politics. Though the show has always had a "newsy bent" inscribed by founder Barbara Walters, the show's platform has more recently taken a stronger turn toward politics. In particular, many cite Rosie O'Donnell's short tenure on the show as a major catalyst. Early on, O'Donnell held her own with the rest of the panelists, creating a forum of intense debates that immersed millions of daytime viewers in the guts of political intrigue and controversy.[30] Later on, O'Donnell was ousted for being too controversial and replaced by the less divisive but equally political Whoopi Goldberg. Since then, Goldberg has helped move the show to relatively more civil though equally political territory, effectively rounding out the panel of hostesses that also includes Sherri Shepherd, Joy Behar, and the unabashedly conservative Elisabeth Hasselbeck.

DAYTIME TELEVISION AS A VENUE FOR WOMEN'S EMPOWERMENT

As more political candidates continue to stream into daytime television, elections are becoming increasingly relevant for traditionally feminine and often marginalized audiences. The trend is occurring at a time when women in politics are breaking new ground and redefining expectations about female leadership. In just the last couple of years, Hillary Clinton came within a hair of nabbing the Democratic primary race in 2008 (and likely the White House) before taking over Condoleezza Rice's post of secretary of state, while Sarah Palin was barnstorming the country as the right wing's fundraiser in chief and star maker for unknown up and coming Tea Party candidates. During her tenure as Speaker of the House, Nancy Pelosi adapted "gritty maneuvering" to herd catlike Democratic legislators to oppose all of George W. Bush's major initiatives and, more recently, to rally behind and vote for Barack Obama's biggest first-term gambles, including the economic stimulus package and health care reform.[31] Across from the capitol building, Elena Kagan recently joined Sonia Sotomayor and Ruth Bader Ginsburg on the Supreme Court, leaving an unprecedented number of women in charge of interpreting the law of the land. For a country that took nineteen amendments to its Constitution before finally allowing women to vote in 1920, things seem to have come a long way. Nevertheless, women's voices on television have only recently begun to emerge amid the long-male-dominated anchor and pundit positions on news shows, while descriptive representation continues to fall short for women across all branches of government.

In looking for ways to expand the voice and representation of women in politics, daytime television is increasingly becoming a venue with the potential to encourage greater political participation and issue activism among women, as well as greater government responsiveness to female constituents. Hilary Estey McLoughlin, president of Telepictures Productions, which syndicates both *The Ellen DeGeneres Show* and *The Tyra Banks Show,* is an expert on the influence that daytime television can have on politics.[32] In the midst of the 2008 primaries, McLoughlin commented on the potential that daytime talk has for candidates mindful of female voters: "Ellen has a very influential audience of soccer moms that the candidates know are important to reach. . . . Tyra's show [has] a younger audience, which is also key to the election."[33]

During Obama's visit to *The View* in July 2010, the president pointed out the potential that talk show hosts have in influencing public debate. He did so in answering one of Joy Behar's questions about why the president had not done more to address the partisan attacks levied against him. "That's your job," the president quipped.[34] Though the president was half jesting in his response, it stands to reason that the forum afforded to women like Joy Behar and Oprah Winfrey provides a powerful platform for women's empowerment, with both the increasing number of female hosts and the broader audience of women they speak on behalf of.[35] Indeed, Behar and others have tremendous creative control over the content of their programs, which they can take full advantage of by increasingly addressing women's issues, relating their importance to the viewing audience, encouraging greater discourse and political participation to benefit the women's movement, and seeking out female (as well as male) guests that are most likely to engage effectively in such conversation and debate.

WHAT PRESIDENTIAL FIGURES (AND WOMEN) STAND TO GAIN

As noted previously, during the 2004 reelection campaign against John Kerry, then sitting president George W. Bush and first lady Laura Bush made an appearance on *Dr. Phil*.[36] Unlike Obama's visit to *The View* six years later, then president Bush chose not to talk about any serious political issues, focusing instead on topics such as "spanking, teenaged drinking, and what kind of men the Bushes hope their daughters choose as husbands."[37] Asked about his image, Bush billed himself as a man who "loves life . . . can relate to people from all walks of life . . . loves to read history . . . loves to laugh a lot." About a week later, Bush's rival, John Kerry, and his wife, Teresa Heinz Kerry, made their own appearance on *Dr. Phil* and took on similar topics, including some difficult personal experiences such as Teresa's miscarriages and the adjustments John Kerry's daughters had to make when he divorced his first wife, Julia Thorne.[38] Both appearances were considered humanizing for the candidates and having the potential to influence viewer perceptions of the candidates and their families, though the effect on voter choices and the election was apparently minimal. Much like the polling numbers seen after Obama's visit to *The View*, no significant movement in the polls was cited for Bush or Kerry in 2004 (both candidates hovered around the 49 percent mark in polls taken immediately before and after each appearance).[39] This raises the question, do daytime television appearances really make a difference and, if so, how?

THE DOWNSIDE: LIMITATIONS OF SOFT NEWS

Some critics have been overtly skeptical that any good can come from "soft" news programming and political appearances on entertainment shows. David

Horowitz, founder of the former Center for the Study of Popular Culture, once lamented, "We're in the midst of a global war with Islamic fanatics. How is telling jokes with Jay Leno going to help that?"[40] In other words, in a highly complicated world, how can soft news and daytime television possibly provide the tools necessary to help citizens become more knowledgeable, active, and reasoned voters?

For decades, scholars have widely considered a theoretical puzzle, known as the democratic dilemma, which warns that a democracy may not function properly if its voters are unable to make reasoned choices.[41] Reasoned decision making requires that people have at least a minimal awareness of the consequences of their actions. However, the majority of the electorate's knowledge of political information remains very low, calling the viability of effective self-governance into question.[42] At first glance, one would expect that soft news and the "fluff" of daytime television would fall far short of providing the kind of useful information one would need to be politically knowledgeable or motivated enough to act on such knowledge through voting or other forms of political participation.

Philip Converse's classic work pioneered what scholars refer to as the fundamental paradigm of minimalism: the view that mass publics display "minimal levels of political attention and information; minimal mastery of abstract political concepts; minimal stability of political preferences; and minimal levels of attitude constraint."[43] However, this perspective began to change during the mid- to late 1970s as scholars questioned, on theoretical and methodological grounds, whether such a negative evaluation of the capacities of the mass electorate was indeed accurate.[44] The section that follows reviews some major alternative approaches to the assessment of voter capabilities, namely, studies on heuristics, core values and beliefs, and online information processing. I then relate such findings to more recent studies that deal directly with the potential influence that soft news and daytime television may have in shaping and moving public opinion and voting behavior.

THE UPSIDE: ONLINE PROCESSING, VISIBILITY, AND THE RATIONAL VOTER

V. O. Key asserts that "voters are not fools," since they behave rationally and responsibly given the clarity of alternatives presented to them and the character of the information they have available.[45] In this line of thought, the average citizen's responsibilities are portrayed as limited, as is the expected payoff for one's vigilance. Thus, though citizens may be capable of sophisticated political thought and action, it is not rational for them to expend the personal resources necessary to do this.[46] Rather, citizens engage in what Samuel Popkin calls "low-information rationality," which individuals achieve by taking cues from trusted political elites about which policies they should prefer and by harnessing a variety of heuristic strategies to deduce their political preferences.[47] In this way, individuals are able to avoid the need to infer preferences from factual bits of knowledge stored in long-term memory.[48]

Henry Brady and Paul Sniderman argue that citizens can draw an impressively accurate map of politics (of who wants what politically, of who takes the same side as whom, and of who lines up on the opposing sides of key issues) by relying on their political affect.[49] Political affect denotes the "likability heuristic" that is rooted in people's likes and dislikes of politically strategic groups. Party identification and retrospective evaluations of the economy have also been interpreted as efficient "information shortcuts" for "cognitive misers."[50] It is worth noting as well that aside from members of the public engaging in low information rationality, political actors such as legislators engage in similar behavior, particularly when it comes to decisions about legislation.

In more recent studies, scholars point to the online process model (i.e., the "impression-driven" model of candidate evaluation), which suggests that many people process information using a running tally at the time they are exposed to it, update their opinion accordingly, and then quickly forget the information itself, while retaining an updated affective summary judgment. Scholars of online process models thus argue that, rather than measuring a voter's actual level of political knowledge, those who use memory-based methods may in fact be testing voter recall ability.[51] This is because people may express informed preferences even though they may be unable to recall the factual information used to shape those preferences.

All things considered, the summary tally allows voters to construct opinions in a reasoned manner. The specific information used to create such a tally is irrelevant because it is not necessary to recall it correctly in order to make proper judgments. Thus real-time impression processes are what influence vote choice. This is why individuals know how much they like or dislike a candidate or an issue but are (1) unable to recount exactly why and (2) may instead provide stereotypes or other rationalizations that vary from the original information they utilized for evaluation.[52] Daytime television provides a good venue for this thought process, as hosts often touch on a variety of topics—serious and substantive as well as personal and character based—that viewers may find appealing and informative enough to shape lasting views about certain issues and political figures.

THIS JUST IN: RECENT FINDINGS ON THE "OPRAH EFFECT"

Despite some of the limitations mentioned above, scholars have begun to take notice of what has been termed the "Oprah Effect," referring to the manner in which appearances on soft news and talk shows can sometimes influence undecided voters and those less likely to have a direct interest in political information.[53] Looking at soft news coverage of foreign policy, Baum argues that such media platforms help attract and influence viewers who are typically less interested in politics and more independent.[54] Others, such as Markus Prior, have countered that the soft news audience is much smaller than those interested in hard news and that a preference for soft news decreases the likelihood of gains in political knowledge or participation.[55] However, audiences for soft news and daytime television have grown exponentially, and video clips from the telecasts often reach millions of additional viewers through the Internet. As pollster John Zogby has put it, "The clips of the politicians get played over and over again on cable television and on YouTube, making these shows more important to candidates."[56]

Conversely, Matthew Baum posits that by adopting recent findings from cognitive and social psychology studies (as noted in the foregoing sections), scholars can better understand the merits of soft news media, particularly in the manner that otherwise inattentive viewers can, at the very least, potentially increase their political knowledge and, under certain conditions, even engage in learning that influences political behavior, if only in the short term.[57] Baum argues that chat shows provide candidates "their best chance at reaching people they could actually persuade, while doing it in a relatively friendly context."[58] Indeed, having a friendly context is particularly useful because it allows candidates to put forth their message without the kind of probing more often seen in investigative journalism and among the White House press corps. Thus candidates and presidents can use such venues to more easily set the terms of a debate and have greater control over the way their message is framed.[59]

More recently, Baum and Angela Jamison have drawn on the "Oprah Effect" to argue that news quality depends not so much on the extent of substance in content as on how well it enables individuals to choose candidates based on their personal preferences.[60] For the large portion of the electorate that tends to be less attentive, scholars find that soft news programs such as *The Daily Show* and *The Colbert Report* may actually trump traditional hard news venues in helping viewers determine preferences.[61] As for daytime television, the "Oprah Effect" began with the megastar's shift away from tabloid coverage and onto more serious, substantive conversation and debate. Consequently, it should not be so surprising that President Obama chose to visit to *The View*, nor that he also addressed substantive policy matters in addition to the entertaining fodder that transpired between the hosts and their guest. The implication of these changing trends in daytime television is that such programming has much potential for cultivating greater political knowledge among the masses, engaging viewers who are otherwise inactive politically, and perhaps even mobilizing key demographics under the right context and conditions.

Although some may continue to debate the appropriateness of Obama's historic visit to *The View*, the findings from recent studies imply that the president had some foresight in perceiving the potential benefits of appearing on a show more likely to engage women and other key voting blocs than the more traditional hard news outlets. If presidential figures (and other politicians) increasingly seek out the public in such venues and continue to draw large audiences, it stands to reason that daytime television hosts will double their efforts to make such appearances count, both in motivating viewers to take interest in national debates and in amplifying their own megaphones in trying to influence the debate themselves. For female hosts such as the gang of five that headline *The View*, as well as their female viewers, daytime television holds much promise for providing a new venue for political discourse.

Notes

1. Julie Pace, "Obama Talks Race, Pop Culture on *The View*," Associated Press, July 29, 2010, http://news.yahoo.com/s/ap/20100729/ap_on_go_pr_wh/us_obama_the_view; Karen Travers and Brian Braiker, "Obama, on *The View* Discusses the 'Roses' and 'Thorns' of the Presidency," ABC News, July 28, 2010, http://abcnews.go.com/Politics/daytime-tv-appearance-obama-win-back-support-women/story?id=11262381; Patricia Zengerle, "Obama Seeks His 'Mojo' on Daytime TV's *The View*," Reuters, July 29, 2010, http://in.reuters.com/article/idINIndia-50504420100729. Technically, it was not the first time a sitting U.S. president appeared on daytime TV. On September 29, 2004, then president George W. Bush and first lady Laura Bush appeared on *Dr. Phil* (see David Skinner, "The Bushes Do Dr. Phil, and Wouldn't You Know It? They're Just Like You!" *Weekly Standard*, September 29, 2004). Unlike Obama, however, Bush made his appearance during a hard-fought campaign for reelection against Democratic candidate John Kerry, who also made an appearance on the show a week later with his wife, Teresa Heinz Kerry (see David Skinner, "John and Teresa Do Dr. Phil, and How Very Different They Are from the Bushes," *Weekly Standard*, October 7, 2004). Thus

it may be more appropriate to cite Obama as the first U.S. president to appear on daytime TV *outside of a presidential election cycle.*

2. James Hibberd, "Obama's *The View* Gets Presidential Ratings," *Hollywood Reporter,* July 30, 2010, http://livefeed.hollywoodreporter.com/2010/07/obamas-the-view-gets-presidential-ratings.html.

3. "Obama's Appearance on *The View* Sets Ratings Record," *New York Post,* July 30, 2010.

4. "Obama to Appear on Daytime Talk Show *The View,*" CNN, July 26, 2010, http://www.cnn.com/2010/POLITICS/07/26/obama.talk.show/index.html?hpt=Sbin; "Should President Obama Appear on *The View*? PD Writers Weigh In," *Politics Daily,* July 27, 2010, http://www.politicsdaily.com/2010/07/28/should-president-obama-appear-on-the-view-pd-writers-weigh-in/.

5. Matt Lewis, "Ed Rendell Compares *The View* to *Jerry Springer,*" *Politics Daily,* July 27, 2010, http://www.politicsdaily.com/2010/07/27/ed-rendell-compares-the-view-to-jerry-springer/.

6. "Sarah Palin Hits Obama for *View* Appearance," *Huffington Post,* July 29, 2010, http://www.huffingtonpost.com/2010/07/29/sarah-palin-obama-the-view_n_664467.html; Rosie O'Donnell, "Rosie O'Donnell: Obama Shouldn't Go on *The View,*" *Huffington Post,* July 28, 2010, http://www.huffingtonpost.com/2010/07/28/rosie-odonnell-obama-shou_n_662618.html.

7. Joan E. Dowlin, "I Am Glad We Have a Media Accessible President," *Huffington Post,* August 13, 2010, http://www.huffingtonpost.com/joan-e-dowlin/i-am-glad-we-have-a-media_b_672553.html; Araminta Wordsworth, "Obama Goes to Where the Women Are," *National Post,* July 30, 2010, http://fullcomment.nationalpost.com/2010/07/30/obama-goes-to-where-the-women-are/.

8. Jessica Derschowitz, "*The View*: Obama Talks about His iPod, Lindsay Lohan, and His Daughters," CBS News, July 29, 2010, http://www.cbsnews.com/8301-31749_162-20012103-10391698.html.

9. Ibid.; Robert Winnett, "Barack Obama Criticised over Daytime TV Appearance," *Telegraph,* July 29, 2010.

10. "President Obama Job Approval," *Real Clear Politics,* September 1, 2010, http://www.realclearpolitics.com/epolls/other/president_obama_job_approval-1044.html; George C. Edwards, *On Deaf Ears: The Limits of the Bully Pulpit* (New Haven, CT: Yale University Press, 2003).

11. Matthew A. Baum, *Soft News Goes to War: Public Opinion and American Foreign Policy in the New Media Age* (Princeton, NJ: Princeton University Press, 2003); Matthew A. Baum, "Soft News and Political Knowledge: Evidence of Absence or Absence of Evidence?" *Political Communication* 20, no. 2 (2003): 173–90; Matthew A. Baum and Angela S. Jamison, "The Oprah Effect: How Soft News Helps Inattentive Citizens Vote Consistently," *Journal of Politics* 68, no. 4 (2006): 946–59.

12. John Haydon, "The List: TV Shows with Presidential Appeal," *Washington Times*, August 11, 2010.

13. Ibid.

14. Ibid.

15. Ibid.; Matthew A. Saal, "Bill Clinton's Presidential Campaign," *Washington Monthly*, January 1, 1993.

16. Clinton also garnered positive attention by appearing on Don Imus's radio show, *Imus in the Morning*, just before his appearance on *The Arsenio Hall Show*. In addition to hitting the radio waves, Clinton's campaign worked out a deal with ABC's *Nightline*, which taped and later broadcasted the Imus radio appearance to add visual imagery of the candidate as relaxed and down-to-earth (see Saal, "Clinton's Presidential Campaign").

17. Jennifer Parker, "Talk Shows Pursue White House Contenders: Presidential Candidates Are Ratings Winners on Daytime and Late-Night Talk Programs," ABC News, August 30, 2007, http://abcnews.go.com/Politics/Decision2008/Story?id=3536348&page=4.

18. Rebecca Traister, "How the Election Ate Daytime Television," *Salon*, October 9, 2008, http://www.salon.com/mwt/feature/2008/10/09/daytime_politics/.

19. Ibid.

20. Janice Peck, *The Age of Oprah: Cultural Icon for the Neoliberal Era* (Boulder, CO: Paradigm, 2008).

21. Lauren Brown, "Nader Targets Youth with Talk Show Appearance," CNN, September 28, 2000, http://articles.cnn.com/2000-09-28/politics/nader.queenlatifah_1_youth-vote-ralph-nader-green-party?_s=PM:ALLPOLITICS.

22. Parker, "Talk Shows Pursue"; Traister, "How the Election."

23. Parker, "Talk Shows Pursue."

24. See Peck, *Age of Oprah*.

25. Traister, "How the Election."

26. Beverly Guy-Sheftall and Johnnetta Betsch Cole, eds., *Who Should Be First? Feminists Speak Out on the 2008 Presidential Campaign* (Albany: State University of New York Press, 2008).

27. Ibid.

28. Tony Allen-Mills, "Women Turn on 'Traitor' Oprah Winfrey for Backing Barack Obama," *Sunday Times* (London), January 20, 2008.

29. "*Oprah's Lifeclass*," Oprah Winfrey Network, http://www.oprah.com/topics/oprah-winfrey-network/oprahs-lifeclass.htm.

30. Traister, "How the Election."

31. Camille Paglia, "Pelosi's Victory for Women," *Salon*, November 10, 2009, http://www.salon.com/news/opinion/camille_paglia/.

32. Joe Flint, "How I Made It: Hilary Estey McLoughlin," *Los Angeles Times*, March 21, 2010.

33. Parker, "Talk Shows Pursue."

34. Dowlin, "I Am Glad."

35. Though the focus here is on women's empowerment on daytime television, the same may certainly be said with respect to other prime-time and late-night shows, with anchors such as Rachel Maddow leading the way in lending a voice not just to like-minded viewers but often to females (as well as LGBT and other minority voters) on the key political issues of the day.

36. Toward the end of his term, President George W. Bush also made a brief but notable appearance on NBC's prime-time show *Deal or No Deal* in April 2008 to commend show contestant Captain Joseph Kobes, a U.S. war veteran who had served in Iraq, stating: "I'm thrilled to be on *Deal or No Deal* with you tonight. . . . Come to think of it, I'm thrilled to be anywhere with high ratings these days" (see Haydon, "The List"). As a lame duck president suffering in the polls, Bush nevertheless made the appearance to try to at least remind some of his viewers of the down-to-earth persona he had first displayed as Texas governor and then during the height of his popularity as president.

37. Skinner, "Bushes Do Dr. Phil."

38. Skinner, "John and Teresa Do Dr. Phil."

39. "The Poll Tracker," CNN, November 2, 2004, http://www.cnn.com/ELECTION/2004/special/polls/index.html.

40. Parker, "Talk Shows Pursue."

41. Arthur Lupia and Matthew D. McCubbins, *The Democratic Dilemma: Can Citizens Learn What They Need to Know?* (New York: Cambridge University Press, 1998).

42. Donald R. Kinder and David O. Sears, "Public Opinion and Political Action," in *Handbook of Social Psychology*, ed. Gardner Lindzey and Elliot Aronson (New York: Random House, 1985), 659–741; Russell W. Neuman, *The Paradox of Mass Politics: Knowledge and Opinion in the American Electorate* (Cambridge, MA: Harvard University Press, 1986); Michael X. Delli Carpini and Scott Keeter, *What Americans Know about Politics and Why It Matters* (New Haven, CT: Yale University Press, 1996).

43. Philip E. Converse, "The Nature of Belief Systems in Mass Publics," in *Ideology and Discontent*, ed. David E. Apter (Ann Arbor: University of Michigan Press, 1964), 206–61, quoted in Paul M. Sniderman, "The New Look in Public Opinion Research," in *The State of the Discipline II*, ed. Ada Finifter (Washington, DC: American Political Science Association, 1993), 219.

44. Christopher H. Achen, "Mass Political Attitudes and the Survey Response," *American Political Science Review* 69, no. 4 (1975): 1218–31; Robert Erikson, "The SRC Panel Data and Mass Political Attitudes," *British Journal of Political Science* 9, no. 1 (1979): 89–114; Donald P. Green, *Self-Interest, Public Opinion and Mass Political Behavior,* 2 vols. (Berkeley: University of California Press, 1988); Jon A. Krosnick,

"The Stability of Political Preferences: Comparisons of Symbolic and Non-Symbolic Attitudes," *American Journal of Political Science* 35, no. 3 (1991): 547–76.

45. V. O. Key, *The Responsible Electorate: Rationality in Presidential Voting, 1936–1960* (Cambridge, MA: Belknap, 1966). See also Gerald M. Pomper, "From Confusion to Clarity: Issues and American Voters, 1956–1968," *American Political Science Review* 66, no. 2 (1972): 459–65; Benjamin Page, *Choices and Echoes in Presidential Elections* (Chicago: University of Chicago Press, 1978); Benjamin Page and Richard Brody, "Policy Voting and the Electoral Process: The Vietnam War Issue," *American Political Science Review* 66, no. 3 (1972): 979–95; Norman Nie, Sidney Verba, and John Petrocik, *The Changing American Voter* (Cambridge, MA: Harvard University Press, 1979); Lupia and McCubbins, *Democratic Dilemma*.

46. Delli Carpini and Keeter, *What Americans Know*, 45.

47. Samuel L. Popkin, *The Reasoning Voter: Communication and Persuasion in Presidential Campaigns* (Chicago: University of Chicago Press, 1991).

48. Richard A. Brody and Philip E. Tetlock, *Reasoning and Choice: Explorations in Political Psychology* (Cambridge, MA: Cambridge University Press, 1991); Jeffrey J. Mondak, "Cognitive Heuristics, Heuristic Processing, and Efficiency in Political Decision Making," in *Research in Micropolitics*, vol. 4, ed. Michael X. Delli Carpini, Leonie Huddy, and Robert Y. Shapiro (Greenwich, CT: JAI, 1994), 117–42; John R. Zaller, *The Nature and Origins of Mass Opinion* (New York: Cambridge University Press, 1992).

49. Henry E. Brady and Paul M. Sniderman, "Attitude Attribution: A Group Basis for Political Reasoning," *American Political Science Review* 79, no. 4 (1985): 1061–78.

50. David Robertson, "A Predictive Theory of Competitive Democracy," in *A Theory of Party Competition*, ed. David Robertson (London: Wiley, 1976), 23–54; Morris P. Fiorina, *Retrospective Voting in American National Elections* (New Haven, CT: Yale University Press, 1981).

51. Memory-based models suggest that people draw on information in their minds that is readily available to them, which helps them to form their political attitudes and opinions. There are three memory-based schools of thought—the sociological model (Columbia school), the social-psychological model (Michigan school), and the rational-choice model (Rochester school)—that explain how voting behavior works (see Milton Lodge, Patrick Stroh, and John Wahlke, "Black-Box Models of Evaluation," *Political Behavior* 12, no. 1 [1990]: 11; Milton Lodge, Kathleen McGraw, and Patrick Stroh, "An Impression-Driven Model of Candidate Evaluation," *American Political Science Review* 83, no. 2 [1989]: 399–419; Milton Lodge, Marco R. Steenbergen, and Shawn Brau, "The Responsive Voter: Campaign Information and the Dynamics of Candidate Evaluation," *American Political Science Review* 89, no. 2 [1995]: 309–26).

52. Milton Lodge and Charles Taber, "Three Steps toward a Theory of Moti-

vated Political Reasoning," in *Elements of Reason: Cognition, Choice, and the Bounds of Rationality,* ed. Arthur Lupia, Matthew D. McCubbins, and Samuel L. Popkin (New York: Cambridge University Press, 2000); Charles Taber and Milton Lodge, "Motivated Skepticism in Political Information Processing," *American Journal of Political Science* 50, no. 3 (2006): 755–69.

53. Baum and Jamison, "Oprah Effect."

54. Matthew A. Baum, "Sex, Lies, and War: How Soft News Brings Foreign Policy to the Inattentive Public," *American Political Science Review* 96, no. 1 (2002): 91–109; Baum, "Soft News and Political Knowledge"; Baum, *Soft News Goes to War.*

55. Markus Prior, "Any Good News in Soft News? The Impact of Soft News Preference on Political Knowledge," *Political Communication* 20, no. 2 (2003): 149–71.

56. Parker, "Talk Shows Pursue."

57. Baum, "Soft News and Political Knowledge"; Paul R. Brewer and Xiaoxia Cao, "Candidate Appearances on Soft News Shows and Public Knowledge about Primary Campaigns," *Journal of Broadcasting & Electronic Media* 50, no. 1 (2006): 18–35; Barry A. Hollander, "Late-Night Learning: Do Entertainment Programs Increase Political Campaign Knowledge for Young Viewers?" *Journal of Broadcasting & Electronic Media* 49, no. 4 (2005): 402–15.

58. Parker, "Talk Shows Pursue."

59. Nevertheless, such an advantage could quickly dissipate if talk show hosts become more aggressive. Already, observers have noted an increase in the amount of probing that takes place on daytime interviews. One prominent example is the manner in which Elisabeth Hasselbeck challenged President Barack Obama on *The View* when the president addressed the issue of unemployment and his administration's efforts to save jobs (see Danny Shea, "Elisabeth Hasselbeck: Obama 'Crafty' on *The View* but 'Wonderful Citizen,'" *Huffington Post,* July 30, 2010, http://www.huffingtonpost.com/2010/07/30/elisabeth-hasselbeck-obam_n_664883.html). Another example may be the way Ellen DeGeneres "subjected [John] McCain to one of his most uncomfortable interviews, using her upcoming nuptials as a platform on which to grill the candidate about the issue of gay marriage" (Traister, "How the Election").

60. Baum and Jamison, "Oprah Effect"; Young Mie Kim and John Vishak, "Just Laugh! You Don't Need to Remember: The Effects of Entertainment Media on Political Information Acquisition and Information Processing in Political Judgment," *Journal of Communication* 58, no. 2 (2008): 338–60.

61. R. Lance Holbert et al., "Primacy Effects of *The Daily Show* and National TV News Viewing: Younger Viewers, Political Gratification, and Internal Political Self-Efficacy," *Journal of Broadcasting & Electronic Media* 51, no. 1 (2007): 20–38; Michael A. Xenos and Amy B. Becker, "Moments of Zen: Effects of *The Daily Show* on Information Seeking and Political Learning," *Political Communication* 26, no. 3 (2009): 317–32.

9

THE CHECKOUT LINE PERSPECTIVE

Presidential Politics as Celebrity Popular Culture in *People*

Elizabeth Fish Hatfield

Just a few weeks after *People* magazine launched in 1974, readers were greeted by a cover image featuring Gerald Ford, vice president of the United States, in a most casual setting—his swimming pool. Celebrity news magazine *People* self-proclaims a focus on personalities, not issues, yet the headline of Ford's cover story read: "With Richard Nixon's Impeachment Looming, Can Gerald Ford Keep a Family Promise Not to Run Again?"[1] Although political drama made this story timely, it was the "family" aspect that worked for *People*. What readers learn about Gerry Ford, as the magazine calls him, is surprising; even though he was poised to be a frontrunner in the 1976 presidential race, he had promised his family that after twenty-eight years of serving in elected positions, he would retire. *People* does not discuss how the Republican Party would be affected or what would happen in the case of impeachment. Instead the publication's anecdotes of Vice President Ford serve to make him even more likable: pranks on his vice presidential plane, a commitment to his family, a long career free from scandal, and the fact that for Ford campaigning seemed to be a natural fit rather than a well-constructed effort.[2] When Ford did eventually run as the Republican presidential candidate in 1976, this article would certainly have been an asset to his campaign.

Celebrity gossip magazines such as *People* communicate with voters in a different way than many mainstream news outlets. Presenting Vice President Ford at home in his bathing suit is hardly "news" but rather an opportunity to show readers Ford's personality. Narrowcasting, the communication of targeted messages to small, specific populations, is a long-standing element of campaigns:

"Although presidents may publicly present themselves as representing the nation, the reality is that presidents win elections and then govern by assembling a coalition of disparate interests and groups."[3] Reporting a readership that is 70 percent female, *People* offers a communication outlet where messages can be narrowcast for voters.[4] As a long-term staple of the media environment, women's magazines (including entertainment weeklies) offer a unique and resilient print communication directly targeting a female audience and, so far, avoiding the impact of competition from the Internet.

Though entertainment weeklies emphasize an absence of policy substance in their publications, their soft news approach becomes significant when one considers that approximately one out of five individuals in the United States closely follows soft news, described by Joseph Turow as news that deals with the "less urgent aspects of life."[5] Twenty percent of the voting population comprises a substantial audience in a media environment that continues to expand and, more important, fragment. Such a large, consistent readership positions the messages contained within entertainment weeklies as legitimate mass communications about the political process regardless of their apolitical content claims.

Women's magazines have a long history of communicating with women about the political process, beginning with the issue of women's suffrage. Replacing public speaking, women's magazines became a way to spread messages of women's rights, fostered by technological advances in printing around 1880. A content analysis of magazines in the nineteenth century noted that all women's publications took a stance on suffrage, many promoting it.[6] As the first mass medium that spoke directly to a female audience, magazines catered to particular demographic groups and cultivated cultural knowledge of appropriate gender roles, framing everything from parenthood and housework to maintaining beauty as the primary responsibility of women. Natalie Fuehrer Taylor argues traditional women's magazines such as *Good Housekeeping* and *Redbook* continue to play an important role in discussing and promoting women's issues, even when readers refuse to identify politically as "feminists."[7] These publications manage to promote both a women's agenda, with what Taylor calls "suspiciously feminist" writing, and an adherence to traditional domesticity.[8] For politicians, women's magazines offer an important complement to the overall campaign communications strategy, one that often places their family, values, and private life in the spotlight.

With a focus on celebrity gossip rather than women's home lives, entertainment weeklies arguably offer one of the least explicitly political genres of women's magazines. Little research has focused on the content of messages contained in these publications as they relate to the modern political process. This chapter examines one publication, *People* magazine, as a mechanism of communication that bypasses bipartisan politics by focusing on the personal lives of political figures, creating in the process a subgenre of political messages framing candidates as people within the broader media atmosphere.

The Evolution of Entertainment Weeklies and the Political Celebrity

Entertainment weeklies fall into a category of news called soft news, a term often used without a clear definition; in the broadest sense of the term, soft news is any news that is not "hard" news and includes "a set of story characteristics, including the absence of a public policy component, sensationalized presentation, human-interest themes, and emphasis on dramatic subject matter, such as crime and disaster."[9] While the term encompasses a large variety of news outlets, this chapter focuses on one subcategory of soft news: the tabloid news outlet. Tabloid news may offer the most extreme down market example of soft news, with a focus solely on celebrity, scandal, and popular culture.[10] Historically, tabloids descended from the "yellow journalism" of the early twentieth century—newspapers that focused on the salacious and sensational news of the day, often adding dramatic appeal to stories of the unusual to increase sales.[11] The most notable tabloid remains the *National Enquirer,* which was founded in 1926 as a newspaper and received a major overhaul in 1957 when its distribution in supermarkets began. Supermarket tabloids became a popular entity, and a new genre of news was created. These magazines compete with each other for breaking stories and have pushed the boundaries of journalism through intense coverage of celebrities' day-to-day lives. The celebrities covered by these magazines include not only the Hollywood elite but also the Washington elite. Around the time the *National Enquirer* reached its peak in the 1970s, *People* magazine was created as a spin-off from the popular "People" section of *Time.*[12] Characterized by its focus on celebrities, human interest stories, and vivid images, *People* boasts a circulation of 3.7 million per week, making it the most widely read entertainment weekly and tenth-most popular magazine overall.[13] The admired magazine *Life,* credited with developing photojournalism, stopped publication just two years prior to *People*'s introduction, and though editors from both *Time* and *Life* argued the magazine was not meant to mimic either publication, in many ways, the new format merged the visuals of *Life* with the focus on "people" from *Time.*[14]

The earliest issues of *People* focused on the personal side of newsworthy people with an adherence to journalistic values (more so than its newspaper-style tabloid cousins), investigating stories the mainstream press might not cover while avoiding the extreme or unbelievable. *People's* first Washington bureau correspondent, Clare Crawford-Mason, asserts that the desire for increased profits changed *People* magazine over the decades.[15] *People* no longer has a Washington bureau and "all it's interested in is sensational stuff to do with Hollywood and entertainment."[16] The magazine now clearly falls into the tabloid category, covering news that would have initially been off limits for the magazine. For example, Crawford-Mason notes that "back with President Kennedy and Johnson, they never printed the fact that people were having romances or affairs."[17] But with Monica Lewinsky, coverage of politicians' sexual affairs became newsworthy material. Richard Davis and Diana Owen argue, "Tabloids are in a unique position to investigate and break these more sordid political stories, as they conform to the news values of the medium."[18] Even with entertainment news defining the tabloid medium, tabloid stories have infiltrated almost all media forms as an inexpensive way to fill space in a twenty-four-hour-a-day news environment.

The nature of politics—elevating individuals into the public sphere—positions elected officials as potentially newsworthy for these publications. Readers of tabloid publications such as entertainment weeklies often do not closely follow politics, making communications about politicians within these publications even more significant for their female readers.[19] Matthew Baum's research demonstrates tabloid audience members do learn about politics watching soft news programs such as *Entertainment Tonight*, a celebrity-focused news program.[20] He surveyed soft news audiences about a frequent media topic in the early 1990s, Operation Just Cause. His audiences had an emotional reaction to these soft news stories on the situation in Panama indicating that, while story retention remained low, the information gathered was used by viewers to determine how they felt about the issue, adding to their existing feeling of like or dislike. This is what Baum calls a positive or negative charge. The importance of this "charge" is highlighted by today's cluttered media environment as various outlets compete for the same audience members' time and attention.

POLITICS, SCANDAL, AND AUTHENTICITY

When the publication was launched, *People's* managing editor noted: "Our focus is on people, not issues."[21] Indeed, as a profit-driven news outlet, *People* does not desire to uncover hard news but instead to find sellable stories with mass appeal. For entertainment weeklies, that means coverage of politics entails a morality-coded story of family life rather than a debate over policy.[22] This coverage transforms the politician and his or her family from icons of democratic policy making into celebrity figures. This was exemplified by President Obama's recent presidential run, as commented on by *Entertainment Weekly* writer Benjamin Svetkey: "Nobody in Hollywood or elsewhere would disagree that Obama has already become the biggest celebrity in the world. Even before the election, he was drawing more TV viewers than *American Idol* and larger crowds than Bono (with speeches that were almost as political!)."[23] That Obama has become a pop culture icon was not accidental—his campaign managers specifically focused on the soft media to first sell the person and then the politics.[24]

Authenticity becomes a key element in "selling the person." Audiences view celebrities as both public and private individuals; a celebrity may be valued for consistency between their public and private lives or for the surprising difference between the two. Central to the idea of authenticity is the stability portrayed in an individual's display of his or her private and public lives. When a gap emerges between the public's expectation of a person and that person's actions, scandal occurs.[25] Stephen Hinerman and others argue that tabloids shape how a scandal unfolds by acting as an unofficial "guarantor of public morality": sorting out details, applying a cultural code of accepted behavior, and seeking the truth for the reader.[26] Scandalous behavior can be highlighted only against a communicated norm for accepted behavior. By finding out the "truth" of a scandal, tabloids construct stories that allow them to comment on an individual's morality and values.

For example, news of Bill Clinton's relationship with Monica Lewinsky was first reported by the *Dallas Morning News* but quickly retracted when source credibility was questioned.[27] Though the story's sources were not satisfactory for the *Dallas Morning News*, they were acceptable for tabloid media to continue with the story. With the proliferation of the Internet, the story spread quickly across both traditional and new media, which could not ignore it. Newspapers covered the story by citing other newspapers (rather than investigating the story themselves), instilling an approach called "copycat journalism," now a prominent method of reporting stories first covered by the tabloids.[28]

CELEBRITY CULTURE

As news outlets and celebrity journalism converge with more and more newspapers covering what previously characterized the entertainment weeklies and tabloids, the result blends public and private behavior for famous individuals in what Ellis Cashmore calls "celebrity culture."[29] John Street argues that politicians come into celebrity during the election process, which legitimizes their position as a public figure and thrusts them into the spotlight.[30] Politicians may "use the forms and associations of celebrity to enhance their image and communicate their message" through media communications that "privilege style and appearance over substance."[31] Cashmore uses examples such as Presidents Clinton and Reagan to demonstrate how celebrity culture and politics intersect as the media create a space where political stories serve as entertainment rather than informative news.[32] Women's magazines in particular are guilty of this—as Baum found, political issues are often left out entirely from stories on politicians appearing in soft news media.[33] This contrasts with research that found traditional women's magazines do indeed support a liberal political agenda with their content, including issues such as abortion, government spending programs, and health care.[34] A conundrum then exists within these publications: though women's magazines may take up political issues, these issues are detached from coverage of the politicians who actually impact policy. As Rosalind Ballaster and colleagues note, "The weeklies dwell on stories of personal tragedy, yet rarely relate them to underlying political processes and trends."[35] Most likely, this separation of politician and policy within women's magazines reflects today's profit-driven media culture and a desire to appeal to the broadest audience. This type of presentation opens up a critical media space for politicians, allowing a personable portrait of the individual that potentially bypasses an audience member's existing partisan bias.

THE PRESIDENTIAL FAMILY

For today's politicians, celebrity and politics fuse in the form of personal stories that put private life on display as part of a consistent image.[36] As a key part of this private life, Barbara Kellerman argues the presidents' families have become more important in an era of increased primaries, television, the women's movement, and the "glamour and power" of the president in the public's eye.[37] She writes of presidential families: "Since the most visible personal ties are to members of his family, they quickly become endowed with their own mystique."[38] Liesbet van Zoonen argues that "the dominant angle in family stories is the opposition between the obligations of a political career and the possibility of having a fulfilling family life."[39] Even in *People*'s earliest days, reporter Crawford-Mason used political family members in her articles to answer questions such as "Who are these people? How did they meet? Where does their money come from? Why did they decide to go into politics?"[40] One family member of particular importance was the first lady. Crawford-Mason covered the White House during the 1960s and argues that Jacqueline Kennedy Onassis "invented the role of the first lady, and it was because of Jackie Onassis that they even put women covering the White House. . . . That was the first time really, except for Eleanor [Roosevelt], a woman had been a news story at all."[41]

With the first lady in the spotlight, her expected role of "helpmeet" presented an obvious frame for news coverage of the first family. Meaning a helpful partner, the gendered term *helpmeet* descends from the biblical creation of Eve for Adam and refers to women as they support men. This term in many ways perfectly describes the ambiguous role of first lady—she is defined solely by her husband's elected position. Kellerman argues the helpmeet role can "at its best, be a crucial determinant of [the president's] overall performance," presenting the presidential couple as "trusted and respected business partners sharing the tasks which the business of politics demands."[42] Adherence to the helpmeet identity is seen by some as critical for public acceptance. For example, Karlyn Kohrs Campbell argues that during her time as governor's wife, Hillary Clinton's reform of the Arkansas school system was accepted by voters who felt the traditionally feminine domain of education did not constitute acting toward Hillary's own agenda; instead her actions were viewed as those of a typical "helpmeet" supporting her husband's policies in an appropriate way.[43] Later in her career, however, Hillary's work on health care reform as first lady was not received in the same way, stripping Hillary of the helpmeet identity and reducing her popularity with voters.[44]

Similarly, Ashli Quesinberry Stokes found the news media punished women's campaign behavior that did not adhere to traditional first lady "frames": Laura Bush's repetitive media clips supporting her husband's platform during the 2000 election fell within the accepted behaviors of a first lady, allowing her to avoid criticisms leveled against Teresa Heinz Kerry for being "too bold."[45] Erica Scharrer and Kimberly Bissell's research supports this finding, noting that the more political the first lady, the more negative the media coverage of her.[46] This public scrutiny forces the role of the first lady to become a highly managed public image strictly contained by the public's potential criticism.

This containment was cited by Lewis Gould, who found the press critical of Betty Ford and Rosalynn Carter, active first ladies who advised and contributed to their husbands' work.[47] He writes: "Beyond actually being president or having the institution of First Lady formalized into the function of the office, Mrs. Carter took the role of surrogate, partner, and advocate to the current limits of its capacity in our system of government."[48] These findings point to the critical role taken by the first lady, and to a lesser degree other presidential family members, in the political process. Interactions with the media communicate the working relationship between the president and first lady—a relationship that now appears to be much more carefully managed than in the 1970s and 1980s.

COVERING POLITICAL CELEBRITIES

Within women's magazines, politicians (and celebrities) typically fulfill two story types, which can be neatly categorized into positive and negative coverage. As Graeme Turner writes, "The tabloids deal with the celebrity industries through a see-sawing pattern of scandalous exposures and negotiated exclusives—at one point threatening the professional survival of the celebrities they expose, and at another point contracting to provide them with unparalleled personal visibility."[49] Daniel Boorstin argues our modern heroes are "mass produced, to satisfy the market" and "have been fabricated on purpose to satisfy our exaggerated expectations of human greatness."[50] Magazine articles on celebrity home life exemplify this manufactured element—allowing the celebrity to maintain control of his or her image in the popular press and pairing text with images that bring celebrities' private worlds to life. As long as scandal is avoided, articles on a politician's family life offer a chance to subtly position his- or herself as a family-focused American who shares the values and interests of female readers. The first type of coverage portrays politicians within their family context as a committed father or husband, often through direct participation in the story's generation. This is evidenced by direct quotes or interviews with the politician and his or her family and the inclusion of images that indicate a cooperative photo shoot. P. David Marshall argues: "Celebrity journalism is one of the key locations for the convergence of publicity, promotion and journalism in terms of the generated editorial content."[51] As a public relations tool, these stories frame politicians in a positive light free from scandal or criticism and discrete from their stance on political issues.

A second story type characterizing soft media outlets, particularly entertainment weeklies, is the scandal or unauthorized story. As noted earlier, this is not political scandal per se but personal scandal. Affairs and indiscretions are identified and teased out through heavy media coverage of the politician and his family. All angles of the story are debated, even theoretical, unproven details, and often the politician's coverage in magazines does not become positive again until a lengthy period of time has passed (for example, years after Clinton's many affairs, Bill and Hillary were pictured happily walking along a New England beach as she geared up for her own senate run) or the politician engages the media in a series of stories meant to show repentance and a period of familial repair. One way this is done is through the exclusive interview, an interview that provides a high level of news value for the magazine.[52]

A review of *People* magazine's coverage of candidates since its introduction in 1974 demonstrates this pattern. Most candidates during their presidential campaign have been vetted for damaging personal scandal, and therefore the campaign period most likely follows the first story type, with positive, endorsed coverage. During President Bill Clinton's first campaign, the Clinton family was shown posed together on the White House front lawn, and details such as Chelsea's braces portray the family as "normal." Yet when scandal emerges—through mainstream news media or entertainment media—this idealized family setting shifts to critical coverage of the actions in question. As do other media, the entertainment weeklies use story frames to efficiently cover scandal. Once a politician's "bad" side has been uncovered, it is challenging or impossible to return to the blissful family image. Future coverage will always be tinged by scandal.

MAKING THE PEOPLE POLITICAL?

Reflecting on thirty years of *People* covers, the magazine identifies the types of covers that sell: "Among the basic rules: Celebrities: Good. Royals: Good. Celebrities marrying celebrities: Very, very good. Politicians: Not so good."[53] Even so, around one hundred *People* covers in more than thirty-five years have featured politicians and their families. The remainder of this chapter explores *People*'s extensive online archive to consider the role of politics within the publication. Data for this project were collected from www.people.com, which contains full digital versions of every issue ever published. All political cover stories were included in the data set, for a total of approximately one hundred articles that spanned from 1974 to 2010. A qualitative thematic analysis was then used to organize and assess the articles. While the stories in *People* stick to the magazine's original goals—highlighting people and not issues—a subtle infusion of politics within stories provides apolitical readers with information about the country's elected politicians.

The Personal Is Political: Candidates' Politics and Family Profiles

During election years, profiles of the candidates, their wives, and their families intertwine the personal with the political. Indeed, though political party is clearly identified in these articles, more notable for readers are the narratives of a candidate's values, positions on issues, and life history. Getting to know the candidate personally, via *People,* may be what politicizes this communication—using family life to support issue positions in a new twist on the feminist slogan. Using one's personal life to demonstrate political views creates a cohesive life story consistent with and committed to party ideals, while subtly targeting controversial campaign issues. These articles involve direct interviews with the candidates, their families, or their close acquaintances—a show of cooperation between the publication and politicians.

The first election covered by *People* was the 1976 presidential election between Democrat Jimmy Carter and Republican Gerald Ford. The magazine introduced the Georgia peanut farmer to readers the week of the 1976 Democratic National Convention, where he was nominated as the Democratic candidate.[54] Readers of the article clearly take away several key characteristics of this presidential candidate: his strong, extended family ties to a small town in Georgia, his dedicated work ethic in an unglamorous industry, and his intelligence. Yet his politics provide the undercurrent of the article, as anecdotal stories and quotes from both black and white supporters frame Carter as a liberal who supported integration. Readers learn that his son was beaten up at school for his dad's "liberal" politics and that daughter Amy attends an integrated school (visually depicted by a chummy picture of Amy with two black classmates). Carter is depicted as progressive and committed to issues of equality, an outlook portrayed as uncharacteristic of southern politicians. Rather than discussing issues in a straightforward manner, the family offers a lived narrative illustrating Carter's views on segregation and presenting his work ethic as an unstated qualification for the role of president.

Similarly, Reagan's politics are outlined through conversations with those around him.[55] Reagan made bids for the Republican nomination in 1976 and 1980. In 1980, he became his party's candidate and later won the presidency. That year, *People* ran a cover story on his "authentic American family" featuring interviews with Reagan's four children from two marriages. Making inroads to normalize families of divorce, the article carefully uses a neutral tone to discuss the "unique" family.[56] Through the interviews with each of his children, the article demonstrates how each acts as a potential political liability: Patti's apolitical stance and distance during her father's 1976 campaign, Michael's support but feelings of inferiority on the campaign trail as an adopted child of divorce, young Ron's choice to pursue the gay-stereotyped ballet, and Maureen's public support for the Equal Rights Amendment (ERA), which her father opposed. Reagan's family life was peppered with drama and contradiction—something that Nancy Reagan counters in the story with her narrative of marriage for life and conventional family values. Reagan's politics bleed through the stories of his children—communicating that he does not support the ERA, that having a homosexual son would not be acceptable, and that he supports nuclear weapons. As a conservative Republican, Reagan's personal beliefs trump family loyalties—a communication of constancy and dependability to voters. Reagan is shown to be unwavering.

Presenting a very different family dynamic from the Reagans, Hillary and Bill Clinton spoke with *People* during the 1992 campaign.[57] The Clintons' family life contrasts with the Reagans' in size, challenges, and personality. Chelsea Clinton, President Clinton's only daughter, comes across as an all-around student, balancing school with extracurriculars, and most important, demonstrating her strong relationship with her parents. In light of accusations of infidelity that surfaced earlier that year, daughter Chelsea Clinton is a key part of an article that works to position the Clinton family as strong, steady, and unfazed by potential scandal. Politics is not directly discussed, but several clear issues that might keep voters from supporting Clinton are taken up, namely, his youth, Hillary's prominent role, and their family life. Clinton and his opponent, incumbent George H. W. Bush, are contrasted as young and old, traditional and modern. The Clintons clearly used *People* magazine to present their unified front, spending much of their conversation talking about their role as parents to only-child Chelsea. With a majority of *People*'s readers being parents, this offers the chance to showcase parenting values and an understanding of the challenges facing working women. As the first first lady to come to the office with her own significant career achievements, Hillary presented both a risk and an opportunity. The Clintons' life story within the article is not about Bill's successes but their combined work. Especially as compared to first ladies such as Nancy Reagan and Pat Nixon, Hillary defies the "helpmeet" role of traditional first ladies through her independence and professionalism. An appeal to female readers (and voters) comes through Hillary, as she comments: "A lot of the problems I face are the same ones all working women face. I may have, for example, more help, but I have somewhat more obligations, so I am engaged in the same kind of juggling act that most women I know are."[58] Hillary speaks to modern women—a voting population that was later credited with winning her husband the presidency. Though Hillary was ultimately a divisive political figure, within this article she presents herself as more closely adhering to normative gender roles in promotion of her husband's campaign.

Finally, *People*'s coverage of presidential candidate John McCain's family demonstrates changes in cultural acceptance in an article that candidly discusses his divorce, in contrast to the tentative language used to discuss that of President Reagan. A 2008 article on the Republican presidential candidate compares McCain's large, blended family to television's popular *Brady Bunch*.[59] As in the article on the Clintons, politics is not directly discussed. Yet McCain's military service provides the backbone to his life story: the potential cause of his first marriage dissolving, the expectations for his marriage to Cindy, his time as a prisoner of war, and the continued military service of several of his seven children. Loyalty to family and country underpin this introduction to John McCain as a typical conservative candidate.

These articles offer examples of how candidates become familiar to readers during the campaign process. *People*'s articles in the 1970s and 1980s were more likely to directly engage political issues through labeling and summary quotes of candidates within a family exposé, but recent articles engage the reader in different ways—while the articles communicate who the candidates are as people, particular issues are not highlighted. This may reflect the greater role of public relations in campaign management. Public relations have grown as an industry, and message production and control have become a central part of campaigning. Speaking to female voters, recent candidates may realize the value in an issue-free publicity piece, leaving readers with a positive "charge" based on who they are rather than the issues they support.

Helpmeet in the Pink Ghetto?

The first lady is not a paid position but one that comes with unofficial requirements for wives of the president who set up office in the East Wing of the White House, also known as the "pink ghetto." When a new president takes office, *People* profiles the first lady, discussing her approach to the role, her adjustment to the new lodgings, and her goals while in office. Every first lady since *People*'s 1974 first issue has been covered this way. A review of these articles demonstrates both personal ideologies of the first ladies and public images crafted to satisfy voters. In many ways, the coverage of active first ladies in *People* demonstrates the constant negotiations surrounding what it means to be the first lady, an undefined, gendered part of the presidency, and her critical role of appealing to female voters during presidential campaigns. For decades, not only the president's popularity but that of first ladies has been the subject of public opinion polling. Coverage of first ladies indicates a spectrum of personal styles, ranging from hostess to partner to advocate of independent agendas. Though Republican women have generally framed themselves as supporting mates to the president rather than equals impacting policy and decisions, the position of first lady seems to be largely defined by the standing first lady, and examples of both traditional and more egalitarian personifications can be found from both major political parties. How a first lady positions herself appears to be a crafted element of a public image that adheres to current politics and accepted gender roles. It was Republican Betty Ford, at *People*'s start, who first referred to the role of first lady as a "job" in an article that labeled her as a "tempered feminist." Indeed, Betty Ford and her successor, Rosalynn Carter, are portrayed as forerunners for Hillary Clinton's professional approach to being first lady. Ford's articles identify the changing position of women in the 1970s as feminism grew; she is described as a breadwinner (from her book and other activities) and a proactive first lady taking on issues of her own, yet she simultaneously communicates traditional family values as a "helpmeet" for her husband, President Gerald Ford.[60] *People* frequently uses the term "helpmeet" to describe first ladies who frame the role as supportive rather than equal. In an article describing Ford's role as "First Lady–Diplomat," *People* writes: "While the President met with foreign leaders to shore up the wobbly North Atlantic alliance, Mrs. Ford compared notes with their wives."[61] Though positioned by *People* in a feminine, less substantial role, Ford is quoted as saying: "There is no frivolity. The wives of these leaders are very strong and very bright. They take their jobs seriously."[62] Ford negotiates the perception and importance of these meetings, attempting to bridge traditional ideas that frame the first lady as political accessory with more modern views of an active partner. Though the language used by *People* ultimately frames Ford as helpmeet, she can be seen as a critical bridge between those who came before and after her.

Betty Ford's predecessor, Patricia Nixon, described as "fragile" in the wake of the Watergate scandal, and whose main duties included "greeting the poster child of the month, playing host to women's groups," offered a much more domestic image of the first lady.[63] Following Ford, Rosalynn Carter pushed beyond her to position the first lady as partner rather than helpmeet.[64] For female readers, Ford offered a critical transition—still cloaked as helpmeet yet with an undercurrent of political change and female capability. In Carter, we see the first woman to be portrayed as a partner and advisor to the president. *People* writes of Carter: "An equal partner in the Carter political combine, she is keenly aware of a first lady's potential for leadership. Although Rosalynn's public concerns—care for the mentally ill, problems of the aged—are well-known, her behind-the-scenes impact may be far more wide-ranging ('If I have to, I'll push him on women's rights,' she vows)."[65] This is a new situation for an American first lady, and though the article describes the couple positively, an air of uncertainty about Rosalynn

Carter's dominant personality filters through the text. The magazine points to her disputes with President Carter's mother and anger and disappointment at returning to farm life after several years on the move as a navy wife. Yet her expected role as first lady is unambiguous: "Rosalynn will be a power in the White House, not merely an ornament."[66]

Nancy Reagan purposefully displayed the helpmeet role, adhering to her husband's conservative political stance and her own personal values. Maurine Beasley argues that both Reagans brought their acting experience to the White House, using their knowledge of public presentation to expertly control how the media portrayed their relationship.[67] When interviewed by *People,* Nancy Reagan contrasted herself with her predecessor Carter, noting she would never influence policy through pillow talk and that the only time she steps in is when President Reagan's time gets overbooked, "like any political wife would do."[68] Of Reagan, *People* writes:

> "Nancy is an anachronism," says one California woman on the Reagan team. "She lives in the '50s, when it was a man's world and women were there to be perfect wives. She lacks compassion for the issues of the day because they have never been in her sphere of life." Her projects are expected to be noncontroversial and First Lady–like: notably Foster Grandparenting, a program that matches senior citizens with mentally retarded youngsters, and the rehabilitation of drug abusers. Yet it is clear from the relentless strength Nancy showed in the long months of campaigning that she is far from uninvolved in the grittier, more basic stuff of politics.[69]

People explores Reagan's traditionally feminine aspirations, such as her greatest ambition: "to have a successful, happy marriage."[70] With regard to politics, Reagan's views are clearly outlined as contrasting to Carter's, identifying her as opposing many lifestyle issues such as the ERA, abortion, premarital sex, and living together before marriage. As Reagan works to demonstrate her return to 1950s first lady norms, *People* reminds us that it is with decided opinions and potential impact on presidential decisions.

The recent first ladies—Barbara Bush, Hillary Clinton, Laura Bush, and Michelle Obama—have all negotiated and redefined the presentation of the role of first lady. As Ford, Carter, Barbara Bush, Clinton, and Laura Bush are portrayed by *People* as expanding the role and importance of the office of first lady, it is surprising to consider the case of Michelle Obama. Generally, the present analysis has found Democratic first ladies have taken a more liberal and active role in the White House. And yet Obama, a Harvard-educated lawyer, epitomizes the stay-at-home, opt-out mom. Voters like Obama more than any other recent first lady, with approval ratings of around 50 percent.[71] Just as *People* communicated social discomfort with Rosalynn Carter's approach to the White House, the magazine wrote of Clinton's aggressive redefinition of the roles and responsibilities of the first lady,[72] "Of course, some feel the First Lady has come too far too fast."[73] This might be just the type of commentary that Obama seeks to avoid when portraying herself as a young, engaged mother to her school-age daughters. Indeed, with Obama we see a return to the language of helpmeet (here seen in its alternate form helpmate) not used since Nancy Reagan was first lady: "She recognizes that 'helpmate' has taken on a whole new meaning as she watches her husband getting grayer by the month. As Agriculture Secretary Tom Vilsack recently told Mrs. Obama, she may have the hardest job in Washington because, when times get tough for the President, 'he has got to have someone he can lean on who understands and cares about him.' She says—and his aides agree—that it's never been her style to weigh in at his policymaking table. The last thing he consulted her on? Spring break, she says."[74] In many ways, Obama enters the White House with professional experiences similar to Hillary Clinton's. Obama's approach may then be a reaction to the "polarizing effect" Clinton had on voters.[75] However, Obama instead positions herself as a sort of "everywoman" by reflecting the struggles facing educated women within families and an awareness of her historic influence as the first African American first lady. The Obamas' cohesive and traditional home life, as crafted within *People* magazine, comforts readers about the unknown of a black president while reinforcing President Obama's qualification to lead this country.

What *People*'s coverage of first ladies adds to the political conversation is arguably an important communication on power within the White House. Certainly, *People* adheres to its journalistic mission—discussing the fashions, hairstyles, and domestic abilities of America's first ladies. These details weave through their biographies and approaches to the White House. But within articles on the first ladies comes a perspective on government and gender relations that critically bears on political affairs. Voters are shown a spectrum of approaches to the White House reflecting the current social environment. Ultimately, the role of first lady demonstrates a contentious space for presidential wives—a communication about what type of women they are, what type of marriage they share, and what impact they will have.

A Female President?

For readers of *People* magazine, presidential gender roles are not challenged—traditional views of a male president are reinforced within this publication. *People* has covered the few female political exemplars that have emerged as contenders for the presidential and vice presidential offices. However, their coverage of these women has framed them as just that—exemplars far from the norm. In 1984, Geraldine Ferraro was the first woman to run for one of the top executive offices and since has been followed by Hillary Clinton and Sarah Palin during the 2008 elections. Calling Ferraro a "trailblazer," *People* pointed to the nonnormative behavior surrounding a female candidate: "During the cheering he [running mate Walter Mondale] resisted throwing his arm around her shoulders or grabbing her fist in a victory salute the way he might have done with a man. It didn't seem right to do that with a woman vice-presidential nominee, but then who knows what you do with a woman vice-presidential nominee?"[76] Here, gender-coded rules of conduct dictate appropriate behavior, as readers learn that dealing with a female candidate is vague and awkward terrain. Because politics has traditionally been a male enterprise in the United States, certain feminine characteristics disrupt "typical" behaviors. Similar uncertainty was communicated through a story on Sarah Palin. On the subject of her pregnancy with special-needs son Trig while governor of Alaska, readers learn, "Initially Palin hid her pregnancy—and her pain—from both the public and her children. 'I didn't want Alaskans to fear I would not be able to fulfill my duties,' she says."[77] Pregnancy, a distinctly female function, is communicated as a threat to her reputation with voters. Palin's concern that voters might see her pregnancy as affecting her job capabilities reflects her conservative politics and relays a rhetoric of traditional gender roles. Readers are later told, "Within hours of Trig's birth Palin was signing bills and BlackBerrying colleagues," and she took only a few days of maternity leave—clarifying that motherhood did not slow her down.

Palin and Ferraro are both portrayed as women who simultaneously exemplify and defy gender norms throughout their lives by their professional decisions, hobbies, and family lives. *People* reports that Ferraro kept her maiden name even after getting married to honor her mother and that she became a teacher because, as she stated, "That's what women were supposed to do."[78] However, her professional restlessness soon led her to pursue law school in the 1970s as "an outlet for her ambition"—a typically male endeavor at that point. Though she practiced law after graduating, she also took at least seven years off to raise three children (working part-time)—a more traditional female path.

Fertility also serves as a visual and literal demonstration of Palin's feminin-ity with her large family and young children, along with an interest in fashion and beauty pageant participation during her college years. Readers are told: "To this day she is a fashion addict, favoring flashy high heels and Kazuo Kawa-saki designer glasses perched below her trademark updo. But Palin's heart also leaned toward elk hunting and salmon fishing. Her independent streak was nurtured by her dad, Chuck, 70, a retired science teacher, and her mom, Sally, 67, a secretary, who, she says, 'taught me to be self-sufficient.'"[79] Palin's love of hunting and fishing, traditionally male pastimes, offers a contrasting gender portrait identifying her more masculine hobbies. An additional display of her masculinity comes as husband Todd Palin assumes "Mr. Mom" duties by tem-porarily leaving his job to stay home with the kids. Indeed, Palin's family life offers a reinterpretation of family gender roles that manages to adhere to her conservative political stance.

Though these articles reflect openness to female candidates, the publication generally uses a language of traditional presidential gender roles. For example, in an article outlining the women of the Kennedy family, *People* notes: "[Eunice Kennedy] was so competent [dad Joseph Kennedy] paid her the supreme com-pliment: 'If that girl had been born with balls, she would have been a hell of a politician.'"[80] Stephen Birmingham's 1978 article on Jackie Onassis described her as the ideal woman: "She is indeed the prototype of the successful American woman: intelligent, beguiling, adept at stroking the male ego."[81] For President and Mrs. Nixon, a gender order is conveyed: "Always, publicly, her life has taken second place to her husband's, and she has never been known to complain."[82] While *People* depends on language of traditional gender roles as a general prin-ciple, its coverage of female candidates expands our understanding of the word "politician." The magazine demonstrates a willingness to explore how female candidates can bring the same skills to the table as male candidates, particularly by weaving together traditional femininity with an appropriated masculinity. Women and male candidates are featured in *People* similarly through chronicles of their journey and challenges faced along the way. Highlighting masculine qualities in particular brings female candidates into a realm most commonly dominated by men.

Exploiting Scandal

The scandals experienced by politicians appear to fall into three categories: badly behaving children, love affairs, and tell-all books. Scandal sells, and when personal scandal befalls public figures, a cover story is born—ready to entice readers into details of lust, greed, and sin. Often it is scandal that truly pushes a politician into the celebrity realm. The many cover stories that *People* has done on political scandal have primarily revolved around threats to family life; only twice are cover stories about true political scandals, when *People* covered Watergate and the assassination attempt on President Reagan. Yet these stories still circle back to the impact on the family. One unwavering fact of *People*'s scandal stories: they all involve women. Scandal therefore brings to the table not just a story that sells but also a gendered tale of political life. Common to many stories in *People*, the drama is teased out through a seesaw of criticism and empathy. For example, readers are asked, "The question in Hillary Clinton's case, of course, is how much humiliation can one woman take? When does the unforgivable become unendurable?" Yet later the publication concedes: "In truth, of course, every marital crisis is different. And friends suggest that Hillary, in dealing with hers, is guided by the same resources she has always drawn on in bad times."[83] This language provides a dramatic story line for readers while leaving the story open to the unknown unfolding of future events.

Though children behaving badly can influence voters' perceptions of a president, it is extramarital affairs that cause the most damage to a political reputation. John Edwards's campaign was significantly affected by his relationship with Rielle Hunter and the birth of their child together. Many women alleged or admitted to relationships with President Clinton—building his reputation as a womanizer. Yet the most notorious philanderers come from the Kennedy family—the epitome of celebrity political families. Because all presidents have been male, a pattern of transgression emerges making women "victims" of their husbands and yet highlighting the key to the political marriage—that women also desire what the presidency will bring their family. Of Elizabeth Edwards's choice to stay with presidential candidate John Edwards, *People* stated: "Some wondered if she stayed in the marriage out of political ambition."[84]

Often celebrity becomes the explanation for infidelity—as in John Edwards's case: "Over time, 'he started to think the rules didn't apply to him.'"[85] Similarly, *People* advised that Hillary Clinton "consider the experiences of other highly visible wives and lovers who have weathered infidelity and salvaged their relationships," including celebrities such as Kathy Lee Gifford and Elizabeth Hurley.[86] Morality comes through women—readers learn that political wives often look to religion, a commitment to the principles of marriage, and their moral compass to guide them through such crises. Though women are clearly wronged in cheating stories, their choice to stay is often portrayed as difficult, and usually the relationship does not end in divorce like celebrity marriages. Political marriages survive infidelity simply because both partners have put so much into achieving office—and wives are left without status should they divorce. These scandal stories highlight the dependent state of political wives, whose position is entirely reliant on their husbands' success.

Gendering the Presidency, Tabloid Style

People's coverage of politicians offers a soft news, pop culture outlet targeting women. The publication discusses politicians in a way that allows readers to get to know candidates and elected officials on a more "personal" level. During election periods, candidates' families are interviewed and become a part of the process—Reagan, Clinton, and McCain each were covered in articles that discussed the dynamics of their very different families. Reagan's children were portrayed as a liability but served to reinforce his strong principles and willingness to put politics first. For Clinton, presenting a unified family front and a focus on clean-cut preteen daughter Chelsea offered a wholesome family image. McCain used his family and background as a tool to present his political strengths and commitment to serving his country.

In expanded coverage of politicians' families, profiles of the standing first ladies show differing approaches to the role, depicting women who chose to adhere more or less closely to the gendered role of the presidential helpmeet. Independence and personal initiatives by first ladies are presented in a variety of ways, as these articles mirror the changes resulting from the women's movement over the past three and a half decades. A surprising first lady is Michelle Obama, who presents herself as one of the more traditional first ladies—very clearly avoiding the criticism a too-zealous first lady historically receives.

Female candidates for the elected offices have also been covered by *People*. The articles on these women, Sarah Palin and Geraldine Ferraro, demonstrate the publication's challenge in covering nontraditional candidates and nontraditional gender roles. The language used by the publication reflects both support for a future female president and, simultaneously, uncertainty about dealing with a new situation. Reformatting candidates to fit with "typical" male traits, such as describing Sarah Palin's love of hunting, helps make sense of changing gender roles.

Finally, scandals of infidelity hurt a politician's career. *People*'s coverage dramatizes these tales and highlights the difficult position a husband's infidelity puts women in. A politician's wife who desires political office may choose to ignore her husband's indiscretions or risk the loss of a status that is earned solely through her relationship with her husband. Many argue celebrity status contributes to politicians' extramarital relationships.

This analysis exposes how *People* covers the political process. But how does *People* influence elections? First, it speaks to a target audience who may not be paying attention to other media outlets' coverage of elections and politics. More importantly, it allows voters to decide if they *like* candidates. Voters get to know candidates through coverage of their families, hobbies, and histories. *People*'s stories subtly infuse details about a candidate's morals and personality. Even scandals communicate information about a politician that can be helpful for voters, revealing details about candidates such as their choice to lie about or admit to an affair. The cooperative nature of *People*'s content creation gives politicians more control over their image—even negative images—while potentially serving as an incentive for *People* to temper their stories to ensure future collaboration. Analyzing the types of stories that dominate political coverage, *People* demonstrates a reflective nature influenced by current social conditions that reiterates social norms. Though the publication is open to social change, its goal of covering "people, not issues" mandates that articles generally avoid change-oriented discussion of politics and gender relations. Female voters do not see the current status quo questioned within the publication. Though *People* is not engaged in political discussion, it is part of a news genre that speaks to those otherwise inactive in the political process—a valuable communication as fewer and fewer Americans vote during elections.

Notes

1. Clare Crawford, "With Richard Nixon's Impeachment Looming, Can Gerald Ford Keep a Family Promise Not to Run Again?" *People,* April 1, 1974, 4–6, http://www.people.com/people/archive/article/0,,20063906,00.html.

2. Ibid.

3. Lawrence Jacobs, "Communicating from the White House: Presidential Narrowcasting and the National Interest," in *The Executive Branch,* ed. Joel Aberbach and Mark Peterson (New York: Oxford University Press, 2005), 174–218.

4. "Demographics and Circulation," *People* media kit, 2009, http://www.people.com/people/static/mediakit/main.html.

5. Michael J. Robinson, "Two Decades of American News Preference," Pew Research Center, August 22, 2007, http://pewresearch.org/pubs/574/two-decades-of-american-news-preferences; Joseph Turow, "Local Television: Producing Soft News," *Journal of Communication* 33 (1983): 111.

6. Lee Jolliffe, "Women's Magazines in the 19th Century," *Journal of Popular Culture* 27, no. 4 (1994): 125–41.

7. Natalie Fuehrer Taylor, "The Personal Is Political: Women's Magazines for the 'I'm Not a Feminist' Generation," in *You've Come a Long Way, Baby: Women, Politics, and Popular Culture,* ed. Lilly J. Goren (Lexington: University Press of Kentucky, 2009), 215–32.

8. Ibid., 230.

9. Matthew A. Baum, "Sex, Lies, and War: How Soft News Brings Foreign Policy to the Inattentive Public," *American Political Science Review* 96, no. 1 (2002): 92.

10. Ibid.

11. Richard Davis and Diana Owen, *New Media and American Politics* (New York: Oxford University Press, 1998).

12. Susan Douglas and Meredith Michaels, *The Mommy Myth: The Idealization of Motherhood and How It Has Undermined Women* (New York: Free Press, 2005).

13. "Average Circulation for Top 100 ABC Magazines (2005)," Magazine Publishers Association, http://www.magazine.org/CONSUMER_MARKETING/CIRC_TRENDS/16117.aspx.

14. "The Press: *People*'s Premiere," *Time,* March 4, 1974, http://www.time.com/time/magazine/article/0,9171,944778,00.html.

15. Clare Crawford-Mason, Telephone interview with the author, October 20, 2010.

16. Ibid.

17. Ibid.

18. Davis and Owen, *New Media,* 93.

19. Ibid.

20. Matthew A. Baum, *Soft News Goes to War: Public Opinion and American Foreign Policy in the New Media Age* (Princeton, NJ: Princeton University Press, 2003).

21. "The Press."

22. Liesbet van Zoonen, "'Finally I Have my Mother Back': Politicians and Their Families in Popular Culture," *Harvard International Journal of Press/Politics* 3, no. 1 (1998): 48–64.

23. Benjamin Svetkey, "Barack Obama: Celebrity in Chief," *Entertainment Weekly,* November 21, 2008, http://www.ew.com/ew/article/0,,20241874,00.html.

24. Amy Chozick, "The Making of a Celebrity President," *Wall Street Journal,* April 29, 2009.

25. Stephen Hinerman, "(Don't) Leave Me Alone: Tabloid Narrative and the Michael Jackson Child-Abuse Scandal," in *The Celebrity Culture Reader,* ed. P. David Marshall (New York: Routledge, 2006), 454–69.

26. Ibid., 458.

27. Marvin L. Kalb, *One Scandalous Story: Clinton, Lewinsky, and Thirteen Days That Tarnished American Journalism* (New York: Free Press, 2001).

28. Ibid., 261.

29. Ellis Cashmore, *Celebrity/Culture* (New York: Routledge, 2006).

30. John Street, "Celebrity Politicians: Popular Culture and Political Representation," *British Journal of Politics and International Relations* 6, no. 4 (2004): 435–52.

31. Ibid., 437, 440.

32. Cashmore, *Celebrity/Culture*.

33. Matthew A. Baum, "Soft News and Political Knowledge: Evidence of Absence or Absence of Evidence?" *Political Communication* 20, no. 2 (2003): 173–90.

34. Evan Gahr, "Uncovering the Politics of Women's Magazines," *Wall Street Journal,* April 21, 1997. This does not include entertainment weeklies.

35. Rosalind Ballaster et al., *Women's Worlds: Ideology, Femininity, and Women's Magazines* (Hampshire, UK: Palgrave Macmillan, 1991), 159.

36. Liesbet van Zoonen, *Entertaining the Citizen: When Politics and Popular Culture Converge* (Lanham, MD: Rowman and Littlefield, 2005).

37. Barbara Kellerman, "The Political Functions of the Presidential Family," *Presidential Studies Quarterly* 8, no. 3 (1978): 304.

38. Ibid., 305.

39. Van Zoonen, *Entertaining the Citizen,* 77.

40. Crawford-Mason, interview.

41. Ibid.

42. Kellerman, "Political Functions," 306.

43. Karlyn Kohrs Campbell, "The Discursive Performance of Femininity: Hating Hillary," *Rhetoric & Public Affairs* 1, no. 1 (1998): 1–20.

44. Ibid.

45. Ashli Quesinberry Stokes, "First Ladies in Waiting: The Fight for Rhetorical Legitimacy on the Campaign Trail," in *The 2004 Presidential Campaign: A Communication Perspective,* ed. Robert J. Denton Jr. (Lanham, MD: Rowman and Littlefield, 2005), 190.

46. Erica Scharrer and Kimberly Bissell, "Overcoming Traditional Boundaries: The Role of Political Activity in Media Coverage of First Ladies," *Women in Politics* 21, no. 1 (2000): 55–83.

47. Lewis L. Gould, "Modern First Ladies in Historical Perspective," *Presidential Studies Quarterly* 15, no. 3 (1985): 532–40.

48. Ibid., 537.

49. Graeme Turner, "Celebrity, the Tabloid, and the Democratic Public Sphere," in *The Celebrity Culture Reader,* ed. P. David Marshall (New York: Routledge, 2006), 487–500.

50. Daniel Boorstin, *The Image: A Guide to Pseudo-Events in America* (New York: Vintage, 1961), 74, 79.

51. P. David Marshall, "Intimately Intertwined in the Most Public Way: Celeb-

rity and Journalism," in *The Celebrity Culture Reader,* ed. P. David Marshall (New York: Routledge, 2006), 323.

52. Ibid.

53. "Big Hits," *People,* April 12, 2004, http://www.people.com/people/archive/article/0,,20149821,00.html.

54. Joyce Leviton, "This Is Carter Country: They Love Jimmy and the Quiet Lives They Lead," *People,* July 19, 1976, 8–13, http://www.people.com/people/archive/article/0,,20066680,00.html.

55. Andrew Schneider and Barbara Wilkins, "In Icy New Hampshire, Nancy with the Smiling Face Is a Primary Asset," *People,* February 23, 1976, 4–9, http://www.people.com/people/archive/article/0,,20066179,00.html; "Patti, Ron, Maureen & Mike: A Look at What Could Be the Nation's Next First Family," *People,* July 21, 1980, 22–27, http://www.people.com/people/archive/article/0,,20077011,00.html.

56. "Patti, Ron, Maureen & Mike."

57. Landon Y. Jones, "Road Warriors: At Home in Arkansas, the Clintons Talk about Friends, Family, Faith—and Pierced Ears," *People,* July 20, 1992, 68–76, http://www.people.com/people/archive/article/0,,20113135,00.html.

58. Ibid.

59. Alex Tresniowski et al., "The Real McCains: The Candidate and His Wife Talk about Their Life Together, All Seven—Count 'em—Kids and What It's Like to Grow Up McCain," *People,* September 22, 2008, 72–77, http://www.people.com/people/archive/article/0,,20230575,00.html.

60. Clare Crawford, "Up Front: A Confident Betty Ford Tests Her Wings in Europe," *People,* June 16, 1975, 4–9, http://www.people.com/people/archive/article/0,,20065339,00.html; Clare Crawford, "Betty Ford Has the Deed to a Gorgeous New Home—and a New Lease on Life," *People,* March 26, 1979, 118–27, http://www.people.com/people/archive/article/0,,20073259,00.html.

61. Crawford, "Up Front."

62. Ibid.

63. "Pat Nixon: How Does She Hold Up?" *People,* May 27, 1974, 30–35, http://www.people.com/people/archive/article/0,,20064103,00.html.

64. Clare Crawford and Joyce Leviton, "The Leap from Plains to Pennsylvania Avenue: How Rosalynn Will Do It," *People,* November 15, 1976, 22–27, http://www.people.com/people/archive/article/0,,20067099,00.html.

65. Ibid.

66. Ibid.

67. Maurine Beasley, *First Ladies and the Press: The Unfinished Partnership of the Media Age* (Evanston, IL: Northwestern University Press, 2005).

68. Garry Clifford, "The New First Lady Is a Former Debutante, but Watch Out, 'She's a Fighter,'" *People,* November 17, 1980, 44–47, http://www.people.com/people/archive/article/0,,20077881,00.html.

69. Ibid.

70. Ibid.

71. "Michelle Obama: The New First Lady (2009)," CBS News, January 7, 2009, http://www.cbsnews.com/htdocs/pdf/Feb09b-MichelleObama.pdf.

72. For example, Clinton remains the only first lady to establish her office in the West Wing. All others have used the traditional East Wing offices for their affairs and activities. She did relocate to the East Wing later in the presidency.

73. Michelle Green, "Her Own Woman: Hillary Clinton—Mom, Wife, Policy Wonk—Redefines the First Lady's Role with Hard Work and High Hopes," *People,* May 10, 1993, 82–90, http://www.people.com/people/archive/article/0,,20110388,00 .html.

74. Sandra Sobieraj Westfall, "Michelle Obama: 'We're Home,'" *People,* March 9, 2009, 112–18, http://www.people.com/people/archive/article/0,,20264255,00.html.

75. Susan Schindehette, "The First Lady Next Door," *People,* January 29, 2001, 50–57, http://www.people.com/people/archive/article/0,,20133518,00.html.

76. Louise Lague, "The Making of a Trailblazer," *People,* July 30, 1984, 24–29, http://www.people.com/people/archive/article/0,,20088346,00.html.

77. Lorenzo Benet and Jill Smolowe, "Gov. Sarah Palin's Family Matters," *People,* September 15, 2008, 70–76, http://www.people.com/people/archive/ article/0,,20230644,00.html.

78. Lague, "Making of a Trailblazer."

79. Benet and Smolowe, "Palin's Family Matters."

80. Paula Chin, Joe Treen, and Karen S. Schneider, "Camelot after Dark," *People,* May 27, 1991, 58–68, http://www.people.com/people/archive/article/0,,20115192,00 .html.

81. Stephen Birmingham, *Jacqueline Bouvier Kennedy Onassis* (New York: Pocket Books, 1978).

82. "Pat Nixon."

83. Susan Schindehette, "High Infidelity," *People,* September 7, 1998, 53–59, http://www.people.com/people/archive/article/0,,20126181,00.html.

84. Sandra Sobieraj Westfall, Sharon Cotliar, and Nicole Weisensee, "Inside the Edwards Split: I Want My Life Back," *People,* February 8, 2010, 88–91, http://www .people.com/people/archive/article/0,,20342817,00.html.

85. Ibid.

86. Schindehette, "High Infidelity."

10

VIRAL VIDEOS

Reinforcing Stereotypes of Female Candidates for President

Todd L. Belt

Following the midterm elections in 2006, the Pew Internet and American Life Project surveyed Americans about their preferred news sources.[1] Television remained the favorite source of news, preferred by 69 percent of respondents; newspapers were a distant second at 34 percent; and Internet sources brought up the rear with a mere 15 percent.[2] By 2008, the number of respondents favoring Internet sources had more than doubled to 33 percent.[3] One explanation for the increase is the growing symbiosis among Internet, print, radio, and television media. The interdependence among these sources has grown to such a degree that stories cycle through the various media at lightning speed, with Internet sources creating a lasting record of audio, visual, and textual content.[4] To some extent, it is becoming difficult to distinguish media content as belonging to one platform or another.

Borrowing Harold Lasswell's enduring framework for communications analysis, this chapter examines "Who says what, in what channel, with what effect?"[5] As the channel changes with the advent of "new media," the speakers have changed. Beyond the candidates and the mainstream press, these speakers now include interest groups and individuals to a greater degree than ever before. This chapter specifically investigates the second element of Lasswell's framework: what these new political players say. Inferences are then drawn as to the new content's effect on democratic politics.

Female Candidates in the Election of 2008

Since there are no female presidential incumbents to consider, elections offer the only opportunity to evaluate gender issues and the role of mass media as they relate to presidential politics. Although Shirley Chisholm (1972) and Elizabeth Dole (2000) mounted presidential nomination campaigns, Chisholm was not considered a viable contender and only participated in the primaries of twelve states, whereas Elizabeth Dole withdrew before the first Republican primary because of fundraising difficulties.[6] The 2008 election campaign provides the best opportunity for a case study analyzing the role of gender in presidential politics. On the Democratic side, the election featured the first viable female candidate for a major-party nomination, Hillary Clinton. On the Republican side it included the second major-party nominee for vice president, Sarah Palin.[7] Thus the field of candidates in the media spotlight featured a woman throughout nearly the entire race, excluding the weeks between early June and late August 2008—from when Barack Obama had secured enough delegates to be assured the Democratic nomination and McCain's announcement of Sarah Palin as his running mate.

Early on, many saw Hillary Clinton as such an insider that she was branded the establishment candidate.[8] Previously, female presidential candidates had been considered outsiders. Clinton's near miss at securing the Democratic Party's nomination provides evidence of the viability of female presidential candidates in the twenty-first century, but will voters elect a woman in the general election? Historically, and of particular consequence to the Democratic primary, being a female candidate has been a greater burden on candidates than being a black candidate.[9] Reflecting on her political life, Shirley Chisholm said as much: "Of my two 'handicaps,' being female put more obstacles in my path than being black."[10] But the evidence today is mixed. Caitlyn Dwyer and her colleagues found in 2009 that racism had a significant impact on attitudes in the 2008 election, whereas sexism did not.[11]

In 2007, 88 percent of Americans said that they would vote for a well-qualified woman for president, up from 39 percent in 1972.[12] But there is still a gap between men's and women's preferences for female candidates. The gap between females and males voting for female candidates ranges from 6 to 8 percent depending upon the office.[13] But research indicates that there may be a social acceptability bias in these findings, as 26 percent of respondents say that they are "angry" or "upset" with the possibility of a female president, and this level of antipathy is constant across demographic groups.[14] There may be a current of sexism lying beneath the surface of survey responses that affects how the public views candidates. Significant to this study is the possibility that these sexist stereotypes held by the public can now be broadcast through new media.

Certainly, female politicians know the risks they run when they enter the vicious arena of electoral politics, and 2008 was no exception. Female candidates are cognizant of presenting themselves in ways to downplay the omnipresent potential for sexist coverage. Candidates know, as research has shown, that appearance is a more frequent source of media comment for female than for male candidates.[15] In order to guard against this, the Republican National Committee spent $150,000 on wardrobe for Palin and her family.[16] But even when female candidates do their best to combat the issue of appearance, it still tends to seep into coverage. For example, Hillary Clinton's banal "uniform" of pantsuits became the focus of many jokes on late-night television.[17] While fashion is an occasional focus in the coverage of male presidential candidates (e.g., Howard Dean's rolled sleeves, Al Gore's earth tones, or Lamar Alexander's plaid shirts), this sort of coverage does not generate nearly as much criticism or serve as a personality indicator of male candidates as it does of female candidates.

But appearance is not the only area where female candidates must guard against asymmetrical media focus. Certain issues are often considered to be handled better by males than by females, forcing female candidates to take strident political stands in order to fend off judgments based on gender stereotypes.[18] It was against this backdrop that candidates waded into a media landscape that included commentary from the public to a greater degree than ever before in 2008.

The literature on media coverage of female political candidates is clear and unequivocal: female candidates are taken less seriously than their male counterparts. Although gender stereotyping is less prevalent today than it has been in the past, differences exist in the way female and male candidates are covered in the media. For example, studies of congressional and gubernatorial candidates reveal systematic trends: coverage of male candidates largely focuses on experience, accomplishments, and issue positions, whereas coverage of female candidates is more likely to focus on personal information, physical appearance, and personality.[19]

Research focusing on specific election campaigns repeatedly demonstrates these patterns. In her studies of U.S. senate elections, Kim Fridkin Kahn finds that female candidates receive more negative coverage than male candidates regarding their prospects for victory.[20] In their study of Elizabeth Dole's presidential campaign, Caroline Heldman, Susan Carroll, and Stephanie Olson find that 61.3 percent of stories mentioned one or more of Dole's personality traits and 61.9 percent mentioned personal information, specifically her husband— former senate majority leader and former presidential candidate Bob Dole.[21]

Following the pattern of the "issue ownership" thesis that the public perceives Democrats as better able to handle certain issues and Republicans better able to handle others, voters have preconceived notions of which issues are better handled by men and which are better handled by women.[22] Males are generally viewed as being better suited to handling issues of defense, foreign affairs, and the economy. By contrast, women are seen as better able to handle children's issues, education, and health care.[23] This form of stereotyping extends to perceptions of candidates' ideologies. Kathleen Dolan finds that when a female candidate is a Democrat, she is perceived to be more liberal than a male Democratic candidate, but there is no relationship between candidate sex and perceived ideology for Republican candidates.[24] Coverage in the press of female candidates mirrors these stereotypes as well, with the press focusing more on the aforementioned "women's issues" when covering female candidates.[25]

The tendency of the public and the press to stereotype has endured even though female candidates do not set their issue priorities or run their campaigns in ways that conform to these stereotypes. Instead, female candidates tend to campaign on largely the same issues as male candidates and to run their campaigns in many of the same ways.[26] In terms of style versus substance, female candidates are more likely than male candidates to run issue-specific campaigns.[27] Perhaps this is because female candidates recognize the danger of running a campaign that focuses too much on personality. But in terms of votes, Paul Herrnson, J. Celeste Lay, and Atiya Kai Stokes show that women running for the House of Representatives and state legislative offices are advantaged by running on "women's issues."[28] But these levels of office do not require officials to have as much expertise in the so-called male issues that face presidential candidates, such as defense and foreign affairs.[29]

Voters perceive male candidates to be more competent overall than female candidates, and voters prefer more competent-looking candidates, regardless of the candidate's sex.[30] Males are more likely to vote for female candidates who are more attractive, while female voters are more likely to vote for a male candidate who appears more approachable.[31] The more provocatively a female with a high-status occupation dresses, the less both men and women perceive her level of competence.[32] Moreover, when subjects in an experimental manipulation were asked to write about Sarah Palin's physical appearance (as opposed to writing about her as a person), they were less likely to vote the McCain/Palin ticket.[33]

On top of all of these disadvantages, research shows that to be successful, female candidates must engage in behavior that is not associated with femininity, such as self-promotion, aggression, and demonstrations of superiority.[34] It is a double-edged sword, because if a woman fails to demonstrate these traits, she may not appear to be an effective leader and can consequently suffer at the ballot box.[35]

New Media in the Election of 2008

When we think of new media today, we commonly think of blogs and the social media website Facebook. Much has been made about Barack Obama's ability to use new media, specifically cell phones and Facebook, to his advantage.[36] Though the election took place only a few years ago, much has changed. Facebook was not widely used by many candidates throughout the 2008 campaign. In fact, the Obama/Biden campaign was the first to use it, but didn't integrate it with the Obama campaign website until October 20, 2008—weeks before election day.

One important aspect of new media is the ability of ordinary citizens to engage in fact checking. One particular incident that prompted fact checking on the Internet was Hillary Clinton's assertion of the dangers she faced on her trip to Bosnia. Blogs that engage in this type of activity are not unimportant. Indeed, such blogs caught and disseminated Obama's controversial "guns and religion" remark in Pennsylvania.[37] But blogs are still read and commented on by a small audience. It is what this audience sends to the wider public that has greater impact.[38]

A phenomenon with greater public impact than blogs is YouTube. This website allowed candidates and individuals to produce advertising and audiovisual commentary. The ability of the public to produce and share political commentary in a virtually unrestricted marketplace was a phenomenon so impressive that YouTube was used as a medium by which to select questions from the public for Democratic and Republican primary debates.[39]

But existence of web content does not necessarily produce an audience. As always, viewers need a reason to "tune in" to content. And as usual, the content that catches the public's eye is entertainment. During the 2008 campaign, some individuals actively sought out new media coverage on blogs, and by alerting others, these individuals set off a cascade of e-mails alerting still others to the presence of entertaining content pieces, especially videos. The public's attention was then directed to the videos by e-mails, blogs, social networking sites, news sites, and even radio and television personalities. As time went on, awareness of the videos snowballed, and web hits grew geometrically—the videos "went viral."

People redirected these videos to their family and friends precisely because they were funny. Laughing at the powerful and those who aspire to power is a tradition that dates back at least to ancient Greece.[40] A popular form of political humor is satire, which is based on exaggerating stereotypes.[41] Satire works comedically because it is based on a widely held version of the truth, or as *Saturday Night Live* (*SNL*) executive producer Lorne Michaels calls it, "heightened reality." It is stretching the truth that creates the humor. Humor is not politically trivial; it can grab and hold viewers' attention and decrease citizens' trust in governmental institutions.[42] This raises the question, What were the "viral videos" of the 2008 presidential campaign all about? What did they contain, and what effects did they have on our long-term perceptions of presidential candidates?

The findings of prior research studies lend themselves to certain expectations about the portrayal of female candidates for president in "viral videos." Standard gender stereotyping is important in predicting video depictions of the female candidates, but so are the images that the candidates themselves put forward. In 2007–2008, Hillary Clinton ran her campaign largely on the basis of her experience as first lady and as senator from New York. These experiences, combined with her elite education at Wellesley and Yale, helped to fend off potential criticism of riding on her husband's coattails. During the campaign, Clinton earned a reputation as a tough and tenacious campaigner.[43] And as noted above, she kept her appearance and clothing conservative.

Particularly important for making predictions about the 2008 election is the fact that voters are more likely to employ gender stereotypes for less well-known candidates.[44] In 2008, Hillary Clinton was the known quantity and was remembered by many voters for her past as a trailblazing feminist who originally refused to take her husband's last name and who once remarked that she could have "sat home and baked cookies" instead of getting involved in politics and public service. In the past, Clinton had associated herself with "women's issues" such as health care and child care.

By contrast, Sarah Palin was unknown even to many attentive political observers. She presented herself as a "maverick" who, like John McCain, did not always follow the Republican Party's platform. However, she did appeal to Christian evangelicals and other social conservatives. Palin was known for her "folksy" demeanor in her speaking engagements, and she played this up during the course of the campaign, often referring to herself as a "hockey mom." Like Clinton, Palin cultivated the image of tenacity, joking that the only difference between a "hockey mom" and a pit bull was "lipstick." Palin emphasized her dedication to Christian family values and to her large family. Additionally, the campaign promoted the nickname Palin earned for her dogged determination as a high school basketball player: "Sarah Barracuda."

But one portrayal that Palin could not live down was her appearance. Palin was a former beauty pageant winner (Miss Wasilla) and placed third in the Miss Alaska pageant. This, combined with the $150,000 campaign expenditure on her wardrobe, put Palin's appearance center stage in the campaign, whether she liked it or not.

When it came to issues, Palin was associated with two in particular: guns and hunting, both generally considered "male" issues. For example, Palin played up the fact that she was an avid hunter and a lifelong member of the NRA. In fact, news about her hunting escapades included hunting by helicopter and a widely circulated photo of her next to a moose carcass that she had presumably bagged.

Given the trends in political coverage in the mass media combined with the self-portrayals of the candidates, certain hypotheses can be drawn regarding the amount of attention each candidate received in the viral videos, the topics addressed, and the tone of the content. First, more portrayals of female candidates (Clinton and Palin) are expected than portrayals of videos of male candidates (Obama, McCain, and Biden) because of the novelty of female candidates in the presidential race and the greater amount of material expected to be on the table. That is to say, the videos will follow the trend in press coverage of female candidates by focusing on appearance, personality, and issue positions.

This leads to a second hypothesis: that appearance and personality are likely to be addressed more for female candidates than for male candidates. Between the female candidates, Palin should receive more attention overall than Clinton. This attention should be paid specifically to her appearance and personality for several reasons. First, Clinton was the better-known candidate, so opportunity for commentary on her personality and appearance would be more limited than that for the less well-known Palin. Second, the McCain/Palin campaign's choice to focus on Palin's personality as a "maverick" offered opportunities for evaluation and commentary. Finally, Palin's history of self-objectification through participation in beauty pageants opened the door to a focus on her appearance.

As far as issue topics addressed in the videos, Hillary Clinton should be associated more with "women's issues," given her trademark issue interests. By contrast, given Republican "issue ownership" on issues such as foreign affairs and national security, Palin should be associated more with male issues than female issues.[45] This should also be true given her penchant for guns and hunting.

The last set of hypotheses has to do with the tone of the videos. First, female candidates should be portrayed with more female stereotypes, and male candidates should be portrayed with more male stereotypes, but more overall stereotypes should be employed in the depictions of female candidates. Clinton, as a woman forgoing traditionally feminine gender roles, should be portrayed with

Table 10.1. Summary of Hypotheses

Content		Candidate differences
Amount of content	Female > Male	Clinton < Palin
Topics		
Appearance	Female > Male	Clinton < Palin
Personality	Female > Male	Clinton < Palin
Women's issues	Female > Male	Clinton > Palin
Men's issues	Female < Male	Clinton < Palin
Tone		
All stereotypes	Female > Male	Clinton < Palin
Female stereotypes	Female > Male	Clinton < Palin
Male stereotypes	Female < Male	Clinton < Palin

fewer female stereotypes than Palin, who stressed her role in a traditional family. Palin should be portrayed with masculine stereotypes for her aggressiveness and association with men's issues. On the whole, more stereotypes overall should be applied to Palin than Clinton (see table 10.1 for a summary of hypotheses).

Data, Methods, and Analysis

The data for this study are drawn from the viral videos that circulated during the campaign. Tracking the number of hits on a story or video has become increasingly complicated because of embedding technologies and redirecting links. That being the case, videos in this study were drawn from online lists of the top viral videos of the campaign, including sources such as politicalhumor .about.com and politico.com, as well as those collected by the author. The number of videos accumulated for this study totaled twenty-eight (see the appendix to this chapter for the full list of videos). Although these are not all of the videos focusing on the candidates that were circulated over the Internet during the 2008 campaign, they were the most prevalent.

    Videos were coded for the candidate(s) portrayed, personality stereotypes attributed to the candidates, and gendered issues associated with each candidate. Stereotypes included the specific personality traits attributable to men or women. Drawing on previous literature, lists of both masculine and feminine stereotypes were drawn up, including both positive and negative stereotypes.[46]

Table 10.2. Stereotypical Personality Portrayals

Masculine	Feminine	Neutral
Dominant	Sensitive	Intelligent
Aggressive	Warm	Articulate
Self-reliant	Motherly	Unintelligent
Strong	Compassionate	Inarticulate
Controlling	Insensitive	
Submissive	Cold	
Passive	Unmotherly	
Dependent		
Weak		

Each video could have a number of different issue and personality portrayals for multiple candidates. Male stereotypes included depictions such as "dominant," "self-reliant," and "aggressive" as well as their reverse depictions. Female stereotypes included portrayals such as "sensitive," "warm," and "compassionate" and depictions of the opposite of these traits (see table 10.2 for a complete list of gender stereotypes coded in this study).

Gendered issues were also adopted from prior literature. Issues classified as "men's issues" included foreign policy, terrorism, the Iraq War, foreign trade, guns, and hunting. "Women's issues" included health care, the environment, abortion, and education.

Gendered issues and personality stereotypes were recorded each time an issue was associated with a given candidate. Two coders were employed in the coding, and agreement between coders was measured at 92.3 percent. The length of the videos ranged from 1 minute and 51 seconds for the shortest to 11 minutes and 40 seconds for the longest. All videos featured at least one candidate, nine featured two candidates, and four featured three candidates. Analysis of the videos incorporates both quantitative and qualitative study. Quantitative measures were compared in order to test the aforementioned hypotheses. Qualitative interpretive analysis was performed to help read between the lines—a particularly important aspect of interpreting satire.

The hypotheses were tested by comparing the content of the videos for portrayals of male versus female candidates and then for Hillary Clinton versus Sarah Palin. For each comparison, the total number of portrayals of interest

Table 10.3. Comparison of Content by Candidates

| Content | Candidate portrayals per video | | | | | |
	Female	Male	t	Clinton	Palin	t
Amount of content	1.036	0.750	2.121*	0.179	0.643	3.300**
Topics						
Appearance	0.286	0.143	1.162	0.107	0.179	0.812
Personality	3.110	1.964	1.959†	0.643	2.464	3.070**
Women's issues	0.429	0.179	1.426	0.143	0.286	1.072
Men's issues	0.964	0.214	2.725*	0.107	0.857	3.000**
Tone						
All stereotypes	2.250	1.420	1.752†	0.500	1.750	2.525*
Female stereotypes	0.786	0.357	1.721†	0.107	0.679	2.661*
Male stereotypes	1.464	1.071	1.110	0.393	1.071	1.884†

Note: Paired samples t-tests, † < .10, * < .05, ** < .01

were aggregated for each candidate and then divided by the total number of stories. This quotient measures how much of each type of portrayal existed per story. As the number increases, the more of that portrayal exists in the totality of the videos. This measure reflects the overall milieu of the content created by the viral videos.

As expected, the female candidates were more frequently portrayed in the videos than the male candidates. Female candidates appeared twenty-nine times in the twenty-eight videos, yielding a score of 1.036 per video (see table 10.3). In comparison, male candidates appeared twenty-one times in the videos, for .750 portrayals per video. In line with the first hypothesis, there were more portrayals of female candidates than male candidates, and the difference was statistically significant (t = 2.121, p < .05). Among the candidates, Palin was portrayed most often—nineteen times—followed by Obama and McCain at ten portrayals each. Hillary Clinton was portrayed in five of the videos and Biden only once. The expected difference occurred in the amount of content for Clinton versus Palin (.179 per video versus .643 per video, respectively). This difference was in the expected direction and statistically significant (t = 3.300, p < .01). Table 10.3 shows the frequency of appearances by male and female candidates and specifically by Clinton and Palin in relation to overall content, topics, and stereotypes depicted.

Physical depictions of the candidates that reflected them in either a positive or negative light were few. There were more depictions of female candidates' appearances than there were of male candidates' appearances, but the difference was small and insignificant (.286 versus .143 per video, respectively). Palin, the former beauty queen, was depicted in terms of her appearance more than Clinton, but again, the difference was insignificant (.179 versus .107 per video, respectively). In line with the literature, female candidates were depicted more in terms of their personality than male candidates. On average, each video contained 3.110 depictions of female candidates' personalities, whereas male candidates' personalities were depicted at a rate of 1.964 per video. This result supports the hypothesis that personality is a more frequent topic of commentary for female candidates than for male candidates (t = 1.959, $p < .10$).[47] Also as expected, Palin received a greater share of depictions of her personality than did Clinton. In fact, Palin received four times as many depictions of her personality (2.464 per video) as Clinton did (.643). This difference between the female candidates was not only statistically significant, it was the strongest found in all of the comparisons tested (t = 3.070, $p < .01$).

The varying issue content among the videos yielded some interesting and unexpected results. The trends in the data are not strong enough to support the hypothesized relationships of women's issues to the candidates, but they are for men's issues. Contrary to expectations, videos associated the female candidates significantly more with male issues (.964 per story) than they associated male candidates with those same issues (.214 per story, $p < .05$). But as expected, Palin was much more often associated with men's issues than was Clinton (.857 versus .107 per story respectively, $p < .01$). There are three explanations for these findings. The first is that many of the issues that face a presidential candidate are men's issues, so it is not surprising that the commentary on the videos evaluates the female candidates in these terms. Second, the McCain/Palin campaign made an issue of campaigning on traditionally male—and Republican—issues such as foreign policy. Third, Palin brought male issues to the forefront in terms of the public's evaluations of her. Her interview gaffes regarding foreign policy set her up for criticism and ridicule, as did her hunting hobby.

Delving deeper into the results for personality portrayals of the candidates reveals patterns of gender stereotypes. Interestingly, and similar to the results for gendered issues, female candidates were more often the targets of both male and female stereotypes than male candidates. Overall, stereotypes were attributed to female candidates at a rate of about 2.25 per video, whereas they were attributed to male candidates at a rate of 1.420 per video (t = 1.752, $p < .10$). Not surprisingly, female candidates were more likely than men to be depicted along the lines of female stereotypes (.786 versus .357 per video, respectively, t = 1.721, $p < .10$). But contrary to expectations, female candidates were more likely than male candidates to be portrayed in terms of male stereotypes, although the difference was smaller and not statistically significant.

As expected, the lion's share of stereotypical portrayals was directed at Palin. In all three categories—female, male, and total stereotypes—Palin was significantly more often the target than Clinton (see table 10.3). Of the few stereotypes attributed to Clinton, "aggressive" and "controlling" were the most common. For Palin, the most common masculine stereotype was "aggressive," and the second-most common was "weak." Stereotypes of Palin were just as likely to be negative ("weak," "submissive," and such) as they were positive ("aggressive," "strong," "controlling," etc.). The feminine stereotypes attributed to Palin were more negative than the masculine stereotypes, and she was most commonly portrayed as "insensitive." Put another way, Palin was more frequently portrayed in an *un*feminine way.

These top-line quantitative data indicate patterns that offer a good deal of support for hypotheses regarding the content of viral videos, but they do not tell the full story. The quantitative results represent the quantity of the amount of content in the videos, but they mask the intensity. When one reads between the lines, the portrayals of Clinton were terse and stodgy, certainly not flattering. The depictions of Palin were even less charitable. Most of the viral videos from the 2008 campaign targeted Sarah Palin, and many were critical of her intelligence. To be sure, Governor Palin set herself up for criticism through remarks that indicated that she was not aware of the "Bush Doctrine" of preemptive war and her lack of knowledge on certain issues in her interviews with Charles Gibson and Katie Couric. But the portrayals of Palin were particularly harsh and portrayed her as relying completely on her charm as a candidate, utterly devoid of policy ideas.

Particularly instructive is the *SNL* video featuring both Clinton and Palin. The upshot of this video is that both candidates were portrayed strongly on the lines of the expected stereotypes and gendered issues (see chapter 3 of this book for detailed descriptions of the *SNL* videos). At one point in the video, Palin asks the audience, "Please, stop Photoshopping my head on sexy bikini pictures." This comment refers to a number of pictures where Palin's head was digitally altered to appear on the bodies of scantily clad women.[48] Conversely,

Hillary Clinton is portrayed as extraordinarily bland and unattractive. These juxtaposed portrayals of Palin and Clinton indicate that a female politician will be scrutinized for being either too attractive or not attractive enough. Unlike male candidates, female politicians cannot escape the omnipresent media focus on appearance.

John McCain's decision to place Sarah Palin on the GOP ticket was panned in two widely circulated viral videos. The first video is a satirical re-creation of a telephone call from McCain to Palin, asking her to join the ticket. McCain is heard leaving a message for Palin, and the dialogue points to the dark-horse elements of her selection. McCain is portrayed as not even knowing who Palin was—he mistakenly refers to her as "Sandra" and "Senator" and thinks that she is from Arkansas, not Alaska. For the formal announcement of her candidacy, he tells her to look presentable but "don't dress too slutty . . . definitely show a little cleavage." The content further devolves into a discussion of her appearance, as McCain can be heard asking an assistant if Palin "has nice gams" and discussing the length of her skirt.[49] As in the *SNL* skits, Palin is objectified even though McCain ostensibly does not even know her, and the dialogue again emphasizes the catch-22 of physical appearance for female politicians: looking attractive is just as bad as looking unattractive.

Another video circulated on the topic of McCain's overtures to Palin as a running mate. This video portrays the two engaged in a phone conversation. Palin interrupts target practice to take the call from a worried McCain. Palin asserts her dominance over him by telling him to "stop whining" and admonishing him, "I'm gonna tell you how this is going to go, John McCain. I'm going to put a smile on, look real pretty—which isn't hard, OK, for me—talk about being a hockey mom, and take this shit home. So you stop being a little pussy and send me that private jet and I'll see you in Dayton." Palin then hangs up and yells, "Who wants to go polar bear huntin'?" This video was circulated with the title: "Is McCain Palin's Bitch?" and exemplifies the overtly masculine portrayals of Palin found in other videos. Palin is depicted as aggressive and domineering. The video also associates Palin with the male gendered issues of guns and hunting. The question about hunting an endangered species, the polar bear, serves to push her insensitivity over the top.

The video "Sarah Palin's Greatest Hits" is a montage of Palin's biggest misstatements, gaffes, and awkward interview moments. The video begins with a quote from the movie *Apocalypse Now*: "The horror. The horror" and then launches into the montage of actual footage of Palin. These clips include her interview gaffes with Katie Couric and Charles Gibson and Palin's claim that she reads "all" of the news weeklies. While not a comic portrayal of Palin per se, the video adopts a cinema verité documentary style to portray Palin as unintelligent, inarticulate, and unfit for the presidency.

Another video regarding Palin's nomination was produced by the political comic-pundit duo of Jackie and Dunlap for their show *Red State Update*. While their weekly YouTube show received a fair amount of attention throughout the campaign, it was this particular video that was most widely circulated.[50] The show features the pundits espousing their views while sitting before an American flag, smoking, and slugging back cans of Budweiser beer. Jackie and Dunlap have developed personas as southern "rednecks" who, though only mildly informed on the issues, nonetheless offer strident conservative commentary. In this video, the younger Dunlap informs the elder Jackie about McCain's choice of Palin as his running mate. Jackie expresses his skepticism about the pick, stating, "I don't know nothing about the woman." Dunlap counters, "I can tell you all you need to know right now, Jackie—she hot! She hot as hell, man! Looky here." The video shows a picture of Palin on the campaign trail as Dunlap continues, "She got that Alaska librarian, let her hair down, take her on the tundra kinda thing goin' on." Jackie protests, saying that "she's an alright lookin' woman, but I don't see what you're gettin' all worked up about." Dunlap responds, "Well, maybe I didn't show you the right picture, lookit this one." The screen changes to a photo of Palin peering through the scope of an assault rifle at the camera. Jackie is convinced, proclaiming, "Oh. Good Lord! Look out! You better take that picture down. I better not be lookin' at that picture too long, I'm a married man!" For these stereotypical "red staters," Palin's appeal comes not only from her physical appearance but her position on the gendered issue of guns and, later in the video, on moose hunting. In a last moment of objectification of the two female candidates, Jackie and Dunlap contend that Palin is ready to break through the glass ceiling because Hillary Clinton caused 18 million cracks in it by looking at it.

A prank phone call to Sarah Palin also went viral during the campaign. The caller pretends to be French president Nicolas Sarkozy but is in fact a member of the prankster group known as the Masked Avengers, two comedians from Montreal, Canada. The YouTube video contains the audio content of the prank call paired with a picture of Nicolas Sarkozy while the prankster is talking. The video then switches to a picture of an animated pink "My Little Pony" figure with rainbows and stars in the background as Palin speaks. The visual added to the telephone call serves to reinforce the message of Palin as fluff—all show and no substance. Other pictures flash in the background showing eagles and caricatures of Palin and "Joe the Plumber." Sarkozy suggests that they go hunting together, saying that he just loves "killing those animals, mmm, mmm, take away life, that is so fun!" As Sarkozy says this, the widely circulated picture of Palin next to her moose kill fills the screen, which then switches to a baby seal being clubbed. Later, as Palin talks, an old photo of her competing in a beauty pageant appears briefly, only to be replaced by a photo of Paris Hilton. While Palin's responses are fairly professional in nature, the presentation of the audio content alongside the visuals sent out a clear message of appearance over substance.

A video that was ostensibly a Disney movie trailer for a movie called *Head of Skate* was widely circulated during the campaign. The video was produced by the group collegehumor.com. The video shows Palin as an All-American mom who is recruited by McCain to be vice president. As the video proceeds, McCain dies in office and Palin ascends to the presidency. In order to solve the crisis in the former Soviet Republic of Georgia, Palin challenges Russian prime minister Vladimir Putin to a game of hockey, warning him that he has "pucked with the wrong ice president." While not focusing on Palin's appearance, the video parodies Palin's penchant for zippy one-liners and her lack of gravitas on foreign policy issues. The upshot is that Palin is unintelligent and unprepared for the presidency.

Some of the viral videos that made the rounds on the Internet were not humorous. Two of them included criticism of Palin's intelligence by public figures (CNN reporter Jack Cafferty and actor Matt Damon). Another featured Hillary Clinton in New Hampshire, welling up with tears in her eyes when she was asked what keeps her going when times get tough on the campaign trail. This video came out the weekend prior to the state's primary election, and along with racial factors, is considered to have had an effect on the marked difference between public opinion polls prior to the election and Clinton's large returns at the ballot box. This video broke the stereotype of Clinton as unfeminine, as she gave a number of women's issues as reasons for her motivation to run against what appeared to be increasingly unlikely odds following her third-place finish in the Iowa caucuses.

One video in the sample was circulated shortly after the election. The video is a news clip showing the Alaska governor's pardoning of a turkey just prior to the Thanksgiving holiday. Ironically, Palin pardons the turkey at a slaughterhouse while turkeys behind her continue to be killed. The video is a critique of Palin's intelligence, demonstrating her obliviousness to the contradiction between what she says and what she does. Subsequent to the campaign and her resignation of the governorship of Alaska, Palin became a spokesperson for the

Tea Party movement, a commentator on Fox News, and wrote an autobiography. To this day, she continues to be panned on late-night TV for her intelligence, but focus on her appearance has lessened. Fewer videos are circulated on the Internet today, as she has generated less interest over time and is no longer a candidate for office.

The press is often criticized for its tendency to sensationalize news, but is the public any better when it can control the content?[51] These viral videos, mostly produced by members of the public, show little difference in content from the trends in the press identified by prior research. This study finds that the content, specifically portrayals of candidates' appearances and personalities, as well as the issues associated with the candidates, mirror broader trends established in past practice.

This is not surprising given the definition of satire as "heightened reality." A new generation of Internet content creators takes its cues from what it already sees in old media and augments it. Moreover, citizen-produced videos lack an editorial filter. The combination of these two elements results in an even greater intensity of sexist and simplistic portrayals of female candidates. The videos demonstrate frequent gender stereotypes in portrayals of female candidates' personalities and the issues associated with them. Considering that this is the type of public-generated discourse that is becoming most circulated on the Internet, it looks as though the struggle for gender equity in politics is taking a step backward.

Research demonstrates that the portrayal of female presidential candidates is important because female politicians act as role models for adolescent girls, stimulating their involvement in politics.[52] Moreover, visible and competitive female candidates increase women's engagement in the electoral process.[53] This study demonstrates that gender stereotypes and sexist objectification are still rampant in the twenty-first century. Moreover, they are now packaged in videos that express them even more intensely.

The results attained here further demonstrate that female candidates aspiring to the highest office in the land run the risk of being either too masculine or too feminine. There does not seem to be a middle ground. These results correspond to what Kathleen Hall Jamieson calls the "double-bind"—the perception that female candidates cannot simultaneously be both feminine and competent in politics.[54]

Counterfactuals are always difficult, but could we presume that the new media landscape would have been as hard on Sarah Palin if she were a man?

Would Dan Quayle have garnered the same sort of critical portrayals in citizen-produced videos? Certainly, Palin is not totally without fault for creating the reality that was then exaggerated by satirists. Palin's statements in the press often made her seem to be a rural simpleton.[55] Palin was also widely remembered for winking at the camera during the vice presidential debate—a suggestive act that many women found demeaning.

What can be learned from this study is that both the content and context of political satire are important. While the quantitative data generated by this sample of videos reflect many trends in gender stereotyping, it is just as important to read between the lines. The humorous portrayals of Clinton and Palin indicate the difficult balance that must be struck by a female candidate—if it can be struck at all. Being seen as too feminine is a burden, but so is being seen as too masculine. And to campaign for the presidency, female candidates must wade into the sea of issues that are traditionally considered men's issues. This creates another difficulty for female candidates—managing a gender-neutral personality while discussing gendered issues. Even a candidate who pulls off this balance remarkably well, as Hillary Clinton did, still faces ridicule. More than 135 years since the *Bradwell v. Illinois* decision that created the public/private split between the sexes, our cultural milieu dictates that politics is still widely viewed as a "man's game."[56]

Appendix: Viral Videos of the 2008 Campaign

VIRAL VIDEOS FROM SATURDAY NIGHT LIVE

Democratic debate: Barack Obama and Hillary Clinton (originally aired March 1, 2008): http://www.hulu.com/watch/11208/saturday-night-live-democratic-debate-2

Hillary Clinton guest stars (originally aired March 1, 2008): http://www.hulu.com/watch/11204/saturday-night-live-editorial-response-sen-clinton

Spoof of Hillary Clinton and Sarah Palin opening *Saturday Night Live* (originally aired September 13, 2008): http://www.nbc.com/saturday-night-live/video/palin-hillary-open/656281/?_cid=thefilter

Spoof of Sarah Palin's interview with Katie Couric (originally aired September 27, 2008): http://www.nbc.com/saturday-night-live/video/couric-palin-open/704042/

Spoof of the vice presidential debate (originally aired October 4, 2008): http://www.nbc.com/saturday-night-live/video/vp-debate-open-palin-biden/727421/?_cid=thefilter

Sarah Palin guest stars (originally aired October 18, 2008): http://www.nbc.com/saturday-night-live/video/gov-palin-cold-open/773761/?_cid=thefilter

Palin rap (originally aired October 18, 2008): http://www.nbc.com/
   saturday-night-live/video/update-palin-rap/773781/?__cid=thefilter
John and Cindy McCain guest star, Tina Fey as Sarah Palin (originally aired November 1,
   2008): http://www.nbc.com/saturday-night-live/video/mccain-qvc-open/805381/

OTHER VIRAL VIDEOS

Spoof of John McCain's voicemail to Sarah Palin: http://www.youtube.com/
   watch?v=nszcwZ60Y18
Spoof of John McCain's call to Sarah Palin: http://www.youtube.com/watch?v=
   d-QevraCQUc
Sarah Palin's greatest hits: http://www.youtube.com/watch?v=NrzXLYA_
   e6E&feature=related
Red State Update videos on Palin's nomination: http://www.youtube.com/
   watch?v=W5IAPK0hbU
Sarah Palin's turkey pardon fiasco: http://www.youtube.com/watch?v=nJd_vm9VhpU
Prank phone call to Sarah Palin: http://www.youtube.com/watch?v=4H2qPyo4ALM
Sarah Palin Disney trailer: http://www.collegehumor.com/video:1831461
Hillary Clinton cries on camera in New Hampshire: http://www.youtube.com/
   watch?v=MVlwH7–05Fk
CNN's Jack Cafferty video clip criticizing Sarah Palin's interview with Katie Couric:
   http://www.youtube.com/watch?v=L8__aXxXPVc
Matt Damon condemns Sarah Palin: http://www.youtube.com/watch?v=anxkrm9uEJk
"Yes We Can"—Barack Obama music video: http://www.youtube.com/
   watch?v=35tI-8TaKmU
Dear Mr. Obama: http://www.youtube.com/watch?v=TG4fe9GlWS8
"I Got a Crush . . . on Obama" by Obama Girl: http://www.youtube.com/
   watch?v=wKsoXHYICqU
"Obama and McCain—Dance Off!": http://www.youtube.com/watch?v=
   wzyT9–9lUyE
Jib Jab, "Time for Some Campaignin'": http://sendables.jibjab.com/originals/
   time_for_some_campaignin
Sarah Silverman and the Great Schlep: http://www.youtube.com/
   watch?v=AgHHX9R4Qtk
"The McCain-Palin Mob": http://www.youtube.com/watch?v=KjxzmaXAg9E
Terry Tate, "Reading Is Fundamental": http://www.youtube.com/
   watch?v=07kO9TtHYzQ
Diddy Obama Blog 16, "John McCain Is Buggin the F%^k Out!": http://www
   .youtube.com/watch?v=p-fC1T3zH5E
Paris Hilton responds to McCain ad: http://www.funnyordie.com/videos/64ad536a6d/
   paris-hilton-responds-to-mccain-ad-from-paris-hilton-adam-ghost-panther-
   mckay-and-chris-henchy

Notes

1. Deborah Fallows, "Election Newshounds Speak Up: Newspaper, TV and Internet Fans Tell How and Why They Differ," Pew Internet and American Life Project February 6, 2007, http://pewresearch.org/pubs/406/election-newshounds-speak-up.

2. Percentages total more than 100 percent because they are derived from a multiple-response question.

3. Pew Research Center for the People and the Press, "Internet Now Major Source of Campaign News Continuing Partisan Divide in Cable TV News Audiences," October 31, 2008, http://pewresearch.org/pubs/1017/internet-now-major-source-of-campaign-news.

4. Richard Davis, "A Symbiotic Relationship: Bloggers and Journalists," in *Media Power in Politics*, 6th ed., ed. Doris A. Graber (Washington, DC: Congressional Quarterly Press, 2011), 293–301.

5. Harold Lasswell, "The Structure and Function of Communication in Society," in *The Communication of Ideas*, ed. Lyman Bryson (New York: Institute for Religious and Social Studies, 1948), 37–51.

6. Ruth B. Mandel, "She's the Candidate! A Woman for President," in *Women and Leadership: The State of Play and Strategies for Change*, ed. Barbara Kellerman and Deborah L. Rhode (San Francisco: Jossey-Bass, 2007), 283–307.

7. In 1984, Geraldine Ferraro became the first female major-party nominee by joining the Democratic ticket with Walter Mondale.

8. Mandel, "She's the Candidate!"

9. Lee Sigelman and Susan Welch, "Race, Gender and Opinion toward Black and Female Candidates," *Public Opinion Quarterly* 48, no. 2 (1984): 467–75.

10. Jone Johnson Lewis, "Shirley Chisholm Quotes," About.com, http://womenshistory.about.com/od/quotes/a/shirleychisholm.htm.

11. Caitlin E. Dwyer et al., "Racism, Sexism, and Candidate Evaluations in the 2008 U.S. Presidential Election," *Analyses of Social Issues and Public Policy* 9, no. 1 (2009): 223–40.

12. Andrew Kohut, "Are Americans Ready to Elect a Female President? Past Statewide Elections Suggest Gender Is Not an Obstacle—at Least for Democratic Candidates," Pew Research Center for the People and the Press, May 9, 2007, http://pewresearch.org/pubs/474/female-president; Myra Marx Ferree, "A Woman for President? Changing Responses: 1958–1972," *Public Opinion Quarterly* 38, no. 3 (1974): 390–99.

13. Kohut, "Are Americans Ready"; Stefanie Simon and Crystal L. Hoyt, "Exploring the Gender Gap in Support for a Woman for President," *Analyses of Social Issues and Public Policy* 8, no. 1 (2008)): 157–81.

14. Matthew J. Streb et al., "Social Desirability Effects and Support for a Female American President," *Public Opinion Quarterly* 72, no. 1 (2008): 76–89.

15. Sean Aday and James Devitt, "Style over Substance: Newspaper Coverage of Elizabeth Dole's Presidential Bid," *International Journal of Press/Politics* 6, no. 2 (2001): 52–73.

16. Patrick Healy and Michael Luo, "$150,000 Wardrobe for Palin May Alter Tailor-Made Image," *New York Times,* October 22, 2008.

17. Ariel Alexovich, "Here's Your Pantsuit Joke . . . ," *New York Times,* May 5, 2008.

18. Jennifer L. Lawless, "Women, War, and Winning Elections: Gender Stereotyping in the Post–September 11th Era," *Political Research Quarterly* 57, no. 3 (2004): 479–90.

19. Aday and Devitt, "Style over Substance"; Maria Braden, *Women Politicians and the Media* (Lexington: University Press of Kentucky, 1996); James Devitt, "Framing Gender on the Campaign Trail: Female Gubernatorial Candidates and the Press," *Journalism & Mass Communication Quarterly* 79 (2002): 445–63; Kim Fridkin Kahn, *The Political Consequences of Being a Woman: How Stereotypes Influence the Conduct and Consequences of Political Campaigns* (New York: Columbia University Press, 1996).

20. Kim Fridkin Kahn, "The Distorted Mirror: Press Coverage of Women Candidates for Statewide Office," *Journal of Politics* 56, no. 1 (1994): 154–73; Kahn, *Political Consequences.*

21. Caroline Heldman, Susan Carroll, and Stephanie Olson, "Gender Differences in Print Media Coverage of Presidential Candidates: Elizabeth Dole's Bid for the Republican Nomination," paper presented at the Annual Meeting of the American Political Science Association, Washington, DC, 2000.

22. John R. Petrocik, "Issue Ownership in Presidential Elections, with a 1980 Case Study," *American Journal of Political Science* 40, no. 3 (1996): 825–50.

23. Barbara Burrell, *A Woman's Place Is in the House: Campaigning for Congress in the Feminist Era* (Ann Arbor: University of Michigan Press, 1994); Michael X. Delli Carpini and Ester R. Fuchs, "The Year of the Woman? Candidates, Voters, and the 1992 Elections," *Political Science Quarterly* 108 (1993): 29–36; Leonie Huddy and Nayda Terkildsen, "Gender Stereotypes and the Perception of Male and Female Candidates," *American Journal of Political Science* 37, no. 1 (1993): 119–48; Lawless, "Women, War, and Winning"; Mark S. Leeper, "The Impact of Prejudice on Female Candidates: An Experimental Look at Voter Inference," *American Politics Quarterly* 19 (1991): 248–61; Kira Sanbonmatsu, "Gender Stereotypes and Vote Choice," *American Journal of Political Science* 46, no. 1 (2002): 20–34.

24. Kathleen A. Dolan, *Voting for Women: How the Public Evaluates Women Candidates* (Boulder, CO: Westview, 2004). See also Jeffrey W. Koch, "Do Citizens Apply Gender Stereotypes to Infer Candidates' Ideological Orientations?" *Journal of Politics* 62, no. 2 (2000): 414–29.

25. Braden, *Women Politicians*; Linda Witt, Karen Paget, and Glenna Mat-

thews, *Running as a Woman: Gender and Power in American Politics* (New York: Free Press, 1994).

26. Kathleen A. Dolan, "Do Women Candidates Play to Gender Stereotypes? Do Men Candidates Play to Women? Candidate Sex and Issue Priorities on Campaign Websites," *Political Research Quarterly* 58, no. 1 (2005): 31–44; Kristin la Cour Dabelko and Paul S. Herrnson, "Women's and Men's Campaigns for the U.S. House of Representatives," *Political Research Quarterly* 50, no. 1 (1997): 121–35.

27. Kim Fridkin Kahn and Ann Gordon, "How Women Campaign for the U.S. Senate: Substance and Strategy," in *Women, Media, and Politics,* ed. Pippa Norris (New York: Oxford University Press, 1997), 59–76.

28. Paul S. Herrnson, J. Celeste Lay, and Atiya Kai Stokes, "Women Running 'as Women': Candidate Gender, Campaign Issues, and Voter-Targeting Strategies," *Journal of Politics* 65, no. 1 (2003): 244–55.

29. Shirley Miller Rosenwasser and Norma G. Dean, "Gender Role and Political Office: Effects of Perceived Masculinity/Femininity of Candidate and Political Office," *Psychology of Women Quarterly* 13, no. 1 (1989): 77–85.

30. Joan Y. Chiao, Nicholas E. Bowman, and Harleen Gill, "The Political Gender Gap: Gender Bias in Facial Inferences That Predict Voting Behavior," *PLoS ONE* 3 (2008): e3666.

31. Ibid.

32. Peter Glick et al., "Evaluations of Sexy Women in Low- and High-Status Jobs," *Psychology of Women Quarterly* 29, no. 4 (2005): 389–95.

33. Nathan A. Heflick and Jamie L. Goldenberg, "Objectifying Sarah Palin: Evidence That Objectification Causes Women to Be Perceived as Less Competent and Less Fully Human," *Journal of Experimental Social Psychology* 45, no. 3 (2009): 598–601.

34. Susan J. Carroll, *Women as Candidates in American Politics,* 2nd ed. (Bloomington: Indiana University Press, 1994); Huddy and Terkildsen, "Gender Stereotypes."

35. Carroll, *Women as Candidates*; Kathleen Hall Jamieson, *Beyond the Double Bind: Women and Leadership* (New York: Oxford University Press, 1995).

36. Greg Mitchell, *Why Obama Won: The Making of a President 2008* (New York: Sinclair Books, 2009).

37. Claire Ann Miller, "How Obama's Internet Campaign Changed Politics," *New York Times,* November 7, 2008.

38. Other factors of interactive Web 2.0 new media were involved in the 2008 presidential campaign. Though candidates were late in arriving to Facebook, their supporters used it for organizational purposes. Another Web 2.0 application was Second Life, where individuals could move their avatars through a virtual world. Candidates set up campaign headquarters that interacted with individuals online, but the phenomenon was short-lived.

39. These were called the CNN-YouTube debates. The Democratic debate was held on July 23, 2007, and the Republican debate was held on November 28, 2007.

40. Thomas Cronin, "Why and How We Laugh at Politicians," unpublished manuscript, 2007.

41. Jonathan S. Morris, "*The Daily Show with Jon Stewart* and Audience Attitude Change during the 2004 Party Conventions," *Political Behavior* 31, no. 1 (2009): 79–102.

42. Jody C. Baumgartner, "Humor on the Next Frontier: Youth, Online Political Humor, and the 'Jib-Jab' Effect," *Social Science Computer Review* 25 (2007): 319–38.

43. Mark Leibovich and Kate Zernike, "Seeing Grit and Ruthlessness in Clinton's Love of the Fight," *New York Times,* May 5, 2008.

44. Deborah Alexander and Kristi Andersen, "Gender as a Factor in Attribution of Leadership Traits," *Political Research Quarterly* 46, no. 3 (1993): 527–45.

45. Petrocik, "Issue Ownership."

46. Lawless, "Women, War, and Winning." Masculinity and femininity are best conceived as separate dimensions rather than opposite ends of a single continuum. See Sandra L. Bem, "The Measurement of Psychological Androgyny," *Journal of Consulting and Clinical Psychology* 42 (1974): 155–62; Peter J. Burke and Judith C. Tully, "The Measurement of Role Identity," *Social Forces* 55 (1997): 881–97; Janet T. Spence and Robert L. Helmreich, *Masculinity and Femininity: Their Psychological Dimensions, Correlates, and Antecedents* (Austin: University of Texas Press, 1978).

47. Results at the .10 level are appropriate for small data sets such as this one ($n = 28$).

48. This comment stimulated the recycling of other viral content across the Internet, specifically, the altered pictures.

49. "Gams" was a term used in the early twentieth century for a woman's legs. The use of this term implies McCain's advanced age.

50. YouTube play counts show that this video received ten times more hits than most other *Red State Update* videos.

51. Tom Rosensteil et al., *We Interrupt This Newscast: How to Improve Local News and Win Ratings, Too* (New York: Cambridge University Press, 2007).

52. David E. Campbell and Christina Wolbrecht, "See Jane Run: Women Politicians as Role Models for Adolescents," *Journal of Politics* 68, no. 2 (2006): 233–47.

53. Lonna Rae Atkeson, "Not All Cues Are Created Equal: The Conditional Impact of Female Candidates on Political Engagement," *Journal of Politics* 65, no. 4 (2003): 1040–61.

54. Jamieson, *Beyond the Double Bind.*

55. Eliza Jane Darling, "O Sister! Sarah Palin and the Parlous Politics of Poor White Trash," *Dialectical Anthropology* 33 (2009): 15–27.

56. *Bradwell v. Illinois*, 83 U.S. 130 (1873).

Part IV
WOMEN IN THE WHITE HOUSE

First Ladies, First Couples, First Families

11

High Culture, Popular Culture, and the Modern First Ladies

MaryAnne Borrelli

To study the modern first ladies is to study variation and change, generalizing cautiously and with caveats. Even so, one can accurately assert that these presidents' wives have routinely served as representatives, facilitating communication and building relationships between the president and numerous publics. Some first ladies have focused their representation on the rich symbolism of the presidency. Mamie Doud Eisenhower showcased the White House, which had virtually been reconstructed throughout the Truman years; more than nine hundred tours were given while she was first lady. Jacqueline Bouvier Kennedy abolished the social season and redesigned state dinners, altering rituals that had defined elite-presidential relations for generations. Eleanor Roosevelt, Rosalynn Smith Carter, and Hillary Rodham Clinton instead focused on policy making, on substantive representation. They sought to advance social justice and to reform national systems for mental health care and health care insurance, respectively. Still other modern first ladies—among them Lou Henry Hoover, Lady Bird Taylor Johnson, Barbara Pierce Bush, and Laura Welch Bush—have made commitments to both symbolic and substantive representation.[1] In brief, the content of the first ladies' representation has changed to reflect presidential, first lady, and public interests.

The first ladies' performance of descriptive representation has, however, continued throughout the modern presidency. Elites and publics have expected the presidents' wives to evidence the virtues espoused by the nineteenth-century "cult of true womanhood," namely, piety, purity, submissiveness, and domesticity.[2] First ladies criticized for behavior perceived as contradicting this ideal include Eleanor Roosevelt and Nancy Davis Reagan (viewed as obstructing presidential decision making), Lady Bird Johnson and Rosalynn Carter (judged too active during their husbands' reelection campaigns), Betty Bloomer Ford (seen as too outspoken on policy matters), and Hillary Clinton (identified as too much the policy activist). In contrast, Bess Truman, Mamie Eisenhower, Jacqueline Kennedy, and Barbara Bush were applauded for their performance as wives and mothers. The standards set for the first lady have changed very slowly; first ladies have faced increasing criticism as societal disagreements about women's gender roles have intensified.[3] Though their presence on the public stage is required, first ladies have won higher approval ratings when presenting themselves as dedicated to the private sphere.

But whose virtues and traditions, whose conceptions of the private and public spheres are being supported, as support is measured by approval ratings and positive media coverage? The "cult of true womanhood" is an aristocratic construction, obliging a woman to prove herself through her other-directed appreciation of the arts, her hospitality, and her charitable works. In conforming to these ideals, the first lady's gender performance normalizes the privileged circumstances of the socially, economically, and politically powerful.

Such a rigid and essentialist conception of gender is strongly at odds with present-day understandings and behaviors. Recognized as a social construct, gender is now widely perceived as indicative of a society's history and aspirations, especially the fluidity and the inflexibility of its peoples' identities. It is lived, performed, experienced, and diverse. It is one facet of a person and of a society, intertwining with other social constructs such as race and class.[4]

As descriptive representatives, modern first ladies have regularly embraced this conception of gender as evolving, seeking to relax the strictures associated with "true womanhood." Yet this strategy is not necessarily available to Michelle Obama. As a first lady who is a self-identified African American woman, Obama confronts a related but different mixture of presumptions, expectations, and ascriptions. The cultural myths that whites have constructed for African American women contrast markedly with those that they have imposed upon white women. Thus, white women are expected to be pious in religious and civic contexts; African American women are expected to be hostile matriarchs, emasculating men and corrupting children. White women are to be pure; African American women are presumed jezebels, sexually voracious. White women are required to be models of republican motherhood and domesticity; African American women are required to be mammies, raising the oppressor's children and neglecting their own. White women are expected to be submissive; African American women are expected to be Sapphires, "uppity" and angry. Such oppositional and essentialist ideologies may seem historic relics, but they have been refreshed with each generation. Consider, for example, the ways in which these cultural myths are renewed when African American women are identified as "welfare queens."[5] Reinvigorated, abolished, or something in between—how has Michelle Obama's first ladyship been affected by, and affected, these cultural myths and ideologies? What is the significance of this change for the first ladyship and for the presidency?

First Ladies, Representation, and Identity

To identify the first lady as a representative is to take a very different approach to examining the contributions of the presidents' wives. Previously, first lady scholars have conducted extensive biographical investigations, historical studies, and communication and rhetorical analyses.[6] Understanding the first lady as a representative builds upon this research, taking the further step of analyzing her functions and contributions across administrations. Formally, Congress has authorized and funded the first lady's post; the president has "designated" the woman who would serve as first lady; and the federal courts have ruled that she functions as a de facto public official.[7] Informally, the first lady is defined through her marriage to the president, a relationship that is presumed to give her unique insights on the chief executive. Yet this relationship may generate more concern than support if the intimacies of marriage are viewed as precluding the transparency and accountability required of a presidential advisor. The manipulative wife, trading sexual favors for power, is a familiar figure in many political narratives.[8] Thus the first lady finds herself constrained by a series of cultural myths and ideologies. If the formal aspects of the first lady's post seem to promise power and legitimacy, the informal aspects are more suggestive of constraints and limitations.

For white first ladies, the "cult of true womanhood" has sometimes offered a means of assuaging concerns about their accountability, allowing them to capitalize on the formal and informal resources of the post. This strategy has carried high costs. A past president of the Girl Scouts, Lou Henry Hoover resigned from that organization and rarely published or spoke publicly while her husband was president. An accomplished foundation fund-raiser and advocate, Barbara Bush presented herself as a family-centered matriarch while her husband was vice president and president. Other first ladies—including Lady Bird Johnson, Betty Ford, and Nancy Reagan—confined themselves to policy agendas congruent with conceptions of women as moral guardians, caregivers, and satellite wives. These first ladies leveraged "positive" ideologies (the cult of true womanhood and republican motherhood) against other, negative cultural myths (the "domineering dowager" and the "scheming concubine") in an effort to avoid negative media coverage, strong criticism, and low approval ratings.

For an African American first lady, the management of these cultural myths and ideologies is even more difficult. The cultural myths she confronts as an African American woman—the matriarch, the jezebel, the mammy, the Sapphire—strongly reinforce concerns about her lack of accountability as a wife and presidential advisor. Would Michelle Obama, as an African American first lady, be able to reassure the public by leveraging the ideologies ascribed to the white first ladyship against these negative cultural myths? Is this a strategy that she would want to adopt? How would such a strategy affect her credibility as a descriptive representative? For Michelle Obama, these are familiar unknowns: she has studied sociology, race relations, and the law; professionally, she has been a "first" in more than one context. Even so, to find and live the answers to these questions, under the close scrutiny that comes with being first lady, has been a formidable challenge.

This chapter considers how Michelle Obama has met this challenge with her early initiatives in the arts, with the *Let's Move!* campaign against childhood obesity, and with her fashion choices. As different as these three are, they reveal Obama's continuing commitment to blurring the boundaries between high and popular culture, so that high culture becomes richly democratic, popular in the most profound sense of the word. Streaming video of White House concerts has increased access to the arts, and pairing workshops with each concert has provided talented youngsters with the opportunity for a master class. A media campaign featuring the White House kitchen garden has stressed homegrown vegetables, with the goal of increasing access to local and organic foods. And when the first lady agreed to be featured on innumerable magazine covers but retained strong control of the associated photo shoots, she obliged the fashion and media industries to recognize women of color as beautiful and autonomous. As first lady, then, this president's wife has used her political resources to reform established systems of cultural, social, and economic power. Repeatedly, she has deliberately leveraged, challenged, and potentially altered enduring cultural myths and ideologies.

The Arts: Symbolic Representation

The fine arts have historically been associated with the powerful. Their patronage has underwritten great creativity, and artists have, in turn, conveyed and legitimized their patrons' vision. Appreciation of the arts has also, for women adhering to the "cult of true womanhood," been evidence of their refinement, civility, and high-mindedness. Not surprisingly, then, presidents have used the arts to express their vision as a chief of state, and first ladies have assumed the associated responsibilities of staging and delivering this message. These are practices that accent the monarchical qualities of the presidency and the aristocratic aspects of the first ladyship.

Michelle Obama is similar to her predecessors in that she has capitalized on opportunities to convey the values of her husband's administration through the arts. Yet she has also, distinctively, sought to broaden access to cultural capital and to power. In one of her first public statements, delivered at the Metropolitan Museum in New York City, the first lady issued a call to action: "We've been trying to break down barriers that too often exist between major cultural establishments and the people in their immediate communities, to invite kids who are living inches away from the power and prestige and fortune and fame—we want to let those kids know they belong here, too."[9] Rejecting the notion that the arts should be reserved to the few, the first lady insisted that they be part of a mass-based democratic impetus extending through politics ("power and prestige") to the market ("fortune") and society ("fame"). Later, speaking to middle and high school musicians invited to master classes at the White House, she acknowledged that these achievements would require struggle and sacrifice. But Obama stressed the opportunity for achievement and success: "I know your instructors and parents have probably told you this time and time again, but they were right—they're right, I'm sorry—you'll learn that if you believe in yourself and put in your best effort, that there's nothing that you can't achieve. And those aren't just lessons about music. These are really lessons about life."[10] Continuing this argument, she lauded the artists who came to the White House as activist role models: "It wasn't that long ago that these great musicians that you celebrate today were sitting in your seats, standing in your shoes. And that's why they're here—to show you that if you follow that passion and never give up, you too can claim your place in the world of classical music."[11] The wording is telling: recognition must be "claim[ed]," but the individual can look forward to a "place" of his or her own. This is a journey to power that is strongly reminiscent of that described by black feminists, who speak of the importance of a "safe space"—which has often been provided by the arts—in which to find one's voice, in order to move from self-definition to self-valuation to an expressive self-reliance and independence.[12] Other first ladies have stated their confidence in the American dream of socioeconomic mobility, and some could do so on the basis of their personal experiences. But never before had this assertion been made by the descendent of African American slaves, by a woman who publicly acknowledged that she was not always proud of her country but who insisted that black women "be fearless."[13]

The first lady has delivered this message of hard-won optimism and determined inclusivity repeatedly, often across social and political divides. Her early arts programming at the White House showcased the cultural legacies of African American communities in the context of the nation's artistic and expressive identity. The first major arts event at the Obama White House was an East Room concert, "Music of the Civil Rights Era," on February 11, 2009.[14] The White House Music Series was inaugurated with jazz, which Michelle Obama described as "America's indigenous art form."[15] Thus the first lady placed the cultural legacies of African American communities in the context of the nation's artistic and expressive identity. Other genres—among them, country-western, classical, and Broadway—were subsequently featured. The president, always in attendance, delivered remarks that paralleled the first lady's. At the classical music concert, he "counseled those who did not know where to applaud not to worry, but added: 'I have Michelle to help me. The rest of you are on your own.'"[16] Though a bit of self-deprecation may have preempted charges of elitism, the president was also saying that even those unfamiliar with the arts could enjoy and appreciate them. There were to be no boundaries—self- or socially imposed—to these events, which used music to highlight the nation's racial, cultural, and regional pluralism.

An objection could be made that the arts are merely a ceremonial element of the presidency, a nod (sometimes more) to talents and gifts that are honored if not always respected. There are the stories of President Kennedy dozing through White House concerts and more recent references to National Endowment for the Arts funding as "wasteful."[17] Yet the arts and presidential politics have always been intertwined at a deeper level, and the first lady has mediated that relationship. Laura Bush, for example, renewed Washington's interest in literature, with literary salons at the Library of Congress and with book fairs. The Obama administration built upon this work. A White House evening of "Poetry, Music, and the Spoken Word," just weeks into the presidential term, gave literary form to Barack Obama's electoral promises of bipartisan governance. As the press release declared, "This event is designed around the theme of dialogue, showing how dialogue is important in every aspect of who we are as Americans and as human beings, and demonstrating how communication is a constant throughout the ages. The hope is also that this evening's gathering helps ensure that all voices are heard, particularly voices that are often not heard."[18] The sheer repetition of inclusive terminology—"dialogue," "communication," "all voices are heard"—was unmistakable. This was a literary and political event, whose cultural antecedents were diverse and democratic.

Formally, the first ladies' leadership in the arts is based upon an executive order from 1982, which identified the president's wife as the honorary chair of the President's Committee on the Arts and Humanities, the agency charged with "advancing the White House's arts and humanities objectives." In the Obama administration, the power of this authorization has been informally enhanced by close coordination with the president's message. Few prior administrations have so precisely and consistently used the first lady's influence as a symbolic representative in their efforts to advance the president's agenda. And Michelle Obama has not been criticized for her arts-centered outreach. She has spoken against the exclusivity of high culture, and she has featured African American artists and arts at the White House, largely free of the constraints imposed by negative cultural myths and ideologies.

The White House Garden and *Let's Move!*: Substantive Representation

Gardens and food have always been at the center of human survival, but gardens and food have also been status symbols: the pastoral in the midst of the urban, the aesthetic enjoyment of cultivated acreage, has been a prerogative of the powerful for centuries, as evidenced by the gardens that surround innumerable stately homes and palaces. Upper-class women—ladies—have instructed their gardeners and then enjoyed nature's beauty and bounty. Women of lower status have done hard labor and tried to ward off hunger. For a first lady to actually plant a garden, therefore, is a potentially revolutionary undertaking. True, Lady Bird Johnson participated in numerous flower and tree plantings as part of her beautification campaign. But those trees and flowers were decorative, in keeping with aristocratic sensibilities. Michelle Obama stressed that hers was a kitchen garden, providing food and nourishment. Remarkably, this aspect of her work in the garden has received little commentary. As one blogger remarked,

> Just two months into the Obama Era, it seems like now either no one cares about the politics of racial history anymore, or that no one is appreciating the hugeness of yesterday's events . . . or that it is still too charged to be addressed. Digging up a piece of the White House lawn

to plant a garden as the first First Lady who is documented to be a descendant of slavery is a somewhat transgressive act in terms of making a statement about food politics, food policy, healthy eating, nutrition . . . and about cultural/racial history, when you consider that much of the agricultural work in this country was done by slaves, from the Founding through the Civil War, and even beyond the Emancipation. "Field Negros" as a crucial population of agricultural laborers did not vanish even after slaves were "freed."[19]

Perhaps the first lady's Jimmy Choo boots have signaled her distance from her family's historical experience of slavery.[20] Certainly the glamour of the White House kitchen garden distances it from the harsh realities of fieldwork, though it remains a symbol of the first lady's commitment to healthy eating.

Slightly less than one year after the garden was first planted, Michelle Obama began the *Let's Move!* campaign for children's health.[21] She also had been a working mother, the first lady said, and she was well aware of the pressures confronting families. *Let's Move!* would help parents live up to their "best intentions":

Like most parents, I was a working mother trying to put it all together, and I gradually learned that . . . when my family eats fresh food, healthy food, that it really affects how we feel. . . . But I also have learned through my experiences that as a working mother that there are times when putting together a healthy meal is harder than you might imagine. . . . Takeout food was a primary part of our diet. It was quick. (Laughter) It was easy. (Laughter) We did what was easiest and what kids liked, because you didn't want to hear them whining. . . . (Laughter) And sometimes it turns out that the food that is the least healthy for us can sometimes be the cheapest. And even with the best intentions, as I know all of us . . . care about our kids and we're doing the best that we can for them and with the best of intentions. In this society today sometimes it's hard to make regular meals, healthy meals, a part of everyone's existence.[22]

This statement, a staple in the first lady's *Let's Move!* stump speeches, defends her policy work as an extension of her private-sphere commitments. In presenting herself as a caregiver and moral guardian, Michelle Obama draws upon her own experiences as a parent to speak persuasively and confidently, as befits a "mom-in-chief." Dismissing the cultural myths of the mammy and the hostile matriarch, she also rejects the white "cult of true womanhood," speaking of domestic matters assertively rather than subserviently.[23]

Political commentators have had much to say about *Let's Move!* African American analysts, while often wishing that the first lady would advance more comprehensive policies, have observed that Michelle Obama is countering long-standing presumptions that African American women are bad mothers.[24] Doing so has won Obama support throughout society, as the first lady's approval ratings rose and her negatives "plummeted" with respondents "positively influenced" by "her focus on children and family, her devotion to her own family, and by the symbolic gesture of her planting the first White House vegetable garden since Eleanor Roosevelt."[25] Michelle Obama's policy agenda has grown, with momentum generated by the kitchen garden channeled first into a media campaign against childhood obesity and then into a series of government programs and private-public partnerships for healthy eating. The president's task force on childhood obesity recommended budget increases, which have been advanced, for the Departments of Agriculture, Treasury, and Health and Human Services to facilitate the establishment of farmers' markets and grocery stores throughout the country. The program budget for the school lunch program has been increased, and negotiations have been initiated with major suppliers to raise nutrition standards. More than forty food and agribusiness corporations have announced their support for *Let's Move!*[26] In the third year of the initiative, Judith S. Palfrey, M.D., immediate past president of the American Academy of Pediatrics, has been named executive director of *Let's Move!*, suggesting that the first lady will be taking a more comprehensive approach to children's health policy.[27] The mom-in-chief has established herself as a policy entrepreneur, leading a professional and well-respected staff.

"Nanny state" critics have, however, become more emphatic as the first lady's agenda has lengthened and as the presidential election nears. Then presidential candidate Michele Bachmann denounced a proposal by the first lady that would allow tax deductions for breast-feeding expenses as a "'hard left' position that 'government is the answer to everything.'"[28] Former Alaska governor Sarah Palin, in a wide-ranging radio interview, concluded, "Take her anti-obesity thing. . . . What she is telling us is she cannot trust parents to make decisions for their own children, for their own families. . . . Instead of a government thinking that they need to take over and make decisions for us according to some politician or politician's wife priorities, just leave us alone, get off our back, and allow us as individuals to exercise our own God-given rights to make our own decisions and then our country gets back on the right track."[29] In these and other statements, gender, race, and class mix with partisan politics, as white women accuse an African American woman of overreaching, of exercising power to which she has no claim. This churning combination of identity, partisan, and policy politics will require the first lady to develop even more sophisticated strategies to cause change as a descriptive and substantive representative throughout the 2012 campaign.

Fashion: Descriptive Representation

Haute couture is at once art and business. It is intensely personal and highly nationalistic.[30] When Rosalynn Carter wore the same gown to the presidential inaugural balls that she had worn for her husband's gubernatorial inauguration, it was a deliberate act meant to signal the Carter administration's populist values. This would not be an "imperial presidency." Just four years later, Nancy Reagan resurrected the monarchical conception of the presidency with dresses that were brilliantly red and designed by Adolfo, Bill Blass, James Galanos, David Hayes, and Jean Louis. Fashion makes the first lady a symbol of her husband's administration. The challenge for her, in performing this role, is to guard against her own objectification, protecting her status as a representative.

The impact of fashion on and by the first lady is determined, to a significant extent, by her relationships and communications with designers and with the wider public. It is presumed that a president's wife will cultivate and advance the fortunes of American designers, such as Oleg Cassini (Jacqueline Kennedy), Albert Capraro (Betty Ford), James Galanos and Adolfo (Nancy Reagan), Oscar de la Renta and Carolina Herrera (Hillary Rodham Clinton and Laura Bush).[31] As part of this relationship, first ladies are expected to conform to the designers' aesthetic standards of slenderness, whatever their own body types. Harry Truman defended his wife against charges that she was excessively heavy. Barbara Bush simply endured these judgments, which she found very hurtful. Lady Bird Johnson avoided criticism by existing on black coffee and dry toast for days before formal events in order to ensure a "flattering" fit and drape for her gowns. In this relationship, the first lady is more mannequin than person; she is routinely objectified.

The relationship with the public is no less complex, as "appropriate" standards for women's wear are no longer widely shared. If successful in her outreach, however, the first lady will influence—even as she is influenced by—the routine fashion choices of women and men throughout the society. She will, in other words, blur the boundaries of high culture and popular culture, as elite fashion is adopted and adapted to the daily lives of diverse women.[32] Mamie Eisenhower's hairstyle (especially her bangs), Jacqueline Kennedy's hats, and Barbara Bush's pearls are only a few examples of this kind of impact, with an attentive public mimicking the first ladies' style choices.

Close scrutiny of Michelle Obama was to be expected, since whites have routinely defined and displayed fashion throughout the twentieth and twenty-first centuries. Though African American models had appeared regularly on runways and among the ranks of supermodels during the 1980s and 1990s, those decades proved exceptional; only one African American woman had ever been featured on the cover of *Vogue* in the United States.[33] Now there was an African American first lady, whose choices would influence perceptions of what was or was not socially appropriate, what was or was not aesthetically pleasing for a woman's body, what was or was not feminine. Fashion would no longer be quite so white.

But would Michelle Obama be accepted as a descriptive representative by the elite and by the ordinary, by women of color and white women, by women and men in an increasingly diverse and polarizing society? The "history of the traffic in the Black female body," wrote Lisa Collins, leads to a strong association of their bodies with the "sexual and economic marketplace."[34] A first lady framed in this way would not be able to deliver a persuasive message on behalf of her husband's administration. This would be judged her failure, even though popular interpretations of African American women have seldom been respectful of their personal authenticity.[35]

Michelle Obama has encountered negative interpretations of her style choices and of herself. Critics have not hesitated to objectify her, referring to her as body parts rather than as a person. One of the most widely circulated accounts was written by columnist Maureen Dowd, who recounted the following conversation with *New York Times* columnist David Brooks: "In the taxi, when I asked David Brooks about [Michelle Obama's] amazing arms, he indicated it was time for her to cover up. 'She's made her point,' he said. 'Now she should put away Thunder and Lightning. . . . Washington is sensually avoidant. The wonks here like brains. She should not be known for her physical presence, for one body part. . . . Sometimes I think half the reason Obama ran for president is so Michelle would have a platform to show off her biceps.'"[36] Brooks, a white male, does not question why this first lady is so readily objectified, why "wonks" have the power to define a person's identity, why "brains" and "physical presence" are at odds. Presenting this as an accepted and acceptable reality, Brooks implicitly endorses the cultural myth of the hypersexed jezebel, the scheming concubine. Michelle Obama, however, rejects these presumptions and cultural myths; she adopts, modifies, and ignores long-standing first lady fashion conventions.

Michelle Obama has, for example, conformed in wearing clothing by American designers.[37] Rather than choosing from among well-established couturiers, though, this first lady has showcased less famous, independent designers. These include Naeem Khan (who founded his label in 2003), Thakoon Panichgul (2004), Rachel Roy (2004), Kate and Laura Mulleavy (2005), Jasmin Shokrian (2003), and Jason Wu (2006). Several of her designers are first- or second-generation immigrants from countries not associated with western European traditions in fashion design, including India, Iran, Taiwan, and Thailand. These choices are distinctively her own, so that she embodies the priorities of her husband's administration—providing wider access to cultural capital—in ways that are her own. Thus the first lady presents herself as a representative, not an object, with "brains" and a "physical presence."

The first lady has also selected ensembles that draw attention to her body. She favors jewel tones that strongly contrast with her skin color, as also did her white inaugural ball gown. She has frequently worn sleeveless dresses and strapless gowns, without the swathing of shawls, stoles, or scarves. Her self-confidence and self-esteem has earned praise, as when Robin Givhan declared in the *New Yorker,*

> Obama's athletic arms are achievable—in between the kids' soccer practice, the executive suite, and the grocery store. Those arms represent personal time. They are evidence of a forty-five-year-old woman's refusal to give up every free moment in service to husband, kids, and all the nagging distractions that could have filled her days.... The arms imply vanity and power: two things that make many women uncomfortable and yet are fundamental to self-confidence.... Michelle Obama reminds women that they can make a place for vanity in their lives, and that, when they do, a little fashion can be supremely empowering.[38]

This elite endorsement has been matched by popular support. In 2010, the *Harvard Business Review* reported, "Following 189 public appearances between November 2008 and December 2009, Michelle Obama created $2.7 billion in cumulative abnormal returns—value over and above normal market variations—for fashion and retail companies associated with the clothes she wore." The study concluded that Obama was "a powerful force: a woman who, every time she leaves the White House, creates an average of $14 million in value for the companies lucky enough to be chosen by her."[39] Here is a clear instance of pocketbook voting, with the first lady exercising power through, rather than being victimized by, the market.

Summarizing the dilemmas that confront Michelle Obama in making her fashion choices and presenting herself, Jenée Desmond-Harris wrote,

> One might think having a black First Lady who is widely praised as sophisticated and stylish would represent a happy ending to the story of black female beauty and acceptance. Alas, our hair still simultaneously bonds and divides us. "There is not a hair choice you can make that is simple," says Melissa Harris Lacewell, an associate professor of politics and African American studies at Princeton. "Any choice carries tremendous personal and political valence."
>
> Not once when I've seen an image of our First Lady has it been lost on me that she is also a member. I don't see just an easy, bouncy do. I see the fruits of a time-consuming effort to convey a carefully calculated image. In the next-day ponytail, I see a familiar defeat.[40]

In negotiating with designers and the public, embodying her husband's priorities, insisting that her self-definition be respected, Michelle Obama has effected change—an African American woman is now widely accepted as a fashion icon. Yet she has also encountered criticism and objectification, as negative cultural myths have been reinvigorated and wielded against her. Like other first ladies whose descriptive representation has been deemed controversial, Obama has paid a price for her reforms. Precisely which aspects of Obama's first ladyship are rejected or honored throughout the 2012 campaign and into the future and by whom will reveal the extent to which her work as a representative has resulted in lasting change.

As first lady, Michelle Obama has not escaped the negative cultural myths that have dehumanized African American women for generations; the mammy, the hostile matriarch, the jezebel, the Sapphire are all constructions that have been wielded against her. Even so, her arts outreach, *Let's Move!,* and her status as a fashion icon deliver strong messages that harmonize with her husband's initiatives. She persuasively blurs the boundaries between popular and high culture, modeling how cultural capital and power can be widely shared. Her approval ratings remain high. She has, by these measures, experienced more success than failure as a symbolic, substantive, and descriptive representative throughout her first three years in the White House.

Why has Michelle Obama been so successful? What will her success mean for the first ladyship specifically, the presidency generally, and, most important, the public? The answers to the first of these queries lie in the strategic similarities that underlie her initiatives; answers to the second take the form of further questions and speculations. A first lady's influence, like a president's, cannot be measured readily and certainly not immediately. With that caveat firmly in place, some conclusions can be ventured about the reasons for and the consequences of her success.

Michelle Obama has, first, kept her agenda short and then has made a strong and consistent investment in her priorities. Whether it is her choice of events to host and address (the arts) or initiatives to establish and lead (*Let's Move!*) or fashion to present, the first lady's message has been consistently and repeatedly delivered: high culture and the power it brings are to be shared, advancing everyone's health and well-being. By articulating these priorities clearly and keeping "on message," she has avoided the criticisms directed at other activist Democratic first ladies, whose agendas have been stigmatized as too ambitious (Roosevelt), too lengthy (Carter), or too complex (Clinton).

Second, Michelle Obama has coordinated her work as a representative with that of the president. Though there are emerging reports of "East Wing"–"West Wing" tensions in 2012, the outward appearance has been one of constructive collaboration.[41] Issue agendas have been perceived as complementary, as when the *Let's Move!* campaign was launched in the midst of health care reform battles.[42] Throughout, the first lady has reinforced the major themes of the administration. The greatest exception to this pattern occurred during the 2010 midterm elections, when Michelle Obama engaged in significantly less campaigning than a number of her first lady predecessors.

Third, Michelle Obama has relied upon diverse media sources, communicating her messages to a wide cross section of the public. The kitchen garden (minus the first lady) was featured on an episode of *The Biggest Loser*; it was referenced in interviews Obama conducted with Martha Stewart and Mike Huckabee, as well as on soft news programs such as *Today*; it was covered by a series of print outlets. The *New York Times* described her appearance on *Iron Chef America* as

> the latest example of her willingness to get her message across to the public in ways few of her predecessors would have considered. . . .

Each episode of "Iron Chef America" is seen by almost 1.5 million viewers, and its core audience is 25- to 54-year-olds. . . .

[Iron Chef Mario] Batali, who might seem an unlikely spokesman for eating in moderation, has thrown himself into the project.

"What's exciting for us is this is the first time I can remember the White House taking an active interest in doing something about diet and health," he said. "They understand this kind of P.R."[43]

In the arts and in fashion, also, this first lady has used popular and targeted media campaigns to inform and mobilize the public. Eleanor Roosevelt, Jacqueline Kennedy, Lady Bird Johnson, Betty Ford, Rosalynn Carter, Nancy Reagan, Barbara Bush, and Laura Bush all conducted communications campaigns. Yet Obama's use of a wider array of media outlets connects the delivery of her message to its substance, providing further evidence of her commitment to democratic inclusivity.

Fourth, this first lady has exercised great control over her self-definition and self-presentation. In the early months of the administration, she limited her outreach to two days—sometimes two events—each week. She inaugurated her representation with the arts, an arena in which the first ladies have long been accepted as arbiters and leaders. Her substantive initiatives unfolded in stages, building momentum slowly. She set firm conditions for photo shoots. By being deliberate, incremental, and uncompromising, she dramatically altered popular perceptions of her character and person. A cover of *New York* magazine proclaimed "The Power of Michelle Obama: From terrorist fist-bumper to American icon in eight months flat."[44] She sustained popular approval in the months and years that followed, maintaining control and resisting the appeals of African American women, feminists, and liberal Democrats who wanted her to take more risks, embrace more controversial causes, and set more ambitious policy goals.

To assess the implications of Michelle Obama's first ladyship for the future, an observer must first acknowledge the heavy, routine constraints confronting the first African American first lady. These include the cultural myths and ideologies that have traditionally been ascribed to president's wives, rooted in nineteenth-century white, Anglo-Saxon, aristocratic conceptions of womanhood; they also include the cultural myths and ideologies that have been ascribed to African American women as justifications for their sexual and economic exploitation. And there is the absence of mentors or guides, obliging this president's wife to find her way alone. These were just some of the problems that Michelle Obama faced as a new first lady, after a protracted campaign in which she had been repeatedly attacked. On January 20, 2009, it must have seemed that Obama's only options were to define her work incrementally, weighing the responses to each innovation; to diversify her communication outlets, so that one could be used to check another; to coordinate her message closely with that of the president, in order to strengthen her credibility; and to keep her agenda short, focusing her efforts.

Three years later, the first lady's political and historical circumstances were very different. In the intervening years, she has built constructive relationships with an array of publics, many of them of great importance to her husband's reelection campaign. She has refined her skills as a communicator, learning the nuances of persuasion and mobilization. She has established her identity as an African American woman who is an empathetic mother and an engaged first lady. Though she has strong opponents, especially among conservatives, Michelle Obama is not seen as a polarizing figure. These are formidable resources, and it remains to be seen whether the first lady and the presidential campaign will choose to expend them on behalf of Barack Obama's reelection. Not all first ladies have been willing to campaign, and not all first ladies have been valued by their husbands' campaign organizations. Will the "East Wing" and the "West Wing" work together in campaigning, or will the tensions that have sometimes emerged in governing come to dominate? As the first lady's representation is centered less in collaborative processes of governing and more in the unfettered competition of campaigning, how will her communications and her relationships change? This question, in turn, leads to others about the persuasiveness of her outreach. Will Michelle Obama continue to be endorsed by whites and by people of color? Or will her campaigning change popular expectations, ideologies, and judgments? It may be that partisan and presidential politics will so strongly affect the first lady that she is more influenced by than influencing the elections. What will happen then, to the performance of representation by this first lady—and by the next?

Notes

    1. MaryAnne Borrelli, *The Politics of the President's Wife* (College Station: Texas A&M University Press, 2011).
    2. Barbara Welter, "The Cult of True Womanhood: 1820–1860," *Ameri-*

can Quarterly 18, no. 2 (Summer 1966): 151–74; Betty Boyd Caroli, *First Ladies,* expanded ed. (New York: Oxford University Press, 1995); Shawn J. Parry-Giles and Diane M. Blair, "The Rise of the Rhetorical First Lady: Politics, Gender Ideology, and Women's Voice, 1789–2002," *Rhetoric & Public Affairs* 5, no. 4 (Winter 2002): 565–600. See also Maurine H. Beasley, "Eleanor Roosevelt's Press Conferences: Case Study in Class, Gender, and Race," *Social Science Journal* 37, no. 4 (2002): 517–28.

3. Lewis L. Gould, "Modern First Ladies in Historical Perspective," *Presidential Studies Quarterly* 15, no. 3 (1985): 537–38; Jill Abraham Hummer, "First Ladies and American Women: Representation in the Modern Presidency," Ph.D. diss., University of Virginia, 2007.

4. Nikol G. Alexander-Floyd, "Theorizing Race and Gender in Black Studies: Reflections on Recent Examinations of Black Political Leadership," *International Journal of Africana Studies* 9, no. 1 (2003): 58; Georgia Duerst-Lahti, "'Seeing What Has Always Been': Opening Study of the Presidency," *PSOnline* (October 2008): 733–37; Kimberle Crenshaw, "Mapping the Margins: Intersectionality, Identity Politics, and Violence against Women of Color," *Stanford Law Review* 43, no. 6 (July 1990): 1241–99; Judith Butler, *Gender Trouble: Feminism and the Subversion of Identity* (New York: Routledge, 1990).

5. Julia Jordan-Zachary, "Black Womanhood and Social Welfare Policy: The Influence of Her Image on Policy Making," *Sage Race Relations Abstracts* 26, no. 3 (2001): 5–24; Patricia Hill Collins, *Black Feminist Thought: Knowledge, Consciousness, and the Politics of Empowerment,* 2nd ed. (New York: Routledge, 2000); K. Sue Jewell, *From Mammy to Miss America and Beyond: Cultural Images and the Shaping of US Social Policy* (New York: Routledge, 1993); Gina Athena Ulysse, "She Ain't Oprah, Angela, or Your Baby Mama: The Michelle O Enigma," *Meridians* 9, no. 1 (2009): 174–76.

6. See, for example, Caroli, *First Ladies*; Lewis L. Gould, ed., *American First Ladies: Their Lives and Their Legacy* (New York: Garland, 1996); Gil Troy, *Mr. and Mrs. President: From the Trumans to the Clintons,* 2nd ed. (Lawrence: University Press of Kansas, 2000); Myra Gutin, *The President's Partner: The First Lady in the Twentieth Century* (New York: Greenwood, 1989).

7. MaryAnne Borrelli, "The First Lady as Formal Advisor to the President: When East (Wing) Meets West (Wing)," *Women & Politics* 24, no. 1 (2002): 25–45.

8. Suzanne Dixon, "The Enduring Theme—Domineering Dowagers and Scheming Concubines," in *Stereotypes of Women in Power: Historical Perspectives and Revisionist Views,* ed. Barbara Galick, Suzanne Dixon, and Pauline Allen (New York: Greenwood, 1992), 209–26.

9. Sarah Baxter, "Michelle Paints Herself as the Queen of Arts," *Times* (London), May 24, 2009.

10. Michelle Obama, "Remarks by the First Lady at Classical Music Series Workshops," October 26, 2009.

11. Ibid.

12. Patricia Hill Collins, *Black Feminist Thought: Knowledge, Consciousness, and the Politics of Empowerment,* 2nd ed. (New York: Routledge, 2000), 99–119.

13. Michelle Obama, "Be Fearless," *Essence,* September 2010, 174–75.

14. "In Performance at the White House: Music of the Civil Rights Era," Rocky Mountain PBS, n.d.

15. Karen Travers, "Obamas Spotlight American Music at White House," ABC News, July 22, 2009, http://www.abcnews.go.com/print?id=8140337.

16. Antony Tommasini, "Classic Music Takes Center Stage at the White House," *New York Times,* November 5, 2009.

17. Thomas Brown, *JFK: History of an Image* (Bloomington: Indiana University Press, 1998), 14–15.

18. Jesse Lee, "Poetry, Music and Spoken Word," *The White House Blog,* May 12, 2009, http://www.whitehouse.gov/blog/Poetry-Music-and-Spoken-Word/.

19. "White House Kitchen Garden at the Intersection of Race, Politics, Food, and History," *Obama Foodorama* (blog), March 21, 2010, http://obamafoodorama .blogspot.com/2009/03/white-house-kitchen-garden-intersection.html. Michael C. Thornton notes that coverage of the Obama presidency by the black press, while giving consideration to race, is similar in its routine failure to analyze the deeper significance of this presidency for the descriptive and substantive representation of African American interests. Michael C. Thornton, "'He Loves Strong Women. They're His Kryptonite.': Michelle Obama, Gender, Race, and the Black Press," *Research in Race and Ethnic Relations* 16 (January 2010): 29–53.

20. Rachel L. Swarns and Jodi Kantor, "In First Lady's Roots, a Complex Path from Slavery," *New York Times,* October 8, 2009.

21. On the controversies associated with an African American woman as an ethicist, see Katie Geneva Cannon, *Katie's Cannon: Womanism and the Soul of the Black Community* (New York: Continuum, 1995).

22. Michelle Obama, "Remarks by the First Lady at the Opening of Fresh Farm Farmers' Market," September 17, 2009.

23. On black women, mothering, and domesticity, see Brittney Cooper, "Ain't I a Lady? Race Women, Michelle Obama, and the Ever-Expanding Democratic Imagination," *MELUS* 35, no. 4 (Winter 2010): 39–57; Deborah K. King, "Mom-in-Chief, Community Othermothering, and Michelle Obama: The First Lady of the People's House," *Research in Race and Ethnic Relations* 16 (January 2010): 77–123.

24. Melissa Harris-Lacewell, "The Notion: Michelle Obama, Mom-in-Chief," *Nation,* May 5, 2009. For a discussion of mothering as the premise and context for Michelle Obama's initiatives and first ladyship, see King, "Mom-in-Chief."

25. Lois Romano, "Michelle's Image: From Off-Putting to Spot-On," *Washington Post,* March 31, 2009. For polling results, see also "Michelle Obama's Favorability Ratings, NBC News / *The Wall Street Journal* Poll," *New York,* March 23, 2009.

26. See *Let's Move!* http://www.letsmove.gov/. See also Michelle Obama, "Remarks of First Lady Michelle Obama," February 9, 2010; Michelle Obama, "Remarks by First Lady Michelle Obama at a *Let's Move!* Event," March 3, 2010; Michelle Obama, "Remarks by the First Lady at Event on Surgeon General's Report," January 28, 2010; Michelle Obama, "Remarks by the First Lady at 'Let's Move' Action Plan Announcement with Cabinet Secretaries," May 11, 2010.

27. Michelle Obama, "First Lady Names Respected Pediatrician Judith S. Palfrey, M.D. to Lead *Let's Move!* Program," The White House, Office of the First Lady, September 2, 2011, http://www.whitehouse.gov/the-press-office/2011/09/02/first-lady-names-respected-pediatrician-judith-s-palfrey-md-lead-lets-mo.

28. Kate Zernike, "A Breast-Feeding Plan Mixes Partisan Reactions," *New York Times,* February 17, 2011.

29. Quoted in "During Radio Interview, Sarah Palin Attacks Michelle Obama & *Let's Move!*" *Obama Foodorama* (blog), November 24, 2010, http://obamafoodorama. blogspot.com/2010/11/during-radio-interview-sarah-palin.htm.

30. For a particularly insightful discussion of African diasporic theory, identity politics, and fashion theory, see Susan B. Kaiser and Sarah Rebolloso McCullough, "Entangling the Fashion Subject through the African Diaspora: From *Not* to *(K)not* in Fashion Theory," *Fashion Theory* 14, no. 3 (2010): 361–86.

31. Booth Moore, "Six Ways to Shape Fall," *Los Angeles Times,* February 22, 2009; Booth Moore, "Following Her Lead," *Los Angeles Times,* January 17, 2010.

32. On rejecting binary approaches to fashion, see Kaiser and McCullough, "Entangling the Fashion Subject."

33. Constance C. R. White, "Black Out: What Has Happened to the Black Models?" *Ebony,* September 2008, 98–100. See also Amy Larocca, "Michelle O," *New York,* February 2009.

34. Lisa Collins, "Economies of the Flesh: Representing the Black Female Body in Art," in *Skin Deep, Spirit Strong: The Black Female Body in American Culture,* ed. Kimberly Wallace-Sanders (Ann Arbor: University of Michigan Press, 2002), 113, 118.

35. Carla Williams, "Naked, Neutered, or Noble: The Black Female Body in America and the Problem of Photographic History," in *Skin Deep, Spirit Strong: The Black Female Body in American Culture,* ed. Kimberly Wallace-Sanders (Ann Arbor: University of Michigan Press, 2002), 196. On references to the jezebel cultural myth in coverage of Michelle Obama, see Carmen R. Lugo-Lugo and Mary K. Bloodsworth-Lugo, "Bare Biceps and American (In)security: Post-9/11 Constructions of Safe(ty), Threat, and the First Black First Lady," *Women's Studies Quarterly* 39, no. 1–2 (Spring/Summer 2011): 200–217.

36. Maureen Dowd, "Should Michelle Cover Up?" *New York Times,* March 8, 2009. Negative portrayals were also a staple throughout the presidential campaign. See Tiffany J. Shoop, "From Professionals to Potential First Ladies: How Newspapers Told the Stories of Cindy McCain and Michelle Obama," *Sex Roles* 63 (2010): 807–19.

37. On Obama's wearing American and foreign designers while traveling, see, for example Cathy Horyn, "Mrs. Obama's American-British Day," *New York Times,* May 24, 2011.

38. Robin Givhan, "Baring Arms," *New Yorker,* March 16, 2009. See also Liz Robbins, "She's Pumped. Your Turn," *New York Times,* March 19, 2009.

39. David Yernick, "How This First Lady Moves Markets," *Harvard Business Review,* August 2010, http://hbr.org/2010/11/vision-statement-how-this-first-lady-moves-markets/ar/1. Not all designers have been able to sustain this profit-generating momentum; Maria Pinto closed her boutique and her line in 2010. Susan Saulny, "Designer Has Fan at Top, but Too Few at the Stores," *New York Times,* May 1, 2010.

40. Jenée Desmond-Harris, "Why Michelle's Hair Matters," *Time,* September 7, 2009, http://www.time.com/time/magazine/article/0,9171,1919147,00.html. See also Bertram D. Ashe, "'Hair Drama' on the Cover of *Vibe* Magazine," *Race, Gender & Class* 8, no. 4 (2001): 64–77.

41. Jodi Kantor, "Michelle Obama and the Evolution of a First Lady," *New York Times,* January 6, 2012.

42. See Rachel L. Swarns, "First Lady in Control of Building Her Image," *New York Times,* April 25, 2009.

43. Marian Burros, "Someone's in the Kitchen with Michelle: The Secret Ingredient Is Politics," *New York Times,* November 4, 2009. See also Cristeta Comerford, "Of Iron Chefs and Healthy Eating," *The White House Blog,* January 8, 2010, http://www.whitehouse.gov/blog/2010/01/05/iron-chefs-and-healthy-eating.

44. *New York,* March 23, 2009.

12

THE FIRST FAMILY

Transforming the American Ideal

Melissa Buis Michaux

> The Obama family presents itself before the American eye at a time when
> there is no real typical American family. Gay couples uphold strong family
> values as do single-parent households. The problem with poster images is
> that posters sometimes cover walls of reality. Still, we like what we see in the
> Obama family. It tells us that our government and the economy might not
> be working well, but something still is. Cultural images don't pay the bills
> but for a moment, they can provide warmth during this winter in America.
> —E. Ethelbert Miller, January 25, 2009

As President Barack Obama's job approval numbers fell from the high six-
ties following his inauguration to the low forties just before the 2010 midterm
elections, his ratings on personal attributes remained high.[1] Even conservative
political opponents find it difficult to criticize Obama's personal life and commitment to family. In fact, despite the American electorate's delivering a devas-
tating rebuke to Obama and the Democratic Party in the midterm election, his
children's book, *Of Thee I Sing: A Letter to My Daughters,* which was released
a mere two weeks after the election, became the fastest-selling picture book in
Random House history.[2] And when Obama invoked the memory of the youngest
shooting victim in his Tucson memorial speech and encouraged all Americans
to be "worthy of those we have lost," his speech received accolades from across
the political spectrum.[3] Although politicians regularly speak of family values
and the importance of children, Obama's emphasis on family seems different.
He often suggests that being a parent changes his perspective: the phrase "as a
father" frequently peppers his speeches.[4] With Michelle Obama's self-designated

mantle of "mom-in-chief" and the numerous photos of the couple with their daughters, the Obamas project a self-conscious public family image.

The Obama family (and the massive media campaign focusing on it) has captured the public's imagination in remarkable ways, which arguably reflects an intensity that has not been witnessed since the Kennedys. During the heady days surrounding his election and inauguration, commentators across the globe noted how the "secure, affectionate Obama family [has become] a symbol of reassurance and hope."[5] Another observer wrote: "Here, in President-elect Obama, was a handsome and charismatic father exuding adoration for his daughters . . . [and] in Michelle Obama, was a brilliant wife and attentive mother, eyes trained on her children, protective and strong."[6] They have been described as "more human, more real, more accessible" than, presumably, past residents of the White House.[7] The Obamas are "just the first family next door," observed the *Washington Post*.[8] Michelle does not miss her daughters' soccer games or school events.[9] Family time and family dinners are sacred. Malia and Sasha have to make their own beds, set the table, and clean their plates.[10] As the *Independent* (London) reported, "There has never been the smallest suggestion that the Obamas are anything more or less than the close-knit and committed family they appear to be."[11] Simultaneously, they are just like ordinary Americans *and* they represent the American family ideal.

Given how unusual any presidential family must be, the Obamas' ability to look perfectly normal is an incredible public relations feat. As the first black family in the White House, the Obamas' image as the quintessential all-American family is all the more remarkable, perhaps offering a glimpse of the transformative power of his presidency for reflecting back to us who we are as Americans and who we want to be. And while her husband's political fortunes have waxed and waned, Michelle Obama's popularity remains high as the icon of motherhood, the keeper of the family. This is a significant repudiation of her critics during the campaign that worried she would be overly assertive and a liability to her husband.[12] These concerns played out in the wake of her comments that she had "never really been proud" of her country before her husband ran for office, followed by the *New Yorker*'s caricatured image of Michelle as an afro-coiffed angry black woman in fatigues fist-bumping her turban-wearing husband.[13] More than three years after their ascension to the White House, criticism of Michelle and her daughters has been mostly muted.[14] Even the popular Sarah Palin has found that she could not criticize the first lady without being rebuked by her usual supporters.[15]

The image or use of the first family as the ideal American family is not new.

George Washington's family portrait could be found in homes, needlework, and lithographs in varying renditions designed to emphasize Washington's role as the father of his country; over time, new versions appeared that reflected changes in cultural and political attitudes through the removal of the slave and the domestication of the military man.[16] As historian Scott Casper argues, the Washington family portrait "remained a familiar visual trope for seventy years, offering new cultural meanings in changing times."[17] The president's family was the site of disagreements between Federalists and Jeffersonian Republicans during the Adams administration; the Jeffersonians questioned Mrs. Adams's entertaining (extravagant and partisan) as well as the marriage of their son to a prominent British woman.[18] Critical attention to the way the first family lives (and spends money) has been political fodder ever since.[19] Still, presidents and their families enjoyed some privacy in their personal lives before the development of an increasingly ubiquitous media in the post–World War II years. For example, Franklin Delano Roosevelt's separated daughter and her two children lived in the White House on and off over twelve years without scandal or public disapprobation.[20]

The Cold War arguably marked a turning point when the constant need to prove the superiority of the American way of life over communism placed the politics of family on the world stage.[21] A reinvigorated domesticity with traditional gender roles in a nuclear family stood as a bulwark against the encroachments of socialist thinking that sought to level citizens and increase the role of the state. Although the ideological war was political, the battles were not just military and diplomatic but also deeply cultural. So, although the politics of family have been present in presidential politics since the founding, the post–World War II emphasis on the "traditional" family created a new standard by which to judge presidential families and family lifestyles. Kennedy's election in 1960, Elaine May successfully argues, did not just represent youthfulness as is often portrayed: "With his stylish wife at his side and his two small children, he seemed to embody the virtues of the American domestic ideal par excellence: the tough cold warrior who was also a warm family man."[22] The images of the Kennedy family reinforced the domestic ideal, with "Jackie's self-positioning as a supportive wife and doting mother, rather than as a politician."[23] As Robert Dallek argues, the Kennedys became "democratic royalty" through photographs of the family designed to elicit both admiration and "a renewed belief in America's capacity."[24]

However, as the Cold War consensus around the traditional family came under attack both by feminists and as a result of economic developments that brought more women into the workforce in the following decades, the first family became a locus of cultural debates over gender roles and sexuality, the work/family balance, and parenting styles. Betty Ford invited an outpouring of negative publicity when she candidly discussed her support for *Roe v. Wade* and told *60 Minutes* that if her daughter told her she was having an affair, she would not be surprised because she was like other young women her age.[25] Nevertheless, she enjoyed popular support and admiration for her outspoken views.[26] Although Rosalynn Carter's feminism was more muted in comparison, she, like Ford, actively supported the Equal Rights Amendment and rejected traditional gender roles for women.[27] While the Clintons participated in these cultural arguments at a time when women had already moved dramatically into the workforce, Hillary Clinton was both admired and subjected to censure because of her own open political ambitions. After Hillary Clinton was recorded on camera saying, "I suppose I could have stayed home and baked cookies and had teas, but what I decided to do was to fulfill my profession which I entered before my husband was in public life," she ignited a cultural firestorm and provided fodder for the Bush campaign.[28]

While former presidents and their families (especially their wives) have been subject to these cultural battles over appropriate gender roles and family expectations before, the Obama family navigates this terrain in a nation still profoundly divided by race. The ascendance of the first black family into the White House enhanced the idealization of the first family. As one African American wrote to the new first lady, "For all the history you and Barack have and will continue to make, one of the simplest and most treasured is your showing the world the face of black America; the beautiful, faithful, accomplished, nurturing, caring, loving, smart, strong, and moral face of black America. What a wonderful picture you have drawn for the world."[29] In "An Open Letter to Barack Obama," published just after his election, Pulitzer Prize–winning author Alice Walker wrote, "You have no idea, really, of how profound this moment is for us. Us being the black people of the Southern United States. . . . Seeing you take your rightful place, based solely on your wisdom, stamina and character, is a balm for the weary warriors of hope, previously only sung about."[30]

Few families have taken up residence in the White House with more scrutiny or higher expectations than the Obamas. Media coverage of the family has been extensive, from Malia and Sasha's first day of school to Michelle Obama's workout schedule. In contrast to Hillary Clinton's endorsement of a copresidency, Michelle Obama eschewed formal politics, asserting that her first duty was to get her children settled. In fact, her focus on family despite her Princeton and

Harvard degrees and history of high-profile jobs caused some to question the extent to which the Obamas were reinforcing a rather traditional understanding of family.

After all, "mom-in-chief" was a fairly limited role during the yearlong health care debate for a woman who was actually in the health care industry as a hospital administrator. As flattering as the *Vanity Fair* article comparing the fashions of Michelle Obama and Jackie Kennedy was no doubt intended to be, Jackie Kennedy was a silent (and often absent or suffering) spouse. The first lady's major focus beyond motherhood was an antiobesity initiative that began with gardening and exhorting us all to eat our vegetables. As one commentator satirized: "For the first time in her adult life, Michelle Obama is really proud of her cauliflower. . . . It is a domestic agenda—extremely domestic."[31] She did not sit in on cabinet meetings or confer with senators about finance reform. Even her staunchest supporters say they would like to see more of Michelle and her incredible talents and education applied more directly to policy. Is this just the image of the 1950s nuclear family updated in color? Has Michelle Obama succumbed to the demands of domesticity in taking on the role of first lady?

Certainly, the focus on family and Michelle Obama's mothering has helped to "insulate her from criticism" and "demystify her racial heritage."[32] But instead of thinking of the Obamas and their family presentation as a throwback to another era and a reifying of traditional gender roles, I argue that Michelle Obama and the first family are charting a new path forward for feminists, one that provides an alternative to the mommy wars, between traditional stay-at-home mothers and those in paid employment, and is more in the spirit of Joan Williams's call for a reconstructive feminism that seeks a restructuring of market and family work that can unite women (and men) across race and class boundaries.[33]

Reconstructive feminism addresses the gendered dynamics of market and family work that make balancing caregiving and paid employment difficult. The term "reconstructive feminism" is an explicit attempt to move beyond the stifled sameness-difference debate of second-wave feminism by rejecting both an "assimilationist feminism" focused on gaining access for women to male spheres and an "essentialist feminism" that insists sex differences necessarily have social consequences. Reconstructive feminism recognizes that even as women have made major advances in employment and educational attainment, the United States "is probably the worst industrialized country for women living traditionally feminine lives." Yet rejecting essentialism positions reconstructive feminism to be more inclusive in acknowledging the "racialization of gender bias," namely, the fact that gender dynamics differ by race. The aim of reconstructive feminism is not an analysis of identity but a call for new work and family structures that promote equality for all.[34]

The first lady's model of parenting and work recognizes that, like most Americans, she does not want to operate as an ideal worker who is expected to ignore family caregiving responsibilities. Reconstructive feminism acknowledges the norm of parental care without marginalizing caregivers.[35] Acknowledging the norm of parental care means understanding that most mothers and fathers do not want to be merely freed from child care responsibilities; they seek a reasonable balance of paid employment and time to care for families. From the perspective of reconstructive feminism, then, the antiobesity campaign is less about eating one's vegetables or about an individual effort to help oneself and more about setting up the conditions—social, educational, governmental—for all Americans to be better parents. In the process, the experiences of the first family—and especially the work of Michelle Obama—offers observers a new American family ideal, one that reaches beyond the traditional family model to embrace (1) shared parenting, (2) a more balanced but meaningful work life, and (3) greater connections with extended family and the wider community. Ultimately, this model seeks the necessary structural changes to support healthy families for more Americans across racial and class divides.

Parenting in the White House

When President George W. Bush opened up the White House to a private residential tour for the president-elect, Barack Obama reportedly wanted to see the bedrooms where his girls were going to sleep, leading Bush to comment: "Clearly, this guy is going to bring a great sense of family to the White House."[36] Whether it is telling the nation on election night that he promised his girls a dog if he forced them to move to Washington, DC, or explaining that being awarded the Nobel Peace Prize did not impress his daughters, Obama makes frequent mention of his children and their centrality in his life. When asked the best thing about being president, Obama answered: "I get to live above the office and see Michelle and the kids every day. I see them in the morning. We have dinner every night. It is the thing that sustains me."[37] Parenthood is not an abstraction or metaphor but a key component of the president's identity, both personal and public.

Of course, the constraints on presidential time are severe, but his involvement with his children while holding the most demanding of jobs speaks to a commitment to share in the parenting role. Reconstructive feminism recognizes that the old model of male breadwinner who has no child-caring or household responsibilities consigns men to a stressful, even potentially oppressive, life. Although masculinity has historically been tied to paycheck size, studies suggest that fathers are willing to take reduced salaries in exchange for more family time.[38] The president is not just a model of involved fatherhood; he is representative of his generation of men who are more likely to value caregiving in addition to breadwinning.

Not only did the Obamas bring their young daughters—aged seven and ten at the time of the president's inauguration—to the White House and the limelight, they brought a support system from Chicago that includes Michelle's mother, Marian Robinson, who also resides there and takes the children to school every morning. Exceedingly self-conscious about stereotypes of black families as dysfunctional, Michelle Obama walks a difficult line between being the ultimate role model and wanting her family to appear normal and ordinary. As Michelle herself noted: "Sometimes in the black community those stereotypes define us. Sometimes we start internalizing something that is not even true. . . . So maybe [our family] can be a reminder that all you need to do is look around your own community and you will see this same family in churches and in schools."[39] The addition of Robinson especially resonates with African American and working-class families whose ties to kinship care tend to be greater. As Williams explains, many working-class families feel that they can only access high-quality child care through family members; indeed, one study found that "40 percent of women in manufacturing used relatives for child care as opposed to only 8 percent of professional women."[40] Doing well by one's children frequently means honoring family work. If the former model for solving child care responsibilities rested on public subsidies for day care, reconstructive feminism emphasizes finding new ways to organize families to meet caregiving needs.

Dialogue about the very public Obama family should be situated in the context of both American desires for family and dramatic changes in the nuclear family over the last fifty years. Although Americans report greater acceptance of trends in cohabitation without marriage, there is still strong support for the two-parent model of child rearing.[41] The overall percentage of children living with both parents married to each other is 66 percent, according to the latest Annual Social and Economic Supplement data from the Census Bureau.[42] Only 35 percent of black children, however, live with both parents married to each other, and the numbers are even lower for children living under the poverty line (20 percent).[43] Even for married mothers of children under fifteen, only 26 percent fit the stereotype of the "traditional" stay-at-home model.[44] In the face of the decline of the traditional nuclear family, new family arrangements and nonmarriage patterns have formed. Further, the longer-term trends in single parenthood and cohabitation have been supplemented with a recession-inspired boost in multigenerational households, up to 16 percent by 2008, the highest level since before 1960.[45]

It is this reconstruction of the family and shared responsibilities that make the Obama image more than just a "neo-1950s vision of the first family as the embodiment of traditional American mom, dad and the kids' values."[46] Although it is true the Obamas have been careful to craft this family image, or "brand," as former White House social secretary Desiree Rogers rather indelicately referred to it, they both openly discuss the need for a family-work balance and sharing parental responsibility.[47] Michelle Obama has never presented herself as the demure wife whose only role is to support her husband; both have been forthcoming about her frustrations with Obama's absences while she worked professionally and cared for small children at home.[48] In a candid interview with a *Vanity Fair* reporter during the campaign, Michelle explained that although she had rather traditional notions of family when she came into the marriage, she soon realized that she needed more help than her husband's career would permit him to provide, so she "built that community myself."[49] The president conceded this point as well: he has not always met his share of parenting responsibilities.[50] Still, when he can, the president participates in parent-teacher conferences and even attends Saturday soccer games.[51]

In the White House, of course, Michelle has an entire staff at her disposal. Nevertheless, the girls still have their chores, and the president must walk the dog at night. Furthermore, she is careful to acknowledge the work of the household staff. When she first arrived, Michelle made a point of introducing East Wing aides to the household workers made up of plumbers, electricians, butlers, maids, and an entire kitchen crew, telling her closest aides that they would be judged on whether the aides know the names of household staff, not the other way around.[52]

Those critics who call for Michelle to take a more overt political role on public policy issues may be missing the significance of upholding the primacy of family for many African Americans. As Williams notes, "Because one of the key expressions of white supremacy, from slavery until today, is the assault on the black family, African Americans have often seen the preservation of family life as a deeply important political goal."[53] Because black women have historically engaged in market work at higher rates than white women, the traditional feminist emphasis on moving women into the paid labor force did not have the same impact or urgency for many women of color or working-class women. For Michelle, the first African American first lady, her ability to tend to her family and engage in meaningful work on her own terms are in themselves a political statement, exhibiting not a passive or muted acceptance of gendered roles but the work of a powerful woman. As black motherhood has all too often been blamed for social problems,[54] her image as the loving mother concerned with the well-being of her children is more than just a domestic agenda. As Patricia Hill Collins has explained, "Black women wanted to withdraw from the labor force, not to duplicate middle-class white women's cult of domesticity but, rather, to strengthen the political and economic position of their families."[55] Racial pride in the Obama family model is frequently expressed. One *Essence* magazine profile enthused: "Finally, the world could see what we've always known: Black families can be loving, intact, nurturing worlds that produce confident, talented children."[56] Parenting under such expectations and conditions is unavoidably political.

Redefining the Work of the First Lady

Early reports compared Michelle Obama to Jackie Kennedy. As Barack Obama supplanted John F. Kennedy as the youngest president ever elected to office and Kennedy also brought young children to the White House, such comparisons are understandable. Like Jackie Kennedy, Michelle quickly became a fashion icon for her grace and standing. As *Vanity Fair*'s feature article, "Jackie and Michelle: The White House Wardrobes"—which compares the two women, complete with side-by-side photographs—noted, "Comparisons between Michelle Obama and Jacqueline Kennedy are inevitable: two elegant women, catapulted into the national spotlight by their charismatic, ambitious husbands." Yet the comparison quickly falls short. On the campaign trail, one reporter found that Michelle's "pride visibly chafes at being asked to subsume her personality."[57] In interviews across a variety of media, Michelle Obama comes across as more confident, more sure and yet warm and inviting than the charming but private Jackie O. Michelle has helped remake the image and work of the first lady by leveraging her status as "mom-in-chief" and speaking candidly about race and racial inequality in an attempt to bring together disparate white and African American concerns. So while much of her work as first lady appears conventional on the surface, it reflects a careful blending of family care work with institutional change.

Citing her children as a priority, Michelle Obama tries to model a reconstructed work environment by reducing the hours and days she works in the East Wing, telling reporters that she never has meetings before her girls go to school, and she is careful to schedule her public events over just a few days a week.[58] And although the midterm election campaign schedule impinged on her carefully constructed home life and required her to travel more, she duly protected her family as well as her broader priorities. Somehow, she seems to manage a dizzying array of activities, notwithstanding her reduced work time. In addition to the myriad domestic duties of the first lady in hosting state dinners and various cultural events, the antiobesity initiative *Let's Move!* has an impressively far-reaching set of goals. While many parents sacrifice flexibility and time with children to achieve interesting work, Michelle Obama has used her celebrity "mom" status to further her work.

While Michelle's visits with military families have obvious political dividends, her outreach to the Washington, DC, community involves leveraging her status and power to reach out to the less visible—federal workers, African American youth, and those in need. Community outreach, of course, is a staple of any modern first lady's agenda. Michelle's predecessor Laura Bush was an advocate of community service and spent considerable time in local schools on literacy initiatives. However, community outreach has a long history for the first family, with a father who was a community organizer and a mother who worked professionally on getting more youth involved in community service. What is striking about Michelle's outreach to the DC community is the extent to which she thinks programmatically, leveraging resources to scale up the level of her initiatives so that the work is not just about her personal involvement.

Michelle's celebrity is probably her greatest resource, despite the growing budget and reach of the Office of the First Lady. Although not a constitutional office, the first lady now occupies the East Wing in the White House and has enjoyed a budget line since 1978. Michelle herself is not salaried, but she manages a staff of twenty-two, including a number of policy experts of her own.[59] In contrast, Eleanor Roosevelt had two secretaries set up in a spare bedroom.[60] Still, Michelle does not fit the model of "associate president" that characterized the work of Rosalynn Carter or Hillary Clinton.[61]

Despite the modern advantages of the current Office of the First Lady, Michelle spent considerable time getting out of her office and into the community. This meant that she visited thousands of federal workers during her first few months in office. Michelle Obama has hugged her way through a labyrinth of federal agencies. A visit to the Environmental Protection Agency drew over a thousand workers to see and hear Michelle speak.[62] At the Office of Personnel Management, Michelle shook hundreds of hands and thanked them for their work, leading one worker to comment that the first lady has "the interest of people at heart."[63] Her outreach to the enormous federal bureaucracy of normally invisible employees is new territory for a first lady and represents an interesting twist on the standard role of "goodwill emissary" from the administration.[64] Reaching out to the community of federal workers, Michelle has been credited with "boosting morale in agencies that have been maligned for years."[65]

More conventionally, Michelle has worked to inspire local youth to achieve more and believe in themselves. Less conventionally, Michelle has not hesitated to discuss racial and class dynamics, telling a group of Latino teens, "I want you all to see me and see Barack, and to have access to whatever we can offer."[66] While speaking to a group of African American students, she pushed the importance of hard work and taking school seriously, explaining that she did not grow up wealthy. Some of her classmates told her she "spoke like a white girl," but she refused to accept the idea that a good education and erudition is "white."[67] The message of self-help and resilience in the face of tough conditions is not radical but part of a long-standing African American tradition aimed at increasing expectations and expanding the realm of the possible through inspiration. Within the first six months of coming to Washington, Michelle had contact (through visits or invitations) with students from thirty area schools, and she established the first White House summer internship program for DC students.[68] Her work with area youth of color reflects her understanding of the legacies of racism. As Michelle explained to a reporter during the campaign, "You know, when you have cultures who feel like second-class citizens at some level . . . there's this natural feeling within the community that we're not good enough . . . we can't be as smart as or as prepared—and it's that internal struggle that is always the battle."[69] So she hugs people to make them feel comfortable, like her, and she tries to raise their aspirations. For Women's History Month, the first lady brought a group of accomplished women and role models to visit DC schools and then hosted those same women and one hundred students at the White House for dinner. The recruits included the first female four-star general and the first African American female astronaut.[70]

Broader community work follows a similar trajectory. Michelle helps to bring more resources into the community's food banks, domestic violence shelters, and other organizations. These community service endeavors are often tied to a White House event. For example, the Obamas held a service day before the inauguration. Together with Jill Biden, Michelle brought a group of political spouses to bag food at a local food bank.[71] She asked congressional families to stuff backpacks for the children of military personnel before coming to a White House barbeque.[72] And she has raised attention to local causes that cross class lines in their engagement with the community.

Recognizing that many working-class women and women of color felt alienated from the historical women's movement, reconstructive feminism seeks to address that divide in the service of all families. The multiracial identity of the Obama family became a symbol itself of the potential for racial reconciliation. It was during the campaign that Michelle learned details about her slave ancestors and spoke to reporters about this history. Census records show that Jim Robinson, who was a slave on Friendfield Plantation in Georgetown, South Carolina, likely fathered Michelle's great-grandfather Fraser Robinson.[73] Later, with the help of a genealogist and the *New York Times,* Michelle (and the public) learned that her great-great-great-grandmother on her mother's side was a slave who was impregnated by a white man two years before the Civil War began in rural Georgia.[74] After the Civil War, the former slave's "mulatto" son, Dolphus Shields, migrated to Birmingham, becoming a homeowner, businessman, and cofounder of a Baptist church.[75] Like many African Americans, Michelle did not know these details of her own ancestry. Now she can trace her direct ancestral line from slavery, revealing her own biracial past and reminding all Americans, as Edward Ball put it, "of how we have evolved and who we are. We are not separate tribes of Latinos and whites and blacks in America. We've all mingled, and we have done so for generations."[76] As first lady, she has not shied away from talking about race and the intersection of race with her endeavors to reach out to the broader Washington, DC, community and in launching her antiobesity efforts.

The Antiobesity Campaign

Although it is true that Michelle Obama has walked a careful line, largely within the context of more standard first lady parameters (good parenting and community outreach), she has also stretched and remade those boundaries. The *Let's Move!* antiobesity campaign is the perfect example of how she has extended the idea of first lady as "mom-in-chief."[77] The antiobesity initiative began as a conversation about personal responsibility and gardening but ends with school reform, food-chain reform, and urban renewal—the governmental and economic structures that make a healthy diet especially difficult for low-income people. And Michelle is always careful to place this work in the context of what this means for African Americans and Latinos who suffer from even higher rates of obesity.

The story Michelle Obama has now told many times over is that she was at the pediatrician's office when the doctor pointed out the girls' body mass index was inching up and that she ought to be careful about what they eat. Then she discovered corn syrup in everything and the high calories of fast food. Whether or not this story is apocryphal, the thrust of it is that she comes to her concern for the issue as most Americans would, through the eyes of her own parental experiences. She is an Ivy League–educated professional, but she introduces her audience to the topic through a story about her own family, and immediately every middle-class family who has battled the ubiquity of sugar and bad food in children's diets and school menus can relate to her mission. If Michelle's antiobesity initiative just ended there—exhorting parents to read labels and make their children eat more vegetables—it would not have the same powerful dynamic it has to link individual decisions to a broader system of choices structured by governments and corporations. In other words, this work enables parents to better understand that their own choices are structured and constrained by these broader forces.

The White House garden started by Michelle has served multiple purposes, not least of which is producing hundreds of pounds of vegetables each year for the first family, White House guests, and the homeless who come to Miriam's Kitchen for food and help.[78] The garden involved a local fifth-grade class that was instrumental in the first planting; since that time, Michelle has used the garden to invite schoolchildren to learn about gardening and vegetables, encourage community gardens, and generally popularize the idea of eating fresh and local foods. She's taken this message to *Sesame Street* and even hosted an *Iron Chef* cook-off using ingredients found in the White House garden.[79] Her efforts have been credited with boosting seed sales and getting more people to take up home gardens. The success of the garden initiative laid the foundation for *Let's Move!*, a broad-based initiative aimed at reducing childhood obesity through healthier eating and exercise.[80]

In encouraging healthy eating and exercise, however, Michelle has turned to the barriers to both, especially for inner-city minority communities. She notes that the high rates of obesity in African American and Hispanic communities leads to "conversations about accessibility and affordability."[81] Twenty-three million Americans live in low-income rural and urban areas where fresh food is not easily available.[82] Michelle has commented on the fact that many of these "'food deserts' are in underserved communities."[83] So she not only attends the garden but also was at the opening of a Fresh Grocer in a black Philadelphia neighborhood, highlighting the fact that there had not been a full-service grocery store there in more than ten years.[84] Many low-income neighborhoods rely on inexpensive fast food, which explains the counterintuitive link between food insecurity and obesity.[85] A conversation about exercise turns to the importance of having safe neighborhoods and zoning regulations. As Michelle explains, "Urban sprawl and fears about safety often mean the only walking [many people] do is out their front door to a bus or a car."[86] The initiative moves from the need to reduce sugary drinks in kids' diets to tackling a panoply of urban problems.

What began as a campaign emphasizing vegetables has expanded to include critiques not just of parenting or school nutrition but also of inequality and the relationship between inequality and the entire food distribution system. As Andra Gillespie explains, "A black person might see it as a racial justice issue, and somebody interested in class could see it from a poverty perspective, but the suburban white housewife with chubby kids can identify with it as well. It's about [Obama] being an everywoman, though she has a different sensibility and thinks about cities and issues through an urban perspective."[87] It is really an approach informed by reconstructive feminism's push to speak to intersecting interests across race and class.

Criticisms of the program have surfaced. On the left, critics complain that despite the talk of healthy eating and organic vegetables, the Obama administration has followed a very conventional agricultural policy overall that primarily subsidizes big agriculture.[88] Some conservative critics have argued that the antiobesity campaign is yet another major governmental takeover. Most notably, Sarah Palin has called *Let's Move!* an example of "the nanny state run amok" and blasted Michelle for trying to ban desserts.[89] Still, then-potential presidential rival Mike Huckabee defended the program and Michelle's role, stating: "I still think her approach is the right one. I do not think that she is out there advocating that the government take over our dinner plates. In fact, she has not. She has been criticized unfairly by a lot of my fellow conservatives. I think it is out of a reflex rather than out of a thoughtful expression."[90]

It remains to be seen whether Michelle will continue to be able to stand above the political fray as "mom-in-chief" as the comprehensive nature of the antiobesity campaign unfolds. Already a few who see it as more transformative seek to politicize her work and bring her more fully into the fold of contestations with the Obama administration writ large. Nevertheless, her work to date suggests that there is political room for overcoming the left-right, social responsibility versus individual responsibility dualism that animates so much of American social policy.

Reconstructive feminism is a model for overcoming traditional divides across race and class in feminist political action. Michelle Obama is modeling this reconstructive feminism to expand the conversation to not just work-family balance or healthy eating but asking who our neighbors are and what makes up our community. She presents us with a holistic vision that has the capacity to transcend the personal debate over responsibility versus government obligation. This is extraordinarily delicate work, as it has long been true that the "exercise of power [in the office of the first lady] is largely dependent upon the extent to which [first ladies] conform to formulations of the 'ideal woman' of their generation."[91] Key to her popularity has been the careful manner in which she has operated, which is not traditionally recognized as political at all—through parenting, community outreach, and gardening. But in the context of the first African American first family, in a community marked by widespread inequality, during a time of major corporate power, her marshaling of resources and frank discussions of race are profoundly important (and political) work.

Notes

Epigraph is from "An Image of Obama Family," NPR, January 25, 2009, http://www.npr.org/templates/story/story.php?storyId=99851361.

1. Obama continued to score very high on "warm and friendly," "trustworthy," and "cares about people like me." See "Obama's Job Ratings, Personal Image Unchanged by Recent Washington Events," Pew Research Center for People and the Press, January 13, 2011, http://people-press.org/files/legacy-pdf/693.pdf.

2. Caroline May, "Obama's *Of Thee I Sing* Children's Book an Ode to Diversity—and Sitting Bull, Jane Addams, and Cesar Chavez," *Daily Caller,* November 30, 2010, http://dailycaller.com/2010/11/30/obamas-of-thee-i-sing-childrens-book-an-ode-to-diversity-and-sitting-bull-jane-addams-and-cesar-chavez/.

3. Barack Obama, Remarks by the President at a Memorial Service for the Victims of the Shooting in Tucson, Arizona, January 12, 2011, http://www.whitehouse.gov/the-press-office/011/01/12/remarks-president-barack-obama-memorial-service-victims-shooting-tucson.

4. In an analysis of the party platforms and candidate speeches, Laurel Elder and Steven Greene found that "2008 represents an all-time high for Democrats' use of the terms 'family' and 'father.'" See Elder and Greene, "The Politics of Parenthood and the 2008 Electoral Campaign: The Use of Parent and Family Themes in Party

Appeals and Election Coverage," paper presented at the Midwest Political Science Association Annual Meeting, Chicago, 2009.

5. Olivia Ward, "Citizens Look to Obama to Restore Pride," *Toronto Star,* January 20, 2009.

6. Diane McKinney-Whetstone, "Part I: This Is Our Time: The First Family," *Essence,* January 2009, 67–70.

7. "The Obamas? Oh, They're Just the First Family Next Door," *Washington Post,* November 9, 2009.

8. Ibid.

9. Throughout this chapter, I make frequent references to the first lady as "Michelle," reflecting the informality of Michelle Obama and her presentation to the public. While her husband presented himself before formal quasi-presidential trappings—columns, podiums, and flags—during the campaign, her approach was decidedly different. She sought to reinforce the message that she is "just like everyone else."

10. Mary L. Kahl, "First Lady Michelle Obama: Advocate for Strong Families," *Communication and Critical/Cultural Studies* 6, no. 3 (2009): 317.

11. Deborah Orr, "A Sure Sign of Change: A Young Family Is in the White House," *Independent* (London), November 8, 2008.

12. Philip Delves Broughton, "Does Michelle Deserve to Be First Lady?" *Daily Mail,* August 27, 2008.

13. Barry Blitt, "The Politics of Fear" (illus.), *New Yorker,* July 21, 2008.

14. Rush Limbaugh is a significant exception to this general pattern. He has ridiculed her antiobesity campaign and her body shape and size. See "Rush Limbaugh Criticizes First Lady Michelle Obama's Weight, Nutritional Campaign," *Los Angeles Times,* February 22, 2011.

15. Dave Cook, "Mike Huckabee Hits Fellow Conservatives for Criticizing Michelle Obama," *Christian Science Monitor,* February 23, 2011.

16. Scott Casper, "First First Family: Seventy Years with Edward Savage's 'The Washington Family,'" *Imprint: Journal of the American Historical Print Collectors Society* 24 (1999): 2–15.

17. Ibid., 14.

18. Carl Sferrazza Anthony, *America's First Families: An Inside View of 200 Years of Private Life in the White House* (New York: Simon and Schuster, 2000).

19. Ibid., 65–66.

20. See Curtis Roosevelt, *Too Close to the Sun: Growing Up in the Shadow of My Grandparents, Franklin and Eleanor* (New York: Public Affairs, 2009).

21. Elaine Tyler May, *Homeward Bound: American Families in the Cold War Era* (New York: Basic Books, 2008).

22. Ibid., 218.

23. Richard Avedon and Shannon Thomas Perich, *The Kennedys: Portrait of a Family* (New York: Collins Design, 2007), 231.

24. Robert Dallek, foreword to Avedon and Perich, *The Kennedys*, 13.

25. Jeffrey Ashley, *Betty Ford: A Symbol of Strength* (Hauppauge, NY: Nova Science, 2003), 102–3.

26. Betty Boyd Caroli, *First Ladies: From Martha Washington to Michelle Obama* (Oxford: Oxford University Press, 2010).

27. Ibid., 271, 275–77.

28. "Making Hillary Clinton an Issue," *Nightline* transcripts, March 26, 1992, http://www.pbs.org/wgbh/pages/frontline/shows/clinton/etc/03261992.html; Margaret Carlson and Priscilla Painton, "All Eyes on Hillary," *Time*, September 14, 1992; Deborah Rhode, "Media Images, Feminist Issues," *Signs* 20, no. 3 (Spring 1995): 698.

29. Lori Jones, in *Go, Tell Michelle: African American Women Write to the New First Lady*, ed. Barbara A. Seals Nevergold and Peggy Brooks-Bertram (Albany, NY: Excelsior Editions, 2009), 24.

30. Alice Walker, "An Open Letter to Barack Obama: Alice Walker on Expectations, Responsibilities and a New Reality That Is Almost More Than the Heart Can Bear," *The Root*, November 5, 2008, http://www.theroot.com/views/open-letter-barack-obama.

31. Dana Milbank, "Michelle Obama's Garden-Variety Agenda," *Washington Post*, April 1, 2010.

32. Kahl, "First Lady," 317.

33. Joan Williams, *Unbending Gender: Why Work and Family Conflict and What to Do about It* (Oxford: Oxford University Press, 2000).

34. Joan C. Williams, "Reconstructive Feminism: Changing the Way We Talk about Gender and Work Thirty Years after the Pregnancy Discrimination Act," *Yale Journal of Law and Feminism* 21 (2009): 79–116, quotations at 98, 114.

35. Ibid.

36. "Obama Most Concerned about Kids' Bedrooms," *New Zealand Herald*, November 12, 2008.

37. Nancy Gibbs and Michael Scherer, "The Meaning of Michelle Obama," *Time*, May 21, 2009, http://www.time.com/time/politics/article/0,8599,1900067,00.html.

38. Williams, "Reconstructive Feminism," 59.

39. Sarah Baxter, "Michelle Paints Herself as the Queen of Arts," *Sunday Times* (London), May 24, 2009.

40. Williams, "Reconstructive Feminism," 157.

41. Rich Morin, "The Public Renders a Split Verdict on Changes in the Family Structure," Pew Research Center Social and Demographic Trends, February 16, 2011, http://pewsocialtrends.org/2011/02/16/the-public-renders-a-split-verdict-on-changes-in-family-structure/#prc_jump.

42. Author calculations based upon "Living Arrangements of Children under 18 Years," U.S. Census Bureau (2010), http://www.census.gov/apsd/techdoc/cps/cpsmar10.pdf.

43. Ibid.

44. Rose M. Kreider and Diana B. Elliott, "Historical Changes in Stay-at-Home Mothers: 1969–2009," paper presented at the Annual Meeting of the American Sociological Association, Atlanta, GA, 2010.

45. "The Return of the Multi-Generational Family Household," Pew Research Center Publications, March 18, 2010, http://pewresearch.org/pubs/1528/multi-generational-family-household?src=prc-latest&proj=peoplepress.

46. Kathleen Hennessey, "He's Just Dad. Oh, and Leader of the Free World: The Obamas' Carefully Crafted Image of Ordinariness May Be Working," *Los Angeles Times*, January 25, 2010.

47. Baxter, "Michelle Paints Herself."

48. See Barack Obama, *The Audacity of Hope: Thoughts on Reclaiming the American Dream* (New York: Crown, 2006); Leslie Bennetts, "First Lady in Waiting," *Vanity Fair*, December 27, 2007, http://www.vanityfair.com/politics/features/2007/12/michelle_obama200712.

49. Quoted in Bennetts, "First Lady in Waiting," 2007.

50. Mimi Hall and Maria Puente, "With Cultural 'Flair,' Obamas Updating First Family's Image," *USA Today*, November 3, 2009.

51. Ibid.

52. Quoted in Gibbs and Scherer, "Meaning of Michelle."

53. Williams, "Reconstructive Feminism," 165.

54. Verna Williams, "The First (Black) Lady," *Denver University Law Review* 86 (2008): 842.

55. Quoted in Williams, "Reconstructive Feminism," 166.

56. McKinney-Whetstone, "This Is Our Time."

57. Laura Collins, "The Other Obama," *New Yorker*, March 10, 2008, http://www.newyorker.com/reporting/2008/03/10/080310fa_fact_collins.

58. Gibbs and Scherer, "Meaning of Michelle."

59. Executive Office of the President, "Annual Report to Congress on White House Office Staff," July 1, 2009, http://www.whitehouse.gov/assets/documents/July1Report-Draft12.pdf.

60. Robert P. Watson, *The Presidents' Wives: Reassessing the Office of First Lady* (Boulder, CO: Lynne Rienner, 2000).

61. Robert P. Watson, "The First Lady Reconsidered: Presidential Partner and Political Institution," *Presidential Studies Quarterly* 27, no. 4 (1997): 805–18.

62. Linda Feldman, "Michelle Obama Rocks the Bureaucracy with Her Star Quality," *Christian Science Monitor*, March 5, 2009.

63. Richard Leiby, "First Lady's Job? Slowly, It's Hers to Define," *Washington Post*, 20 February 2009.

64. Ibid.

65. Feldman, "Michelle Obama Rocks."

66. Quoted in Leiby, "First Lady's Job."

67. Robin Givhan, "First Lady Reaps What She Sowed: The Mom in Chief Changed How Some Americans Saw Her and How Some American Kids Saw Themselves," *Washington Post*, January 17, 2010.

68. Lois Romano, "A First Lady Who Demands Substance," *Washington Post*, June 25, 2009.

69. Quoted in Collins, "The Other Obama."

70. Gibbs and Scherer, "Meaning of Michelle."

71. Leiby, "First Lady's Job."

72. Romano, "A First Lady."

73. Shailagh Murray, "A Family Tree Rooted in American Soil: Michelle Obama Learns about Her Slave Ancestors, Herself and Her Country," *Washington Post*, October 2, 2008.

74. Rachel L. Swarns and Jodi Kantor, "In First Lady's Roots, a Complex Path from Slavery," *New York Times*, October 8, 2009.

75. Ibid.

76. Quoted in ibid.

77. See http://www.letsmove.gov/.

78. Givhan, "First Lady Reaps."

79. Darlene Superville, "Michelle Obama's White House Garden Is a Growing Success," *Christian Science Monitor*, January 12, 2010.

80. See "Learn the Facts," http://www.letsmove.gov/learn-facts/epidemic-childhood-obesity.

81. Quoted in Nia-Malika Henderson, "Michelle: No Longer a 'Caricature,'" *Politico*, March 4, 2010, http://www.politico.com/news/stories/0310/33883.html.

82. Tom Vilsack, "USDA's Food Atlas Highlights Challenges and Opportunities to Bring Healthy Options to American Families," *Let's Move!*, http://www.letsmove.gov/blog/2011/01/21/usdas-food-atlas-highlights-challenges-and-opportunities-bring-healthy-options-ameri.

83. Quoted in Henderson, "No Longer."

84. Nia-Malika Henderson, "Michelle Speaks Frankly about Race," *Politico*, February 19, 2010, http://www.politico.com/news/stories/0210/33162.html.

85. White House Task Force on Childhood Obesity, "Report to the President: Solving the Problem of Childhood Obesity in a Generation," http://www.letsmove.gov/pdf/TaskForce_on_Childhood_Obesity_May2010_FullReport.pdf.

86. Quoted in Henderson, "Michelle Speaks Frankly."

87. Ibid.

88. Mark Crispin Miller, "Michelle Obama's Garden Is a Propaganda Masterpiece," *News from Underground*, January 30, 2011, http://markcrispinmiller.com/2011/01/michelle-obamas-garden-is-a-propaganda-masterpiece/; Christopher Beam, "Organic Panic: Michelle Obama's Garden and Its Discontent," *Slate*,

June 4, 2009, http://www.slate.com/articles/news_and_politics/politics/2009/06/
organic_panic.html.

89. Eddie Gehman Kohan, "Michelle Obama Talks Sarah Palin, Taco Bell, and
the Coercive Power of Consumers," *Obama Foodorama blog,* January 28, 2011,
http://obamafoodorama.blogspot.com/2011/01/michelle-obama-talks-sarah-palin-
taco.html.

90. Lynn Sweet, "Mike Huckabee Defends Michelle Obama after Palin, Bachmann, Limbaugh Attacks," *Chicago Sun-Times,* February 24, 2011.

91. Kahl, "First Lady," 316.

13

THE PRESIDENTIAL PARTNERSHIP

A Gender Seesaw

Karen S. Hoffman

Throughout history presidents have relied on their spouses in the White House. In jobs as diverse as hostess, political advisor, campaigner, and fund-raiser, first ladies have worked hard to help their husbands. Karlyn Kohrs Campbell describes the presidency as a two-person career that "requires their cooperative efforts if it is to be successful."[1] Not surprisingly, virtually every president has said that he could not have succeeded without his wife. As the possibility of a female president has become greater, discussion of the partnership between the president and a first gentleman has occurred. During Hillary Clinton's campaign for the 2008 Democratic nomination, one journalist noted, "The Clintons have committed themselves now to campaigning as a couple." He went on to say that if Hillary were elected president, Bill "would be a force in American government."[2] Similar discussions were prompted by speculation about Sarah Palin's possible run for the presidency in 2012. Examining her role as the governor of Alaska for clues to her style as chief executive, some found that Todd Palin was a significant partner in the governorship, implying that should Sarah Palin ever become president, he would be an active first gentleman. One headline announced, "First Dude Todd Palin Heavily Involved in Governing Alaska."[3]

That we are talking about a partnership between a female president and male spouse suggests that the idea of female political leadership is gaining more legitimacy. The 2008 candidacies of Hillary Clinton and Sarah Palin—not to mention Nancy Pelosi's election as Speaker of the House in 2007—were "major breakthroughs."[4] The 2012 Republican nominating process featured discussion of Sarah Palin as a serious presidential contender as well as the entrance of

Representative Michele Bachmann into the race. Despite these positive steps, the persistent challenges facing women in the institution of the presidency are sobering. In a discussion of gender and the presidency Georgia Duerst-Lahti argued that media discussion of presidential aspirants for the 2008 election demonstrates "the glacial pace of progress in opening this space for women."[5] Another scholar concluded that despite the advances made by women in the 2008 presidential election, media coverage of both Clinton and Palin "indicates a retreat to gender stereotypes and blatant sexism not generally seen in the past six years."[6] Yet another examination of Clinton's and Palin's candidacies notes that the challenges of gender are "uniquely amplified in candidacies for the highest executive offices—the presidency and vice presidency."[7] Even now that a partnership between a female president and a male spouse is more a question of *when* than *if,* we still perceive the role of first spouse to be extremely gendered and defined strictly in terms of a male presidential role.[8] The first spouse is firmly established in American culture as the partner of the president, an important position, but strictly a feminine supporting character whose talents and accomplishments are expected to complement, not duplicate or overshadow, those of the president.[9]

The entrenched belief in a male president supported by a female spouse is evident in the way popular culture continues to masculinize the presidency and feminize the first spouse. Despite the increasing appearance of female political leaders in television and movies, to a great extent popular culture confirms the gendered boundaries of the first spouse's role. *The West Wing, Commander in Chief,* and *24* were all television shows that included women as part of the presidential partnership, either as president or first lady. On *The West Wing,* the first lady was forced to adjust and subordinate her own goals to the president's. The relationship between the female president and her husband on the *Commander in Chief* similarly reinforced the gendered nature of the partnership. The president was attributed masculine characteristics to demonstrate her fitness for the office, while her husband was viewed in a feminine light and became a national joke. A comparison of *Commander in Chief* with a 1964 movie featuring a female president, *Kisses for my President,* demonstrates the absence of change over time in society's gendered understanding of the first couple. Finally, the female presidents in both *Commander in Chief* and *24* approved the use of violence in order to highlight the office's masculinity. Ultimately, this view of the presidential partnership in popular culture is borne out in political discourse as society struggles to apply the traditional gender standards to female presidential candidates and their spouses, such as the Clintons and Palins, as well as past and present female chief executives, such as Margaret Thatcher and Angela Merkel. While scholars move to distinguish the biological differences of "sex" from "gender" as an analytical strategy to shed light on the socially constructed elements of both masculinity and femininity, cultural attitudes toward women in the White House remain wedded to the view that women and femininity are one and the same.[10]

A Growing Role for Spouses

We seem to have come a long way from the early days of first lady as chief hostess. The first lady's activities grew far beyond those duties. Robert P. Watson summarizes some of the tasks that have been part of the first spouse role: "So too have these wives edited presidential speeches, hit the campaign trail, testified before Congress, lobbied on behalf of legislation, chaired task forces, traveled internationally as unofficial presidential envoys, and championed important social causes."[11] While some first ladies are remembered—sometimes fondly, sometimes not—for their active political partnership with the president (Abigail Adams, Dolley Madison, Edith Wilson, Eleanor Roosevelt, and Hillary Clinton, for example), many others were more involved than we generally remember.[12] Take Florence Harding, for instance. She was a career woman who brought her experience in managing an Ohio newspaper to the White House. She helped the president choose cabinet nominees, edited the inaugural address, and reviewed the budget of the Veteran's Bureau during her time there.[13] Still, although she was clearly talented and politically knowledgeable, her actions served to support the president, and she did not discuss politics in public. She spoke in favor of career women but said that "if the career is the husband's the wife can merge her own with it."[14] Warren Harding's presidency was his career; her career was to help his succeed.

Although the first lady has become increasingly involved in political issues, there are two significant characteristics of this involvement. To begin with, first ladies still tend to be involved in issues that are associated with women's roles.[15] These are often family issues, such as education, housing, equal pay, children, and family values in general.[16] Michelle Obama, for instance, has been a spokesperson against childhood obesity and has been involved in encouraging community service and supporting military families. Laura Bush promoted literacy (fittingly, given her degree in library science). Even Hillary Clinton's controversial policy involvement was in health care. Second, everything the first lady does implicitly supports the president's agenda and is designed to boost his popularity. Those who have used the first ladyship as a political platform have hurt the president's image. The idea of a copresidency, "two for the price of one," as the Clinton campaign put it early in the campaign of 1992, was not popular. Betty Ford is another example. She caused an uproar when she spoke about premarital sex and marijuana on *60 Minutes* in 1975.[17] She did not publicly approve of those behaviors but noted that in the 1970s many children, including her own, had possibly engaged in both. The president's approval rating dropped seventeen points in the two weeks after the broadcast.[18] The firestorms caused by political activism in nontraditional first ladies prove the rule. Even as the role of first spouse has expanded beyond hostess duties, the expectations remain severely constrained: "The national image of the First Spouse is still that of a quiet, coiffed wife beaming adoringly at her husband."[19]

The Masculine Nature of the Presidency

The seeming contradiction between the increased duties and activism of the first lady and the strict limits on the role can be explained best by the steadfastly masculine conception of the presidency. Many scholars have studied the presidency as an inherently masculine institution.[20] Beginning with George Washington, "the father of our country," the maleness of the presidency has been firmly established and continually confirmed and reinforced. Society's understanding of the presidency is critically important, given the centrality of the office to an understanding of our identity as a nation. The president has always been a symbolic figure representing the entire country. We look at the president in order to see who we are: "The presidency is an important site where our national expectations of gender are performed and ritualized."[21] Thus there is a lot at stake. Any change in a definition of the presidency would amount to a seismic shift in our national identity. Our national identity has evolved over time, struggling to accommodate and address an increasingly heterogeneous and racially diverse society, but one element that has not changed is the idea that the national leader is a man with "manly" characteristics.[22]

The first spouse plays an important role in confirming the masculine identity of the president, which is reflected in norms governing the position. Judith Butler suggests that society has constructed gender as a binary system. Feminine and masculine are opposites. People are either one or the other. Traits belong in one category or the other. According to this understanding, woman is the other of man.[23] If the president is considered masculine, the first spouse needs to have the opposite qualities. Georgia Duerst-Lahti concurs, calling the phenomenon gender dualism: "Both biological sex and gender has been constructed as dualism with the sexes and gender being opposites."[24]

One scholar identifies five basic masculine traits—physical strength and control, work and occupational achievement, patriarchy, outdoorsmanship, and heterosexuality.[25] According to this list, the president's ideal partner would be someone who is weaker than the president, values the president's career achievements above his or her own, values the role of taking care of the president's children in the home, and by his or her very existence as spouse attests to the president's heterosexuality. Not coincidentally, this definition aptly captures important elements of the existing first spouse role. It is ironic that, viewed from this perspective, the role of the first spouse as a partner is revealed as more, not less, important. In fact, it demonstrates the absolutely vital part that first spouses play in maintaining the president's position. It is not simply that they are expected to exhibit feminine characteristics. Rather, the spouse is supposed to confirm the masculine nature of the president by being the other.[26] Since the president is considered masculine, first ladies should be feminine (explaining why we persist in thinking about presidential spouses as wives), but it is not simply a matter of first ladies following gender norms. In fact, one cannot really define the first spouse as an individual at all. As the president's partner he or she is defined in opposition to the other role. This helps to explain how the role of first spouse has not followed advances in female leadership in other contexts. Women in positions such as the CEO of a Fortune 500 company or even the Speaker of the House of Representatives or a cabinet secretary must still deal with gender stereotypes, but they are not partners in an institution that requires them to be the very opposite of the president. Several scholars have noted the disconnect between progress for women in society generally and the status of first spouses. Lewis Gould argues that attitudes about first ladies "are a lagging indicator about where women are in the country."[27] The factor setting first spouses apart from other women is their critical role in a masculine institution.

One journalist wrote that Laura Bush was the ideal political spouse: "She makes her husband look good and doesn't offend anyone. She is photogenic, she's intelligent, she hasn't made any major boo-boos and seems to have a certain warmth about her."[28] Although this description omits the gender of "the ideal political spouse," it clearly refers to "female" characteristics and demonstrates how the feminine spouse is defined according to how much she helps the president. An interesting example of this occurred in 1952 when Vice President Richard Nixon gave his "Checkers" speech. During the television broadcast the camera focused primarily on Nixon sitting at a desk in his office, but occasionally Nixon referred to his wife's exemplary character as his partner, and the camera moved to show Pat Nixon sitting demurely in a corner by herself. It was rather odd; there was no reason for Pat to be sitting there. She did not speak and the camera did not even show her most of the time. It makes sense, however, given a binary understanding of gender. She was the other; her silent and devoted presence made visible her husband's masculine leadership qualities.

A Gendered Partnership in Popular Culture

One strategy for examining the role of the first spouse as a political partner to the president is to look at the partnership as it is portrayed in popular media. Popular culture reveals important beliefs in society, partly because it is so widely accessible.[29] Instead of reflecting an elite view of an issue, popular culture reflects the much broader understanding of a mass public. Since "television is decidedly a medium that must by definition express dominant cultural expressions to be successful," we have good reason to take seriously the themes found there.[30]

On the surface, a review of television shows and movies about strong female leadership suggests that the public is increasingly comfortable with women in these positions. There are numerous shows and movies that portray women as strong leaders, in both political positions and other fields. The following are just a few examples. The press secretary on *The West Wing* was the "tough as nails" C. J. Cregg (played by Allison Janney). The show *NCIS* included a female agent, Ziva David (played by Cote de Pablo), who was acknowledged to be tougher and physically stronger than most men on the show. Kyra Sedgwick played criminal investigator Brenda Leigh Johnson on *The Closer*. A "steel magnolia" with a southern accent, Brenda was known for her ability to obtain a confession from any suspect with her tough methods.

The West Wing, Commander in Chief, and *24* shed the most light on expectations of the presidential couple. *The West Wing* addressed the role of first lady, while *Commander in Chief* and *24* included female presidents. *The West Wing* was likely the most popular political drama series on television. Spanning seven seasons, the show followed President Jed Bartlet (Martin Sheen) and his staff as he governed through two terms of office. The president's wife was a prominent physician, Dr. Abigail Bartlet, played by Stockard Channing. Given the first lady's education and accomplishments, it seemed as though the show was going to push the boundaries of the role and demonstrate broader possibilities than the traditional focus on home and family issues. In the end, it failed to do so and ultimately confirmed the image of the first lady as a partner whose responsibility was to help the president succeed by taking care of the family and supporting the president. Abigail did not become politically involved in an independent way during Bartlet's administration. She was interested in the issue of child labor—again, a traditionally female issue—but had to subordinate her goals to the president's every time the two came in conflict. Once, Abigail convinced a senator to add an amendment to a trade bill that addressed child labor issues (demonstrating how first ladies could be substantively involved in political issues). As it turned out, the amendment would likely have killed the bill, one her husband supported. In a confrontation about the issue, Abigail was angry about the limits put on her behavior but ultimately admitted to her husband that she was wrong and had the amendment withdrawn (demonstrating the subordinate role of first ladies' goals). Abigail was also attributed the responsibility for raising their children and taking care of her husband's health, other traditional roles. That Abigail Bartlet was an essentially feminine partner to the president (albeit an outspoken, stubborn partner) suggests that popular culture is still not comfortable with a presidential couple that breaks from the traditional gender roles.

Although the series was cancelled after one year, *Commander in Chief* was the first television show that focused on a female president, Mackenzie Allen, played by Geena Davis. An examination of the type of partnership found in a female presidency/male spouse combination confirms the binary gendering of the relationship.[31] The best way to illustrate the consistently gendered elements of the partnership in popular culture over time is to compare the role of the "first gentleman" in *Commander in Chief* with the "first gentleman" in the movie *Kisses for My President*, a 1964 comedy starring Polly Bergen as President Leslie Harrison McCloud.[32] Given the forty-year span between the TV show and the movie, it is significant that there were so many parallels between the treatment of the president and her spouse.[33] In both, the "first gentleman" felt emasculated and useless, while the female presidents were given prominently masculine characteristics (while struggling at the same time to fulfill the responsibilities of motherhood).

Upon being shown around the White House both men were uncomfortable with the feminine nature of their space (Thad McCloud objected to frills in his bedroom, while Rod Calloway thought his office was too pink). They both also thought the traditional first spouse task of menu planning was not important. In addition, they quickly became unhappy that their wives were so busy they did not have much time for them and, even worse, made important decisions without their input. Ultimately, both first gentlemen, feeling neglected, looked to other women for attention.[34] The first spouses' careers were also a source of dissatisfaction, as neither man felt fulfilled in the first spouse role and wanted to have a career of his own. In general, both men were unhappy and unfulfilled.[35] Thad McCloud referred to his "deceased male ego," while Rod Calloway's son told him that everyone thought he was the "national wuss" and got into a fight to defend his father's honor (thereby demonstrating Rod's lack of manhood because he did not stand up for himself). In contrast, the female presidents were both attributed strong leadership qualities and impressive knowledge of political matters. Yet they were not unfeminine. Aside from attractive appearances, both were also visibly concerned with their families. As it turned out, both women found it difficult to juggle the role of mother with presidential duties, and both faced problems with their children that were implicitly caused by the mother's inability to devote sufficient attention to family issues because of her presidential responsibilities.[36]

More evidence of the binary nature of the presidential partnership in fictional accounts is found in a comparison of *Commander in Chief* and *24*. The latter starred Kiefer Sutherland as a U.S. agent fighting terrorism. In the final two seasons, the show had a female president, Allison Taylor, played by Cherry Jones. Both female presidents were similar in their strength, courage, intelligence, and confidence.[37] However, the shows also attributed to the female presidents the most extreme of masculine traits—the willingness to do violence. National security and military matters are often considered masculine issues, partly because of the violent nature of war. To demonstrate the legitimacy of each woman's leadership, both shows featured episodes in which the presidents approved of heightened interrogation of detained suspects. President Taylor knowingly authorized torture, while President Allen believed she was authorizing only intense interrogation methods, which were short of torture in her mind. The point is that this association with the use of force demonstrated that both women had the requisite characteristics to be a true (masculine) president. One of President Allen's political opponents told her afterward that he did not know she "had the balls" to do it, a backhanded compliment that suggested it was an act of a man. Interestingly, *24* seemed to acknowledge the difficulties inherent in a partnership between a female president and male spouse by eliminating the spouse. President Taylor and her husband were divorced before her second season, freeing her from the seesaw of partnership expectations.

The Gendered Partnership in Politics

Fictional portrayals of female presidents and their husbands demonstrate the challenges of the gendered partnership. Male first spouses struggle against charges of "wimpiness" and feelings of uselessness and neglect. Similarly, female presidents have to portray "manly" characteristics of leadership without relinquishing their femininity. The experience of actual political actors suggests that the fictional characterizations reflect important elements of the partnership.

The current first lady is a case in point. Very ambitious, Michelle Obama followed a career path admired and envied by both men and women. With degrees from Princeton and Harvard and a successful career in corporate law, this is a first lady whose accomplishments would be admired according to any standard. As first lady, however, Michelle has followed the traditional gender expectations fairly closely. There is no doubt that both Obamas view themselves as partners, yet the division of labor is significant: "For all the talk about this being a partnership of equals, the domestic roles Michelle and Barack have assumed are, in many ways, strikingly stereotypical. He is the dreamer, the visionary, the inspirational leader. She is . . . the hyperorganized multitasker who makes sure the trains run on time," the typical mother's role.[38] And even though she had a successful career, Michelle has been the one "to adjust her personal ambitions to accommodate the needs of her clan."[39] When Michelle poked fun at her husband for his sloppiness around the house, Maureen Dowd reported that some "worried that her chiding was emasculating, casting her husband . . . as an undisciplined child."[40] In other words, her statements were not those of an adoring wife working to support her husband's election. As she appeared strong and critical, her husband's masculinity was diminished.[41] In seesaw fashion, when her perceived strength increased, her husband's decreased. When phrases such as "ball breaker" and "henpecked" started appearing in the press, she backed away from this kind of comment. Since she settled into her position as first lady, it is also apparent that she is the one responsible for the children, and she works on family and social issues, being sure to leave Barack's public masculinity intact. She calls herself "mom-in-chief," a title that would apply to first ladies in any era.[42]

Hillary Clinton initially adopted a different strategy as first lady. Intent on breaking down the barriers to political involvement of spouses, she confidently threw herself into health care reform, emphasizing the substantive partnership with her husband by occupying an office in the West Wing. The public response reflected the gendered nature of both the presidency and first spouse. In cartoons

Hillary was portrayed as the "man" of the family, while Bill was shown in a dress, a typical binary interpretation.[43] Responding to criticism, she gradually adjusted her role to fit better into the feminine supporting role. As a presidential candidate Hillary was not constrained as much by the partnership boundaries. She still struggled with the double bind that all female political leaders face—how to demonstrate strength and leadership without sacrificing femininity—but no longer did her "masculine leadership style" threaten the symbol of nationhood her husband represented as president.

If Bill Clinton ever became first gentleman, he would likely not face the same expectations as other first gentlemen would (a former president as first gentleman is an extremely ungeneralizable case); there have been discussions about whether he would have the ability to stay out of politics if Hillary Clinton became president, an implicit criticism of politically active spouses. Even though he says he would take a backseat, some believe he does not realize how hard that would be. During Hillary Clinton's presidential campaign, George H. W. Bush said, "[Bill] Clinton had better be careful what he wishes for; her winning will be harder for him than he can imagine," suggesting that the position of first spouse would force him to make changes in his own behavior that he would find objectionable.[44] Some believed that despite Clinton's promise not to meddle, in practice he would find that impossible, potentially setting up a partnership with *both* spouses trying to assume leadership roles, a situation that has not yet worked in practice, because one of the partners becomes defined as weak because of the other's strength. In the meantime, Hillary Clinton's political leadership now as the secretary of state is acceptable in a way it was not when she was a first lady: "Hillary Clinton permanently has an identity of her own now, separate and distinct from her husband."[45] In this role she is no longer defined as the other of the president, or as a woman trying to become the masculine symbol of the country.

As the speculation grew about whether Sarah Palin would run for the presidency in 2012, discussion about the type of partnership she would have with her husband, Todd, also arose. Although Todd did not receive much media attention in her 2008 vice presidential campaign (daughter Bristol Palin was more familiar to the public), his name came up much more in the context of a potential Palin presidency. While most do not doubt the strength or confidence of the "pit bull" with "lipstick" or "Mama Grizzly" (as Sarah Palin describes herself) some were concerned about information that surfaced about Todd's involvement in helping her govern Alaska: "The idea of a spousal invisible hand influencing Sarah Palin's priorities served to reinforce the traditional stereotype of women's dependence on men in decision making."[46] Published e-mails suggest that Todd was involved in a judicial appointment, monitored contract negotiations with public employee unions, and added his approval or disapproval to state board appointments, to name a few items.[47] While Palin's (masculine) leadership qualities are well established (confidence, aggressiveness, decisiveness, etc.), one columnist worried that Todd's involvement "could make Sarah Palin look like the weak wife who needs protecting."[48] Here again is the dichotomization of traits in the partnership. If Todd Palin speaks out to protect his wife, he is exhibiting toughness and aggression, thereby diminishing Sarah's apparent toughness and aggressiveness. In the binary gendered partnership, only one of the partners can possess those qualities.

A journalist once said that if Hillary Clinton ever became president, Bill would be "America's new, handbag-carrying Denis Thatcher."[49] This is not only an expression of the gendered nature of the presidential partnership but a reference to another well-known female chief executive, Margaret Thatcher, prime minister of Great Britain in the 1980s.[50] The Iron Lady's handbag was a symbol of her power throughout her administration, as well as her husband's feminization.[51] Sir Denis was important in the partnership, and Margaret often said she could not have been prime minister without him, but he also called her "Boss" and was seen carrying her handbag, epitomizing the henpecked spouse.[52] A group of male political spouses in the United States even started a support group in the 1980s called the Sir Denis Thatcher Society. The password was "Yes, dear," jokingly highlighting their subordinate role.[53] Criticism of the role of political spouse is evident, however. One member said of his situation, "As second-income earners, we try to be busy and productive, lest people think we have jobs only as political spouses."[54] Having a job "only as political spouse" is apparently demeaning to men, although it is expected of first ladies. A male first spouse who does not work can be "ridiculed as 'riding on the woman's coat tails, so to speak.'"[55]

German chancellor Angela Merkel and her husband have dealt with the problem differently. Rather than try to manage the gender expectations of a partnership, they have deliberately avoided the appearance of political partnership altogether, eliminating the binary nature of her leadership. Merkel's husband, Joachim Sauer, is a successful scientist in his own right, but he stays completely away from the political scene. Merkel's biographer says his absence is not about gender or ill will, yet he also says of Sauer, "nor does he want to carry her handbag," again referring to the symbol of Denis Thatcher's "feminized" status.[56] For instance, he did not even attend her inauguration as chancellor. The German press calls him "the phantom of the opera" because he is so seldom seen publicly.[57]

Persistent Gender Roles

An examination of the president and first spouse over history demonstrates the extent to which the couple constitutes a partnership. The contributions of the spouse have changed over time, but spouses have always been important for a president's success, if for no other reason than confirming his masculinity. As we contemplate the possibility of the first female president, the gendered expectations of the presidential couple should give us pause. U.S. society persists in viewing the president as a masculine figure supported by a feminine spouse. Depiction of the partnership in both popular culture and politics demonstrates the difficulties for women both as first ladies and potential presidents. As first ladies, women are defined as the "other" of the president, relegated to a subordinate, feminine role, and convincing society that a woman can successfully occupy one of the most masculine offices in the world may be more difficult than imagined.[58] At the very least, spousal support for a female president will be strained, as her leadership qualities diminish her husband's identity or vice versa. Until our definition of the presidency advances beyond the extreme masculinization of the office, it will be difficult for spouses to move beyond the traditional feminine approach in the first ladyship (or for men to comfortably act as first spouse). Even fictional dramas about women in the White House, narratives that were arguably intended to advocate for a more significant role for women, ultimately succumbed to the traditional binary understanding of the presidential couple. Madeleine Kunin is right: "We don't yet know what a female commander in chief should look like, or more importantly, act like."[59] One hopes that the achievements of women like Hillary Clinton and Sarah Palin will also find their expression in popular culture and allow society to see a regendered presidency and an understanding of national identity that is not threatened by women or femininity.[60]

Notes

1. Karlyn Kohrs Campbell, "The Rhetorical Presidency: A Two-Person Career," in *Beyond the Rhetorical Presidency*, ed. Martin J. Medhurst (College Station: Texas A&M University Press, 2004), 180.

2. Dick Meyer, "First Gentleman Bill: A Legitimate Issue," CBS News,

January 31, 2008, http://www.cbsnews.com/stories/2008/01/31/opinion/meyer/main3773825.shtml.

3. Brad Knickerbocker, "First Dude Todd Palin Heavily Involved in Governing Alaska," *Christian Science Monitor,* February 6, 2010.

4. Susan J. Carroll and Richard L. Fox, eds., *Gender and Elections: Shaping the Future of American Politics* (Cambridge: Cambridge University Press, 2010), 1.

5. Georgia Duerst-Lahti, "Presidential Elections: Gendered Space and the Case of 2008," in *Gender and Elections: Shaping the Future of American Politics,* 2nd ed., ed. Susan J. Carroll and Richard L. Fox (New York: Cambridge University Press, 2010), 23. Women on the media's list of presidential aspirants were limited to Senator Hillary Clinton of New York, Democratic governor Janet Napolitano of Arizona, and Republican secretary of state Condoleezza Rice.

6. Diane Bystrom, "Eighteen Million Cracks in the Glass Ceiling: The Rise and Fall of Hillary Rodham Clinton's Presidential Campaign," in *Cracking the Highest Glass Ceiling: A Global Comparison of Women's Campaigns for Executive Office,* ed. Rainbow Murray (Santa Barbara, CA: Praeger, 2010), 84.

7. Susan J. Carroll and Kelly Dittmar, "The 2008 Candidacies of Hillary Clinton and Sarah Palin," in *Gender and Elections: Shaping the Future of American Politics,* 2nd ed., ed. Susan J. Carroll and Richard L. Fox (New York: Cambridge University Press, 2010), 73.

8. "The changes in the First Lady's role as a public communicator have not reflected changes in the status of women or shown corresponding growth." Myra G. Gutin, *The President's Partner: The First Lady in the Twentieth Century* (New York: Greenwood, 1989), 176.

9. The concept of republican motherhood captures the manner in which first ladies are at once empowered and limited: empowered to act in support of the president but limited to specific feminine activities. "Republican motherhood emphasized women's moral influence on men and ascribed importance to their maternal role and 'recognized that women's choices and women's work did serve larger social and political purposes.'" Lisa M. Burns, *First Ladies and the Fourth Estate: Press Framing of Presidential Wives* (DeKalb: Northern Illinois University Press, 2008), 19.

10. Mona Lena Krook and Sarah Childs believe it is important to make the distinction in order to move away from the purely biological analysis of men and women as binary opposites. Krook and Childs, "Women, Gender and Politics: an Introduction," in *Women, Gender, and Politics: A Reader,* ed. Krook and Childs (New York: Oxford University Press, 2010), 3.

11. Robert P. Watson, "Toward the Study of the First Lady: The State of Scholarship," *Presidential Studies Quarterly* 33, no. 2 (2003): 423.

12. Lewis L. Gould, "Modern First Ladies in Historical Perspective," *Presidential Studies Quarterly* 15, no. 3 (1985): 532–40.

13. Allida M. Black, "The Modern First Lady and Public Policy: From Edith Wilson through Hillary Rodham Clinton," *Magazine of History* 15 (2001): 16.

14. Ibid., 16.

15. One study suggests that not only are men and women associated with different policy strengths but women's areas are viewed as less important. Masculine responsibilities include dealing with terrorism, dealing with military crises, and fulfilling the commander in chief role. Feminine areas include solving problems in the educational system, guaranteeing the rights of racial minorities, solving the problems of the disabled and handicapped, and solving the problems of the aged. Shirley Rosenwasser and Jana Seale, "Attitudes toward a Hypothetical Male or Female Presidential Candidate—A Research Note," *Political Psychology* 9 (1988): 591–98.

16. Sue Thomas and Jean Reith Schroedel, "The Significance of Social and Institutional Expectations," in *Rethinking Madam President: Are We Ready for a Woman in the White House?*, ed. Lori Cox Han and Caroline Heldman (Boulder, CO: Lynne Rienner, 2007), 43–68.

17. MaryAnne Borrelli, "Competing Conceptions of the First Ladyship Responses to Betty Ford's *60 Minutes* Interview," *Presidential Studies Quarterly* 31, no. 3 (2001): 397–414.

18. Gil Troy, *Affairs of State: The Rise and Rejection of the Presidential Couple since World War II* (New York: Free Press, 1997), 223.

19. Carl Sferrazza Anthony, "If Hillary Wins the White House, Bill Becomes 'First Gentleman,'" *History News Network,* May 23, 2007, http://hnn.us/blogs/entries/39240.html.

20. See, for example, Mary E. Stuckey, "Rethinking the Rhetorical Presidency and Presidential Rhetoric," *Review of Communication* 10 (2010): 38–52; Georgia Duerst-Lahti, "Masculinity on the Campaign Trail," in *Rethinking Madam President: Are We Ready for a Woman in the White House?*, ed. Lori Cox Han and Caroline Heldman (Boulder, CO: Lynne Rienner, 2007), 87–112; Georgia Duerst-Lahti, "'Seeing What Has Always Been': Opening Study of the Presidency," *PS: Political Science and Politics* 41, no. 4 (2008): 733–37; Susan J. Carroll and Richard L. Fox, eds., *Gender and Elections: Shaping the Future of American Politics* (New York: Cambridge University Press, 2006); John M. Murphy, "'Our Mission and Our Moment': George W. Bush and September 11th," *Rhetoric & Public Affairs* 6, no. 4 (2003): 607–32; and Shawn J. Parry-Giles and Diane M. Blair, "The Rise of the Rhetorical First Lady: Politics, Gender Ideology and Women's Voice, 1789–2002," *Rhetoric & Public Affairs* 5, no. 4 (2002): 565–99.

21. Stuckey, "Rethinking the Rhetorical Presidency," 44.

22. "A central component in the construction of U.S. nationalism is the consistent depiction of gender roles and a decidedly masculine vision of the U.S. as a nation." Trevor Parry-Giles and Shawn J. Parry-Giles, *The Prime-Time Presidency: "The West Wing" and U.S. Nationalism* (Urbana: University of Illinois Press, 2006), 16.

23. Judith Butler, *Gender Trouble: Feminism and the Subversion of Identity* (New York: Routledge, 1999), 14.

24. Duerst-Lahti, "Masculinity," 90.

25. Luke Winslow, "American Manhood: Reinscribing Idealized Masculinity in *Legends of the Fall,*" *Texas Speech Communication Journal Online,* April 2008, http://www.etsca.com/tscjonline/0408-legends/.

26. A television critic makes this precise point about one of the characters on *The West Wing.* She says that Joey Lucas (played by Marlee Matlin), who is set up as a possible love interest for Josh Lyman (played by Brad Whitford), "is most valuable not as a woman or even as a female character, but as a proving ground of masculinity." Lesley Smith, "Reigning Men," Pop Matters, http://www.popmatters.com/tv/reviews/w/west-wing.html.

27. Quoted in Susan Page, "Public Favors a Traditional, Non-Working First Lady," *USA Today,* October 19, 2004. Gil Troy also argues that discussion of first ladies is "stuck" in an earlier era. "The First Lady: Public Expectations, Private Lives," *NewsHour,* PBS, October 25, 2004, http://www.pbs.org/newshour/vote2004/first_ladies/transcript1.html.

28. Georgie Binks, "The In-Between World of a Political Spouse," CBC News, January 20, 2006, http://www.cbc.ca/news/viewpoint/vp_binks/20060120.html.

29. Parry-Giles and Parry-Giles, *Prime-Time Presidency,* 3.

30. Ibid., 5.

31. President Allen was not even elected president in her own right but assumed the office upon the death of the president (against the wishes of dying president and his advisors).

32. In a conscious nod to her movie, Polly Bergen also played Mackenzie Allen's mother on *Commander in Chief.*

33. In *Kisses for My President* the legitimacy of the female president was also undermined by the implication that her election was not based on widespread general support but specifically female support.

34. Here again is the notion that women are necessary to prove a man's masculinity. The female presidents were diminishing their husbands' masculinity, so they needed other women to help them prove it.

35. This is a stark contrast to the way first ladies feel about their role. Although there have been numerous wives who did not especially like being in the White House, most expressed satisfaction in supporting their husbands.

36. There are two implications of the children's problems. The first is that they would not have become problems in the first place if the mother had devoted more time to family concerns. The second is that it is the mother who is responsible for the children. Since both fathers, by their own accounts, were not terribly busy, they could have exerted more effort in the family arena, yet it was the mothers who struggled to cope and face the issues.

37. It is telling that Allison Taylor and her husband were divorced at the end of her first season, thereby eliminating the difficulty of juggling the gender dualism in the partnership. Thereafter, President Taylor could be given masculine traits without diminishing her husband.

38. Michelle Cottle, "Wife Lessons: Why Michelle Obama Is No Hillary Clinton," *New Republic,* March 24, 2008, http://www.tnr.com/article/wife-lessons?page=1.

39. Ibid.

40. Maureen Dowd, "She's Not Buttering Him Up," *New York Times,* April 25, 2007.

41. The wife of a Canadian political leader, Margaret McTeer, also experienced the gendered, binary nature of the husband-and-wife political partnership. Joe Clark, a longtime figure in the Canadian government (even prime minister for a year in 1979), was criticized for letting his wife keep her own last name: "If Joe couldn't 'control' his wife, he must be weak, they reasoned." Binks, "The In-Between World."

42. Andrea Billups, "Laura Bush: A First Lady with Class," *Human Events,* May 17, 2010, http://www.humanevents.com/article.php?id=37002.

43. Charlotte Templin, "Hillary Clinton as Threat to Gender Norms: Cartoon Images of the First Lady," *Journal of Communication Inquiry* 23, no. 1 (1999): 24.

44. Jonathan Darman, "His New Role," *Newsweek,* May 28, 2007, http://www.newsweek.com/2007/05/27/his-new-role.html.

45. Her popularity confirms the change in her public image. "Hillary Clinton has 70% Approval Rating as Secretary of State," *Hillbuzz,* March 25, 2009, http://hillbuzz.org/2009/03/25/hillary-clinton-has-a-70-approval-rating-as-secretary-of-state/. In late 2009 she had a 75 percent approval rating. Even more remarkable, she had a 57 percent approval rating among Republicans. See Eamon Jeavers, "Poll: Clinton Approval Soars," *Politico,* December 16, 2009, http://www.politico.com/news/stories/1209/30679.html.

46. Carroll and Dittmar, "2008 Candidacies," 68.

47. Bill Dedman, "Palin E-mails Reveal a Powerful 'First Dude.'" MSNBC, March 18, 2011, http://www.msnbc.msn.com/id/35238034/ns/politics/.

48. Matt Lewis, "How Do You Solve a Problem like Todd (Palin)?" *Politics Daily,* October 6, 2010, http://www.politicsdaily.com/2010/10/06/how-do-you-solve-a-problem-like-todd-palin/.

49. Andrew Stephen, "U.S. Election Reveals Deep Divisions," *New Statesman,* November 13, 2000.

50. Rainbow Murray notes that in a global comparison, there are more women executives outside the United States. Murray, introduction to *Cracking the Highest Glass Ceiling: A Global Comparison of Women's Campaigns for Executive Office,* ed. Murray (Santa Barbara, CA: Praeger, 2010), 3–4.

51. It is said that Thatcher intimidated people with the handbag, defeating her enemies with information she pulled from it. One critic said of Thatcher, "She could

not see an institution without hitting it with her handbag." Paul Kelso, "Fierce Bidding for Thatcher's Handbag," *Guardian,* July 4, 2000. The term has even found its way into the *Oxford English Dictionary:* "To handbag: transitive verb (of a woman politician), treat (a person, idea, etc.) ruthlessly or insensitively." "Thatcher's Handbag for the Ages?" *New York Times,* October 14, 1998. One interesting element of the handbag symbolism is that it suggests Thatcher's masculine traits (strength, confidence, decisiveness, insensitivity), but it is an extremely feminine object, reflecting the double bind that women face in proving their leadership qualities (as associated with men) without losing their femininity.

52. Nick Assinder, "Remembering Sir Denis," BBC News, June 26, 2003, http://news.bbc.co.uk/2/hi/uk_news/politics/3022420.stm.

53. Sandra McElwaine, "The Political Husbands of 2010," *Daily Beast,* September 7, 2010, http://www.thedailybeast.com/articles/2010/09/08/the-first-husbands-of-2010.html.

54. Dave Johnson, "Denis Thatchers of the World Offer Each Other Support," *Los Angeles Times,* October 18, 2010.

55. Maurine H. Beasley, *First Ladies and the Press: The Unfinished Partnership of the Media Age* (Evanston, IL: Northwestern University Press, 2005), 258.

56. Andrew Purvis, "Just Don't Call Him Mr. Merkel," *Time,* November 8, 2007.

57. David Crossland, "Merkel's Phantom of the Opera," *Spiegel Online,* November 22, 2005, http://www.spiegel.de/international/0,1518,druck-386384,00.html.

58. Indeed, in 2007 Lilly Goren suggested that an African American male might be more acceptable than a white woman, an argument subsequently supported by the result of the 2008 Democratic primary. See Goren, "Fact or Fiction? Are We Ready for the First Female or Minority President?," paper presented at the Annual Meeting of the American Political Science Association, Chicago, IL, 2007. See also Goren, "Fact or Fiction: The Reality of Race and Gender in Reaching the White House" (chapter 5 in this volume). After her own 2004 Democratic primary presidential candidacy, Carol Moseley Braun said that, of the barriers she faced, "gender is more intractable than race." Madeleine M. Kunin, *Pearls, Politics, and Power: How Women Can Win and Lead* (White River Junction, VT: Chelsea Green, 2008), 151.

59. Kunin, *Pearls, Politics, and Power,* 159.

60. Duerst-Lahti, "Masculinity," 110.

ACKNOWLEDGMENTS

The idea for this book came out of several discussions about the icons, symbols, and cultural dynamics of the 2008 election—an election that paid more attention to gender than had any previous presidential election. We were both intrigued by many of the perspectives offered throughout the long election season, particularly those that we found unexpected, taking debates and images much further in some cases and not far enough in other cases. In all, the 2008 election was much more than the total of votes at the end of the night on election November 4, 2008. The question of feminism came up in numerous contexts and made its way to the forefront of policy discussions in ways that had not been seen for quite some time. Although the term and ownership of what feminism might mean remain contested, having a national conversation on a number of levels about the role of women in public life, as they ran for the highest office in the land and as they were nominated for the vice presidential position, was an opening to bring forward many of these unresolved issues that continue to dominate the lives of many Americans.

Many celebrated, and rightly so, the facts that Hillary Clinton went further in pursuing the Democratic nomination for president than had any woman previously and that Sarah Palin did the same as the first female on the Republican ticket as the vice presidential candidate. We were particularly intrigued by the way that conversations about these women and their electoral fortunes unfolded in unexpected arenas: on Oprah's couch, in fashion magazines, on late-night comedy shows, and across the changing media landscape. However, though both Clinton and Palin broke through certain glass ceilings, neither of them achieved the ultimate goal of winning their respective election. As a result—and perhaps partly as an explanation, too—the role, presentation, consumption, and experience of women and American politics in its highest echelon remain contested—especially in the realm of popular culture. As we began to see links between otherwise seemingly disconnected spheres of the public discourse, we were prompted to delve into the intersections of gender, presidential politics, and popular culture and to see what we and a number of our colleagues might have to say about the ongoing dynamics of these phenomena. The result of these investigations is this volume.

Along the way, we have had help and assistance from a host of individuals, all of whom deserve our gratitude. We would like to thank first our generous contributors, who have worked with us over a number of years revising and refining their work and responding to our many e-mails and edits. We thank them for taking this intellectual journey with us. We have learned a great deal from their research and writing, all of which has made this book diverse and engaging. We also would like to thank our respective universities—Cleveland State University, where Justin worked throughout the course of this project, and Carroll University, where Lilly has worked since 2005—for supporting our efforts through travel grants so that we could attend a variety of conferences where many of these chapters were initially presented.

Finally, we would like to acknowledge the individuals who have stood by us as we worked on writing, assembling, editing, and all the other aspects of construction that go into moving a project from an idea to a completed manuscript. We particularly thank the diligent and gracious staff at the University Press of Kentucky. Anne Dean Watkins, Bailey Johnson, Steve Wrinn, and Mack McCormick have been constantly supportive of this project and have worked with us every step of the way. It is a pleasure to work with such a wonderful editorial and marketing staff.

Lilly needs to specifically mention some of the individuals who were particularly vital to this project. From her earliest days door-knocking to driving around on election nights, checking vote tallies at local precincts, her father, Ralph Goren, has instilled in her not only an interest in politics, but also a profound love of our country, warts and all. She also wants to dedicate this book to the memory of a woman who enjoyed popular culture, took her politics seriously, and inspired her and whose memory continues to inspire her, her wonderful aunt Verna Dee Goren. Along with Ralph and Verna Dee, Lilly would like to dedicate this book to Benjamin, who made a lot of noise when he first showed up, but she can't imagine what life would be like without him; to Jory, for his unflagging support and love; to Edward, her beautiful, funny, and patient husband; and to Eli and Sophia, ready to take over *tikkun olum,* healing the world.

Justin thanks those professors and colleagues who have taught him about gender, politics, and political science, in ways large and small, direct and indirect. Among the most important of these are Jen Mercieca, Julia Azari, Lisa Ellis, Neda Zawahri, Manfred Steger, Lane Crothers, and Judy Baer. He also gratefully extends his appreciation to: Aleksandra Misovic, who provided considerable research assistance during the development of this project; Virginia Varaljay, who made all aspects of his professional life at CSU more efficient and enjoyable; and Rodger Govea, who was a loyal chair and valued friend during his time in Cleveland. Most important, he thanks Elena Tomorowitz for the countless moments, both lighthearted and tender, that have so wonderfully and consistently sustained him as this project has come to fruition.

SELECTED BIBLIOGRAPHY

Books and Articles

Aday, Sean, and James Devitt. "Style over Substance: Newspaper Coverage of Elizabeth Dole's Presidential Bid." *Press/Politics* 6 (2001): 52–73.

Alexander, Deborah, and Kristi Andersen. "Gender as a Factor in Attribution of Leadership Traits." *Political Research Quarterly* 46, no. 3 (1993): 527–45.

Altschuler, Bruce E. "From Hero to Anti-Hero: The Transformation of the American Presidency on Stage." *White House Studies* 10 (2011): 211–28.

Anthony, Carl Sferrazza. *America's First Families: An Inside View of 200 Years of Private Life in the White House*. New York: Simon and Schuster, 2000.

Atkeson, Lonna Rae. "Not All Cues Are Created Equal: The Conditional Impact of Female Candidates on Political Engagement." *Journal of Politics* 65, no. 4 (2003): 1040–61.

Bachmann, Ingrid, et al. "News Platform Preference: Advancing the Effects of Age and Media Consumption on Political Participation." *International Journal of Internet Science* 5, no. 1 (2010): 34–47.

Ballaster, Rosalind, et al. *Women's Worlds: Ideology, Femininity, and Women's Magazines*. Hampshire, UK: Palgrave Macmillan, 1991.

Baum, Matthew A. "Sex, Lies, and War: How Soft News Brings Foreign Policy to the Inattentive Public." *American Political Science Review* 96, no. 1 (2002): 91–109.

———. "Soft News and Political Knowledge: Evidence of Absence or Absence of Evidence?" *Political Communication* 20, no. 2 (2003): 173–90.

———. *Soft News Goes to War: Public Opinion and American Foreign Policy in the New Media Age*. Princeton, NJ: Princeton University Press, 2003.

Baum, Matthew A., and Angela S. Jamison. "The Oprah Effect: How Soft News Helps Inattentive Citizens Vote Consistently." *Journal of Politics* 68, no. 4 (2006): 946–59.

Baumgardner, Jennifer, and Amy Richards. *Manifesta: Young Women, Feminism, and the Future*. New York: Farrar, Straus and Giroux, 2000.

Baumgartner, Jody C. "Humor on the Next Frontier: Youth, Online Political Humor, and the 'Jib-Jab' Effect." *Social Science Computer Review* 25 (2007): 319–38.

Baumgartner, Jody, and Jonathan S. Morris. "The *Daily Show* Effect: Candidate Evaluations, Efficacy, and American Youth." *American Politics Research* 34, no. 3 (2006): 341–67.

Beasley, Maurine. *First Ladies and the Press: The Unfinished Partnership of the Media Age.* Evanston, IL: Northwestern University Press, 2005.

Berila, Beth. "Savvy Women, Old Boys' School Politics, and the West Wing." In *Geek Chic: Smart Women in Popular Culture,* edited by Sherrie A. Inness, 153–69. New York: Palgrave Macmillan, 2007.

Blumberg, Rae Lesser. "A General Theory of Gender Stratification." *Sociological Theory* 2 (1984): 23–101.

Boorstin, Daniel. *The Image: A Guide to Pseudo-Events in America.* 1961. Reprint, New York: Vintage Books, 1992.

Borrelli, MaryAnne. "Competing Conceptions of the First Ladyship: Responses to Betty Ford's *60 Minutes* Interview." *Presidential Studies Quarterly* 31, no. 3 (2001): 397–414.

———. *The President's Cabinet: Gender, Power, and Representation.* Boulder, CO: Lynne Rienner, 2002.

Box-Steffensmeier, Janet M., Suzanna De Boef, and Tse-Min Lin. "The Dynamics of the Partisan Gender Gap." *American Political Science Review* 98, no. 3 (2004): 515–28.

Braden, Maria. *Women Politicians and the Media.* Lexington: University Press of Kentucky, 1996.

Brewer, Paul R., and Xiaoxia Cao. "Candidate Appearances on Soft News Shows and Public Knowledge about Primary Campaigns." *Journal of Broadcasting & Electronic Media* 50, no. 1 (2006): 18–35.

Brewer, Paul R., and Emily Marquardt. "Mock News and Democracy: Analyzing *The Daily Show.*" *Atlantic Journal of Communication* 14, no. 4 (2007): 249–67.

Brunsdon, Charlotte. *The Feminist, the Housewife, and the Soap Opera.* New York: Oxford University Press, 2000.

Burns, Lisa M. *First Ladies and the Fourth Estate: Press Framing of Presidential Wives.* DeKalb: Northern Illinois University Press, 2008.

Burrell, Barbara. *A Woman's Place Is in the House: Campaigning for Congress in the Feminist Era.* Ann Arbor: University of Michigan Press, 1994.

Butler, Judith. *Gender Trouble: Feminism and the Subversion of Identity.* New York: Routledge, 1999.

Bystrom, Dianne. "Advertising, Web Sites, and Media Coverage: Gender and Communication along the Campaign Trail." In *Gender and Elections: Shaping the Future of American Politics*, 2nd ed., edited by Susan J. Carroll and Richard L. Fox, 239–62. Cambridge: Cambridge University Press, 2010.

———. "Eighteen Million Cracks in the Glass Ceiling: The Rise and Fall of Hillary Rodham Clinton's Presidential Campaign." In *Cracking the Highest Glass Ceiling: A Global Comparison of Women's Campaigns for Executive Office*, edited by Rainbow Murray and Pippa Norris, 69–90. Santa Barbara, CA: Praeger, 2010.

Campbell, David E., and Christina Wolbrecht. "See Jane Run: Women Politicians as Role Models for Adolescents." *Journal of Politics* 68, no. 2 (2006): 233–47.

Campbell, Karlyn Kohrs. "The Discursive Performance of Femininity: Hating Hillary." *Rhetoric & Public Affairs* 1, no. 1 (1998): 1–20.

———. "The Rhetorical Presidency: A Two-Person Career." In *Beyond the Rhetorical Presidency*, edited by Martin J. Medhurst, 179–95. College Station: Texas A&M University Press, 1996.

Cao, Xiaoxia. "Political Comedy Shows and Knowledge about Primary Campaigns: The Moderating Effects of Age and Education." *Mass Communication and Society* 11 (2008): 43–61.

Carlin, Diana, and Kelly Winfrey. "Have You Come a Long Way, Baby? Hillary Clinton, Sarah Palin, and Sexism in 2008 Campaign Coverage." *Communication Studies* 60 (2009): 326–43.

Caroli, Betty Boyd. *First Ladies: From Martha Washington to Michelle Obama.* Oxford: Oxford University Press, 2010.

Carroll, Susan J. "Reflections on Gender and Hillary Clinton's Presidential Campaign: The Good, the Bad, and the Misogynic." *Politics and Gender* 5 (2009): 1–20.

———. *Women as Candidates in American Politics.* 2nd ed. Bloomington: Indiana University Press, 1994.

Carroll, Susan J., and Kelly Dittmar. "The 2008 Candidacies of Hillary Clinton and Sarah Palin: Cracking the Highest, Hardest Glass Ceiling." In *Gender and Elections: Shaping the Future of American Politics*, 2nd ed., edited by Susan J. Carroll and Richard L. Fox, 44–77. Cambridge: Cambridge University Press, 2010.

Cashmore, Ellis. *Celebrity/Culture.* New York: Routledge, 2006.

Christensen, Terry, and Peter J. Haas. *Projecting Politics: Political Messages in American Films.* New York: M. E. Sharpe, 2005.

Clift, Eleanor, and Tom Brazaitis. *Madam President: Women Blazing the Leadership Trail.* New York: Routledge, 2003.

Conroy, Meredith. "Political Parties: Advancing a Masculine Ideal." In *Rethinking Madam President: Are We Ready for a Woman in the White House?*, edited by Lori Cox Han and Caroline Heldman, 133–46. Boulder, CO: Lynne Rienner, 2007.

Cook, Elizabeth Adell, Sue Thomas, and Clyde Wilcox. *The Year of the Woman: Myths and Realities.* Boulder, CO: Westview, 1994.

Cooper, Christopher A., and Mandi Bates Bailey. "Entertainment Media and Political Knowledge: Do People Get Any Truth Out of Truthiness?" In *Homer Simpson Goes to Washington: American Politics through Popular Culture*, edited by Joseph J. Foy, 133–50. Lexington: University Press of Kentucky, 2008.

Crawley, Melissa. *Mr. Sorkin Goes to Washington: Shaping the President on Television's "The West Wing."* Jefferson, NC: McFarland, 2006.

Crothers, Lane. "'Get Off My Plane!': Presidents and the Movies." *White House Studies* 10 (2011): 229–42.

———. *Globalization and American Popular Culture.* Lanham, MD: Rowman and Littlefield, 2007.

Dabelko, Kristin la Cour, and Paul S. Herrnson. "Women's and Men's Campaigns for the U.S. House of Representatives." *Political Research Quarterly* 50, no. 1 (1997): 121–35.

Daughton, Suzanne. "Women's Issues, Women's Place: Gender-Related Problems in Presidential Campaigns." *Communication Quarterly* 42 (1994): 106–19.

Davis, Richard, and Diana Owen. *New Media and American Politics.* New York: Oxford University Press, 1998.

Delli Carpini, Michael X., and Ester R. Fuchs. "The Year of the Woman? Candidates, Voters, and the 1992 Elections." *Political Science Quarterly* 108 (1993): 29–36.

Devitt, James. "Framing Gender on the Campaign Trail: Female Gubernatorial Candidates and the Press." *Journalism & Mass Communication Quarterly* 79 (2002): 445–63.

Dolan, Kathleen A. "Do Women Candidates Play to Gender Stereotypes? Do Men Candidates Play to Women? Candidate Sex and Issue Priorities on Campaign Websites." *Political Research Quarterly* 58, no. 1 (2005): 31–44.

———. *Voting for Women: How the Public Evaluates Women Candidates.* Boulder, CO: Westview, 2004.

Douglas, Susan, and Meredith Michaels. *The Mommy Myth: The Idealization of Motherhood and How It Has Undermined Women.* New York: Free Press, 2005.

Dow, Bonnie J. *Prime Time Feminism: Television, Media Culture, and the Women's Movement since 1970.* Philadelphia: University of Pennsylvania Press, 1996.

Duerst-Lahti, Georgia. "Governing Institutions, Ideologies, and Gender: Toward the Possibility of Equal Political Representation." *Sex Roles* 47 (2002): 371–88.

———. "Masculinity on the Campaign Trail." In *Rethinking Madam President: Are We Ready for a Woman in the White House?*, edited by Lori Cox Han and Caroline Heldman, 87–112. Boulder, CO: Lynne Rienner, 2007.

———. "Presidential Elections: Gendered Space and the Case of 2008." In *Gender and Elections: Shaping the Future of American Politics,* 2nd ed., edited by Susan J. Carroll and Richard L. Fox, 13–43. Cambridge: Cambridge University Press, 2010.

Dwyer, Caitlin E., et al. "Racism, Sexism, and Candidate Evaluations in the 2008 U.S. Presidential Election." *Analyses of Social Issues and Public Policy* 9, no. 1 (2009): 223–40.

Elder, Laurel, and Steven Greene. "The Myth of 'Security Moms' and 'NASCAR Dads': Parenthood, Political Stereotypes, and the 2004 Election." *Social Science Quarterly* 88, no. 1 (2007): 1–19.

Fahey, Anna Cornelia. "French and Feminine: Hegemonic Masculinity and the Emasculation of John Kerry in the 2004 President Race." *Critical Studies in Media Communication* 24 (2007): 132–50.

Falk, Erika. *Women for President: Media Bias in Eight Campaigns.* Urbana: University of Illinois Press, 2008.

Feldman, Lauren, and Dannagal G. Young. "Late-Night Comedy as a Gateway to Traditional News." *Political Communication* 25, no. 4 (2008): 401–22.

Ferguson, Michaele L., and Lori Jo Marso, eds. *W Stands for Women: How the George W. Bush Presidency Shaped a New Politics of Gender.* Durham, NC: Duke University Press, 2007.

Ferree, Myra Marx. "A Woman for President? Changing Responses: 1958–1972." *Public Opinion Quarterly* 38, no. 3 (1974): 390–99.

Ferriss, Suzanne, and Mallory Young, eds. *Chick Lit: The New Woman's Fiction.* New York: Routledge, 2006.

Forsyth, Donelson R., Michele M. Heiney, and Sandra S. Wright. "Biases in Appraisals of Women Leaders." *Group Dynamics: Theory, Research, and Practice* 1 (1997): 98–103.

Foschi, Martha, Larissa Lai, and Kirsten Sigerson. "Gender and Double Standards in the Assessment of Job Applicants." *Social Psychology Quarterly* 57, no. 4 (1994): 326–39.

Foy, Joseph J., ed. *Homer Simpson Goes to Washington: American Politics through Popular Culture.* Lexington: University Press of Kentucky, 2008.

Glick, Peter, Sadie Larsen, Cathryn Johnson, and Heather Branstiter. "Evaluations of Sexy Women in Low- and High-Status Jobs." *Psychology of Women Quarterly* 29, no. 4 (2005): 389–95.

Goren, Lilly J., ed. *You've Come a Long Way Baby: Women, Politics, and Popular Culture.* Lexington: University Press of Kentucky, 2009.

Goren, Lilly J., and Justin Vaughn. "Profits and Protest: The Cultural Commodification of the Presidential Image." In *Politics and Popular Culture,* edited by Leah A. Murray, 85–99. Newcastle upon Tyne: Cambridge Scholars Press, 2010.

Gould, Lewis L. "Modern First Ladies in Historical Perspective." *Presidential Studies Quarterly* 15, no. 3 (1985): 532–40.

Gutgold, Nichola D. *Almost Madam President: Why Hillary Clinton "Won" in 2008.* Lanham, MD: Lexington Books, 2009.

———. *Paving the Way for Madam President.* Lanham, MD: Lexington Books, 2006.

Gutin, Myra G. *The President's Partner: The First Lady in the Twentieth Century.* New York: Greenwood, 1989.

Guy-Sheftall, Beverly, and Johnnetta Betsch Cole, eds. *Who Should Be First? Feminists Speak Out on the 2008 Presidential Campaign.* Albany: State University of New York Press, 2008.

Han, Lori Cox, and Caroline Heldman, eds. *Rethinking Madam President: Are We Ready for a Woman in the White House?* Boulder, CO.: Lynne Rienner, 2007.

Heflick, Nathan A., and Jamie L. Goldenberg. "Objectifying Sarah Palin: Evidence That Objectification Causes Women to Be Perceived as Less Competent and Less Fully Human." *Journal of Experimental Social Psychology* 45, no. 3 (2009): 598–601.

Heith, Diane J. "The Lipstick Watch: Media Coverage, Gender, and Presidential Campaigns." In *Anticipating Madam President,* edited by Robert P. Watson and Ann Gordon, 123–30. Boulder, CO: Lynne Rienner, 2003.

Heldman, Caroline. "Cultural Barriers to a Female President in the United States." In *Rethinking Madam President: Are We Ready for a Woman in the White House?,* edited by Lori Cox Han and Caroline Heldman, 17–42. Boulder, CO: Lynne Rienner, 2007.

Herrnson, Paul S., J. Celeste Lay, and Atiya Kai Stokes. "Women Running 'as Women': Candidate Gender, Campaign Issues, and Voter-Targeting Strategies." *Journal of Politics* 65, no. 1 (2003): 244–55.

Holbert, R. Lance, et al. "*The West Wing* as Endorsement of the U.S. Presidency: Expanding the Bounds of Priming in Political Communication." *Journal of Communication* 53 (2003): 427–43.

Hollows, Joanne. *Feminism, Femininity, and Popular Culture*. Manchester: Manchester University Press, 2000.

Hollows, Joanne, and Rachel Moseley. *Feminism in Popular Culture*. New York: Berg, 2006.

Hooper, Charlotte. *Manly States: Masculinities, International Relations, and Gender Politics*. New York: Columbia University Press, 2001.

Horwitz, Linda, and Holly Swyers. "Why Are All the Presidents Men? Televisual Presidents and Patriarchy." In *You've Come A Long Way Baby: Women, Politics, and Popular Culture*, edited by Lilly J. Goren, 115–34. Lexington: University Press of Kentucky, 2009.

Howell, Susan E., and Christine L. Day. "Complexities of the Gender Gap." *Journal of Politics* 62, no. 3 (2000): 858–74.

Huddy, Leonie, and Nayda Terkildsen. "Gender Stereotypes and the Perception of Male and Female Candidates." *American Journal of Political Science* 37, no. 1 (1993): 119–48.

Inness, Sherrie A. *Geek Chic: Smart Women in Popular Culture*. New York: Palgrave Macmillan, 2007.

———, ed. *Tough Girls: Women Warriors and Wonder Women in Popular Culture*. Philadelphia: University of Pennsylvania Press, 1999.

Jamieson, Kathleen Hall. *Beyond the Double Bind: Women and Leadership*. New York: Oxford University Press, 1995.

Kahn, Kim Fridkin. "The Distorted Mirror: Press Coverage of Women Candidates for Statewide Office." *Journal of Politics* 56, no. 1 (1994): 154–73.

———. *The Political Consequences of Being a Woman: How Stereotypes Influence the Conduct and Consequences of Political Campaigns*. New York: Columbia University Press, 1996.

Kahn, Kim Fridkin, and Edie Goldenberg. "Women Candidates in the News: An Examination of Gender Differences in U.S. Senate Campaign Coverage." *Public Opinion Quarterly* 55, no. 2 (1991): 180–99.

Kahn, Kim Fridkin, and Ann Gordon. "How Women Campaign for the U.S. Senate: Substance and Strategy." In *Women, Media, and Politics*, edited by Pippa Norris, 59–76. New York: Oxford University Press, 1997.

Kaid, Lynda Lee, Sandra L. Myers, Val Pipps, and Jan Hunter. "Sex Role Perceptions and Televised Political Advertising: Comparing Male and Female Candidates." *Women & Politics* 4, no. 4 (1984): 41–53.

Kann, Mark E. *A Republic of Men: The American Founders, Gendered Languages, and Patriarchal Politics*. New York: New York University Press, 1998.

Kaufmann, Karen M., and John R. Petrocik. "The Changing Politics of American Men: Understanding the Sources of the Gender Gap." *American Journal of Political Science* 43, no. 3 (1999): 864–87.

Kellerman, Barbara. "The Political Functions of the Presidential Family." *Presidential Studies Quarterly* 8, no. 3 (1978): 303–18.

Lane, Christina. "The White House Culture of Gender and Race in *The West Wing*: Insights from the Margins." In *"The West Wing": The American Presidency as Television Drama*, edited by Peter C. Rollins and John E. O'Connor, 32–41. Syracuse, NY: Syracuse University Press, 2003.

Lawless, Jennifer L. "Women, War, and Winning Elections: Gender Stereotyping in the Post–September 11th Era." *Political Research Quarterly* 57, no. 3 (2004): 479–90.

Lawless, Jennifer L., and Richard L. Fox. *It Takes a Candidate: Why Women Don't Run for Office*. New York: Cambridge University Press, 2005.

Lawrence, Regina G., and Melody Rose, eds. *Hillary Clinton's Race for the White House: Gender Politics and the Media on the Campaign Trail*. Boulder, CO: Lynne Rienner, 2010.

Mandel, Ruth B. "She's the Candidate! A Woman for President." In *Women and Leadership: The State of Play and Strategies for Change*, edited by Barbara Kellerman and Deborah L. Rhode. San Francisco: Jossey-Bass, 2007.

Matviko, John W., ed. *The American President in Popular Culture*. Westport, CT: Greenwood, 2005.

Mueller, Carol M. "Nurturance and Mastery: Competing Qualifications for Women's Access to High Public Office?" In *Women and Politics: Activism, Attitudes, and Office-Holding*, edited by Gwen Moore and Glenna D. Spitze. Greenwich, CT: JAI, 1986.

Parry-Giles, Shawn J., and Diane M. Blair. "The Rise of the Rhetorical First Lady: Politics, Gender Ideology, and Women's Voice, 1789–2002." *Rhetoric & Public Affairs* 5, no. 4 (2002): 565–99.

Rhode, Deborah. "Media Images, Feminist Issues." *Signs* 20, no. 3 (1995): 685–710.

Rochelle, Warren G. "The Literary Presidency." *Presidential Studies Quarterly* 29 (1999): 407–20.

Rollins, Peter C., and John E. O'Connor, eds. *Hollywood's White House*. Lexington: University Press of Kentucky, 2003.

Rosenwasser, Shirley Miller, and Norma G. Dean. "Gender Role and Political Office: Effects of Perceived Masculinity/Femininity of Candidate and Political Office." *Psychology of Women Quarterly* 13, no. 1 (1989): 77–85.

Rosenwasser, Shirley, and Jana Seale. "Attitudes toward a Hypothetical Male or Female Presidential Candidate—A Research Note." *Political Psychology* 9 (1988): 591–98.

Sanbonmatsu, Kira. "Gender Stereotypes and Vote Choice." *American Journal of Political Science* 46, no. 1 (2002): 20–34.

Sapiro, Virginia. "Gender Politics, Gendered Politics: The State of the Field." In *Political Science: Looking to the Future*, edited by William J. Crotty, 165–88. Evanston, IL: Northwestern University Press, 1991.

———. "If U.S. Senator Baker Were a Woman: An Experimental Study of Candidate Images." *Political Psychology* 2 (1982): 61–83.

Scharrer, Erica, and Kimberly Bissell. "Overcoming Traditional Boundaries: The Role of Political Activity in Media Coverage of First Ladies." *Women in Politics* 21, no. 1 (2000): 55–83.

Shapiro, Robert Y., and Harpreet Mahajan. "Gender Difference in Policy Preferences: A Summary of Trends from the 1960s to the 1980s." *Public Opinion Quarterly* 50, no. 1 (1986): 42–61.

Sigelman, Lee, and Susan Welch. "Race, Gender and Opinion toward Black and Female Candidates." *Public Opinion Quarterly* 48, no. 2 (1984): 467–75.

Simon, Stefanie, and Crystal L. Hoyt. "Exploring the Gender Gap in Support for a Woman for President." *Analyses of Social Issues and Public Policy* 8, no. 1 (2008): 157–81.

Smith, Jeff. *The Presidents We Imagine: Two Centuries of White House Fictions on the Page, on the Stage, Onscreen, and Online*. Madison: University of Wisconsin Press, 2009.

Stokes, Ashli Quesinberry. "First Ladies in Waiting: The Fight for Rhetorical Legitimacy on the Campaign Trail." In *The 2004 Presidential Campaign: A Communication Perspective*, edited by Robert J. Denton Jr., 167–94. Lanham, MD: Rowman and Littlefield, 2005.

Streb, Matthew J., et al. "Social Desirability Effects and Support for a Female American President." *Public Opinion Quarterly* 72, no. 1 (2008): 76–89.

Street, John. "Celebrity Politicians: Popular Culture and Political Representation." *British Journal of Politics and International Relations* 6, no. 4 (2004): 435–52.

Sykes, Patricia Lee. "Gender in the 2008 Presidential Election: Two Types of Time Collide." *PS: Political Science & Politics* 41, no. 4 (2008): 761–64.

Templin, Charlotte. "Hillary Clinton as Threat to Gender Norms: Cartoon

Images of the First Lady." *Journal of Communication Inquiry* 23, no. 1 (1999): 20–36.

Troy, Gil. *Affairs of State: The Rise and Rejection of the Presidential Couple since World War II.* New York: Free Press, 1997.

Uscinski, Joseph, and Lilly Goren. "What's in a Name? Coverage of Senator Hillary Clinton during the 2008 Democratic Primary." *Political Research Quarterly* 64, no. 4 (2011): 884–96.

van Zoonen, Liesbet. *Entertaining the Citizen: When Politics and Popular Culture Converge.* Lanham, MD: Rowman and Littlefield, 2005.

———. "'Finally I Have My Mother Back': Politicians and Their Families in Popular Culture." *Harvard International Journal of Press/Politics* 3, no. 1 (1998): 48–64.

Vaughn, Justin S. "Barack Obama's Black Presidential Predecessors: The Myth of Pop Culture Predestination." *White House Studies* 10, no. 3 (2010): 243–58.

Watson, Robert P. "The First Lady Reconsidered: Presidential Partner and Political Institution." *Presidential Studies Quarterly* 27 (1997): 805–18.

———. *The Presidents' Wives: Reassessing the Office of First Lady.* Boulder, CO: Lynne Rienner, 2000.

———. "Toward the Study of the First Lady: The State of Scholarship." *Presidential Studies Quarterly* 33, no. 2 (2003): 423–41.

Williams, Verna. "The First (Black) Lady." *Denver University Law Review* 86 (2008): 833–50.

Winter, Nicholas J. G. *Dangerous Frames: How Ideas about Race and Gender Shape Public Opinion.* Chicago: University of Chicago Press, 2008.

Witt, Linda, Karen Paget, and Glenna Matthews. *Running as a Woman: Gender and Power in American Politics.* New York: Free Press, 1994.

Woodall, Gina Serignese, and Kim L. Fridkin. "Shaping Women's Chances: Stereotypes and the Media." In *Rethinking Madam President: Are We Ready for a Woman in the White House?*, edited by Lori Cox Han and Caroline Heldman, 69–86. Boulder, CO: Lynne Rienner, 2007.

Zeisler, Andi. *Feminism and Pop Culture.* Berkeley, CA: Seal Studies, 2008.

Films

Absolute Power, dir. Clint Eastwood, 1997.
Air Force One, dir. Wolfgang Petersen, 1997.
The American President, dir. Rob Reiner, 1995.
Apocalypse Now, dir. Francis Ford Coppola, 1979.

Armageddon, dir. Michael Bay, 1998.

The Aviator, dir. Martin Scorsese, 2004.

Batman Begins, dir. Christopher Nolan, 2005.

The Birdcage, dir. Mike Nichols, 1996.

Black Sheep, dir. Penelope Spheeris, 1996.

Bruce Almighty, dir. Tom Shadyac, 2003.

Bulworth, dir. Warren Beatty, 1998.

Canadian Bacon, dir. Michael Moore, 1995.

Children of the Corn, dir. Fritz Kiersch, 1984.

The Contender, dir. Rod Lurie, 2000.

The Dark Knight, dir. Christopher Nolan, 2008.

Dave, dir. Ivan Reitman, 1993.

Deep Impact, dir. Mimi Leder, 1998.

Deterrence, dir. Rod Lurie, 1999.

The Devil Wears Prada, dir. David Frankel, 2006.

Disclosure, dir. Barry Levinson, 1994.

The Distinguished Gentleman, dir. Jonathan Lynn, 1992.

Dogma, dir. Kevin Smith, 1999.

Dr. Strangelove or: How I Learned to Stop Worrying and Love the Bomb, dir. Stanley Kubrick, 1964.

Executive Target, dir. Joseph Merhi, 1997.

Falling Down, dir. Joel Schumacher, 1993.

Fatal Attraction, dir. Adrian Lyne, 1987.

The Fifth Element, dir. Luc Besson, 1997.

Friday the 13th, dir. Sean S. Cunningham, 1980.

Frost/Nixon, dir. Ron Howard, 2008.

Get Smart, dir. Peter Segal, 2008.

Head of State, dir. Chris Rock, 2003.

High Noon, dir. Fred Zinnemann, 1952.

Idiocracy, dir. Mike Judge 2006.

Independence Day, dir. Roland Emmerich, 1996.

Juno, dir. Jason Reitman, 2007.

Kisses for My President, dir. Curtis Bernhardt, 1964.

A Knight's Tale, dir. Brian Helgeland, 2001.

Knocked Up, dir. Judd Apatow, 2007.

The Man, dir. Joseph Sargent, 1972.

Man of the Year, dir. Barry Levinson, 2006.

The Manchurian Candidate, dir. Jonathan Demme, 2004.

Mars Attacks!, dir. Tim Burton, 1996.
Miss Congeniality, dir. Donald Petrie, 2000.
Mr. Smith Goes to Washington, dir. Frank Capra, 1939.
Murder at 1600, dir. Dwight H. Little, 1997.
Nixon, dir. Oliver Stone, 1995.
No Way Out, dir. Roger Donaldson, 1987.
The Omen, dir. Richard Donner, 1976.
101 Dalmatians, dir. Clyde Geronimi, Hamilton S. Luske, and Wolfgang Reitherman, 1961.
The Other, dir. Robert Mulligan, 1972.
The Peacekeeper, dir. Frederic Forestier, 1997.
Pet Sematary, dir. Mary Lambert, 1989.
Primary Colors, dir. Mike Nichols, 1998.
Rosemary's Baby, dir. Roman Polanski, 1968.
The Searchers, dir. John Ford, 1956.
The Seduction of Joe Tynan, dir. Jerry Schatzberg, 1979.
Star Wars, Episode IV: A New Hope, dir. George Lucas, 1977.
Star Wars, Episode VI: Return of the Jedi, dir. Richard Marquand, 1983.
The Sum of All Fears, dir. Phil Alden Robinson, 2002.
Swimfan, dir. John Polson, 2002.
Swing Vote, dir. Joshua Michael Stern, 2008.
Traffic, dir. Steven Soderbergh, 2000.
A Very Brady Sequel, dir. Arlene Sanford, 1996.
W., dir. Oliver Stone, 2008.
Wag the Dog, dir. Barry Levinson, 1997.
Welcome to Mooseport, dir. Donald Petrie, 2004.

Television Shows

All My Children, ABC, 1970–2011.
American Morning, CNN, 2002–2011.
The Arsenio Hall Show, Paramount Television, 1989–1994.
Battlestar Galactica, Syfy, 2004–2009.
The Biggest Loser, NBC, 2004–2011.
The Brady Bunch, ABC, 1969–1974.
CBS Evening News with Katie Couric, CBS, 2006–2011.
The Closer, TNT, 2005–2011.

The Colbert Report, Comedy Central, 2005–.
Commander in Chief, ABC, 2005–2006.
The Cosby Show, NBC, 1984–1992.
The Daily Show, Comedy Central, 1996–.
Deadwood, HBO, 2004–2006.
Deal or No Deal, NBC, 2005–2009.
Donahue, WNBC/WGN/WBBM, 1970–1996.
Dr. Phil, Harpo Productions, 2002–.
Dynasty, ABC, 1981–1989.
The Ellen DeGeneres Show, NBC, 2003–.
The Event, NBC, 2010–2011.
Hail to the Chief, ABC, 1985.
Home Improvement, ABC, 1991–1999.
Huckabee, Fox, 2008–.
Iron Chef America, Food Network, 2005–.
The Jerry Springer Show, NBC, 1991–2011.
Jimmy Kimmel Live!, ABC, 2003–.
The King of Queens, CBS, 1998–2007.
The Late Late Show with Craig Ferguson, CBS, 2005–.
Late Night with Conan O'Brien, NBC, 1993–2009.
The Late Show with David Letterman, Worldwide Pants, 1993–.
M*A*S*H*, CBS, 1972–1983.
Murphy Brown, CBS, 1988–1998.
NCIS, CBS, 2003–.
Nightline, ABC, 1980–.
Nightly News, NBC, 1970–.
NYPD Blue, ABC, 1993–2005.
The Oprah Winfrey Show, Harpo Productions, 1986–2011.
Oprah's Lifeclass, OWN, 2011–.
Parks and Recreation, NBC, 2009–.
Real Time with Bill Maher, HBO, 2003–.
Rowan and Martin's Laugh-In, NBC, 1967–1973.
Saturday Night Live, NBC, 1975–.
Sesame Street, PBS, 1969–.
The Simpsons, Fox, 1989–.
Soap, ABC, 1977–1981.
Today, NBC, 1952–.
The Tonight Show with Jay Leno, NBC, 1992–.

24, Fox, 2001–2010.
The Tyra Banks Show, CBS/CW, 2005–2010.
The View, ABC, 1997–.
The West Wing, NBC, 1999–2006.
World News Tonight, ABC, 1953–.

CONTRIBUTORS

Linda Beail is professor of political science and director of the Margaret Stevenson Center for Women's Studies at Point Loma Nazarene University in San Diego, where she teaches courses on gender and race politics, U.S. elections, and feminist theory. She is the author of several articles and book chapters on feminism in popular culture, motherhood as a political identity, and evangelical political behavior, as well as coauthor, with Rhonda Kinney Longworth, of *Framing Sarah Palin: Pit Bulls, Puritans and Politics* (2012). She earned her B.A. summa cum laude from Wheaton College in Wheaton, Illinois, and her Ph.D. from the University of Iowa.

Todd L. Belt is associate professor of political science at the University of Hawaii at Hilo. He received his B.A. in economics and political science from the University of California, Irvine, and his M.A. and Ph.D. in political science from the University of Southern California. Additionally, he did two summers' worth of graduate work at the Inter-University Consortium for Political and Social Research at the University of Michigan. His research focuses primarily on the influence of the mass media on public opinion and its resulting effects on the public's policy and voting preferences. He is coauthor of *We Interrupt This Newscast: How to Improve Local News and Win Ratings, Too* (2007). He has published articles in *Political Communication, Journal of Health and Social Behavior, California Journal of Politics and Policy, Political Linguistics, Columbia Journalism Review,* and *Campaigns & Elections.* Additionally, he has published several chapters in scholarly books and is coauthor of *Getting Involved: A Guide to Student Citizenship* (1999).

MaryAnne Borrelli is professor of government at Connecticut College. Her research has focused on gender dynamics in the U.S. presidency, examining cabinet selection and confirmation processes and the office of the first lady. She is the author of *The Politics of the President's Wife* (2011) and *The President's Cabinet: Gender, Power, and Representation* (2002) and a contributing coeditor of *The Other Elites: Women, Politics, and Power in the Executive Branch* (1997). She has published a number of chapters in edited collections; her articles have appeared in *Political Research Quarterly, Presidential Studies Quarterly, Sex Roles,* and *Women & Politics.* Professor Borrelli has also served as an interviewer at the Presidential Oral History Project at the Miller Center, University of Virginia, and as a member of the White House 2001/2009 Project, which provided briefing materials to the Bush/Gore and Obama/McCain transition teams. Her current research examines the performance and meaning of gender in the executive branch, investigating the inclusion of women in decision making through cabinet appointments and through first ladies' political initiatives. Professor Borrelli earned her Ph.D. in political science from the Graduate School of Arts and Sciences at Harvard University.

Lilly J. Goren is professor of political science and global studies at Carroll University in Waukesha, Wisconsin. She teaches American government, the presidency, the U.S. Congress, politics and culture, gender studies, and political theory. Her research often integrates popular culture, literature, and film as means to understanding politics, especially in the United States. Her published works include *Not in My District: The Politics of Military Base Closures* (2003) and *You've Come a Long Way, Baby: Women, Politics, and Popular Culture* (2009), as well as articles in *Political Research Quarterly, White House Studies,* and Berkeley Electronic Press's *The Forum,* and she has served as guest editor, with Justin Vaughn, for a special issue of *White House Studies* on the presidency and popular culture in 2010. Goren is chair of the American Political Science Association's Politics, Literature, and Film section. She has also served as an executive board member for the Presidents and Executive Politics Section of the American Political Science Association. She is currently revising a manuscript on the role of anger in modern democracies. She is a regular political commentator for both local and national media outlets. Professor Goren earned her A.B. in political science and English from Kenyon College and has an M.A. and a Ph.D. in political science from Boston College.

Elizabeth Fish Hatfield is adjunct professor in the Arts and Humanities Department at the University of Houston, Downtown. She is a graduate of Texas A&M University's doctoral program in communication. Her dissertation, entitled "Motherhood, Media and Reality: Analyzing Female Audience Reception of Celebrity Pregnancy as News," focused on mass media, celebrity, gender, and family communication. Other areas of interest include media effects and interpretive methods. Her research has been published in *Communication Law Journal* and *Communication, Culture and Critique* and presented at several conferences, including the National Communication Association's Annual Convention (2008–2011). She received her M.A. from Fordham University and her B.S. from Georgetown University.

Karen S. Hoffman is visiting assistant professor at Marquette University. Her research and teaching interests include the presidency, the presidency and public opinion, political communication, and political institutions. She has published articles in *Congress and the Presidency* and *Rhetoric & Public Affairs,* and her book, *Presidents and the Public: Origins and Practice,* came out in 2010. She received her Ph.D. from the University of Chicago.

Rhonda Kinney Longworth is professor of political science, interim associate provost, and associate vice president for academic programming at Eastern Michigan University in Ypsilanti. She has taught courses on the presidency; legislative politics; campaigns and elections; and literature, film and politics. Her publications include the coedited volume *Innovation and Entrepreneurship in State and Local Government* (with Michael Harris); coauthored chapters in essay collections including "Voting Technology and Voting Access in Twenty-First Century America" (with TeResa Green) in *Counting Votes: Lessons from the 2000 Presidential Election in Florida* (2004); and coauthored articles in the *American Journal of Political Science* and the *Academy of Managerial Communications Journal.* She has also coauthored with Linda Beail *Framing Sarah Palin: Pit Bulls, Puritans and Politics* (2012). Professor Longworth received her B.A. in political science and history and Ph.D. in political science from the University of Iowa.

Mary McHugh is director of the Stevens Service Learning Center and adjunct faculty member in the Political Science Department at Merrimack College in North Andover, Massachusetts. She teaches a variety of classes in U.S. politics and American political institutions. McHugh earned a B.A. in government and history from Colby College and an M.A. in political science from Boston College. She is currently working on her dissertation on the impact of voluntary retirement on the U.S. Senate.

Stacy Michaelson is policy associate at Children First for Oregon, a nonprofit, nonpartisan child advocacy organization committed to improving the lives of vulnerable children and families. She has previous experience working for the state legislature and in education policy. Her research interests include gender and politics, parenthood and electoral politics, and feminism in rural communities. She has a B.A. in political science from Willamette University.

Melissa Buis Michaux is associate professor in the Politics Department and Women's and Gender Studies Program at Willamette University. She teaches courses in American politics, women in American politics, women and power, and public policy. Michaux has a B.A. from Boston College and a Ph.D. from Brandeis University.

Chapman Rackaway is associate professor of political science at Fort Hays State University. Rackaway's primary teaching interests are in the intersection of popular culture and American government. In research, Rackaway also focuses on the process of planning, organizing, and executing political campaigns. After serving as a political activist and consultant for ten years, Rackaway received his Ph.D. in political science from the University of Missouri in 2002. Rackaway is a coauthor (with William Lyons and John Scheb) of *American Government: Politics and Political Culture*, 5th ed. (2010). In addition, he has published in numerous books and academic journals, including *Journal of Politics, PS: Political Science and Politics, Journal of Political Science Education*, and *Social Science Computer Review.*

Joseph E. Uscinski is assistant professor of political science at the University of Miami. He received his Ph.D. in political science from the University of Arizona, his M.A. from the University of New Hampshire, and his B.A. from Plymouth State College. Dr. Uscinski has published scholarly articles on American politics in journals such as *Political Research Quarterly, Presidential Studies Quarterly, PS: Political Science & Politics, Social Science Quarterly,* and *White House Studies.* Dr. Uscinski has appeared on *CBS Evening News, Special Report with Bret Baier,* Al Jazeera International, and *Sky News.* His current research examines the role that profit motives play in determining news content.

Justin S. Vaughn is assistant professor of political science at Boise State University. His area of expertise is the American presidency, focusing on presidential interaction with the American public as well as the presidential institution. He has authored several studies of presidential politics, including papers recently published in *Presidential Studies Quarterly, Political Research Quarterly, Review* *of Policy Research, International Journal of Public Administration, White House Studies,* and *Administration & Society,* and has served as guest editor, with Lilly Goren, for a special issue of *White House Studies* on the presidency and popular culture in 2010. His current projects include examinations of the various linkages between the rhetoric of Barack Obama and the political fortunes of the Obama administration, as well as a study of the evolution of presidential policy czars. He has served as an executive board member for both the Presidents and Executive Politics and the Politics, Literature, and Film sections of the American Political Science Association. He earned his Ph.D. in political science at Texas A&M University.

José D. Villalobos is assistant professor in the Department of Political Science at the University of Texas at El Paso (UTEP). He joined UTEP in June 2009 after receiving his doctoral degree from Texas A&M University. His dissertation work was chosen for the 2009 George C. Edwards III Dissertation Award granted by the Presidency Research Group of the American Political Science Association for best dissertation on the U.S. presidency. His areas of interest are presidential management, presidential-bureaucratic policy making, the public presidency, presidential-congressional relations, and studies on immigration policy and Latino/a politics. He has published articles in *Political Research Quarterly, Presidential Studies Quarterly, Administration & Society; International Journal of Public Opinion Research; Race, Gender & Class; International Journal of Public Administration;* and *Review of Policy Research.* Dr. Villalobos has served as an executive board member for the Presidents and Executive Politics section of the American Political Science Association and as president of the Midwest Latino/a Caucus section of the Midwest Political Science Association.

INDEX

ABC, 61, 63, 109, 119–20n40, 140, 147
African American fictional presidents,
   98–101, 103–7, 114, 118n32;
   accidental presidents, 106–7, 120n45,
   144–45; *Deep Impact* (movie, 1998)
   and, 100, 101, 103, 104, 115nn8–9,
   119n38; *Head of State* (movie, 2003)
   and, 104–5, 118n27, 119n38, 120n45;
   Man, The (movie, 1972) and, 98,
   106–7, 118n35, 118–19n36, 120n43,
   144–45; through normal election
   process, 112, 118n30; *24* (TV series)
   and, 104, 105–6, 109, 110, 118n29
African Americans, 14, 99, 234;
   education and, 106, 118n34,
   118–19n36; family and, 255–56;
   presidential candidates, 99, 101,
   102, 110, 111, 114, 120n43, 165–66,
   285n58; as senators/governors,
   110, 113, 120n43; U.S. Presidential
   Election, 2008 and, 97–98, 168, 252;
   as voters, 79, 90; voting rights, 112;
   women and fashion and, 239, 241;
   women cultural myths, 230–31,
   232, 236–37, 243–44, 256–57, 259.
   See also Obama, Barack; Obama,
   Michelle
Air Force One (movie, 1997), 103,
   116–17n23; white male masculine
   president and, 123, 144, 145, 146;
   woman vice-president and, 101,
   107–8, 115n12, 125, 130, 149–50,
   151
Alaska, 30
Albright, Madeleine, 14, 41
Alda, Alan, 117n26

Allen, Joan, 108, 125, 154
Allen, Tim, 79
*Almost Madam President: Why Hillary
   Clinton "Won" in 2008* (Gutgold), 11
American Academy of Pediatrics, 237
American President, The (movie, 1995),
   116–17n23, 129, 146, 152, 154
American Research Group, 66
American Voter, The (Campbell et al.), 76
Anderson, Karrin Vasby, 142
Anderson, Mary, 77
Angle, Sharon, 43
Apocalypse Now (movie, 1979), 217
Armageddon (movie, 1998), 100,
   115nn8–9
Armisen, Fred, 53, 59–63, 71n17
Arsenio Hall Show, The (TV show), 166

Bachmann, Michele, 9, 43, 101, 110,
   115n4, 132, 237, 270
Bailey, Mandi Bates, 11
Baldwin, Alec, 66–67
Ball, Edward, 260
Ballaster, Rosalind, 186
Barbara Lee Family Foundation, 27, 28
Barnes, Fred, 37
Batman Begins (movie, 2005), 129
Battlestar Galactica (TV show), 104,
   108–9, 140–41, 157n21
Baum, Matthew, 173, 184, 186
Baumgartner, Jody, 50
Beail, Linda, 16
Beasley, Maurine, 194
Beatty, Warren, 105, 115n10
Begala, Paul, 166
Behar, Joy, 169, 170

Belson, Michael, 101
Belt, Todd, 18
Bening, Annette, 129, 152
Benjamin, Walter, 6
Bennett, Dick, 66
Bergen, Candice, 82
Bergen, Polly, 107, 145, 275, 283n32
Bernard, Michelle, 40
Biden, Jill, 259
Biden, Joe, 34, 39, 42, 55, 56, 66, 87, 136
Bielby, Denise, 4
Biggest Loser, The (TV show), 242
bin Laden, Osama, 135–37
Birmingham, Stephen, 197
Bissell, Kimberly, 187
Black Sheep (movie, 1996), 125, 128
blogs, 209
Boorstin, Daniel, 188
Borger, Gloria, 62
Borrelli, MaryAnne, 19
Boston Globe, 60
Box-Steffensmeier, Janet, 77
Bradwell v. Illinois, 221
Brady, Henry, 172
Brazaitis, Tom, 138
Brewer, Paul, 52
Bridges, Jeff, 108, 116–17n23, 130
Brooks, Clem, 76
Brooks, David, 36, 239
Brown, Campbell, 41, 59
Bullock, Sandra, 99, 100
Bulworth (movie, 1998), 105, 115n10
Bush, Barbara, 194, 229, 230, 231, 238,
    239, 243
Bush, George H. W., 85, 111, 116–17n23,
    120n46, 278; late-night television
    and, 53, 165; U.S. Presidential
    Election, 1992 and, 83, 84, 166, 191
Bush, George W., 12, 35, 37, 97, 116–
    17n23, 151, 169, 254; daytime
    television and, 167, 170, 174–75n1,
    177n36; late-night television and,
    53, 56; U.S. Presidential Election,
    2004 and, 81, 82, 91, 170; women
    presidential appointees and, 14, 111

Bush, Laura, 187, 194, 229, 243, 273;
    daytime television and, 170, 174–
    75n1; first lady issues of, 234, 258,
    271
Bush Doctrine, 63, 148, 216
Butler, Judith, 6–7, 272

Cafferty, Jack, 219
Cain, Herman, 101, 115n4
Campbell, Karlyn Kohrs, 187, 269
Cao, Xiaoxia, 50, 51
Carnahan, Jean, 113
Carne, Judy, 165
Carroll, Susan, 29, 207
Carter, Jimmy, 143, 190, 193–94
Carter, Rosalynn, 187, 193–94, 195, 229,
    230, 238, 243, 252, 258
Carvey, Dana, 53
Carville, James, 166
Casey, Susan, 83
Cashmore, Ellis, 185, 186
Casper, Scott, 251
CBS, 51, 64, 77
Center for American Women and
    Politics (Rutgers University), 84
Center for Media and Public Affairs, 56
Center for the Study of Popular Culture,
    171
Channing, Stockard, 274
Chase, Chevy, 53
Children of the Corn (movie, 1984), 127
Chisholm, Shirley, 27, 97, 114, 120n43,
    165, 206
Christensen, Terry, 103
Clift, Eleanor, 138
Clinton, Bill, 35, 100, 186, 199, 252;
    extramarital affairs and, 185, 188,
    198; female presidential appointees
    and, 14, 111; late-night television
    and, 53, 166, 176n16; as possible
    first gentleman, 269, 278, 279; U.S.
    Presidential Election, 1992 and,
    83, 166, 176n16, 189, 191, 272; U.S.
    Presidential Election, 1996 and,
    83–84, 85, 89, 90

Clinton, Chelsea, 189, 191, 199
Clinton, Hillary: as female presidential
  candidate, 9, 52, 69, 82, 87, 102,
  113, 120n43, 121, 131–32, 155,
  206; fashion and, 21n19, 34, 207,
  210; femininity and, 34, 38, 187,
  191, 211–12, 219; as first lady, 90,
  113, 191, 193–95, 198, 204n72, 230,
  252, 258, 271–72, 277–78; first lady
  issues of, 187, 210, 229, 277; late-
  night television and, 52–56, 59–63,
  64, 66, 67, 69, 216–17; as possible
  first woman president, 99, 110, 196,
  269, 278, 279; run for presidential
  nomination, 2008, 12, 14, 62, 101–2,
  121, 155, 168, 169, 206, 210, 219;
  Sarah Palin and, 40, 41, 42, 64,
  216–17; as secretary of state, 14,
  136–37, 156n6, 169, 278, 284n45; as
  senator, 14, 120n43, 188, 210; sexism
  and stereotypes and, 42, 59, 60–62,
  63, 64, 69, 121, 211–16, 219, 221,
  270; U.S. Presidential Election, 1992
  and, 189, 191, 272; U.S. Presidential
  Election, 2008 and, 1, 206–7, 209,
  210, 269; viral videos and, 210–17,
  219, 221
Clooney, George, 99
Close, Glenn, 101, 107–8, 125, 128, 130, 149
Closer, The (TV show), 274
CNN, 62, 63, 219, 226n39
Colbert, Stephen, 53, 55, 57, 69
Colbert Report, The (TV show), 50, 52,
  53, 55, 70, 173
Collins, Lisa, 239
Collins, Patricia Hill, 257
Comedy Central, 52
Commander in Chief (TV show),
  103, 108–10, 119–20n40, 120n41,
  274, 283n32; accidental female
  presidency, 140, 147, 283n31; female
  president relying on men, 141, 147;
  sexuality and, 153–54, 275–76; use of
  violence and, 149, 270
Conroy, Meredith, 142

Contender, The (movie, 2000), 108, 116–
  17n23, 119n37, 125, 130, 131, 154
Converse, Philip, 171
Cooper, Christopher, 11
Copeland, Libby, 35, 38
Cosby, Bill, 97
Cosby Show, The (TV show), 97–98, 99
Costner, Kevin, 81
Cottle, Michelle, 33
Couric, Katie, 40, 41, 64, 65, 132, 216, 217
Crawford-Mason, Clare, 184, 186–87
Crews, Terry, 106, 118n30, 147
Crisis of the Negro Intellectual, The
  (Cruse), 99
Cromwell, James, 103, 116–17n23
Crothers, Lane, 138, 144, 146
Cruse, Harold, 99

Daily Show with Jon Stewart, The (TV
  show), 50, 52–53, 55, 57, 70, 166, 173
Dallas Morning News, 185
Dallek, Robert, 251
Damon, Matt, 100, 219
Dark Knight, The (movie, 2008), 129
Daughton, Suzanne, 142
Dave (movie, 1993), 106, 116–17n23
Davis, Geena, 103, 108, 109–10, 120n41,
  140, 147, 275
Davis, Richard, 184
Day, Christine, 89
daytime television, 166–74, 177n35;
  online process models and, 172,
  178n51; the "Oprah Effect," 173–74;
  presidential politics and, 163–64,
  166–74, 174–75n1, 177n36, 179n59.
  See also "soft news"
Deadwood (TV series), 79
Deep Impact (movie, 1998), 100, 101,
  103, 104, 115nn8–9, 119n38
DeGeneres, Ellen, 168, 179n59
democracy, 3–4
Democratic Party, 26, 208, 263–64n4;
  gender of voters and, 42, 75–79,
  90–91; race of voters and, 78, 79;
  Reagan Democrats, 81–85

de Pablo, Cote, 274
Desmond-Harris, Jenée, 241
Deterrence (movie, 1999), 148–49
Devil Wears Prada, The (movie, 2006), 128
Disclosure (movie, 1994), 128
Distinguished Gentleman, The (movie, 1992), 105, 129
Dittman, Dave, 37
Dodd, Chris, 55
Dolan, Kathleen, 152, 208
Dole, Bob, 83, 84, 89, 207
Dole, Elizabeth "Liddy," 27, 101, 120n43, 206, 207
Douglas, Michael, 80, 116–17n23, 128, 152–53
Dowd, Maureen, 37–38, 239, 277
Dr. Phil (TV show), 170, 174–75n1
Dr. Strangelove or: How I Learned to Stop Worrying and Love the Bomb (movie, 1964), 150–51
Duerst-Lahti, Georgia, 142, 270, 273
Dukakis, Michael, 166
Duke, Patty, 108
Dynasty (TV series), 79

Edwards, Elizabeth, 102, 198
Edwards, John, 55, 102, 198
Eisenhower, Mamie Doud, 229, 230, 239
Ellen DeGeneres Show, The (TV show), 169
Entertainment Tonight (TV show), 184
Entertainment Weekly, 185
Environmental Protection Agency, 258
Equal Rights Amendment (ERA), 76, 190, 191, 252
Essence, 257
Event, The (TV series), 104
executive power, 7–8

Facebook, 209, 225n38
Fahey, Anna, 148
Falk, Erica, 27
Falling Down (movie, 1993), 80–81
Farhi, Paul, 58
fashion, 20n3, 28; first ladies and, 238–41; Hillary Clinton and, 21n19, 34, 207, 210; Michelle Obama and, 239–41, 248n39, 253, 257; presidential politics and, 21n19, 33–34, 102, 207; Sarah Palin and, 21n19, 30, 33–34, 37–38, 102, 197, 207, 208, 210–11
Fatal Attraction (movie, 1987), 128
Feldman, Lauren, 50
female fictional presidents/vice-presidents, 103, 111, 270, 277, 283nn32–34, 283n36; accidental presidents, 98, 108–10, 112–13, 140–41, 147, 283n31; *Air Force One* (movie, 1997) and, 101, 107–8, 115n12, 125, 130, 149–50, 151; *Contender, The* (movie, 2000) and, 125, 130, 131; *Kisses for My President* (movie, 1964) and, 107, 145, 154–55, 270, 275–76, 283n33; masculine attributes and, 100, 109, 149–50, 284n37; *24* (TV series) and, 98, 108, 109, 110, 270, 274, 276, 284n37; vice-presidents and, 119n37, 124–25, 130, 149–50. See also *Commander in Chief* (TV show); first ladies; popular culture; presidential movies/TV
female political candidates: beyond 2008, 42–44, 101, 115n4, 132, 237, 269–70; femininity and, 38, 197, 208–9, 211–12, 271; as governors, 27–28, 29, 43, 110, 113, 120n43; late-night television and, 49, 50, 54, 57–58, 59–70, 86–87, 216–17; mass media and, 16–17, 205–9; motherhood and, 29, 32–33, 83, 127, 196–97; as presidential appointees, 13–14, 111; public acceptance of, 121–22, 206–7, 280, 285n58; as senators, 28, 43, 110, 113, 120n43, 207; sexism and, 41–42, 207; stereotyping and, 15, 26–28, 122, 207–8, 220–21; women's issues and, 15, 40, 44, 208, 210, 282n15. *See also* Clinton, Hillary; first gentlemen; gender; Palin, Sarah; presidential politics

female voters, 16, 112, 169, 174;
"compassion" issues and, 89–90; as
Democratic Party supporters, 42,
75, 76, 77, 78–79, 90–91; as hockey
moms, 87–89; as mothers, 83,
84, 86, 88, 91; in popular culture,
82–83; the security mom, 85–86;
the "soccer mom" as swing voter, 81,
83–85, 87–88, 91, 164; the "soccer
mom" vs. the "hockey mom," 33,
87–89; studies of, 75–79; women's
magazines and, 181–82, 191, 192,
195, 200
feminism, 7, 9, 182; first ladies and, 193,
252; reconstructive feminism, 19,
253–54, 255, 262, 263; Sarah Palin
and, 38, 39–42, 44, 102. *See also*
Clinton, Hillary; Obama, Michelle
Ferguson, Michaele, 12
Ferraro, Geraldine, 13, 29, 111, 120n43,
196, 199, 223n7
Ferrell, Will, 53
Fey, Tina, 36–37, 42, 43, 49, 53, 59–60,
64–65, 66–67, 69, 86–87
fictional presidents. *See* African
American fictional presidents;
female fictional presidents/vice-
presidents; Hispanic Americans;
presidential movies/TV
Fifth Element, The (movie, 1997), 106,
119n38
first families, 18, 19, 186–88, 249–57.
See also Obama, Barack; Obama,
Michelle
first gentlemen, 35, 197, 269–71, 278–79,
280; fictional portrayals, 107, 108,
154–55, 270, 275–76, 277, 283n34
first ladies: the arts and, 232–35; fashion
and, 238–41; femininity and,
272–73, 280; feminism and, 193, 252;
fictional first ladies, 270, 274–75; as
helpmeets, 187, 191, 192–95, 199,
270, 272–73, 281n9; issues and, 229,
272, 277–78, 282n15; as partners
in presidency, 19, 269, 272–74,

277–78, 284n41; roles of, 18–19,
229–31, 271–72, 281n8, 283n35; true
womanhood and, 230, 231–32, 237;
women's magazines and, 18, 186–88,
192–95, 199, 253, 257. *See also* first
gentlemen; Obama, Michelle
food deserts, 261–62
Ford, Betty, 187, 193, 194, 230, 231, 243,
252, 272
Ford, Gerald, 53, 181, 190, 193
Ford, Harrison, 101, 116–17n23, 123,
144, 145
Forsythe, John, 79
Fortini, Amanda, 42
Fox, Richard, 152
Fox News, 41, 70, 220
Foy, Joseph, 2–3
framing, 16, 25–26; frontier woman
frame, 29–31; hockey mom frame,
31–34; the maverick reformer,
36–37; the outsider frame, 34–36;
political framing beyond 2008,
42–44; the sexy puritan, 37–39
France, 148
Frankfurt School, 5, 6
Freeman, Morgan, 100, 101, 103–6,
117n24, 118n27
Friday the 13th (movie, 1980), 127
Fridkin, Kim L., 15

Gates, Robert, 136
gays and lesbians. *See* homosexuality
gender: American presidency and,
135–37, 206–8, 270; femininity and,
126–29, 281n10; general movies and,
99–100; leadership and, 13–14, 146,
169, 177n35, 273; popular culture
and politics and, 1–2, 7, 9, 11, 21n19,
77–78, 79–81, 82–83, 91, 122–32,
137–55; presidential politics and,
12, 13–15, 16–17, 19, 22n29, 148;
U.S. Presidential Election, 2008 and,
1, 121, 131–32, 196, 205–9; voting
patterns and, 16, 33, 76–82. *See also*
female fictional presidents/

gender *(cont.)*
  vice-presidents; female political
  candidates; female voters; first ladies;
  male voters; masculinity; popular
  culture; women's magazines
gender gap, in political participation,
  75, 76–77; political knowledge and,
  77–78; U.S. Presidential Election,
  1996 and, 84, 85, 86, 89, 90, 91; U.S.
  Presidential Election, 2004 and, 86,
  87; U.S. Presidential Election, 2008
  and, 87. *See also* female voters
Get Smart (movie, 2008), 129
Gibson, Charles, 41, 63, 64, 216, 217
Gillespie, Andra, 262
Ginsburg, Ruth Bader, 169
Givhan, Robin, 240
Glover, Danny, 106
Goldberg, Whoopi, 168–69
Gonzales, Alberto, 14
Goodman, Ellen, 69
Gore, Al, 53, 120n48, 167
Goren, Lilly, 17, 138, 141
Gould, Lewis, 187, 273
Gray, John, 79
Grodin, Charles, 106
Gutgold, Nichola D., 11, 138, 155

Haas, Peter J., 103
Hackman, Gene, 103, 116–17n23
Hail to the Chief (TV series), 108, 109,
  111
Haley, Nikki, 43
Hamilton, Alexander, 15, 117n25
Hammond, Darrell, 53
Han, Lori Cox, 12
Harding, Florence, 271
Harding, Warren, 271
Harrington, Lee, 4
Hart, Gary, 165
Harvard Business Review, 240
Hasselbeck, Elisabeth, 169, 179n59
Hatfield, Elizabeth, 18
Haysbert, Dennis, 104, 105–6, 110,
  118n27

Head of Skate trailer (viral video), 219
Head of State (movie, 2003), 104–5,
  118n27, 119n38, 120n45
health care reform: Barack Obama and,
  8–9, 169, 242; Hillary Clinton and,
  187, 210, 229, 242, 271; Michelle
  Obama and, 242, 253; as women's
  issue, 40, 44, 90, 186, 208, 210, 213
Heldman, Caroline, 12, 123–24, 125,
  128, 139–40, 141, 207
Herrnson, Paul, 208
Hilton, Paris, 219
Hinerman, Stephen, 185
Hirshman, Linda, 77–78
Hispanic Americans, 14; as fictional
  presidents, 98, 104, 106, 112, 118n31,
  158n44
Hoffman, Karen, 19
Holder, Eric, 14
Home Improvement (TV show), 79, 80
homosexuality, 29, 98, 115n4
Hooper, Charlotte, 14
Hoover, Lou Henry, 229, 231
Horowitz, David, 170–71
Horwitz, Linda, 14, 140, 141, 157n21
Howell, Susan, 89
Huckabee, Mike, 55, 242, 262
Hunter, Rielle, 198

Idiocracy (movie, 2006), 106, 146–47,
  158n44
Ifill, Gwen, 37, 66
Independence Day (movie, 1996), 116–
  17n23, 123, 130
Independent (London), 250
Independent Women's Forum, 40
Internet, 11, 18, 173, 185; U.S.
  Presidential Election, 2008 and, 205,
  209, 210–12
Iron Chef America (TV show), 242–43,
  261

Jackie and Dunlap, 218
Jackson, Andrew, 35
Jackson, Jesse, 111, 165–66

James, Kevin, 79
Jamieson, Kathleen Hall, 220
Jamison, Angela, 173
Janney, Allison, 274
Jerry Springer Show, The (TV show), 163
Johnson, Lady Bird Taylor, 229, 230, 231, 235, 238, 243
Jones, Cherry, 108, 110, 276
Jones, James Earl, 106, 118n27, 118n 33, 144–45
Jones, Jeffrey P., 51, 54
Juno (movie, 2007), 126

Kagan, Elena, 169
Kahn, Kim Fridkin, 28, 207
Kauffman, Karen, 76, 77
Kellerman, Barbara, 186, 187
Kelley, Tina, 33
Kennedy, Eunice, 197
Kennedy, Jacqueline. *See* Onassis, Jacqueline Kennedy
Kennedy, John F., 198, 234, 250, 251, 257
Kennedy, Joseph, 197
Kerry, John, 81, 82, 85, 88, 148, 170, 174–75n1
Kerry, Teresa Heinz, 170, 174–75n1, 187
Key, V. O., 171
Keyes, Paul, 165
Khan, Naeem, 240
King of Queens, The (TV show), 79, 80
Kingsley, Ben, 106, 116–17n23
Kisses for My President (movie, 1964), 107, 145, 154–55, 270, 275–76, 283nn32–33
Kline, Kevin, 106, 116–17n23
Knight's Tale, A (movie, 2001), 129
Knocked Up (movie, 2007), 126
Kubrick, Stanley, 150
Kucinich, Dennis, 55
Kunin, Madeleine, 280
Kurtz, Howard, 61

Lacewell, Melissa Harris, 241
Lake, Celinda, 81, 85
Lakoff, George, 6, 25

Lasswell, Harold, 205
late-night television, 16; female political candidates and, 49, 50, 54, 57–70, 86–87, 216–17; journalistic commentary on, 60–63, 68–70; politics and, 50–51; presidential politics and, 54–58, 165–66, 176n16; talk shows vs. political comedy shows, 51–53; U.S. Presidential Election, 2008 and, 49–70, 71n17, 86–87; writers' strike and, 58, 62–63. *See also* Clinton, Hillary; daytime television; Obama, Barack; Palin, Sarah; "soft news"
Late Show with David Letterman, The (TV show), 50, 51, 54, 55, 70
Lawless, Jennifer, 15, 152
Lawrence, Regina, 12
Lay, J. Celeste, 208
Leno, Jay, 51, 55, 56, 57, 65, 68, 70
Let's Move! campaign, 232, 236–37, 242, 258, 260–61, 262
Letterman, David, 50, 51, 55, 56, 57, 65, 69
Lewinsky, Monica, 184, 185
Lewis-Beck, Michael, 76, 78
Lichter, Robert, 57
Life magazine, 183
Limbaugh, Rush, 37, 264n14
Lister, Tommy "Tiny," 106, 118n30
Longworth, Rhonda Kinney, 16
Lurie, Rod, 147

MacFarquhar, Neil, 85
MacMurray, Fred, 107
male voters: "NASCAR dad," 81–82, 86, 88; in popular culture, 80–81
Man, The (movie, 1972), 98, 106–7, 118n35, 118–19n36, 120n43, 144–45, 158n35
Manchurian Candidate, The (movie, 2004), 128
Manly States: Masculinities, International Relations, and Gender Politics (Hooper), 14

Manza, Jeff, 76
Marquardt, Emily, 52
Mars Attacks! (movie, 1996), 147
Marshall, P. David, 188
Marso, Lori Jo, 12
Martin, Geoff, 4, 144
Marx, Karl, 5
masculinity, 8, 14, 28, 135–37, 142,
    282n22; aggression and physicality
    of fictional presidents, 143–46;
    decisiveness and authority of
    fictional presidents, 148–51;
    expertise and wisdom of fictional
    presidents, 146–47, 158n41; family
    and sexuality of fictional presidents,
    152–55; of female fictional
    presidents/vice-presidents, 100,
    109, 149–50, 284n37; of fictional
    presidents, 17, 123–24, 125, 143–55,
    270; presidential qualities and,
    272–74, 280
Masked Avengers, 218
mass media. *See* Internet; popular
    culture; presidential politics
May, Elaine, 251
McCain, Cindy, 30, 192
McCain, John: daytime television and,
    168, 179n59; late-night television
    and, 36–37, 54–55, 56, 66, 69, 166;
    People magazine and, 191–92, 199;
    U.S. Presidential Election, 2008 and,
    10, 31, 34, 35, 36–37, 39, 49, 56, 69,
    88, 191–92, 215; viral videos and, 214,
    217, 219, 226n49. *See also* Palin, Sarah
McDonnell, Mary, 109
McHugh, Mary, 16
McLoughlin, Hilary Estey, 169
McRobbie, Angela, 6, 7
McShane, Ian, 79
Media Monitor, 56
Melling, Phil, 124
Mendez, Jeanette, 87
Merkel, Angela, 271, 279–80
Meyers, Seth, 68
Michaels, Lorne, 53, 67, 68, 210

Michaelson, Stacy, 17
Michaux, Melissa Buis, 19
Miller, E. Ethelbert, 249
Mondak, Jeffrey, 77
Mondale, Walter, 13, 29, 165, 196, 223n7
Moore, Demi, 128
Morris, Barbara, 131
Morris, Jonathan, 50
Mr. Smith Goes to Washington (movie,
    1939), 129
Mueller, Carol, 76
Mukerji, Chandra, 4
Mulleavy, Kate and Laura, 240
Murphy, Eddie, 105, 129
Murphy Brown (TV show), 82
Myers, Dee Dee, 166

Nader, Ralph, 167
narrowcasting, 181–82
"NASCAR dad," 81–82, 86, 88
Nathanson, Paul, 80
National Election Studies, 76, 85
National Endowment for the Arts, 234
National Enquirer, 183
National Review, 29
NBC, 49, 51, 58, 64, 119–20n40, 120n48,
    138, 140, 165
NCIS (TV show), 274
New Republic, 42
Newsweek, 30, 32, 102, 147
New York, 243
New Yorker, 240, 250
New York Times, 27, 29–30, 36, 61, 77,
    146, 239, 242, 260
New York Times Magazine, 77
Nicholson, Jack, 147
Nielsen ratings, 64
Nixon, Patricia, 191, 193, 197, 274
Nixon, Richard, 116–17n23, 165, 181,
    197, 273–74
Norton, Anne, 5

Obama, Barack, 209, 214, 244, 246n19;
    as African American, 102, 113, 114,
    116n14, 118n34, 120n43; approval

ratings, 249, 263n1; the arts at the White House and, 234–35; bin Laden's death and, 135–37; daytime television and, 163–64, 168–70, 174, 174–75n1, 179n59; election of, 13, 90, 97, 99, 120n46, 163, 250, 257; family and, 151, 249–50, 252–56, 277; female/minority presidential appointees and, 14, 111, 115–16n13; late-night television and, 53, 55–63, 68–69, 70, 71n17; policies and, 8–9, 169, 242; presidential qualities and, 105, 118n27, 264n9; primary election battle with Hillary Clinton and, 101–2, 155, 168, 169, 206; U.S. Presidential Election, 2008 and, 10, 31, 37, 39, 42, 62, 68–69, 88, 185, 206
Obama, Malia, 250, 252
Obama, Michelle, 42, 55, 244; the arts and, 232–35; community outreach in Washington, DC, and, 258–60, 271; cultural myths and ideologies in role as first lady, 232, 241–42, 243–44; family and, 97, 249–50, 252–53, 255–57; fashion and, 239–41, 248n39, 253, 257; feminism and, 19, 253–54, 262, 263; gender roles expected of, 230–31, 277; genealogy and, 260; media and, 243, 250, 264n14; military families and, 258, 271; motherhood and, 236–37, 249–50, 258, 277; physical appearance and, 239–40, 247n36, 264n14; public presentation of, 199, 250, 256, 264n9; race and, 260, 261–62; staff and, 256, 258; success of, as first lady, 194–95, 241–44, 263; White House garden and childhood obesity, 232, 235–38, 242, 253, 260–63, 264n14, 271
Obama, Sasha, 250, 252
O'Connor, Sandra Day, 13
O'Donnell, Christine, 43
O'Donnell, Rosie, 163, 168
Of Thee I Sing: A Letter to My Daughters (Obama), 249

Ogunnaike, Lola, 63
Oldman, Gary, 144, 150
Olson, Stephanie, 207
Omen, The (movie, 1976), 127
Onassis, Jacqueline Kennedy, 187, 197, 229, 230, 239, 243, 251, 253, 257
101 Dalmatians (movie, 1996), 128
"Open Letter to Barack Obama, An" (Walker), 252
Operation Just Cause, 184
"Oprah Effect," 17, 173–74
Oprah's Lifeclass (TV show), 168
Oprah Winfrey (TV show), 50
Oprah Winfrey Network (OWN), 168
O'Regan, Valerie, 76
Orman, John, 143
Osborn, Tracy, 87
Other, The (movie, 1972), 127
Owen, Diana, 184

Palfrey, Judith S., 237
Palin, Bristol, 40
Palin, Sarah, 110, 120n43; beyond 2008 and, 42–44, 69, 70, 163, 169, 219–20, 237, 250, 262; fashion and, 21n19, 30, 33–34, 37–38, 102, 197, 207, 208, 210–11; femininity of, 33–34, 38–39, 64, 196–97; feminism and, 38, 39–42, 44, 102; as frontier woman, 29–31; as hockey mom, 31–34, 86–89, 210; late-night television and, 49, 51–57, 63–70, 86–87, 216–17; "male" issues and, 199, 211, 212, 215, 217, 218; as "Mama Grizzly," 43–44, 278; as maverick reformer, 36–37, 210, 211; as outsider, 34–36; sexism and stereotyping and, 41–42, 64, 66–70, 86–88, 132, 211–21, 270; as sexy puritan, 37–39; U.S. Presidential Election, 2012 and, 70, 269–70, 278–79; vice-presidential candidacy, 1, 9, 16, 25, 101, 102, 132, 155, 196, 206, 210–11; viral videos and, 210–21
Palin, Todd, 35, 197, 269, 278–79
Palin, Trig, 32, 196

Panichgul, Thakoon, 240
Parker, Jennifer, 167
Parker, Kathleen, 29
Parks and Recreation (TV show), 82
Parry-Giles, Shawn J., 12, 137–39, 141
Parry-Giles, Trevor, 12, 137–39, 141
Parvin, Landon, 38
patriarchy, 14, 114, 139, 140, 142
Pelosi, Nancy, 169, 269
People magazine, 32; establishment of, 183–85; first ladies and, 18, 192–95, 199; political celebrities and, 189; presidential family and, 186–87; presidential politics and, 181–82, 189–92; scandals and, 197–200; women presidential candidates and, 196–97, 199
Perot, Ross, 166
Perrotta, Tom, 38–39
Peterson, Wolfgang, 144
Petrocik, Jon, 76, 77
Pet Sematary (movie, 1989), 127
Pew Internet and American Life Project, 205
Pew Research Center, 51, 62
"pink ghetto," 192. *See also* first ladies
Poehler, Amy, 53, 59–65, 82
Polanski, Roman, 127
Political Network Election Study, 87
politics: online process models and, 172; political institutions and, 3; popular culture and, 1–4, 6, 8, 17, 20n3, 91, 171; satire and, 209–10, 220; the voter and, 171–74, 178n51; women's magazines and, 181–86, 188–92. *See also* female political candidates; first ladies; late-night television; popular culture; presidential movies/TV; presidential politics; U.S. Presidential Election, 2008
Pollak, Kevin, 148–49
Pollitt, Katha, 40–41
Popkin, Samuel, 78, 89, 172
popular culture: defining, 4–5; female fictional leaders, 274; framework for

analysis of, 5–7, 9; gender treatment in, 1–2, 7, 9, 11, 21n19, 77–83, 91, 122–32, 137–55; "Huxtable effect," 97–98; the male voter in, 80–81; mass media and, 3, 10–11, 17–18; motherhood and, 126–27; politics and, 1–4, 6, 8, 17, 20n3, 91, 171; presidential politics and, 5, 8–9, 11–13, 17–18; social change and, 98, 115n4; study of, 2–15; viral videos, 18, 209, 210–17, 226nn48–49. *See also* African American fictional presidents; daytime television; female fictional presidents/vice-presidents; gender; late-night television; *People* magazine; presidential movies/TV; presidential politics; women's magazines
Portman, Natalie, 130
Powell, Colin, 14, 114
presidential movies/TV, 103–14, 115nn8–10, 122–32, 137–42; family and sexuality and, 152–55; male presidential candidates and, 103, 106; male presidents and, 108, 109, 111, 116–17n23, 144–45; minority presidents, 17, 106, 112, 118n31, 147, 158n44; nuclear weapons and, 148–49, 150–51; presidential partnerships and, 274–76, 280, 284n37; science fiction films and, 108–9, 118n32, 119n38, 157n21; white male presidents and, 100–101, 103, 116–17n23, 117n26, 120n44, 123, 144, 145, 146, 148–49, 152–53, 158n44. *See also* African American fictional presidents; female fictional presidents/vice-presidents; masculinity
presidential politics: celebrity culture and, 10, 181–82, 185–86; daytime television and, 163–64, 166–74, 174–75n1, 177n36; executive power, 7–8; family and, 151–52, 181, 186–92, 195, 249; fashion and, 21n19, 33–34,

102, 207, 238; female candidates, 1, 13–14, 101, 110, 111–14, 115n4, 121–22, 124, 129, 206–8, 210–21, 223n7, 285n58; female candidate stereotyping and, 27–28, 131–32, 141; framing and, 25–26, 42–44; gender and, 12–17, 19, 22n29, 135–37, 148; governors as candidates, 113, 120n43, 120nn46–47; late-night television and, 54–58, 165–66, 176n16; likeability and, 172; magazine articles and, 181–82, 189–92; masculinity and, 8, 14, 28, 123–25, 135–37, 142–43, 272–74, 280, 282n22; mass media and, 8, 10–11; minority candidates, 97, 101, 110–14, 115n4, 115–16n13, 119n38, 206, 285n58; patriarchy and, 14, 114, 139, 140, 142; possibility of first gentleman and, 269–71, 278–79, 280; presidential partnerships and, 19, 269, 272–74, 277–80, 284n41; presidential qualities and, 15, 104, 105, 117nn25–26, 118n27, 124, 138, 142, 143, 148, 264n9, 272–74, 280; senators as candidates, 110, 113, 120n43, 120n47. *See also* Clinton, Hillary; first ladies; Obama, Barack; Palin, Sarah; popular culture; presidential movies/TV
President's Committee on the Arts and Humanities, 235
Presidents We Imagine, The (Smith), 5, 12
Primary Colors (movie, 1998), 100, 116–17n23
Prime-Time Presidency: "The West Wing" and U.S. Nationalism, The (Parry-Giles and Parry-Giles), 138
Prior, Markus, 173
Prochnow, Jürgen, 144
Projecting Politics (Christensen and Haas), 103
Pullman, Bill, 116–17n23, 123

Quayle, Dan, 221
Queen Latifah, 37, 66, 167

Rackaway, Chapman, 16
Ralph, Sheryl Lee, 148–49
Reagan, Maureen, 190
Reagan, Michael, 190
Reagan, Nancy, 190, 191, 194, 195, 230, 231, 238, 243
Reagan, Patti, 190
Reagan, Ronald, 13, 35, 76, 85, 143, 186, 190–92, 194, 198, 199
Reagan, Ronald, Jr., 190
Reasoning Voter, The (Popkin), 78
reconstructive feminism, 19, 253–54, 255, 262, 263
Red State Update, 218, 226n50
Remini, Leah, 79, 80
Rendell, Ed, 163
Reno, Janet, 14
Republican Party, 26, 31, 148, 181, 208; Clinton Republicans, 81, 82, 85; female and minority candidates, 42, 101; gender of voters and, 33, 76, 77; outsider frame and, 35–36; sexy puritan frame and, 38
Rethinking Madam President (Han and Heldman), 12, 139–40
Rice, Condoleezza, 14, 169
Richardson, Patricia, 79, 80
Roberts, Julia, 99, 100
Robinson, Marian, 255
Rochelle, Warren, 146
Rochester Democrat and Chronicle, 136
Rock, Chris, 99, 104–5, 106, 118n27, 119n38, 120n45
Roe v. Wade, 252
Rogers, Desiree, 256
Romney, Mitt, 56, 120n44
Roosevelt, Eleanor, 229, 230, 237, 243, 258
Roosevelt, Franklin D., 13, 251
Rose, Melody, 12
Rosemary's Baby (movie, 1968), 127
Rove, Karl, 97–98
Rowan and Martin's Laugh-In (TV show), 165
Roy, Rachel, 240

Rudolph, Maya, 147
Russert, Tim, 60

Saltzman, Joe, 57
Sanchez, Leslie, 31
"Sarah Palin's Greatest Hits," 217–18
Sargent, Joseph, 106
Sarkozy, Nicolas, 218–19
Saturday Night Live (SNL), 71n17, 165,
    166; effect on 2008 election, 1, 16, 50,
    62–63, 68–69; Hillary Clinton and,
    53, 54, 59–63, 64, 66, 67, 69; political
    satire and, 53–54, 57, 210; Sarah
    Palin and, 36–37, 39, 49, 53, 54, 55,
    63–68, 86–87, 216–17; viral videos
    and, 216–17, 221–22; writers' strike
    and, 58, 62–63
Sauer, Joachim, 279–80
Sawyer, Diane, 62
Scharrer, Erica, 187
Schroeder, Patricia, 27, 83
Schudson, Michael, 4
Sedgwick, Kyra, 274
Seelye, Katharine, 61
September 11, 2001 events, 27, 85, 135
Serling, Rod, 106
Sesame Street (TV show), 261
Sheehan, Michael, 28
Sheen, Martin, 103, 105, 116–17n23,
    152–53, 274
Shepherd, Sherri, 169
Shindle, Kate, 37
Shokrian, Jasmin, 240
Siena College Research Institute, 121
Simpsons, The (TV show), 57, 79
sitcoms, 79–80
60 Minutes (TV news show), 252, 272
Smith, Greg, 4, 10, 143
Smith, Jeff, 5, 137, 145
Smith, Margaret Chase, 114
Smits, Jimmy, 103, 104
Sniderman, Paul, 172
"soft news": celebrities and, 181–84;
    defined, 182, 183; downside of,
    170–71; entertainment weeklies,
182–89; first ladies and, 186–88;
    gender and, 11, 17–18, 77–78, 182;
    vs. "hard news," 11, 77–78, 173; the
    "Oprah Effect," 173–74; political
    celebrities and, 181, 185–86, 188–89,
    242; politics and, 50–51, 165–66;
    scandals, 183–85, 188–89; tabloids,
    183–85, 188; upside of, 171–72. *See
    also* daytime television; late-night
    television; *People* magazine; women's
    magazines
Sorkin, Aaron, 119–20n40, 146, 152,
    158n41
Sotomayor, Sonia, 169
Souza, Pete, 136
Spreading Misandry (Nathanson and
    Young), 80
Stambough, Stephen, 76
Star Wars trilogy, 130
Steuter, Erin, 4, 144
Stewart, Jon, 53, 54, 55, 57, 68
Stewart, Martha, 242
Stiller, Jerry, 80
Stockwell, Dean, 150
Stokes, Ashli Quesinberry, 187
Stokes, Atiya Kai, 208
Streep, Meryl, 128
Street, John, 4, 185–86
Stuckey, Mary, 4, 10, 143
Sudeikis, Jason, 66, 87
Sutherland, Kiefer, 105, 276
Sutter, Jane, 136
Svetkey, Benjamin, 185
Swift, Jane, 29
Swimfan (movie, 2002), 128
Swing Vote (movie, 2008), 81, 82
Swyers, Holly, 14, 140, 141, 157n21
Syfy, 140
Sykes, Patricia, 142, 143

tabloids, 183–85, 188
Talent, Jim, 113
Tapper, Jake, 61
Taylor, Natalie Fuehrer, 182
Telepictures Productions, 169

Terry, Mary Sue, 29
Thatcher, Denis, 279
Thatcher, Margaret, 13, 271, 279, 284–85n51
Thompson, Fred, 54, 55
Thorne, Julia, 170
Thorson, Gregory, 76
Time, 183
Tisinger, Russell, 50
Today (TV show), 242
Tomason, Audrey, 136
Tonight Show with Jay Leno, The (TV show), 50, 51, 54, 55, 57, 70
Traister, Rebecca, 167
Travolta, John, 100, 116–17n23
Trevor, Margaret, 76
Truman, Bess, 230, 238
Truman, Harry, 229, 238
Turner, Graeme, 188
Turow, Joseph, 182
24 (TV series): African American presidents and, 103, 104, 105–6, 118n29; female president and, 98, 103, 108, 109, 110, 270, 274, 276, 284n37
2012 (movie, 2009), 106
Tyra Banks Show, The (TV show), 169

Underwood, Blair, 99, 104
United States past presidential elections: 1964, 114; 1968, 165; 1972, 114, 206; 1976, 181, 190; 1980, 76, 81, 84, 90, 190; 1984, 13, 29, 84, 111, 165, 196, 223n7; 1988, 111, 166; 1992, 83, 84, 166, 176n16, 191, 272; 1996, 83–85, 86, 89, 90, 91; 2000, 79, 85, 101, 120n48, 167, 187, 206, 207; 2004, 79, 81–82, 85, 91, 101, 148, 170, 174–75n1, 187. *See also* U.S. Presidential Election, 2008; U.S. Presidential Election, 2012
Uscinski, Joseph, 17
U.S. Presidential Election, 2008, 86–89, 192, 263–64n4; African Americans and, 97–98, 168, 252; daytime television and, 168, 169; gender and,

1, 121, 131–32, 196, 205–9; late-night television and, 49–70, 71n17, 86–87; new media and, 205, 209, 210–12, 225n38, 226n39; vice-presidential debate, 66, 87; viral videos and, 210–21, 226n48; women and minority candidates and, 49, 52, 97, 101–3, 115n4, 115–16n13, 206, 210–21. *See also* popular culture
U.S. Presidential Election, 2012, 70, 101, 132, 269–70
U.S. Supreme Court, 13, 169

Valdes-Rodriguez, Alisa, 98, 99
Vanity Fair, 253, 256, 257
van Zoonen, Liesbet, 4, 5, 186
Vaughn, Justin, 17, 138
View, The (morning TV talk show), 163–64, 168–70, 174, 179n59
Villalobos, José, 17–18
Vilsack, Tom, 195
viral videos, 18, 209, 210–21, 226n48, 226n50; data analysis of, 212–16; Sarah Palin and, 210–21
Vogue, 239
Voth, Ben, 54

Wag the Dog (movie, 1997), 101
Walker, Alice, 252
Wallace, Irving, 106
Walters, Barbara, 168
Washington, George, 251, 272
Washington Post, 38, 58, 61, 250
Washington Times, 41
Watson, Robert P., 271
Weaver, Sigourney, 106
Weekly Standard, 37
Weiner, Jay, 33
Westen, Drew, 26
West Wing, The (TV series), 50, 119–20n40, 120n48, 152; gender and, 12, 138–39, 270, 274–75; minority presidential candidates and, 104, 106, 118n31; U.S. nationalism and, 12, 138–39; white male presidential

West Wing, The (TV series) *(cont.)*
    characters and, 105, 116–17n23,
    117n26, 139, 140, 146; women
    characters in, 138, 139, 270, 274–75,
    283n26
White House Project, the, 114
White House tours, 229
Wiig, Kristen, 59
Williams, Brian, 58, 60
Williams, Joan, 253, 256
Wilson, Gretchen, 31
Wilson, Luke, 147
Wilson, Marie, 114
Winfrey, Oprah, 99, 167–68, 170. *See
    also* "Oprah Effect"; *specific shows*
Winter, Nicholas, 99
Women's History Month, 259
women's magazines, 181–200, 239;
    celebrity culture and, 183, 185–86;
    first ladies and, 18, 186–88, 192–95,
    199, 253, 257; political celebrities
and, 181–82, 188–89; politics and,
    181–85, 186; presidential family
    and, 186–87; presidential politics
    and, 189–92; scandals and, 197–200;
    women presidential candidates and,
    196–97, 199
women voters. *See* female voters
Woodall, Gina Serignese, 15
Woodside, D. B., 104, 106
Writers Guild of America, 58
W Stands for Women (Ferguson and
    Marso), 12
Wu, Jason, 240

Young, Dannagal, 50, 69
Young, Katherine, 80
YouTube, 53, 64, 173, 209, 218, 226n39,
    226n50. *See also* viral videos

Zeisler, Andi, 4
Zogby, John, 173

CPSIA information can be obtained at www.ICGtesting.com
Printed in the USA
BVOW071250211012

302899BV00001B/6/P